VINAYA TEXTS

SACRED BOOKS OF THE EAST

VINAYA TEXTS

TRANSLATED FROM THE PÂLI

BY

T. W. RHYS DAVIDS

AND

HERMANN OLDENBERG

PART III

THE *K*ULLAVAGGA, IV—XII

Atlantic Publishers & Distributors
4215/1, Ansari Road, Darya Ganj, New Delhi

Published by :
Atlantic Publishers & Distributors,
4215/1, Ansari Road, Darya Ganj,
New Delhi-110002

Head Office :
B-2, Vishal Enclave, Najafgarh Road,
New Delhi-110027
Phone : 5413460

***Printed at* :**
MEHRA OFFSET PRESS
1979, Chandni Mahal
DELHI-110006

CLASSICAL REPRINTS PUBLISHED BY US

History of India: From the Earliest Time to the 20th Century, H.G.Keene, Vol.I & Vol.II

History of India Under Baber, William Erskine

History of India Under Humayun, William Erskine

A Comprehensive History of India, 3vols., Henry Beveridge

The History of British India, 3vols., James Mill

History of the Indian Mutiny, T.R.E.Holmes

The History of Humayun (Humayun-Nama), Gul-Badan Begam

Babur-Nama (Memoirs of Babur), 2vols.set, A.S.Beveridge

The Akbar Nama, 3vols., Abu-L-Fazal

Tuzuk-i-Jahagiri, 2vols. bound in one, A.Royers & H.Beveridge

Alberuni's India, 2vols. bound in one, Edward C.Sachau

Travels in the Mogul Empire, Franscois Bernier

Trevernier's Travels in India, 2vols. set, Jean-Baptiste Travernier

History of the Rise of the Mahomedan Power in India, 4vols., Mahomedan Kasim Ferishta & John Briggs

Mogul India or Storia Do Mogor, Niccolao Maucci, Translated by William Irvine, 4vols. set

The Emperor Akbar: A Contribution towards the History of India in the 16th Century, Vol. I & II, Frederick Augustus

A Classical Dictionary of India, John Garrett

A History of Muslim Philosophy: With short Accounts of other Disciplines and the Modern Renaissance in Muslim Lands, 2vols., M.M.Sharif

SACRED BOOKS OF THE EAST

EDITOR: F. Max Müller

These volumes of the Sacred Books of the East Series include translations of all the most important works of the seven non-Christian religions. These have exercised a profound influence on the civilizations of the continent of Asia. The Vedic Brahmanic System claims 21 volumes, Buddhism 10, and Jainism 2; 8 volumes comprise Sacred Books of the Parsees; 2 volumes represent Islam; and 6 the two main indigenous systems of China, thus placing the historical and comparative study of religions on a solid foundation.

VOLUMES

1, 15. THE UPANISADS: in 2 Vols. *F. Max Müller*

2, 14. THE SACRED LAWS OF THE ARYAS: in 2 Vols. *Georg Bühler*

3, 16, 27, 28, 39, 40. THE SACRED BOOKS OF CHINA: in 6 Vols. *James Legge*

4, 23, 31. THE ZEND-AVESTA: in 3 Vols. *James Darmesteter & L. H. Mills*

5, 18, 24, 37, 47. PAHALVI TEXTS: in 5 Vols. *E. W. West*

6, 9. THE QUR'AN: in 2 Vols. *E. H. Palmer*

7. THE INSTITUTES OF VIṢṆU: *J. Jolly*

8. THE BHAGAVADGĪTĀ with the Sanatsujātiya and the Anugitā: *K. T. Telang*

10. THE DHAMMAPADA: *F. Max Müller*
SUTTA-NIPĀTA: *V. Fausböll*

11. BUDDHIST SUTTAS: *T. W. Rhys Davids*

12, 26, 41, 43, 44. THE ŚATAPATHA-BRĀHMAṆA: in 5 Vols. *J. Eggeling*

13, 17, 20. VINAYA TEXTS: in 3 Vols. *T. W. Rhys Davids & H. Oldenberg*

19. THE FO-SHO-HING-TSAN-KING: *Samuel Beal*

21. THE SADDHARMA-PUṆḌARĪKA or THE LOTUS OF THE TRUE LAWS: *H. Kern*

22, 45. JAINA SUTRAS: in 2 Vols. *Hermann Jacobi*

25. MANU: *Georg Bühler*

29, 30. THE GṚIHYA-SŪTRAS: in 2 Vols. *H. Oldenberg & F. Max Müller*

32, 46. VEDIC HYMNS: in 2 Vols. *F. Max Müller & H. Oldenberg*

33. THE MINOR LAW-BOOKS: *J. Jolly*

34, 38. THE VEDĀNTA SŪTRAS: in 2 Vols. with Śaṅkarācārya's Comm.: *G. Thibaut*

35, 36. THE QUESTIONS OF KING MILINDA: in 2 Vols.: *T. W. Rhys Davids*

42. HYMNS OF THE ATHARVA-VEDA: *M. Bloomfield*

48. THE VEDĀNTA-SŪTRAS with Rāmānuja's Śribhāṣya: *G. Thibaut*

49. BUDDHIST MAHĀYĀNA TEXTS: *E. B. Cowell, F. Max Müller & J. Takakusu*

50. INDEX : *M. Winternitz*

CONTENTS.

PAGE

THE *K*ULLAVAGGA.

Fourth Khandhaka (The Settlement of Disputes among the Fraternity) 1

Fifth Khandhaka (On the Daily Life of the Bhikkhus) . 66

Sixth Khandhaka (On Dwellings and Furniture) . . 157

Seventh Khandhaka (Dissensions in the Order) . . 224

Eighth Khandhaka (Regulations as to the Duties of the Bhikkhus towards one another) 272

Ninth Khandhaka (On Exclusion from the Pâtimokkha Ceremony) 299

Tenth Khandhaka (On the Duties of Bhikkhunîs) . 320

Eleventh Khandhaka (On the Council of Râ*g*agaha) . 370

Twelfth Khandhaka (On the Council of Vesâlî) . . 386

Note on the Bhâ*n*avâras 415

Index of Subjects 421

Index of Proper Names 428

Index of Pâli Words explained or referred to in the Notes . 433

Transliteration of Oriental Alphabets adopted for the Translations of the Sacred Books of the East . . . 441

[Similar paragraphs, ending:]

'A Bhikkhunî is not, O Bhikkhus, to use [illegible] clay at her bath. Whosoever does so, shall be guilty of a dukka*t*a. I allow, O Bhikkhus, the use of common clay.'

Now at that time Bhikkhunîs [illegible] the steam-bath room made [illegible].

They told this matter to [illegible].

'Bhikkhunîs are not, O Bhikkhus, [illegible] steam-bath. Whosoever does so, shall be guilty of a dukka*t*a.'

Now at that time Bhikkhunîs [illegible] stream allowed the rush of water [illegible].

They told this matter to [illegible].

'A Bhikkhunî is not, O Bhikkhus, [illegible] against the stream. Whosoever does so, shall be guilty of a dukka*t*a.'

Now at that time Bhikkhunîs bathed [illegible] not a common bathing-place, and men [illegible] life violated them.

They told this matter to the Blessed One.

'A Bhikkhunî is not, O Bhikkhus, [illegible] place not a common bathing-place. Whosoever does so, shall be guilty of a dukka*t*a.'

Now at that time Bhikkhunîs bathed at a [illegible] place used also by men. People [illegible] indignant, and complained, saying [illegible] do who are [illegible] in [illegible] world.'

They told this matter to the Blessed One.

[1] [illegible]
[illegible]

[2] This is apparently covered by the [illegible] Pâkittiya.

*K*ULLAVAGGA.

FOURTH KHANDHAKA.

THE SETTLEMENT OF DISPUTES AMONG THE FRATERNITY.

1.

1. Now at that time the Blessed Buddha was dwelling at Sâvatthi, in the Ârâma of Anâthapi*nd*ika. And at that time the *Kh*abbaggiya Bhikkhus used to carry out the formal Acts—the Ta*gg*aniya, and the Nissaya, and the Pabbâ*g*aniya, and the Pa*t*isâra*n*iya, and the Ukkhepaniya—against Bhikkhus who were not present.

Then those Bhikkhus who were modest were annoyed, murmured, and became indignant, saying, 'How can the *Kh*abbaggiya Bhikkhus [act thus][1]?' And those Bhikkhus told the matter to the Blessed One.

'Is it true, O Bhikkhus, as they say, that the *Kh*abbaggiya Bhikkhus carry out the (aforesaid)[1] formal Acts against Bhikkhus who are not present?'

'It is true, Lord!'

The Blessed Buddha rebuked them, saying, 'This is improper (&c., as in I, 1, 2, down to the end).'

And when he had thus rebuked them, and had

---

[1] The words above are repeated.

delivered a religious discourse, he addressed the Bhikkhus, and said: 'The formal Acts, O Bhikkhus, the Ta*gg*aniya-, the Nissaya-, the Pabbâ*g*aniya-, the Pa*t*isâra*n*iya-, and the Ukkhepaniya-kammas, ought not to be carried out against Bhikkhus who are not present. Whosoever does so, shall be guilty of a dukka*t*a offence.'

2.

1. The single Bhikkhu who speaks not in accordance with the right, the many who speak not in accordance with the right, the Sa*m*gha which speaks not in accordance with the right. The single Bhikkhu who speaks in accordance with the right, the many who speak in accordance with the right, the Sa*m*gha which speaks in accordance with the right [1].

Now (it may happen that) the one Bhikkhu who speaks not in accordance with the right may point out (the right course) to a single Bhikkhu who speaks in accordance with the right, or gives him to understand what it is [2], or urges him to see or consider the matter in that light [3], or teaches him, or

---

[1] This short enumeration of the different categories occurring in the subsequent paragraphs is quite in the style of the Abhidhamma texts, in which such lists are accustomed to be called mâtikâ; compare the expression mâtikâ-dharo as applied to a learned Bhikkhu in the stock phrase at Mahâvagga X, 2, 1; *K*ullavagga I, 11; IV, 14, 25, &c.

[2] The Samanta Pâsâdikâ here says: ni*ggh*âpetîti yathâ so ta*m* attha*m* ni*ggh*âyati oloketi eva*m* karoti.

[3] Pekkheti anupekkhetîti yathâ so ta*m* attha*m* pekkhati *k*' eva punappunañ *k*a pekkhati eva*m* karoti. (Samanta Pâsâdikâ.)

instructs him, saying, 'This is the Dhamma, this the Vinaya, this the teaching of the Master. Accept this, and approve this.' If the dispute should be thus settled, it is settled contrary to the Dhamma, and with a mere counterfeit of the Vinaya rule of procedure (that cases of dispute must be settled before a duly constituted meeting of the Sa*m*gha, and in the presence of the accused person)[1].

[And in like manner, if he instruct the many, or the Sa*m*gha, who speak according to the right;—or if the many or the Sa*m*gha who speak not according to the right instruct the one, or the many, or the Sa*m*gha who speak according to the right;—then the dispute is settled contrary to the Dhamma (&c., as before).]

End of the nine cases in which the wrong side decides.

3.

[This chapter is the contrary of the last; the cases put being those in which the three last members of

[1] Sammukhâ-vinaya-pa*t*irûpakena. The rule of procedure, called Sammukhâ-vinaya, hereafter rendered 'Proceeding in Presence,' is one of the seven modes of settling disputes already referred to in the closing chapter of the Pâtimokkha ('Vinaya Texts,' vol. i, p. 68), and is more fully described below in *K*ullavagga IV, 14, 16, and following sections.

It will be seen below, from §§ IV, 14, 27–30, that it is involved in, or rather is supposed to accompany, each of the other Proceedings mentioned in this chapter.

the mâtikâ in the first paragraph of chapter 2 instruct, &c., the three first members.]

End of the nine cases in which the right side decides.

4[1].

1. Now at that time the Blessed Buddha was staying at Râgagaha, in the Kalandaka Nivâpa, in the Bamboo Grove.

Now at that time the venerable Dabba the Mallian, who had realised Arahatship when he was seven years old, had entered into possession of every (spiritual gift) which can be acquired by a disciple; there was nothing left that he ought still to do, nothing left that he ought to gather up of the fruit of his past labour[2]. And when the venerable Dabba the Mallian had retired into solitude, and was sunk in thought, the following consideration presented itself to his mind: 'Arahatship had I

[1] The whole of the following story of Dabba down to the end of section 9 (except the last sentence) recurs in the Sutta-vibhaṅga as the Introductory Story to the Eighth Saṃghâdisesa. The Samanta Pâsâdikâ has therefore no commentary upon it here, and the few extracts that we give from it are taken from the notes of that work on the corresponding passage in the Sutta-vibhaṅga. The stupidity of Udâyi, who once supplanted Dabba the Mallian in the performance of his duty as bhattuddesaka, forms the burthen of the Introductory Story to the Gâtaka on 'the Measure of Rice' (No. 5 in the Gâtaka book; 'Buddhist Birth Stories,' pp. 172 and following).

[2] On this phrase compare Mahâvagga V, 1, 21, and the verses at V, 1, 27.

acquired when I was seven years old. I have gained everything that a learner can reach to. There is nothing further left for me to do, nothing to gather up of the fruit of that which I have done. What service is it possible for me to render to the Sa*m*gha?' And it occurred to the venerable Dabba the Mallian: 'It would be a good thing for me to regulate the lodging-places for the Sa*m*gha, and to apportion the rations of food.'

2. And when, at eventide, the venerable Dabba the Mallian had arisen from his meditations, he went to the place where the Blessed One was; and when he had come there he saluted the Blessed One, and took his seat on one side; and when he was so seated the venerable Dabba the Mallian spake thus to the Blessed One:

'When I had retired, Lord, into solitude and was sunk in thought, the following consideration presented itself to my mind (&c., as before, down to) It would be a good thing for me to regulate the lodging-places for the Sa*m*gha, and to apportion the rations of food. I desire, Lord, [so to do].'

'Very good, Dabba. Do you then regulate the lodging-places for the Sa*m*gha, and apportion the rations of food!'

'It is well, Lord,' said the venerable Dabba the Mallian, accepting the word of the Blessed One.

3. And the Blessed One on that occasion and in that connection, when he had delivered a religious discourse, addressed the Bhikkhus, and said:

'Let then the Sa*m*gha, O Bhikkhus, appoint Dabba the Mallian as the regulator of lodging-places, and as the apportioner of rations. And thus, O Bhikkhus, should the appointment be made.

'First Dabba should be asked (whether he is willing to undertake the office). When he has been asked, some able and discreet Bhikkhu should lay the resolution before the Sa*m*gha, saying,

'"Let the venerable Sa*m*gha hear me.

'"If it be convenient to the Sa*m*gha, let the Sa*m*gha appoint Dabba the Mallian as regulator of lodging-places, and as apportioner of rations.

'"This is the resolution (*ñ*atti).

'"Let the venerable Sa*m*gha hear me.

'"The Sa*m*gha appoints the venerable Dabba the Mallian as regulator of lodging-places, and as apportioner of rations. Whosoever of the venerable ones agrees that Dabba should be so appointed, let him remain silent; whosoever does not agree, let him speak. The venerable Dabba is appointed by the Sa*m*gha as regulator of the lodging-places, and as apportioner of rations. The Sa*m*gha approves thereof. Therefore is it silent. Thus do I understand."'

4. And the venerable Dabba the Mallian, being so chosen, appointed one lodging-place in the same place for the Bhikkhus who belonged to the same division. For those Bhikkhus who were repeaters of the Suttantas he appointed a lodging-place together, thinking, 'They will be able to chant over the Suttantas to one another.' For those Bhikkhus who were in charge of the Vinaya he appointed a lodging-place together, thinking, 'They will be able to discuss the Vinaya one with another.' For those Bhikkhus who were preachers of the Dhamma he appointed a lodging-place together, thinking, 'They will be able to talk over the Dhamma one with another.' For those Bhikkhus who were given to

meditation [1] he appointed one lodging-place together, thinking, 'They will not disturb one another.' For those Bhikkhus who were wise in worldly lore, and abounding in bodily vigour [2], he appointed one lodging-place together, thinking, 'These venerable ones, too, will thus remain settled according to their pleasure.' And for such Bhikkhus as came in late, for them he caught fire [3], and by the light of the flame thereof he pointed out to them a lodging-place.

So much so [4] that Bhikkhus of set purpose would come in late, thinking, 'We shall thus behold the power of the Iddhi of the venerable Dabba the Mallian.' And they went up to the venerable Dabba the Mallian, and said: 'Appoint us, O venerable Dabba, a lodging-place.'

And to them the venerable Dabba the Mallian would speak thus: 'Where do the venerable ones desire to rest? Where shall I appoint it?'

And they of set purpose would designate some place afar, saying, 'May the venerable Dabba appoint us a lodging-place on the Vulture's Peak; may the venerable one appoint us a lodging-place at the Robber's Cliff; may the venerable one appoint us a lodging-place at the Black Rock on the Isigili Passa; may the venerable one appoint us a lodging on the Vebhâra Passa; may the venerable one appoint us a lodging-place in the Sattapa*nn*i Cave; may the

[1] *Gh*âyino possibly used with the technical connotation of being addicted to the practice of the Four *Gh*âna meditations; but compare Mahâvagga I, 1, 3, 5, 7.

[2] See the comment as quoted by H. O.

[3] Compare the use of te*g*odhâtu*m* samâpa*gg*itvâ at Mahâvagga I, 15, 4.

[4] Compare api ssu at *K*ullavagga I, 9, 1.

venerable one appoint us a lodging-place in the mountain cave of the Snake's Pool in Sîta's Wood; may the venerable one appoint us a lodging-place in the Goma*t*a Grotto; may the venerable one appoint us a lodging-place in the cave of the Tinduka Tree; may the venerable one appoint us a lodging-place at the Tapoda Ghât; may the venerable one appoint us a lodging-place in the Tapoda Ârâma; may the venerable one appoint us a lodging-place in *G*îvaka's Mango Grove; may the venerable one appoint us a lodging-place in the deer-park at Maddaku*kkh*i.'

And the venerable Dabba the Mallian would burst into flame, and walk on in front of them with his finger burning, and they by the light thereof would follow close upon the venerable Dabba the Mallian. And the venerable Dabba the Mallian would appoint them a lodging-place, saying, 'This is the couch, and this the stool, and this the mat, and this the pillow, and this the privy place, and this the drinking-water[1], and this the water for washing, and this the staff[2], and this the form of (the result of) the consultation of the Sa*m*gha[3], that at such and such a time are you to enter thereon, and at such and such a time are you to depart therefrom[4].' And when the

[1] That paribhoga*n*iya*m* does not mean drinking-water, as Childers renders it, is clear from VIII, 1, 2, where it is implied that it is to be used for washing feet. Our translation of Mahâvagga II, 20, 5 should be corrected accordingly.

[2] Compare below, VIII, 6, 3.

[3] Katika-sa*nth*âna*m*. Compare *G*âtaka I, 81, and Mahâvagga VIII, 32, and *K*ullavagga VIII, 1, 2.

[4] That this is the correct rendering of this otherwise doubtful

venerable Dabba the Mallian had thus appointed unto them their lodging-place, he would return back again to the Bamboo Grove.

5. Now at that time the Bhikkhus who were followers of Mettiya and Bhummag*a*ka[1] had been but recently received into the Sa*m*gha, and were wanting in merit, and such among the lodging-places appertaining to the Sa*m*gha as were inferior fell to their lot, and the inferior rations[2].

Now at that time the people of Râg*a*gaha were desirous of presenting to the Thera Bhikkhus a wishing-gift[3], to wit, ghee and oil and dainty bits[4]; while to the Bhikkhus who were followers of Mettiya and Bhummag*a*ka they used to give an ordinary gift according to their ability, to wit, scraps of food and sour gruel with it[5].

---

passage is clear from the closing words of VIII, 1, 2, where most of these phrases recur. In the text, for the last word nikkhipitabba*m* read nikkhamitabba*m*, as pointed out in the note at p. 363 of the edition of the text.

[1] These were two of the six leaders of the notorious *Kh*abbaggiya Bhikkhus.

[2] Compare the 22nd Nissaggiya.

[3] Abhisa*m*khârika*m*; that is, a gift by the giving of which the donor expressly wished that a particular result (as, for instance, that the donor should be re-born as a king or queen, or should enter the paths, or have opportunity to hear a Buddha preach) should be brought about by the normal effect of that good act in a future birth. There are not a few instances of such wishes, and of their fulfilment, recorded in various parts of the sacred literature.

[4] Uttaribhaṅgam. See the passages quoted in the note on Mahâvagga VI, 14, 3. These three things are also mentioned together at VIII, 4, 4.

[5] These expressions recur at *G*âtaka I, 228. The Samanta Pâsâdikâ says merely ka*n*âg*a*kan ti sakuntaka-bhatta*m*. Bilaṅgadutiyan ti kañ*g*ika-dutiya*m*.

When they had returned from their receipt of alms, and had eaten their meal, they asked the Thera Bhikkhus, 'What did you get, Sirs, at the place of alms; what did you get?'

Some of the Theras answered, 'We had ghee, Sirs; we had oil; we had dainty bits.'

The Bhikkhus who were followers of Mettiya and Bhummagaka replied: 'We got nothing at all, Sirs; just an ordinary gift such as they could manage, scraps of food, and sour gruel with it.'

6. Now at that time a certain householder, possessed of good food[1], used to give a perpetual alms to the Samgha, a meal for four Bhikkhus. He with his wife and children used to stand at the place of alms and serve; and offer to some Bhikkhus boiled rice, and to some congey, and to some oil, and to some dainty bits.

Now at that time the meal for the Bhikkhus who were followers of Mettiya and Bhummagaka had been fixed for the morrow at the house of this prosperous householder. And the prosperous householder went to the Ârâma for some business or other, and went up to the place where the venerable Dabba the Mallian was. And when he had come there, he saluted the venerable Dabba the Mallian, and took his seat on one side. And him so seated did the venerable Dabba instruct, and arouse, and gladden, and incite with religious discourse.

And when the prosperous householder had thus been instructed, and aroused, and gladdened, and incited by the venerable Dabba the Mallian with

[1] The Samanta Pâsâdikâ says simply kalyâ*n*a*m* bhatta*m* assâ ti kalyâ*n*a-bhattiko.

religious discourse, he said to the venerable Dabba the Mallian: 'For whom, Sir, has the meal been appointed to-morrow at our house?'

'The meal has been appointed, my friend, at your house to-morrow for those Bhikkhus who are followers of Mettiya and Bhummagaka.'

Then the prosperous householder was ill-pleased, thinking, 'How can bad Bhikkhus enjoy themselves at our house?' And going home he gave command to the slave-girl: 'For those who come to-morrow for the meal, spread out the mats in the entrance hall[1], and serve them with scraps of food, and with sour gruel with it!'

'Even so, Sir!' said the slave-girl, accepting the word of the householder.

7. Then the Bhikkhus who were followers of Mettiya and Bhummagaka spake one to another: 'Yesterday a meal has been appointed for us at the house of the prosperous householder. To-morrow he, with his wife and children, will attend upon us at the place of alms, and serve us. And he will offer to some of us boiled rice, and to some congey, and to some oil, and to some dainty bits.' And through joy thereat they slept uneasily that night.

Then the Bhikkhus who were followers of Mettiya and Bhummagaka, having robed themselves in the early morning, went duly bowled and robed to the dwelling-place of the prosperous householder. And that slave-girl saw the Bhikkhus who were followers

[1] Kotthake, which means the battlemented gateway which formed the entrance to an important house; and in which there was a room. See Gâtaka I, 227.

of Mettiya and Bhummag*a*ka approaching from afar; and spreading out the mats in the entrance hall, she said to them, 'Be seated, Sirs.'

And the Bhikkhus who were followers of Mettiya and Bhummag*a*ka thought: 'For a certainty the meal cannot yet be ready, since we are told to take our seats in the entrance.'

Then the slave-girl coming up with scraps of food, and sour gruel with it, said to them, 'Eat, Sirs!'

'We, sister, are of those for whom perpetual meals are provided.'

'I know, Sirs, that you are so. But only yesterday I received command from the householder that for them who should come to-morrow for the meal I was to spread out the mats in the entrance hall, and serve them with scraps of food, and some gruel with it. Eat, Sirs!'

Then the Bhikkhus who were followers of Mettiya and Bhummag*a*ka thought: 'It was yesterday that the householder, the prosperous one, came to the Ârâma to visit Dabba the Mallian. For a certainty the householder must have been set against us by Dabba the Mallian.' And through sorrow thereat they ate uneasily. And the Bhikkhus who were followers of Mettiya and Bhummag*a*ka, when they had finished their meal, returned from the receipt of alms, went to the Ârâma, and laid aside their bowls and their robes, and sat down outside the porch of the Ârâma, squatting against their waist cloths [1],

[1] Sa*m*ghâ*t*i-pallatthikâya. There is a misprint in the text (°ttikâya). On this curious expression, see below, V, 28, 2.

silent, and ashamed, with fallen hearts [1], and sunken faces, moody, and bewildered [2].

8. Now the Bhikkhunî Mettiyâ came up to the place where the Bhikkhus who were followers of Mettiya and Bhummagaka were: and when she had come there she said to them: 'My salutation to you, Sirs [3]!'

When she had so said the Bhikkhus who were followers of Mettiya and Bhummagaka did not speak to her. So a second time she said to them: 'My salutation to you, Sirs!' and they did not speak. And a third time she said to them: 'My salutation to you, Sirs!' Still the third time the Bhikkhus who were followers of Mettiya and Bhummagaka did not speak. And she said: 'Wherein have I offended you, Sirs? Wherefore do you not speak to me?'

'Are you then so indifferent [4], sister, when we are tormented by Dabba the Mallian?'

'But what can I do, Sirs?'

---

[1] Pattakkhandhâ, which the Samanta Pâsâdikâ explains by patitakkhandhâ. Khandhâ here seems to mean 'faculties.' Compare the use of Dhammâ in a similar connection at Mahâ-parinibbâna Sutta II, 32 = Mahâvagga V, 13, 9; and see Buddhaghosa's commentary on that passage, quoted by Rh. D. in 'Buddhist Suttas from the Pâli,' p. 36.

[2] Appa*t*ibhânâ. Pa*t*ibhâna*m* is the rapid suggestion of an idea in a case of doubt or difficulty, an illumination; so that pa*t*ibhânako, the man of ready wit, may be compared with upâyakusalo, the man fertile in resource. 'Absent-minded' would be an incorrect rendering; they had no idea what to think or do, and the appearance of the nun on the scene (in the next paragraph) supplied the want. Till then they hesitated, drifted.

[3] The following narrative, down to § 9, is repeated almost word for word in V, 20, only that the person there persuaded to bring the false accusation is different.

[4] Agg*h*upekkhati. Compare *G*âtaka I, 147.

'If you like, sister, you could this very day make the Blessed One expel the venerable Dabba the Mallian.'

'But what shall I do, Sirs? What is it that it is in my power to do?'

'Come now, sister; do you go to the place where the Blessed One is, and when you have come there say as follows: "This, Lord, is neither fit nor proper that the very quarter of the heavens which should be safe, secure, and free from danger, that from that very quarter should come danger, calamity, and distress—that where one might expect a calm, one should meet a gale. Methinks the very water has taken fire. I have been defiled, Lord, by Dabba the Mallian!"'

'Very well, Sirs!' said the Bhikkhunî Mettiyâ, accepting the word of the followers of Mettiya and Bhummagaka. And she went to the Blessed One [and spake even as she had been directed].

9. Then the Blessed One, on that occasion and in that connection, convened a meeting of the Samgha, and asked the venerable Dabba the Mallian:

'Are you conscious[1], Dabba, of having done such a thing as this Bhikkhunî says?'

'Even as my Lord, the Blessed One, knows me.' [And a second and a third time the Blessed One asked the same question, and received the same reply.]

[1] Literally, 'Do you recollect?' But it is quite clear from the technical words at the close of this section that the verb sarati had already acquired the secondary meaning 'to be conscious of.' The whole story is peculiarly valuable as illustrating the growth of the connotation of the verb and its allied meanings, and indirectly the origin and growth of the idea of 'conscience' which has played so great a part in theological and ethical speculation.

Then said the Blessed One: 'The Dabbas, O Dabba, do not thus repudiate[1]. If you have done it, say so. If you have not done it, say you have not.'

'Since I was born, Lord, I cannot call to mind[2] that I have practised sexual intercourse even in a dream, much less when I was awake!'

And the Blessed One addressed the Bhikkhus, and said: 'Expel then, O Bhikkhus, the Bhikkhunî Mettiyâ, and examine those Bhikkhus about it.' And so saying he rose from his seat and entered into the Vihâra.

Then those Bhikkhus expelled the Bhikkhunî Mettiyâ. But the Bhikkhus who were followers of Mettiya and Bhummagaka said to those Bhikkhus: 'Do not, Sirs, expel the Bhikkhunî Mettiyâ. She has not committed any offence. She has been set on by us with angry and bitter intentions of causing his fall.'

'What then, Sirs? is it you who are thus harassing the venerable Dabba the Mallian with a groundless charge and breach of morality?'

'That is true, Sirs.'

Then those Bhikkhus who were moderate were indignant and annoyed and complained, saying, 'How can these Bhikkhus the followers of Mettiya and Bhummagaka harass the venerable Dabba the Mallian with a groundless charge of breach of

---

[1] That is, 'Men of character and standing such as yours, O Dabba, are not in the habit of repudiating a charge in so indirect a manner by adverting merely to their standing and known character.'

[2] Here the word used is abhigânâmi.

morality?' And they told the matter to the Blessed One.

'Is this true, O Bhikkhus?'

'It is true, Lord.'

Then he rebuked them, and when he had delivered a religious discourse, he addressed the Bhikkhus, and said:

'Let then the Saṃgha grant to Dabba the Mallian, whose conscience in respect of this matter is quite clear, the Proceeding for the consciously innocent[1].

10. 'And thus, O Bhikkhus, is it to be granted.

'Let that Dabba the Mallian go before the Saṃgha, and having arranged his robe over one shoulder, let him bow down at the feet of the senior Bhikkhus, and crouching down[2], let him stretch

[1] Dabbassa sati-vepulla-ppattassa sati-vinayaṃ detu. The explanation of the compound sati-vepulla-ppatto given by Childers, though it rests on so good an authority as that of Vigesiṃha Mudaliar, cannot be right. He makes it mean 'a man of great intellectual development.' But sati must here refer to the fact that Dabba has been formally called upon to remember (sârito) whether he did or did not commit the offence. And though the exact sense of the compound is subject to some doubt, the general sense of the clause must be very much as we have conjecturally rendered it. On this formal appeal to the conscience, or memory (sati), of a Bhikkhu charged with an offence, or supposed to have offended, see Kullavagga I, 2, and 5 at the end; and X, 20.

[2] Ukkuṭikaṃ nisîditvâ. This verb does not mean 'to sit on the hams,' as rendered by Childers. The exact posture, unknown in Europe, is to crouch down on the feet (keeping both toes and heels on the ground) in such a way that the hams do not touch the ground, but come within an inch or two of it. Europeans find it very difficult to retain this posture for any length of time, but the natives of India find it easy, and it is regarded in the Piṭakas as a posture of humility.

forth his hands with the palms joined together, and let him say, "These Bhikkhus, Sirs, the followers of Mettiya and Bhumma*g*aka, are harassing me by a groundless charge of breach of morality. But I, Sirs, in respect thereof have a clear conscience, and I ask the Sa*m*gha for the acquittal to be accorded to those who are conscious of innocence." Then some able and discreet Bhikkhu is thus to lay the resolution (*ñ*atti) before the Sa*m*gha. "Let the venerable Sa*m*gha hear me. These Bhikkhus, Sirs, the followers of Mettiya and Bhumma*g*aka, are harassing the venerable Dabba the Mallian with a groundless charge of a breach of morality, and the venerable Dabba the Mallian has in respect thereof a conscience that is clear, and asks the Sa*m*gha for the acquittal of those who are conscious of innocence. If the time is convenient to the Sa*m*gha, let the Sa*m*gha accord to the venerable Dabba the Mallian the acquittal of those who are conscious of innocence. This is the resolution. Let the venerable Sa*m*gha hear me. These Bhikkhus (&c., as before, down to) asks the Sa*m*gha for the acquittal of those who are conscious of innocence. The Sa*m*gha accords to the venerable Dabba the Mallian the acquittal of those who are consciously innocent. Whosoever of the venerable ones approves of the grant to Dabba the Mallian of the acquittal of those who are conscious of innocence, let him keep silence. Whosoever approves not thereof, let him speak. And a second time I say the same thing. And a third time I say the same thing. Let the venerable Sa*m*gha hear me. These Bhikkhus (&c., as before, down to) let him speak. The acquittal of those who are conscious of innocence has been granted by the Sa*m*gha to Dabba the Mallian. The Sa*m*gha approves thereof. Therefore is it silent. Thus do I understand[1].''

11. 'There are five things which make a grant of acquittal to those who are conscious of innocence to be according to law. The Bhikkhu must be innocent and without offence, others must have censured him, he must ask the Sa*m*gha for acquittal as being conscious of innocence, the Sa*m*gha must grant it, the Sa*m*gha must be duly held and duly constituted. These, O Bhikkhus, are the five things which make a grant of the acquittal of those who are conscious of innocence to be according to law.'

5[2].

1. Now at that time the Bhikkhu Gagga was insane and out of his mind; and by him, when so insane and out of his mind, many things unworthy of a sama*n*a had been committed, as well in speech as in act[3]. The Bhikkhus warned the Bhikkhu Gagga of a fault so committed by him when insane and out of his mind, saying, 'Does the venerable one call to

---

[1] This section is repeated below, chap. 14, § 27, with the necessary alterations for a general rule instead of a particular case.

[2] The particular decision given in this chapter for the particular case is elaborated in chap. 14, § 28 below into a general rule for every similar case.

[3] Buddhaghosa explains this word as follows: 'Bhâsitaparikantan ti vâ*k*âya bhâsita*m* kâyena parikkanta*m* parikkametvâ katan ti attho.' The similar word Parikanta*m*, which occurs in the Sutta-vibhaṅga, Pârâ*g*ika IV, 1, 2, in the sense of lacerated, is from the root k*ri*nt.

mind that he has committed such and such an offence?'

He replied, 'I, my friends, was insane and out of my mind. (No doubt) many things unworthy of a sama*n*a, as well in speech as in act, may have been committed by me when so insane and out of my mind. But I do not recollect it. It was done by me by reason of my insanity.'

But though they received that answer from him[1], they warned him still, saying, 'Does the venerable one call to mind that he has committed such and such an offence?'

'Those Bhikkhus who were moderate were annoyed, murmured, and became indignant, saying, "How can those Bhikkhus warn the Bhikkhu Gagga . . . saying . . . such and such an offence?" And when he replies, "I, my friends, was insane . . . by reason of my insanity"—how can those Bhikkhus still warn him, saying . . . of such and such an offence?'

And those Bhikkhus told the matter to the Blessed One.

'Is it true, O Bhikkhus, that those Bhikkhus (&c., as before, down to) such and such an offence?'

'It is true, Lord.'

Then he rebuked them, and when he had delivered a religious discourse he addressed the Bhikkhus, and said:

'Let then the Sa*m*gha grant to Gagga the

---

[1] Na*m* in the text is correct. It is identical with the *nam* so frequently found in Jain Prakrit; on which see Weber in his Bhagavatî 'Abhandlungen der Berliner Akadamie,' 1865, pp. 422 and fol.

Bhikkhu who is now sane the dispensation for those who are no longer insane.

2. 'And thus, O Bhikkhus, should it be granted.

'Let that Bhikkhu Gagga [here follow the words of the formal request, of the resolution, and of the grant by decision of the Sa*m*gha, exactly in the same way as in the last case, chapter 4, § 10].'

6.

1. 'There are three cases, O Bhikkhus, in which grants of dispensation for those who are no longer insane are not valid: and three cases in which such grants are valid.

'What are the three cases in which grants of dispensation for those who are no longer insane are not valid?

'In the first place, O Bhikkhus, in case a Bhikkhu have committed an offence: and in respect thereof either the Sa*m*gha, or a number of Bhikkhus, or a single Bhikkhu, warn him, saying, "Does the venerable one call to mind that he has been guilty of such and such an offence?" And he, notwithstanding that he does remember it, says, "I do not remember, Sirs, that I have been guilty of such and such an offence." Then if the Sa*m*gha grant him the dispensation of those who are no longer insane, that grant is not valid.

'Again, O Bhikkhus, in case a Bhikkhu (&c., as before, down to) And he, notwithstanding that he does remember it, says, "I remember it, Sirs, but as if in a dream." Then if the Sa*m*gha grant him the dispensation of those who are no longer insane, that grant is not valid.

'Again, O Bhikkhus, in case a Bhikkhu have committed an offence, and in respect thereof either the Sa*m*gha, or a number of Bhikkhus, or a single Bhikkhu, warn him, saying, "Does the venerable one call to mind that he has been guilty of such and such an offence?" And he, though he is not insane, acts in the (deceptive) way of an insane person[1], saying, "I act so, and you act so likewise. It beseems me, and it likewise beseems you." Then if the Sa*m*gha grant him the dispensation of those who are no longer insane, that grant is not valid.

'These are the three cases, O Bhikkhus, in which a grant of the dispensation for those who are no longer insane is not valid.

2. 'What are the three cases in which grants of dispensation for those who are no longer insane are valid?

'In the first place, O Bhikkhus, in case a Bhikkhu be insane and out of his mind; and by him, when so insane and out of his mind, many things unworthy of a sama*n*a have been committed, as well in speech as in act. And either the Sa*m*gha, or a number of Bhikkhus, or a single Bhikkhu, warns him in respect thereof, saying, "Does the venerable one call to mind that he has committed such and such an offence?" And he really not remembering it, answers, "I do not remember, Sirs, that I have been guilty of such and such an offence." Then if the Sa*m*gha grants him the dispensation for those who are no longer insane, that grant is valid.

---

[1] Ummattakâlaya*m* karoti, on which Buddhaghosa says nothing. The word recurs in the following section.

'Again, O Bhikkhus, in case a Bhikkhu be insane and out of his mind (&c., as before, down to) And he, not really remembering it, answers, "I remember it, Sirs, but as if in a dream." Then if the Sa*m*gha grants him the dispensation for those who are no longer insane, that grant is valid.

'Again, O Bhikkhus, in case a Bhikkhu be insane and out of his mind (&c., as before, down to) "Does the venerable one call to mind that he has been guilty of such and such an offence?" And he, being still insane, acts in the way of an insane person, saying, "I act so, and you act so likewise. It beseems me, and it likewise beseems you." Then if the Sa*m*gha (afterwards) grant him the dispensation for those who are no longer insane, that grant is valid.

'These are the three cases, O Bhikkhus, in which the grant of the dispensation for those who are no longer insane is valid.'

7.

1. Now at that time the *Kh*abbaggiya Bhikkhus carried out official acts against Bhikkhus who had not confessed themselves guilty—the Ta*gg*aniya-kamma, or the Nissaya-kamma, or the Pabbâ*g*aniya-kamma, or the Pa*t*isâra*n*iya-kamma, or the Ukkhepaniya-kamma.

Those Bhikkhus who were moderate were annoyed, murmured, and became indignant, saying, 'How can the *Kh*abbaggiya Bhikkhus (&c., as before).' And those Bhikkhus told the matter to the Blessed One.

'Is it true, O Bhikkhus, that the *Kh*abbaggiya Bhikkhus do so?'

'It is true, Lord.'

Then he rebuked them, and when he had delivered a religious discourse, he addressed the Bhikkhus, and said:

'No official act, O Bhikkhus,—whether the Tag*g*aniya-kamma, or the Nissaya-kamma, or the Pabbâ*g*aniya-kamma, or the Pa*t*isâra*n*iya-kamma, or the Ukkhepaniya-kamma,—is to be carried out against Bhikkhus who have not confessed themselves guilty[1]. Whosoever does so, shall be guilty of a dukka*t*a offence.'

8.

1. 'Now, O Bhikkhus, an official act carried out against a Bhikkhu who has confessed himself guilty is invalid as follows, and is valid as follows. And how does such an official act become invalid? In case a Bhikkhu have committed a Pârâ*g*ika offence, and in respect thereof either the Sa*m*gha, or a number of Bhikkhus, or a single Bhikkhu warns him, saying, "The venerable one has been guilty of a Pârâ*g*ika." And he replies thus, "I have not, Sirs, been guilty of a Pârâ*g*ika. I have been guilty of a Sa*m*ghâdisesa." And in respect thereof the Sa*m*gha deals with him for a Sa*m*ghâdisesa. Then that official act is invalid.'

---

[1] The mode in which such a confession ought to be made is set out in full in IV, 14, 30-34.

[And so also if on being warned of any one of the seven offences[1] he confesses himself to be guilty of any one of the offences different from the one charged, then the official act is invalid.]

2. 'And when, O Bhikkhus, is such an official act valid? In case a Bhikkhu have committed a Pârâ*g*ika offence, and in respect thereof the Sa*m*gha, or a number of Bhikkhus, or a single Bhikkhu warns him, saying, "The venerable one has been guilty of a Pârâ*g*ika." And he replies, "Yea, Sirs, I have been guilty of a Pârâ*g*ika." And in respect thereof the Sa*m*gha deals with him for a Pârâ*g*ika. Then that official act is valid[2].'

[And so for each of the other offences mentioned in § 1, the whole of § 2 is repeated.]

9[3].

Now at that time the Bhikkhus in chapter (Sa*m*gha) assembled, since they became violent, quarrelsome, and disputatious, and kept on wounding one another with sharp words[4], were unable

---

[1] The same, namely, as those in the list given at Mahâvagga IV, 16, 12, &c.

[2] In other words, if a Bhikkhu confesses an offence different from that with which he has been charged, the confession cannot be used against him even as regards a decision with respect to the offence confessed.

[3] On this chapter, see further below, IV, 14, 16.

[4] A*ññ*ama*ññ*a*m* mukhaisattîhi vitudantâ viharanti. Literally, 'with mouth-javelins.' Vitudati, and not vitûdati as Childers gives, is the right spelling. So Fausböll reads at *G*âtaka II, 185, 186.

to settle the disputed question (that was brought before them).

They told this matter to the Blessed One.

[1] 'I allow you, O Bhikkhus, to settle such a dispute by the vote of the majority. A Bhikkhu who shall be possessed of five qualifications shall be appointed as taker of the voting tickets—one who does not walk in partiality, one who does not walk in malice, one who does not walk in folly, one who does not walk in fear[2], one who knows what (votes) have been taken and what have not been taken.

'And thus shall he be appointed.

'First the Bhikkhu is to be requested (whether he will undertake the office). Then some able and discreet Bhikkhu is to bring the matter before the Sa*m*gha, saying,

'"Let the venerable Sa*m*gha hear me. If the time seems meet to the Sa*m*gha, let the Sa*m*gha appoint a Bhikkhu of such and such a name as taker of the voting tickets.

'"This is the motion (*ñ*atti).

'"Let the venerable Sa*m*gha hear me. The Sa*m*gha appoints a Bhikkhu of such and such a name as taker of the tickets. Whosoever of the venerable ones approves of the Bhikkhu of such and such a name being appointed as taker of the

[1] From here to the end of the chapter recurs in IV, 14, 24.

[2] These are the qualifications always ascribed to one who rightly fills any judicial offence, and are called the four Agatis. They are the especial attributes of a good king sitting as judge, and are mentioned elsewhere (Sa*m*ghâdisesa XIII; Mahâvagga VIII, 5, 2; VIII, 6, 1; and below, VI, 11, 2) of other officials of the order with duties similar to those in the text.

tickets, let him keep silence. Whosoever approves not thereof, let him speak. The Bhikkhu of such and such a name is appointed by the Sa*m*gha as taker of the voting tickets. Therefore is it silent. Thus do I understand.'"

10[1].

1. 'There are ten cases, O Bhikkhus, in which the taking of votes is invalid; and ten in which the taking of votes is valid.

'Which are the ten in which the taking of votes is invalid? When the matter in dispute is trivial[2] —when the case has not run its course (that is, when the necessary preliminaries of submission to arbitration have not been carried out[3])—when regarding the matter in dispute the Bhikkhus have not formally remembered, or been formally called upon to remember, the offence[4]—when the taker of votes[5] knows that those whose opinions are not in accordance with the law will be in the majority,

---

[1] On this chapter, see further below, IV, 14, 24–26.

[2] Oramattaka*m*. Compare the English law maxim, De minimis non curat lex.

[3] Buddhaghosa says, Na *k*a gatigatan ti dve tayo âvâse na gata*m*, tattha tatth' eva vâ dvitikkhattu*m* avini*kkh*ita*m*. See on these proceedings above.

[4] Buddhaghosa says, Na *k*a sarita-sâritan ti dvitikkhattu*m* tehi bhikkhûhi saya*m* sarita*m* va aññehi sârita*m* vâ na hoti.

[5] Gânâtî ti salâka*m* gâhento *g*ânâti. (S. P.)

or probably[1] may be in the majority—when he knows that the voting will result in a schism in the Saṃgha—when he is in doubt whether the voting will result in a schism in the Saṃgha—when the votes are irregularly given[2]—when all do not vote equally[3]—and when they do not vote in accordance with the view (which they really hold). These are the ten cases in which the voting is invalid[4].

2. 'And which are the ten cases in which the voting is valid?'

[The ten cases are precisely the reverse of the other ten.]

11.

1. Now at that time the Bhikkhu Uvâḷa[5], being examined in the midst of the Saṃgha with an offence, when he had denied then confessed it, when he had confessed it then denied it, made

---

[1] App eva nâma. That this phrase does not merely mean 'perhaps' is clear from its use in § 2.

[2] Adhammena gaṇhantî ti adhammavâdino evaṃ mayaṃ bahû bhavissâmâ ti dve dve salâkâyo gaṇhanti. (S. P.)

[3] On vaggâ, here = vi + agga, compare our note on the 21st Pâkittiya, and Kullavagga I, 2, 1. Buddhaghosa here says, Vaggâ gaṇhantî ti dve dhammavâdino ekaṃ dhammavâdi-salâkaṃ gaṇhanti evaṃ dhammavâdino na bahû bhavissantî ti maññamânâ.

[4] With this chapter the 26th section of chapter 14 should be compared, where very curious means are inculcated for avoiding some of the votes here stated to be invalid.

[5] In the Burmese MSS. the name of this monk is written Upavâla.

counter-charges[1], and spoke lies which he knew to be such[2].

Those Bhikkhus who were moderate were annoyed, murmured, and became indignant, saying, 'How can the Bhikkhu Uvâ*l*a do so?' And they told the matter to the Blessed One.

'Is it true, O Bhikkhus, as they say that the Bhikkhu [&c., as before].'

'It is true, Lord.'

Then he rebuked him, and when he had delivered a religious discourse he addressed the Bhikkhus, and said:

'Then, O Bhikkhus, let the Sa*m*gha carry out the Tassa-pâpiyyasikâ-kamma (the Proceeding in the case of the obstinately wrong)[3].'

2. 'And thus, O Bhikkhus, is it to be carried out. In the first place the Bhikkhu Uvâ*l*a must have been warned; when he had been warned, he must have been called upon to remember (whether he has, or has not, consciously committed the offence); when he had been called upon to remember, he must have been caused (by being put on his trial with respect to the offence) to bring upon himself a new

[1] Aññena aññam pa*t*ikarati. We follow Wijesi*m*ha Mudaliyar's interpretation of this phrase as given by Childers (s. v. tassapâpiyyasikâ).

[2] Chapter 14, section 29 below, is in fact an elaboration of this paragraph, giving instances of the kind of prevarication here intended to be referred to.

[3] The exact meaning of the phrase is somewhat doubtful, owing to the ambiguity of the tassa. It should probably be analysed 'the proceeding against one who is more sinful (pâpiyo) than that (tassa);' that is, who adds sin to sin. Childers gives a long note on the Proceeding drawn by Wijesi*m*ha Mudaliyar from this chapter, but does not analyse the word.

offence (namely, of obstinacy or prevarication); when he has brought upon himself this new offence, some discreet and able Bhikkhu ought to lay the matter before the Sa*m*gha, saying,

'"Let the venerable Sa*m*gha hear me. This Bhikkhu Uvâ*l*a, being examined in the midst of the Sa*m*gha with an offence, when he has denied it then confesses it, when he has confessed it then denies it, makes counter-charges, and speaks lies which he knows to be such. If the time seems meet to the Sa*m*gha, let the Sa*m*gha carry out the Tassa-pâpiyyasikâ-kamma against the Bhikkhu Uvâ*l*a.

'"This is the motion.

'"Let the venerable Sa*m*gha hear me. This Bhikkhu Uvâ*l*a (&c., as before). The Sa*m*gha carries out the Tassa-pâpiyyasikâ-kamma against Uvâ*l*a the Bhikkhu. Whosoever of the venerable ones approves of the Tassa-pâpiyyasikâ-kamma being carried out against Uvâ*l*a the Bhikkhu, let him keep silence. Whosoever approves not thereof, let him speak.

'"A second time I say the same thing. This Bhikkhu Uvâ*l*a (&c., as before, down to) let him speak. A third time I say the same thing (&c., as before, down to) let him speak.

'"The Tassa-pâpiyyasikâ-kamma has been carried out by the Sa*m*gha against Uvâ*l*a the Bhikkhu. Therefore is it silent. Thus do I understand[1]."'

---

[1] This Kammavâ*k*â is precisely the same as is laid down in *K*ullavagga I, 1, 4, &c. in the case of all the other penal Kammas.

12.

1. 'There are five things, O Bhikkhus, which are necessary to the valid carrying out of the Tassa-pâpiyyasikâ-kamma. To wit—he is impure, he is shameless—a censure has been set on foot against him[1]—the Samgha carries out the Kamma—it carries it out lawfully, and in a full quorum.

2. 'There are three things, O Bhikkhus, by which, when a Tassa-pâpiyyasikâ-kamma is characterised, it is against the Dhamma, and against the Vinaya, and difficult to be settled; (that is to say), when it has not been carried out in a full assembly of properly qualified persons, according to law and justice, and in the presence of the litigant parties—when it has been carried out without the accused person having been heard—when it has been carried out without the accused person having confessed himself guilty.

'These are the three things, O Bhikkhus, by which, when a Tassa-pâpiyyasikâ-kamma is characterised, it is against the Dhamma, and against the Vinaya, and difficult to be settled.

'There are three things by which (and as in last paragraph) it is in accordance with the Dhamma, and in accordance with the Vinaya, and easy to be settled; (that is to say), when it has been [&c., the rest of this paragraph is the reverse of the last][2].'

---

[1] Compare the use of anuvâdo in *K*ullavagga I, 5.

[2] These paragraphs exactly correspond to paragraphs at *K*ullavagga I, 2. It is probably merely owing to this repetition that it is here also prescribed that the accused person must confess

3. [This paragraph exactly corresponds to *K*ulla-vagga I, 4, paragraph 1, as to the three cases in which the Sa*m*gha, if it likes, may carry out the Tassa-pâpiyyasikâ-kamma against a Bhikkhu.]

4. [In this paragraph the 'right conduct' for a Bhikkhu who has been subjected to this Kamma is laid down precisely as in I, 5 for a Bhikkhu subjected to the Ta*gg*aniya-kamma.]

Then the Sa*m*gha carried out the Tassa-pâpiyyasikâ-kamma against Uvâ*l*a the Bhikkhu.

13[1].

1. Now at that time, while the Bhikkhus were continuing in quarrels, strifes, and disputes, they had been guilty of many things unworthy of a Sama*n*a, as well in word as in deed, and it occurred to the Bhikkhus, 'Whilst we were continuing, &c. . . . we have been guilty, &c. . . . as well in word as in deed. If we now deal one with another for those offences, it may happen that that proceeding may result in harshness, in ill-feeling, in divisions. How now should we manage?'

And they told the matter to the Blessed One.

'In case, O Bhikkhus, whilst the Bhikkhus are continuing, &c. . . . they are guilty, &c. . . . as well in word as in deed. And it occurs to them, "Whilst we were continuing, &c. . . . we have been guilty, &c. . . . If we now deal, &c. . . . How now shall

himself guilty, as it must be evident from the Introductory Story, that he will not do so.

[1] The whole of this chapter recurs below, IV, 14, 33.

we manage?" I enjoin upon you, O Bhikkhus, to settle a matter of this kind by Ti*n*avatthâraka (the Covering over as with grass)[1].

2. 'And thus, O Bhikkhus, is it to be settled. All are to meet together in one spot. When they have met together some able and discreet Bhikkhu is to bring the matter before the Sa*m*gha, saying,

'"Let the venerable Sa*m*gha hear me. While we were continuing, &c.... we have been guilty, &c.... as well in word as in deed. And it occurred to us (&c., down to) If we now deal one with another, &c. . . . it may result in harshness, in ill-feeling, in divisions. If the time seems meet to the Sa*m*gha, let the Sa*m*gha settle this matter by the Covering over as with grass—except only as regards serious offences[2], and as regards those things in which the laity have been concerned."

'Then some discreet and able Bhikkhu among those Bhikkhus who belong to the one party is to bring the matter before his own party, saying,

'"May the venerable ones hear me. While we were continuing, &c. . . . we have been guilty, &c. . . . as well in word as in deed. And it occurred to us, &c. . . . (down to) in divisions. If the time seems meet to you, venerable Sirs, I would confess in the midst of the Sa*m*gha, both on your behalf, venerable Sirs, and on my own behalf, both such offence as is yours, venerable Sirs, and such offence

[1] Buddhaghosa's commentary on this expression will be found in the notes to H. O.'s edition of the text, pp. 313, 314.

[2] Buddhaghosa (H. O. loc. cit.) explains this as meaning either Pârâ*g*ika or Sa*m*ghâdisesa offences. So also he explains Du*tth*ullâ âpatti at Mahâvagga X, 5, 4.

as is mine own, to the end that it may be covered over as with grass, except only as regards serious offences, and as regards those things in which the laity have been concerned."

'And some discreet and able Bhikkhu among the Bhikkhus belonging to the other party is to bring the matter before his own party, saying, "May the venerable ones hear me [&c., as before in the last paragraph, down to the end]."

'Then the discreet and able Bhikkhu among the Bhikkhus belonging to the one party is to bring the matter before the Sa*m*gha, saying, "May the venerable Sa*m*gha hear me. While we (&c., as before, down to) in divisions. If the time seems meet to the Sa*m*gha, I would confess[1] in the midst of the Sa*m*gha, both on behalf of these venerable ones and on my own behalf, both such offence as is theirs and such offence as is mine own, to the end that it may be covered over as with grass, except only as regards serious offences, and as regards those things in which the laity have been concerned. This is the motion (*ñ*atti). May the venerable Sa*m*gha hear me. While we (&c., as before, down to) in divisions. I confess (&c., as before, down to) in which the laity have been concerned. Whosoever of the venerable ones approves of the confession of these our offences, to the end that they may so be covered over as with grass, except as before mentioned, let him keep silence. Whosoever approves not thereof, let him speak. These our offences are confessed in the midst of the Sa*m*gha, to the end that they may be covered over as with grass, except

[1] Deseyya*m*. Compare IV, 14, 33, at the end.

as before mentioned. The Sa*m*gha approves thereof. Therefore is it silent. Thus do I understand."

'And the discreet and able Bhikkhu among the Bhikkhus belonging to the other party is to bring the matter before the Sa*m*gha, saying, "Let the venerable Sa*m*gha hear me (&c., as before in the last paragraph, down to the end)."

'Then thus, O Bhikkhus, those Bhikkhus are absolved of those offences, except as regards serious offences, and as regards those things in which the laity have been concerned, and except also as regards those who express their disapproval of the proceedings, or who are not present at them[1].'

14.

1. Now at that time Bhikkhus had disputes with Bhikkhus, and Bhikkhunîs with Bhikkhus. And the Bhikkhu *Kh*anna[2], forcing his way (into the apartments) of the Bhikkhunîs[3], took the part of the Bhikkhunîs and disputed with the Bhikkhus.

---

[1] On these phrases Buddhaghosa has the following note: Di*tth*âvikamman ti ye pana na me ta*m* khamatî ti aññamaññâ di*tth*âvikamma*m* karonti tehi vâ saddhi*m* âpatti*m* âpa*gg*itvâ pi, tattha anâgatâ âgantvâ vâ *kh*anda*m* datvâ parive*n*âdisu nisinnâ, te âpattîhi na vu*tth*ahanti. This is more an exegesis on the rule than an explanation of the words Di*tth*âvikamma*m* *th*apetvâ, the exact meaning of which remains doubtful. The literal rendering would be 'except as regards the manifestation of opinion.'

[2] It was with reference to this conduct of *Kh*anna that the Buddha is stated in the Mahâ-parinibbâna Sutta VI, 4 to have imposed a penalty upon him. He is also mentioned above, I, 25-31, and below, XI, 1, 12-14.

[3] Compare the 16th and 43rd Pâ*k*ittiyas. Buddhaghosa says here, Bhikkhunîna*m* anupakha*gg*â ti bhikkhunîna*m* antopavisitvâ.

Those Bhikkhus who were moderate were indignant, &c. . . . told the Blessed One, &c. . . . he addressed the Bhikkhus, and said:

2. 'There are, O Bhikkhus, the following four kinds of legal questions that require formal settlement by the Sa*m*gha; (that is to say), legal questions arising out of disputes, legal questions arising out of censure, legal questions arising out of offences, legal questions arising out of business[1].

'Among these, what is a legal question arising out of dispute? This, O Bhikkhus, is when Bhikkhus dispute, saying, "This is Dhamma," or "This is not Dhamma," or "This is Vinaya," or "This is not Vinaya," or "This is taught and spoken by the Tathâgata," or "This is not taught nor spoken by the Tathâgata," or "This has been practised by the Tathâgata," or "This has not been practised by the Tathâgata," or "This has been ordained by the Tathâgata," or "This has not been ordained by the Tathâgata," or "This is an offence," or "This is not an offence," or "This is a slight offence," or "This is a grievous offence," or "This is an offence which can be done away," or "This is an offence which cannot be done away[2]," or "This is a most grave offence," or "This is not a most grave

[1] The various ways of settling these four kinds of legal questions are recapitulated in §§ 27-34 of this chapter.

[2] Sâvasesâ-anavasesâ-âpatti. The Parivâra IX, 1, 10 says, Yâ sâ âpatti anavasesâ sâ âpatti na katamena adhikara*n*ena na katamamhi *th*âne na katamena samathena sammati. It is practically equivalent therefore to Pârâ*g*ikâ. Those offences which can be done away, but only by the Sa*m*gha, are called accordingly in the Buddhist Sanskrit Sa*m*ghâva*s*esha, which corresponds to the Pâli Sa*m*ghâdisesa. The translation and note at Mahâvagga X, 2, 4 should be altered accordingly.

offence." Whatsoever quarrel, strife, controversy, difference of opinion, contradiction, opposition, cantankerousness[1], or contention there may be on such a matter, this is called a legal question arising out of dispute.

'And among these, which is a legal question arising out of censure? This, O Bhikkhus, is when Bhikkhus charge a Bhikkhu with a fault of morality, or of conduct, or of opinion, or of means of livelihood. Whatsoever charge, censure, incrimination[2], admonition[2], candid opinion[3], making of excuses[4] for a person, or making fun of him, there may be, that is called a legal question arising out of censure.

'And among these, what is a legal question arising out of offence? The five groups of offences[5] are subjects of legal questions of offences, and the seven groups of offences[6] are subjects of legal questions of offence. This is what is called a legal question arising out of offence.

'And among these, what is a legal question of business? Whatsoever is to the Sa*m*gha a matter which ought to be done, an obligation, a matter for which leave ought to be formally asked, the pro-

---

[1] Vipa*kk*atâya vohâro ti *k*itta-dukkhatthâya vohâro pharusava*k*anan ti attho (S. P.).

[2] Anullapanâ anubha*n*anâ ti ubhaya*m* anuvadana-veva*k*ana-mattam eva (S. P.).

[3] Anusampavaṅkatâ ti punappuna*m* kâya-*k*itta*m* vâ*k*âhi tatth' eva sampavaṅkatâ anuvadanabhâvo ti attho (S. P.).

[4] Abbhussahanatâ ti kasmâ eva*m* na upavadissâmi upavadissâmi yevâ ti ussâha*m* katvâ anuvadanâ (S. P.).

[5] That is to say, Pârâ*g*ika, Sa*m*ghâdisesa, Pâ*k*ittiya, Pâ*t*idesaniya, and Dukka*t*a, as below, in IV, 14, 14; IX, 3, 3.

[6] That is to say, the five mentioned in the last note, and besides them, Thulla*kk*aya and Dubbhâsita.

posal of a resolution[1], the proceeding by *ñ*atti-dutiya-kamma[2], or by *ñ*atti-*k*atuttha-kamma[2], that is called a legal question of business.

3. 'What is that which gives rise to a legal question of dispute? There are six causes of dispute that give rise to legal questions of dispute. And there are three causes of wrong-doing that give rise to legal questions of dispute, and three causes of right-doing that give rise to legal questions of dispute. And which are these six?

'In the first place, O Bhikkhus, there is the Bhikkhu who is angry, and who bears enmity in his heart. Whatsoever Bhikkhu, O Bhikkhus, is such an angry man bearing enmity in his heart, he remains without reverence for, and without delight in the Teacher, the Dhamma, and the Sa*m*gha, and does not fulfil all the duties of a disciple. And whatsoever Bhikkhu, O Bhikkhus, remains without reverence for, and without delight in the Teacher, the Dhamma, and the Sa*m*gha, and does not fulfil all the duties of a disciple, he causes disputes to arise in the Sa*m*gha, and such a dispute becomes a cause

[1] Apalokana-kamman ti-âdi pana tass' eva pabheda-va*k*ana*m*. Tattha apalokana-kamma*m* nâma sîma*tth*akam sa*m*gha*m* sodhetvâ *kh*andârahâna*m* *kh*anda*m* âharitvâ samaggassa anumatiyâ tikkhattu*m* sâvetvâ kâtabba-kamma*m* (S. P.).

[2] See our note at Mahâvagga I, 28, 3. The Samanta Pâsâdikâ here says, *ñ*attidutiyakamma*m* pana apaloketvâ kattabba*m* pi atthi akattabba*m* pi atthi. Tattha sîmasammuti sîmasamûhananâ kathinadâna*m* kathinubbhâro kû*t*avatthudesanâ vihâravatthudesanâ 'ti imâni *kh*a kammâni garukâni apaloketvâ kâtu*m* na va*tt*ati, *ñ*attidutiyakammavâ*k*a*m* sâvetvâ 'va kâtabbâni, avasesâ terasa sammutiyo senâsanagâhakamatuka (? patta) *k*îvaradânâti(°di°?)-sammutiyo *k*â 'ti evarûpâni lahukakammâni apaloketvâ pi kâtu*m* va*tt*anti.

of woe, and of want, and of disaster to the great multitudes, of woe and of want to gods and men. If you, therefore, O Bhikkhus, perceive such a one, a root of disputes both internal and external, do you exert yourselves, O Bhikkhus, to put away from you so evil a person, the root of those disputes. If you perceive, O Bhikkhus, no such person, take pains lest any such evil root of disputes should thereafter arise among you. Thus will so evil a root of disputes be put away from you, and thus will no such evil person, the root of disputes, arise hereafter among you.

'Again, O Bhikkhus, there is the Bhikkhu, who is a hypocrite[1], and who hides his faults; who is envious and jealous; who is crafty and treacherous; who has sinful desires and false beliefs; who is tarnished by love of worldly gain, devoted to getting and taking, for whom to renounce a thing is hard. Whatsoever Bhikkhu, O Bhikkhus, is thus a hypocrite, who hides his faults, he remains [&c., as before, the whole of the last paragraph down to the end being repeated in each of the cases here enumerated].

4. 'And which are the three causes of wrong-doing which give rise to legal questions of dispute?

'Herein, O Bhikkhus, men of greedy mind are given to dispute, men of evil mind are given to dispute, men of foolish mind are given to dispute, saying, "This is Dhamma," or "This is not Dhamma" [&c., as before, in § 2, down to] or "This is not a

[1] Palâsî; no doubt connected with the primary meaning of the word 'leaf,' as is also its use in the sense of 'covering, lining,' in eka-palâsikâ upâhanâ at Mahâvagga V, 1, 29. The expression forms the subject of Puggala II, 2. See also Gâtaka III, 259.

most grave offence." These are the three causes of wrong-doing which give rise to legal questions of dispute.

'And which are the three causes of right-doing which give rise to legal questions of dispute?

'In the first place, O Bhikkhus, men not of greedy mind [&c., as in the last paragraph, inserting the word "not"].

5. 'And what is that, O Bhikkhus, which gives rise to legal questions of censure? There are six causes of censure that give rise to legal questions of censure. And there are three causes of wrong-doing that give rise to legal questions of censure. And there are three causes of right-doing that give rise to legal questions of censure. And the body gives rise to legal questions of censure, and speech gives rise to legal questions of censure.'

[The six are word for word the same as in the last section, reading 'censure' for 'dispute.']

'And which are the three causes of wrong-doing that give rise to legal questions of censure?

'Herein, O Bhikkhus, men of greedy mind are given to censure, men of evil mind are given to censure, men of foolish mind are given to censure, accusing others of breaches of morality, or of behaviour, or of error in doctrine, or of adopting a wrong means of livelihood. These are the three causes of wrong-doing that give rise to legal questions of censure.'

[There follow the three causes of right-doing, reading 'men not of greedy mind,' &c., as before, end of § 4.]

'And how does the body give rise to legal questions of censure? In case a man be ill-favoured, or ugly, or a dwarf[1], or diseased, or blind of one eye, or lame, or humpbacked, or crippled, people find fault with him on that account. This is how the body gives rise to legal questions of censure.

'And how does speech give rise to legal questions of censure? In case a man have a bad voice, or be indistinct, or harsh in speech[2], then people find fault with him on that account. This is how speech gives rise to legal questions of censure.

6. 'And what is it that gives rise to legal questions of offence? There are six origins of offence that give rise to legal questions of offence. There is an offence that originates in deed, but not in word nor in thought. There is an offence that originates in word, but not in deed nor in thought. There is an offence that originates in deed and in word, but not in thought. There is an offence that originates in deed and in thought, but not in word. There is an offence that originates in word and in thought, but not in deed. There is an offence that originates in deed and in word and in thought. These are the six (&c.)

7. 'And what is that which gives rise to legal questions of business? There is one thing that gives rise to legal questions of business, that is to say, the Sa*m*gha.

---

[1] Buddhaghosa has no explanation of these terms here, but on Aṅguttara Nikâya III, 2, 3, where the whole list recurs, he says (as Dr. Morris is good enough to inform us) that oko*t*imako is equal to laku*n**t*ako; and the same explanation is given by the commentary on Puggala IV, 19. Compare the use in English of 'a mere dot of a man,' in a similar sense.

[2] These three epithets of the voice are no doubt intended to be the opposites of the three in Mahâvagga V, 13, 9.

8. 'Legal questions of dispute. Right. Wrong. Undetermined[1].

'A legal question arising out of dispute may be right, and it may be wrong, and it may be undetermined. Of these, which is the legal question arising out of dispute which is right?

'In case, O Bhikkhus, the Bhikkhu of right mind discuss, saying, "This is the Dhamma," or "This is not the Dhamma" (&c., as before, in § 2, down to) or "This is not a most grave offence." Whatsoever quarrel, strife, contention, difference of opinion, contradiction, opposition, cantankerousness, or contention there may be in such a discussion is called a legal question arising out of dispute that is right.'

[And so when the Bhikkhus have a wrong mind, or an undetermined mind, the legal question arising out of such dispute is respectively a legal question arising out of dispute that is wrong or undetermined.]

9. 'Legal questions of censure. Right. Wrong. Undetermined.'

[It may be either of the three, according as the Bhikkhus censuring (as in § 5) have a right, wrong, or an undetermined mind. The form of the paragraph corresponds to § 8 throughout.]

10. 'Legal questions of offence. Right. Wrong. Undetermined.

'There may be a legal question whether an offence is wrong, and there may be a legal question

[1] We have already pointed out (above, IV, 1, 2) that this mode of the commencement of a discussion by setting out a list of the points to be discussed and compared is found also in some of the Abhidhamma books. There it was only the objects themselves, here we have all the predicates which it is proposed to apply (as in § 8), or to declare inapplicable to the object (as in § 10), which are set out, but the principle is the same.

whether an offence is undetermined. There is no legal question whether an offence be right.

'Of these, which is a legal question whether an offence be wrong? Whatsoever transgression be committed knowingly, consciously, and deliberately, this is called a legal question whether an offence be wrong.

'And of these, which is a legal question whether an offence be undetermined? Whatsoever transgression be committed not knowingly, not consciously, not deliberately, this is called a legal question whether an offence be undetermined.

11. 'Legal questions of business. Right. Wrong. Undetermined.'

[It may be all three, according as the Bhikkhus performing the business specified, as in § 2, are right-minded, wrong-minded, or of undetermined mind. The form of the paragraph as in § 8 throughout.]

12. 'Disputes, legal questions arising out of disputes. Dispute which is no legal question. Legal question which is no dispute. Matter which is both legal question and dispute.

'There may be a dispute which is a legal question of dispute. There may be a dispute which is no legal question. There may be such a legal question which is no dispute. There may be such a legal question and also a dispute.

'Of these, which is the dispute which is a legal question of dispute requiring formal settlement? In case Bhikkhus discuss, saying, "This is Dhamma" [&c., as before, in § 2], or "This is not a most grave offence." Whatsoever quarrel, strife [&c., as in § 2] there may be on such a matter is a dispute which is a legal question of dispute requiring formal settlement.

'And of these, which is a dispute which is not a legal question requiring formal settlement? When a mother disputes with her son, or a son with his mother, or a father with his son, or a son with his father, or a brother with a brother, or a brother with a sister, or a sister with a brother, or a friend with a friend. Such a dispute is not a legal question requiring formal settlement by the Sa*m*gha.

'And of these, which is a legal question that is not a dispute? A legal question of censure, or a legal question of offence, or a legal question of business. This is a legal question which is not a dispute.

'And of these, which is a legal question requiring formal settlement which is also a dispute? A legal question of dispute that requires formal settlement by the Sa*m*gha is both such a legal question and also a dispute.'

13. [The same distinction drawn between censure, and a legal question of censure requiring formal settlement.]

14. 'Offence. Legal question arising out of an offence. Offence which is not subject of a legal question. Legal question and no offence. Legal question and offence too.

'There may be an offence which is subject of a legal question of offence. There may be an offence and no legal question. There may be legal question and no offence. There may be legal question and offence too.

'Of these, which is the offence which may be subject of a legal question? The five groups of offences are subjects of legal questions of offence; the seven groups of offences are subjects of legal questions of offence. These are offences which may be subject of a legal question.

'And of these, which is an offence (Âpatti) which is not subject of a legal question? Conversion, higher attainment (sot-âpatti, sam-âpatti), these are âpattis which are not subjects of a legal question[1]. These are âpattis not subjects of a legal question.

'And of these, what is the legal question where there is no offence? A legal question of official duty, a legal question of censure, a legal question of dispute. These are legal questions where there may be no offence.

'And of these, which is the case in which there is both a legal question and an offence too? A legal question regarding an offence is a case in which there is both a legal question and an offence too.

15. 'Official duty which is subject of a legal question of business. Duty and no legal question. Legal question and no duty. Legal question and duty too.

'There may be [each of these four].

'Of these, which is official duty which is subject of a legal question? Whatsoever is to the Sa*m*gha a thing which ought to be done, an obligation, a matter for which leave ought to be formally asked, the proposal of a resolution, the proceeding by *ñ*atti-dutiya-kamma, or by *ñ*atti-*k*atuttha-kamma, that is official duty which may be the subject of a legal question of business.

---

[1] This is merely a play upon words. Âpatti is literally 'attainment to.' Standing alone it is always used with the connotation of 'attainment to guilt, sin, offence,' so that its etymological meaning is always lost sight of. Sotâpatti is the 'attainment to,' the 'entering upon' the stream, that is, the course of the Excellent Way. The Samâpattis, literally, 'complete, or higher, attainments,' are eight successive states of ecstatic insight or meditation practised by Arahats and other men of advanced spiritual culture. The question stated is in fact a riddle, like so many of the questions stated in the Parivâra and the Puggala-pa*ññ*atti.

'And of these, which is the official duty which is not subject of legal question? The duties of an âkariya, of an upagghâya, of a fellow pupil under the same upagghâya or âkariya, that is business, but not subject of a legal question of business.

'And of these, which is a legal question but not official duty? A legal question arising out of dispute, a legal question arising out of censure, a legal question arising out of offence. This is a legal question of business, but not official duty.

'And of these, which is both legal question and official duty too? A legal question arising out of official business is both legal question of business and official duty too[1].

16. 'But by what kind of settlements is a legal question arising out of dispute brought to settlement? By two kinds of settlement, by the Proceeding in presence[2], and by the Proceeding by majority of the Samgha[3].

'If one should ask, "Can it be that a legal question arising out of dispute without recourse having been had to the one mode of settlement—to wit, the Proceeding by majority of the Samgha—can it be that it may be settled by the other mode of settlement, to wit, by the Proceeding in presence?" He should be told "Yes, it can." (If he should say), "How may that be?" the answer should be as follows: "In

[1] Here again the whole section depends upon a play upon the various meanings of the word kikkam. In the technical phrase kikkâdhikaranam, the word means solely the business or the agenda at the formal meetings of the Samgha (compare above, § 7). In the problems or riddles of this section its more common meaning of 'duty' is brought into play.

[2] Sammukhâ-vinayena. See above, chapter 2.

[3] Yebhuyyasikena. See above, chapter 9.

the case when the Bhikkhus dispute, saying, "'This is the Dhamma,' or 'This is not the Dhamma' (&c., as before, in § 2, down to), or 'This is not a most grave offence.'" If, O Bhikkhus, those Bhikkhus, are able to settle their own dispute, that is called, O Bhikkhus, the settlement of the dispute.

'[1] And how has it been settled? By the Proceeding in presence.

'And what must there be in such a Proceeding in presence? There must be the presence of the Sa*m*gha, the presence of the Dhamma, the presence of the Vinaya, and the presence of the particular person.

'And therein, what is the presence of the Sa*m*gha? As many Bhikkhus as are capable of taking part in the proceeding [2], they must be present. The formal consent must be produced of those who are in a fit state to convey their consent [3]. Those who are present must have lodged no objection (against any one of them taking part in the proceeding) [4]. This is the "presence" in such a matter of the Sa*m*gha.

'And of these, what is the presence of the Dhamma, and the presence of the Vinaya? The Dhamma, and the Vinaya, and the teaching of the Master by the aid of which that legal question is settled. That is the "presence" in such a matter of the Dhamma, and of the Vinaya.

'And of these, what is the presence of the par-

---

[1] The following five paragraphs recur in IV, 14, §§ 24, 27, and four of them in IV, 14, 21, 30.

[2] Kammappattâ. See Parivâra XIX, 1, 7, et seq.

[3] See above, Mahâvagga II, 23.

[4] Or rather, perhaps, 'against the proceedings which are being carried out.'

ticular person? He who disputes, and he with whom he disputes—both friends and foes—must be present. That is the "presence" in such a matter of the particular person.

'When a legal question, O Bhikkhus, has been thus settled, if a disputant re-open the question, such re-opening of the question is a Pâ*k*ittiya[1]. If one who has conveyed his consent complain of the decision, such complaint is a Pâ*k*ittiya[2].

17. 'If those Bhikkhus, O Bhikkhus, are not able to settle the legal question within their own residence (Âvâsa), those Bhikkhus should go, O Bhikkhus, to some residence in which there are a larger number of Bhikkhus. Then if those Bhikkhus, O Bhikkhus, should succeed, whilst on their way to that residence, in settling the legal question, that, O Bhikkhus, is called a settlement of it. And how has it been settled? (&c., as in the last paragraph of the previous section, down to the end.)

18. 'If those Bhikkhus are not able, O Bhikkhus, to settle the legal question whilst they are on their way to that residence, then those Bhikkhus, on their arrival at that residence, are to address the Bhikkhus at that residence thus: "Such and such a legal question, Sirs, has arisen thus, and has been carried on thus amongst us. It would be well if you, Sirs, would settle that legal question for us according to the Dhamma, and according to the Vinaya, and according to the teaching of the Master, to the end that that legal question may be thoroughly settled." If the Bhikkhus dwelling in that residence

[1] This is the 63rd Pâ*k*ittiya.

[2] This is the 79th Pâ*k*ittiya. The whole paragraph is repeated several times below in this chapter.

are the senior, and the incoming Bhikkhus are junior, then the Bhikkhus dwelling in that residence are, O Bhikkhus, to address the incoming Bhikkhus thus: "Pray, Sirs, rest a moment apart until we take counsel together!" If, on the other hand, the Bhikkhus dwelling in that residence are junior, and the incoming Bhikkhus are senior, then the Bhikkhus dwelling in that residence are, O Bhikkhus, to address the incoming Bhikkhus thus: "Then remain here, Sirs, a moment until we take counsel together." Then if, O Bhikkhus, the Bhikkhus dwelling in that residence should, on consideration, think thus: "We shall not be able to settle this legal question according to the Dhamma, and according to the Vinaya, and according to the teaching of the Master," then that dispute is not to be entrusted to them. If, on the other hand, O Bhikkhus, the Bhikkhus dwelling in that residence should, on consideration, think thus: "We shall be able to settle this legal question in accordance with the Dhamma, and in accordance with the Vinaya, and in accordance with the teaching of the Master," then, O Bhikkhus, the Bhikkhus dwelling in that residence are to address the incoming Bhikkhus thus: "If you, Sirs, let us know about this legal question, how it arose, and how it was carried on, and if you agree that in the manner in which we may settle the legal question according to the Dhamma, and according to the Vinaya, and according to the teaching of the Master, in that manner it shall be settled, then we will thus accept the legal question at your hands. But if not (&c., the whole being repeated), then we will not accept it." When they have thus, O Bhikkhus, brought it about that the proper way of putting the legal question (the point at issue) has been settled, the Bhikkhus dwelling in that residence should undertake that legal question. And then the Bhikkhus dwelling in that residence should be addressed, O Bhikkhus, by the incoming Bhikkhus thus: "We inform you, Sirs, how this legal question arose and how it was carried on. If you, Sirs, are able in such and such a time[1] to settle this legal question according to the Dhamma, and according to the Vinaya, and according to the teaching of the Master, then will we entrust this legal question to you. But if you, Sirs, should not be able to do so, then will we ourselves retain the custody of the case." Thus, O Bhikkhus, is that legal question to be entrusted by the incoming Bhikkhus to the Bhikkhus dwelling in that residence, causing them duly to accept it. If those Bhikkhus, O Bhikkhus, are able to settle the case, that, O Bhikkhus, is called a settlement of the legal question. And how has it been settled? (&c., as in last paragraph of § 16, down to the end.)

19. 'If, O Bhikkhus, whilst the case is being enquired into by those Bhikkhus, pointless speeches are brought forth, and the sense of any single utterance is not clear[2], I enjoin upon you, O Bhikkhus, to settle the case by referring it (to a jury or commission)[3].

---

[1] Ettakena vâ antarena, on which Buddhaghosa has nothing. On vâ = eva, see Böhtlingk-Roth s. v. vâ, No. 4.

[2] These words recur at XII, 2, 7, where an instance occurs of the mode of proceeding here laid down.

[3] Ubbâhikâya. Childers has quite misunderstood both the meaning and the derivation of this term. It must be derived

'A Bhikkhu to be chosen on such a jury must be possessed of ten qualities—he must be virtuous—he must be living enclosed by the restraint of the rules of the Pâtimokkha—he must be upright in life, trained according to the precepts, taking them upon himself with a sense of the danger in the least offence[1]—he must be versed in the tradition, a custodian of the tradition, a storehouse of the tradition—whatsoever truths, lovely in their origin, lovely in their progress, lovely in their consummation, set forth the higher life, both in its spirit and in its letter, in all its purity and in all its perfectness[2], in such truths must he be well versed, of such must he be full, they must be laid up in his words[3], and dwelt on in his heart, being penetrated throughout through right insight[4]—both the Pâtimokkhas must have

---

from ud + vah; and means simply 'reference'—the turning over of a difficult or intricate case from the general Sa*m*gha to a special committee, as was done at Vesâli (below, XII, 2, 7).

[1] With this passage (so far) compare the Âkaṅkheyya Sutta, § 2 (translated in Rh. D.'s 'Buddhist Suttas,' p. 210), where the wording is somewhat different. See, however, the various readings here.

[2] We prefer to translate, in accordance with IX, 5, 1 below, sâttha*m* savyañ*g*ana*m* as given in the corrections to the text on p. 303; thus making the phrase 'in the spirit and in the letter' refer to the brahma-*k*ariya*m*, and not to the dhammâ. But it should be pointed out that the parallel passage in the stock description of a Buddha (for instance in Tevi*gg*a Sutta I, 46, translated in Rh. D.'s 'Buddhist Suttas,' p. 187) would support the reading given here in the text, referring the phrase in question to the dhammâ, and not to the brahma-*k*ariya*m*.

[3] See the various readings, and compare Sigâlovâda Sutta, p. 301; *G*âtaka II, 247, 293; Mahâvagga VI, 25, 1.

[4] Though di*tth*i is usually found in its bad sense of 'delusion' (it never means 'heresy,' as Childers renders it), it is also used, especially in older texts, in the good sense of 'insight.' Compare the 'Book of the Great Decease,' I, 11.

been completely handed down to him in their full extent, he must have well divided them, well established them, well investigated them, both sutta by sutta and in every detail[1]—further he must be an expert in the Vinaya, irrefutable therein[2]—he must be competent to point out (the right course) to both friends and foes, to get them to understand a thing, get them to see it and recognise it[3], able to pacify them—he must be clever (in judging) both as to the origin and as to the settlement of disputes—he must understand legal questions, the origin thereof, the close thereof, and the way that leads to the close thereof.

'I enjoin upon you, O Bhikkhus, to appoint on the jury a Bhikkhu possessed of these ten qualities[4].

20. 'And thus, O Bhikkhus, is he to be appointed. First, the Bhikkhu should be asked (whether he be willing to undertake the office). Then some discreet and able Bhikkhu should address the Sa*m*gha thus:

'"May the venerable Sa*m*gha hear me. Whilst this case was being enquired into pointless speeches were brought forth amongst us, and the sense of no single utterance was clear. If the time seems meet

[1] Perhaps this may mean 'both as to the Suttas themselves and as to the Old Commentary upon them'—suttato anuvya*ñg*anaso. See 'Vinaya Texts,' vol. i, p. xviii, and note 2, p. xxix.

[2] Vinaye *kh*eko hoti asa*m*hîro. Compare on the use of these words, *G*âtaka I, 290; II, 161; Sutta Nipâta V, 18, 26.

[3] On all these terms, which have occurred above at IV, 2, 1, see the commentary as there quoted in the notes.

[4] It is of course to be understood that the committee or jury does not consist of only one such Bhikkhu. In the instance already referred to as occurring in XII, 2, 7, four are chosen from each side.

to the venerable Sa*m*gha, let it appoint Bhikkhus of such and such a name, and of such and such a name on a committee. This is the motion.

'"Let the venerable Sa*m*gha hear me. Whilst (&c., . . . down to) no single utterance was clear. The Samgha appoints Bhikkhus of such and such names on a committee to settle this case. Whosoever of the venerable ones approves of the appointment of such and such Bhikkhus on the committee for the settlement of this case, let him be silent. Whosoever approves not thereof, let him speak.

'"Such and such a Bhikkhu is appointed by the Sa*m*gha on the committee for the settlement of this case. Therefore is it silent. Thus do I understand."

21. 'If then, O Bhikkhus, those Bhikkhus are able on the reference (or on the committee) to settle the case, that, O Bhikkhus, is called a case that is settled. And how is it settled? By the Proceeding in Presence[1]. And what therein is meant by the Proceeding in Presence? The Dhamma is represented, and the Vinaya is represented, and the particular person is represented[2].

'And of these, what is the presence of the Dhamma (&c., as in § 16, down to the end).

'If a dispute, O Bhikkhus, has been thus settled, if a disputant re-open the question, such re-opening is a Pâ*k*ittiya[3].

22. 'If, O Bhikkhus, whilst the case is being

[1] Sammukhâ-vinayena. See chapter 2.

[2] This is the same as in § 16 of this chapter, except that 'the presence of the Sa*m*gha' is omitted.

[3] See the 63rd Pâ*k*ittiya, and § 17 above.

enquired into by those Bhikkhus, there should be there a Bhikkhu who is a preacher of the Dhamma, but neither has the Sutta[1] been handed down to him nor the Sutta-vibhaṅga, and he not regarding the point of the case, reject the sense for the shadow of the letter, then should the matter be laid before those Bhikkhus by some discreet and able Bhikkhu thus:

'"Let the venerable ones hear me. This Bhikkhu of such and such a name is a preacher of the Dhamma, but neither has the Sutta been handed down to him nor the Sutta-vibhaṅga. And he, not regarding the point of the case, is rejecting the sense for the shadow of the letter. If the time seems meet to the venerable ones, let them send away[2] the Bhikkhu of such and such a name, and let the rest of us settle this case."

'If those Bhikkhus, O Bhikkhus, should be able, after having sent away that Bhikkhu, to settle the case, that is called a case that is settled. And how has it been settled? By the Proceeding in Presence (&c., as in last section, down to the end).'

23. (The same decision if the Sutta has been handed down to him, but not the Sutta-vibhaṅga.)

24. 'If those Bhikkhus, O Bhikkhus, are not able by the committee to settle that case, those Bhikkhus, O Bhikkhus, ought to hand over the case to the Saṃgha, saying, "We, Sirs, are not able by a committee to settle this case, let the Saṃgha settle it." I enjoin upon you, O Bhikkhus, to settle such a case by vote of the majority (&c., as in chapter 9 to the

[1] That is, the Pâtimokkha.

[2] Literally, 'cause him to arise.'

end, as to the appointment of a taker of the voting tickets). By that Bhikkhu, the taker of the voting tickets, are the votes to be collected. And according as the larger number of Bhikkhus who are guided by the Dhamma shall speak, so shall the case be decided. This, O Bhikkhus, is called a legal question that has been settled.

'And how has it been settled? By the Proceeding in Presence and by the vote of the majority. And what herein is meant by Proceeding in Presence? The presence of the Sa*m*gha, and the presence of the Dhamma, and the presence of the Vinaya, and the presence of the particular person. And of these, what is the presence of the Sa*m*gha? (&c., as in § 16, down to) That is the presence in such a matter of the particular person.

'And what herein is meant by the vote of the majority? The carrying out of, the accomplishment of, the proceeding by, the undertaking of, the acceptance of, the pacification by the official act (the Kamma) by the vote of the majority[1]. That is what is meant herein by the vote of the majority.

'When a legal question, O Bhikkhus, has been thus settled, if a disputant re-open the question, such re-opening is a Pâ*k*ittiya. If one who has conveyed his consent complain of the decision, such complaint is a Pâ*k*ittiya[2].'

25. Now at that time a certain legal question had arisen in such and such a manner, and had grown up in such and such a manner at Sâvatthi. And those

[1] This sentence is also used of the other modes of settlement below, §§ 27, 29.

[2] So also above, § 16; and below, §§ 27–29.

Bhikkhus were discontented with the settlement of the case by the Sa*m*gha at Sâvatthi. And they heard that in a certain residence there were dwelling a number of Theras versed in the traditions; men to whom the Âgamas[1] had been handed down; reciters of the Dhamma, of the Vinaya, and of the Mâtikâs[2], learned, discreet, wise, modest, conscientious, anxious to learn. And they thought, 'If those Theras would settle this case according to the Dhamma, and according to the Vinaya, and according to the teaching of the Master, then would this case be indeed well settled.' So those Bhikkhus went to that residence, and spake to those Theras thus: 'This legal question, Sirs, has arisen in such and such a manner, and has grown up in such and such a manner. It would be well if the venerable Theras would settle the case according to the Dhamma, and according to the Vinaya, and according to the teaching of the Master!' Then those Theras, saying, 'Even as the case has been settled by the Sa*m*gha at Sâvatthi, so is it well settled!' decided the case in the same way. Then those Bhikkhus who had been discontented with the decision of the Sa*m*gha at Sâvatthi were discontented with the decision of the number of Theras.

[The paragraph is repeated with the necessary alterations of consecutive applications to three, two, and one Thera with the same result.]

Then those Bhikkhus, discontented with the decision of the Sa*m*gha at Sâvatthi, discontented with the decision of the number of Theras, dis-

[1] That is, the Four Nikâyas, now forming the Sutta Pi*t*aka.

[2] See our note above on *K*ullavagga IV, 1, 2.

contented with the decision of the three Theras, discontented with the decision of the two Theras, discontented with the decision of the single Thera, went up to the place where the Blessed One was, and told the matter to the Blessed One.

'This case, O Bhikkhus, is done with; having been once settled, it is settled for good.

26[1]. 'I enjoin upon you, O Bhikkhus, three ways of taking votes, in order to appease such Bhikkhus[2] —the secret method, the whispering method, and the open method.

'And how, O Bhikkhus, is the secret method of taking votes? The Bhikkhu who is the teller of the votes is to make the voting tickets of different colours, and as each Bhikkhu comes up to him he is to say to him thus: "This is the ticket for the man of such an opinion; this the ticket for the man of such an opinion. Take whichever you like." When he has chosen (he is to add), "Don't show it to anybody." If he ascertains that those whose opinion is against the Dhamma are in the majority, he is to reject the vote as wrongly taken. If he ascertains that those whose opinion is in accordance with the Dhamma are in the majority, he is to report the vote as well taken. This, O Bhikkhus, is the secret method of taking the votes.

'And how, O Bhikkhus, is the whispering method of taking votes? The Bhikkhu who is the teller of the votes is to whisper in each Bhikkhu's ear, "This is the ticket of those of such an opinion; this is the ticket of those of such an opinion. Take whichever

[1] On the following section, compare chapters 9 and 10 above.

[2] On Saññattiyâ, see our note below on VII, 4, 1.

you like." When he has chosen (he is to add), "Don't tell anybody (which way you have voted)." If he ascertains that those whose opinion is against the Dhamma are in the majority, he is to reject the vote as wrongly taken. If he ascertains that those whose opinion is in accordance with the Dhamma are in the majority, he is to report the vote as well taken. Thus, O Bhikkhus, is the whispering method of taking the votes.

'And how, O Bhikkhus, is the open method of taking votes? If he ascertains (beforehand) that those whose opinion is in accordance with the Dhamma are in the majority, the vote is to be taken undisguisedly, openly. Thus, O Bhikkhus, is the open method of taking the votes.

'These, O Bhikkhus, are the three methods of taking the votes[1].'

27. 'By how many kinds of settlement is a legal question arising out of censure settled? A legal question arising out of censure can be settled by four kinds of settlement—by the Proceeding in Presence—by the Proceeding for those who are consciously innocent—by the Proceeding for those who are no longer out of their mind—by the Proceeding for those who are obstinate.

'If one should ask, "Can it be that a legal question arising out of censure, without recourse being had to two modes of settlement—to wit, the Proceeding for those who are no longer out of their mind, and the

[1] This naive chapter would seem to show that the pia fraus was not unknown to the Buddhist monks at the time when the *K*ullavagga was composed. Buddhaghosa's note (given at p. 315 of H. O.'s edition of the text) specifies the different occasions when each of the three methods should be used.

Proceeding for those who are obstinate—may be settled by the two other modes of settlement—to wit, the Proceeding in Presence, and the Proceeding for those who are consciously innocent?" he should be told, "Yes, it can." (If he should say), "How may that be?" the answer should be as follows:

'In case the Bhikkhus bring a groundless charge against a Bhikkhu of a breach of morality. In respect thereof, O Bhikkhus, to that Bhikkhu whose memory in regard to the matter is quite clear, the Proceeding for the consciously innocent is to be accorded.

'And thus, O Bhikkhus, is to be granted (&c., as in chapter 4, § 10, down to the end, with the necessary alterations for a general rule instead of a particular case).

'This, O Bhikkhus, is called a legal question that has been settled. And how settled? By the Proceeding in Presence, and by the Proceeding for the consciously innocent. And what therein belongs to the Proceeding in Presence? The presence of the Sa*m*gha, and the presence of the Dhamma, and the presence of the Vinaya, and the presence of the particular person. And therein what is the presence of the Sa*m*gha (&c., as in § 16, down to the end)? And what therein belongs to the Proceeding for the consciously innocent? The carrying out of, the accomplishment of, the proceeding by, the undertaking of, the acceptance of, the pacification of the Proceeding for the consciously innocent[1]. That is what belongs herein to the Proceeding for the consciously innocent.'

[1] This clause corresponds to the one above, in § 24, and below, in § 29.

28. [This section bears exactly the same relation to chapter 5 as the last section does to chapter 4, the form of the two sections being exactly the same throughout.]

29[1]. 'If one should ask, "Can it be that a legal question arising out of censure, without recourse being had to two modes of settlement—to wit, the Proceeding for those who are consciously innocent, and the Proceeding for those who are no longer out of their mind—may be settled by the two other modes of settlement—to wit, the Proceeding in Presence, and the Proceeding for those who are obstinate?" he should be told, "Yes, it can." If he should say, "How may that be?" the answer should be as follows:

'In case a Bhikkhu warn another Bhikkhu in the midst of the Sa*m*gha of a grievous offence, and call upon him to recollect (whether he have committed it or not), saying, "Has the venerable one been guilty of such and such a grievous offence—a Pârâ*g*ika offence, or an offence equivalent to a Pârâ*g*ika offence?" And he replies thus, "I do not, Sir, call to mind that I have been guilty of such and such a grievous offence—a Pârâ*g*ika offence, or an offence equivalent to a Pârâ*g*ika offence." To him thus denying the other insists, saying, "Come now, Sir, ascertain for certain whether you are conscious of having been guilty of such and such a grievous

[1] This section again bears exactly the same relation to chapter 11 as the previous ones have done to chapters 4 and 5 respectively. The outline of the form is the same, but as in the introductory part (containing the description of the offence) the present section is much fuller than the chapter to which it refers, we prefer to give that part of this section in full.

offence'—a Pârâ*g*ika offence, or an offence equivalent to a Pârâ*g*ika offence." And he replies thus: "I do not, Sir, call to mind that I have been guilty of such and such a grievous offence—a Pârâ*g*ika offence, or an offence equivalent to a Pârâ*g*ika offence. But I do, Sir, recollect that I was guilty of such and such a trifling offence." To him thus denying the other insists [as before]. And he replies thus: "Seeing that I am willing, Sir, though you did not ask me, to confess myself guilty of that trifling offence, why should I not confess, when asked, such and such a grievous offence—a Pârâ*g*ika offence, or an offence equivalent to a Pârâ*g*ika offence?" And the other rejoins, "But you do not confess, Sir, even that trifling offence without being asked. How should you confess, if you were not asked, the commission of such and such a grievous offence—a Pârâ*g*ika offence, or one equivalent to a Pârâ*g*ika offence? Come now, Sir, ascertain for certain whether you are conscious of having been guilty of such and such a grievous offence—a Pârâ*g*ika offence, or one equivalent to a Pârâ*g*ika offence?" And he replies, "Yes, I am conscious, Sir, of having committed such and such an offence—a Pârâ*g*ika offence, or one equivalent to a Pârâ*g*ika offence. In sport did I say, in fun did I say that I was not conscious thereof."

'Then, O Bhikkhus, the Proceeding for those who are obstinate should be carried out against that Bhikkhu.

'And thus should it be carried out (&c., as chapter 11, § 2, down to the end, reading "such and such a Bhikkhu" for "Upavâla," and "grievous offence" for "offence").

'This, O Bhikkhus, is called a legal question that has been settled. And how has it been settled? By the Proceeding in Presence, and by the Proceeding for those who are obstinate. And what therein belongs to the Proceeding in Presence? The Presence of the Sa*m*gha (&c., as in § 16). And what therein belongs to the Proceeding for those who are obstinate? The carrying out of, the accomplishment of, the proceeding by, the undertaking of, the acceptance of, the pacification of the official act (the Kamma) by the Proceeding for those who are obstinate. That is what belongs therein to the Proceeding for those who are obstinate.

'When a legal question, O Bhikkhus, has been thus settled, if a disputant re-open the question, such re-opening is a Pâ*k*ittiya. If one who has conveyed his consent complain of the decision, such complaint is a Pâ*k*ittiya.

30. 'By how many modes of settlement is a legal question arising out of offence settled? A legal question arising out of offence is settled by three modes of settlement—to wit, by the Proceeding in Presence, and by the Proceeding on confession of guilt, and by the Proceeding by covering over as with grass.

'If one should ask, "Can it be that a legal question arising out of offence, without recourse being had to the one mode of settlement—to wit, the Proceeding by covering over as with grass—may be settled by the other two modes—to wit, the Proceeding in Presence, and the Proceeding on confession of guilt?" he should be told, "Yes, it can." If he should say, "How may that be?" the answer should be as follows:

'In case a Bhikkhu has been guilty of a minor offence. That Bhikkhu, O Bhikkhus, should go up to another Bhikkhu, and having arranged his upper robe over one shoulder, and squatted down on his heels, and stretched forth his hands with the palms held together, should speak as follows: "I, Sir, have been guilty of such and such an offence; and that I confess." He should say, "Do you acknowledge it?" "Yes; I acknowledge it." "May you restrain yourself in future[1]!"

'This, O Bhikkhus, is called a legal question which has been settled. And how has it been settled? By the Proceeding in Presence, and by the Proceeding on confession of guilt. And what therein belongs to the Proceeding in Presence? The presence of the Dhamma, and the presence of the Vinaya, and the presence of the particular individual. And what therein is the presence of the Dhamma, and of the Vinaya? The Dhamma, and the Vinaya, and the teaching of the Master, by the aid of which that legal question is settled. That is the presence in such a matter of the Dhamma, and of the Vinaya. And what therein is the presence of the particular individual? He who confesses, and he to whom he confesses, both are present. That is the presence of the particular individual in such a proceeding. And what therein belongs to the Proceeding on confession of guilt? The carrying out of, the accomplishment of, the proceeding by, the performance of, the acceptance of, the pacification of the official act (the Kamma) by the Proceeding on confession of

[1] Âyatim samvareyyâsi. So again in the next section. Compare V, 20, 5.

guilt. That is what belongs therein to the Proceeding on confession of guilt.

'When a legal question, O Bhikkhus, has been thus settled, if a disputant re-open the question, such re-opening is a Pâkittiya[1].

31. 'If he should thus receive (absolution), it is well. If he should not receive it, that Bhikkhu, O Bhikkhus, should go up to a number of Bhikkhus, and having arranged his upper robe over one shoulder, and bowed down before the elder Bhikkhus, and squatted down on his heels, and stretched forth his two hands with the palms held together, he should speak as follows: "I, Sirs, have been guilty of such and such an offence, and that I confess." Then some discreet and able Bhikkhu should lay the matter before those Bhikkhus, saying, "Let the venerable ones hear me. This Bhikkhu, of such and such a name, is conscious of an offence; and he discloses it, reveals it, confesses it. If the time seems meet to the venerable ones, I would absolve[2] that Bhikkhu's offence." And he should say, "Do you acknowledge it?" "Yes; I acknowledge it." "In future may you restrain yourself!"

'This, O Bhikkhus, is called a legal question which has been settled. And how has it been settled? (&c., as in last section, down to the end.)

32. 'If he should thus receive absolution, it is well. If he should not receive it, that Bhikkhu, O Bhikkhus, should go before the Samgha (&c., as in last section, down to the end, then adding): And if one who has given his consent to the pro-

[1] See §§ 16, 29, &c. of this chapter.

[2] Paṭigaṇheyyam. See V, 20, 5.

ceeding thereafter make complaint thereof, that is a Pâkittiya.

33. 'If one should ask, "Can it be that a legal question arising out of offence, without recourse being had to the one mode of settlement—to wit, the Proceeding on confession of guilt—may be settled by the other two modes—to wit, by the Proceeding in Presence, and by the Proceeding by covering over as with grass?" he should be told, "Yes, it can." If he should say, "How may that be?" the answer should be as follows:

'If while the Bhikkhus are continuing in quarrels (&c., as in chapter 13, §§ 1, 2, and 3, down to the end).

'This, O Bhikkhus, is called a legal question that has been settled. And how has it been settled? By the Proceeding in Presence, and by the Proceeding by the covering over as with grass.

'And what therein belongs to the Proceeding in Presence? The presence (&c., as in § 16, down to) And what therein is the presence of the particular person? He who confesses, and he to whom the confession is made[1], both are present. This is the presence of the particular individual in such a case.

'And what therein belongs to the Proceeding by covering over as with grass? The carrying out of, the accomplishment of, the proceeding by, the performance of, the acceptance of, the pacification of the official act (the Kamma) by the Proceeding by covering over as with grass. That is what belongs therein to the Proceeding by covering over as with grass.

---

[1] This refers to the technical term of the Proceeding in question, tinavatthârakena deseyyam (IV, 13, 2); and the singular of course includes the plural, as the confession usually took place before a number of Bhikkhus.

'When a legal question, O Bhikkhus, has been thus settled, if a disputant re-open the question, such re-opening is a Pâ*k*ittiya. If one who has conveyed his consent complain of the decision, such complaint is a Pâ*k*ittiya.

34. 'By how many modes of settlement is a legal question arising out of business settled? A legal question arising out of business is settled by one mode of settlement only—to wit, by the Proceeding in Presence.'

End of the Fourth Khandhaka, on the Settlement of Legal Questions.

FIFTH KHANDHAKA.

On the Daily Life of the Bhikkhus.

1.

1. Now at that time the Blessed One was staying at Râ*g*agaha, in the Bamboo Grove, in the Kalandaka Nivâpa. And at that time the *Kh*abbaggiya Bhikkhus, when bathing, used to rub[1] their bodies—thighs, and arms, and breast, and back—against wood. The people were annoyed, murmured, and became indignant, saying, 'How can the Sakyaputtiya Sama*n*as do so, like wrestlers, boxers, or shampooers[2]?' The Bhikkhus heard the people so murmuring, &c.; and they told the matter to the Blessed One.

Then the Blessed One, on that occasion and in that connection, having convened a meeting of the Bhikkhu-sa*m*gha, asked the Bhikkhus: 'Is this true, O Bhikkhus, what they say, that the *Kh*abbaggiya Bhikkhus, when bathing, rub (&c., as before)?'

'It is true, Lord.'

---

[1] Uggha*m*seti. The simple verb occurs below, V, 9, 2, 4, X, 10, 2, and at *G*âtaka, vol. i, p. 190. It is the Sanskrit root gharsh.

[2] On malla-mu*tth*ikâ Buddhaghosa merely says mu*tth*ika-mallâ. His note on gâma-poddavâ (already given by H. O. at p. 315 of the edition to the text) says, 'town's people given to adorning themselves by painting their skin' (on which compare below, V, 2, 5). But it is difficult to see how that fits in with the connection here.

The Blessed Buddha rebuked them, saying, 'This is improper, O Bhikkhus (&c., as usual, see I, 1, 2, down to the end).' And when he had rebuked them, and had delivered a religious discourse, he addressed the Bhikkhus, and said: 'A Bhikkhu, when bathing, is not, O Bhikkhus, to rub his body against wood. Whosoever does so, shall be guilty of a dukka*t*a.'

2. Now at that time the *Kh*abbaggiya Bhikkhus, when bathing, used to rub their bodies—thighs, and arms, and breast, and back—against a pillar—against a wall (&c., as in last section, down to the end).

3. Now at that time the *Kh*abbaggiya Bhikkhus used to bathe on an A*tt*âna (a sort of shampooing stand[1]). The people (&c., as before). The Bhikkhus (&c., as before). Then the Blessed One (&c., as before, down to) addressed the Bhikkhus, and said: 'You are not to bathe, O Bhikkhus, on an A*tt*âna. Whosoever does so, shall be guilty of a dukka*t*a.'

[Paragraphs similar in every respect to the last follow as to

Using a Gandhabba-hatthaka[2] when bathing.

Using a Kuruvindaka-sutti[3] when bathing.

Rubbing their bodies, when under water, up against each other[4].

---

[1] So Buddhaghosa loc. cit.

[2] A wooden instrument in the shape of a hand, which was first covered with chunam (fine lime), and then rubbed over the body. See Buddhaghosa's note at p. 315 of H. O.'s edition of the text.

[3] Apparently a string of beads which was first covered with the chunam made from Kuruvindaka stone (a ruby-coloured stone), and then held at both ends and rubbed over the body. See Buddhaghosa's note loc. cit.

[4] As Buddhaghosa, loc. cit., explains this by 'rubbing their

Using a Mallaka[1] when bathing.]

4. Now at that time a certain Bhikkhu had the scab, and he could not bathe with comfort without a Mallaka[1].

They told the matter to the Blessed One.

'I allow, O Bhikkhus, to a sick man the use of a Mallaka not (artificially) made[2].'

5. Now at that time a certain Bhikkhu who was weak through old age was not able to shampoo his own body.

'I allow you, O Bhikkhus, the use of an Ukkâsika[3].'

Now at that time the Bhikkhus, (fearing to offend against these rules,) were afraid to shampoo one another.

'I allow you, O Bhikkhus, the ordinary mode of shampooing with the hand[4].'

2.

1. Now at that time the *Kh*abbaggiya Bhikkhus

---

bodies up against each other'(!), vigayha has here probably nothing to do with gâh, but is simply vigr*i*hya.

[1] A kind of back-scratcher, made according to Buddhaghosa, loc. cit., by placing together, by the roots, hooks made of the teeth of crocodiles (makara-dantaka; see V, 11, 6; VI, 3, 2), which had previously been split. Such hooks of split crocodiles' teeth are mentioned in the text itself below, V, 9, 2; and pins or hooks made of nâga's teeth at V, 9, 5, and VI, 3, 5 (nâga-dantaka), and V, 11, 7 (nâga-danta).

[2] Buddhaghosa, loc. cit., makes this phrase mean only 'made of teeth that had not been previously split.'

[3] Buddhaghosa, loc. cit., explains this word by vattava*tt*i; which is to us equally unintelligible.

[4] Pudhu-pâ*n*ikan ti hattha-parikamma*m* vu*kk*ati. Tasmâ sabbesa*m* hatthena pi*tth*i-parikamma*m* kâtu*m* va*tt*ati (B.).

used to wear ear-rings[1], and ear-drops[2], and strings of beads for the throat, and girdles of beads[3], and bangles[4], and necklaces[5], and bracelets, and rings.

The people murmured, &c. . . . . The Bhikkhus heard, &c. . . . . They told the Blessed One (&c., as in V, 1, 1, down to) he addressed the Bhikkhus, and said:

'You are not, O Bhikkhus, to wear any of these things. Whosoever does so, shall be guilty of a dukka*t*a.'

2. [A similar paragraph concluding]

'You are not, O Bhikkhus, to wear long hair. Whosoever does so, shall be guilty of a dukka*t*a. I allow you, O Bhikkhus, hair that is two months old, or two inches long.'

3. [Similar paragraph concluding]

'You are not, O Bhikkhus, to smooth[6] the hair

---

[1] Vallikâ ti ka*nn*ato nikkhanta-mutt-olambakâdîna*m* eta*m* adhiva*k*ana*m*. Na kevala*ñ* *k*a vallikâ eva, ya*m* ki*ñk*i ka*nn*a-pilandhana*m* antamaso tâla-panna*m* pi na va*tt*ati (B.). Compare sata-vallika*m* at V, 29, 4.

[2] Pâmaṅga. The meaning of which is not clear from Buddhaghosa's note loc. cit. It occurs also at Dîpava*m*sa XII, 1, and below in Buddhaghosa's note on maddavi*n*a at V, 29, 2 (twice).

[3] Ka*t*i-suttaka*m*. This is not mentioned in the similar paragraph at V, 29, 2, where all special kinds of girdles are enumerated. It is forbidden below to the Bhikkhunîs at X, 16.

[4] Ova*tt*ika. This word is explained by Buddhaghosa as the same as valaya*m*. Ova*tt*iya occurs, apparently in a different sense, at Mahâvagga VII, 1, 5, and the present word in Buddhaghosa on sata-vallika*m* at V, 29, 4.

[5] Kâyura, on which Buddhaghosa, loc. cit., merely says that the meaning of this, and of the following words, is evident. But the *G*âtaka commentary (Fausböll III, 437, 14) says kâyûran ti gîvâya pilandhana-pasâdhana*m*.

[6] Osa*n*heti. Compare the Sanskrit *s*laksh*n*ayati. The art of hair-dressing had, at the time when the *K*ullavagga was com-

with a comb, or with a smoothing instrument shaped like a snake's hood [1], or with the hand used as such an instrument [2], or with pomade [3], or with hair-oil of beeswax [3]. Whosoever does so, shall be guilty of a dukka*t*a.'

4. [Similar paragraph concluding]

'You are not, O Bhikkhus, to look at the image of your faces in a looking-glass, or a bowl of water [4]. Whosoever does so, shall be guilty of a dukka*t*a.'

Now at that time a certain Bhikkhu had a sore in his face. He asked the Bhikkhus what kind of a sore he had. 'Such and such a kind of sore,' replied they. He did not believe what they said. They told this matter to the Blessed One.

'I allow you, O Bhikkhus, on account of a disease, to look at your faces in a looking-glass, or in a bowl of water.'

5. Now at that time the *Kh*abbaggiya Bhikkhus (&c., down to)

---

posed, been already carried to a high state of efficiency in the valley of the Ganges, as may reasonably be concluded from the numerous kinds of head-dresses figured in bas-relief on some of the oldest Buddhist sculptures.

[1] Pha*n*akenâ ti dantamayâdisu yena kena*k*i (B.).

[2] Hattha-pha*n*akenâ ti hatthen' eva pha*n*aka-ki*kk*a*m* karonti, aṅgulîhi osa*n*henti (B.). It is clear from this last explanation that the pha*n*aka was a kind of very primitive brush, but without bristles. In passing the fingers through the hair the fingers are naturally held separate, slightly forward, and stiff—precisely as one would hold them if one wished to imitate the hood of a cobra. To make a real brush with bristles was evidently beyond the mechanical appliances of those times, or such an article would certainly have been mentioned in this connection.

[3] On the use of Telaka, compare Mahâvagga VI, 13, 1, and Sittha-telaka at *K*ullavagga IV, 3, 1.

[4] Compare *K*ullavagga X, 10, 4.

'You are not, O Bhikkhus, to anoint your faces, nor to rub (ointment, &c.) into your faces, nor to put chunam on your faces, nor to smear red arsenic on your faces, nor to paint your bodies, nor to paint your faces[1].'

Now at that time a certain Bhikkhu had disease in his eyes. They told the matter to the Blessed One.

'I allow you, O Bhikkhus, on account of disease, to anoint your faces.'

6[2]. Now at that time there was a festival on the mountain-top[3] at Râ*g*agaha; and the *Kh*abbaggiya Bhikkhus went to see it.

The people murmured, were annoyed, and became indignant, saying, 'How can the Sakyaputtiya Sama*n*as go to see dancing, and singing, and music, like those who are still enjoying the pleasures of the world?' And they told this matter to the Blessed One.

'You are not, O Bhikkhus, to go to see dancing, or singing, or music. Whosoever does so, shall be guilty of a dukka*t*a.'

---

[1] All these practices are seriatim forbidden to the Bhikkhunîs also in *K*ullavagga X, 10, 3.

[2] The following section recurs, almost word for word, of the Bhikkhunîs, in the Bhikkhunî-vibhaṅga, Pâ*k*ittiya X (Sutta-vibhaṅga, vol. ii, p. 267).

[3] Giragga-sama*gg*a. Compare Dîpava*m*sa XXI, 32, and Mahâva*m*sa, p. 214, line 2. It occurs also in the Introductory Story in the Sutta-vibhaṅga on the 37th Pâ*k*ittiya, and Buddhaghosa there explains it as follows: Giragga-sama*gg*o ti girimhi agga-sama*gg*o girissa vâ agga-dese sama*gg*o. He is evidently in doubt about the word, which is probably connected with ancient local worship or custom, a worship in high-places, as little allied to Vedic Brahmanism as it was to Buddhism.

3.

1. Now at that time the *Kh*abbaggiya Bhikkhus used to sing the Dhamma with the abrupt transitions of song-singing.

The people murmured, were annoyed, and became indignant, saying, 'How can the Sakyaputtiya Sama*n*as [do so]?' The Bhikkhus heard (&c., as usual, down to) he addressed the Bhikkhus, and said:

'These five dangers, O Bhikkhus, befall him who sings the Dhamma with the abrupt[1] transitions of song-singing.—He himself becomes captivated with respect to the sound thereof.—Other people become captivated with respect to the sound thereof.—The laymen are shocked.—The meditation of one who strains after accuracy in the sound is broken.—The common people fall into heresy[2].—These five dangers, O Bhikkhus, befall him who sings the Dhamma with the abrupt transitions of song-singing. The Dhamma is not, O Bhikkhus, to be sung [in that manner]. Whosoever does so, shall be guilty of a dukka*t*a.'

2. Now at that time the Bhikkhus were afraid to make use of intoning[3]. They told this matter to the Blessed One.

'I allow you, O Bhikkhus, to intone.'

---

[1] Âyatakena gîta-ssarena. Compare âyataken' eva papâto at *K*ullavagga IX, 1, 3.

[2] Probably this is supposed to result because dhamma being sung and not said is not intelligible to them—a complaint often made against the singing of prayers among Protestant Christians. On pa*kkh*imâ *g*anatâ, compare the closing words of V, 21, 2; and on the rest of the phrase, Puggala III, 10, 14. The translation of sarakutti*m* is also very doubtful.

[3] Sara-bha*ññ*a*m*. So in the Mahâvagga we hear that So*n*a

4.

1. Now at that time the *Kh*abbaggiya Bhikkhus used to wear woollen cloth with long fleece to it[1].

The people murmured . . . (&c., down to) They told this matter to the Blessed One.

'You are not, O Bhikkhus, to wear woollen cloth with long fleece to it. Whosoever does so, shall be guilty of a dukka*t*a.'

5.

1. Now at that time the mangoes were ripe in the park of Seniya Bimbisâra, the king of Magadha. And Seniya Bimbisâra, the king of Magadha, had given command, saying, 'Let the venerable ones have as much fruit as they like.' Then the *Kh*abbaggiya Bhikkhus plucked even the young fruits and ate them.

Now Seniya Bimbisâra, the king of Magadha, wanted a mango; and he gave orders, saying, 'Go,

intoned before the Buddha a chapter from the Sutta Nipâta. The expression there used is sarena abhâsi, of which our word is used as the verbal noun, the roots bha*n* and bhâs being not only synonymous but interchangeable. (See, for instance, Vin. Pit. vol. iv, p. 353.) Perhaps 'recitative' would be a good rendering. I have several times heard the Dhamma thus recited by living Buddhists in accordance with the traditional interpretation of this passage, and their Sara-bha*ññ*a*m* was precisely like the intoning of prose passages as practised in our cathedral churches (Rh. D.).

[1] Bâhira-lomi*m*-*unn*im. Literally, 'with the fleece outside.' Compare Mahâvagga V, 10, 4, and the Ma*ggh*ima Sîla, § 5 (p. 193 of Rh. D.'s 'Buddhist Suttas').

my good men, to the park, and bring me hither a mango.'

'Even so, Lord,' said the men in assent to Seniya Bimbisâra, the king of Magadha: and they went to the park, and said to the park-keepers, 'Our lord, good friends, has need of a mango. Give us one!'

'There are no mangoes, Sirs. The Bhikkhus have plucked even the young ones, and eaten them.'

Then those men told the matter to Seniya Bimbisâra, the king of Magadha, and he said: 'The mangoes have been well used, my good men, by the venerable ones. Notwithstanding it is moderation that has been exalted by the Blessed One.'

The people murmured, were shocked, and were indignant, &c., saying, 'How can the Sakyaputtiya Samanas, knowing no moderation, use up the king's mangoes?' The Bhikkhus heard those men murmuring, shocked, and indignant. Then those Bhikkhus told this matter to the Blessed One.

'You are not, O Bhikkhus, to eat mangoes. Whosoever does so, shall be guilty of a dukkata.'

2. Now at that time it was the turn of a certain multitude to provide the Samgha with a meal. Mango-peal was put into the curry. The Bhikkhus, fearing to offend, would not partake of it.

'Take it, O Bhikkhus, and eat. I allow you, O Bhikkhus, to eat the peal of the mango.'

Now at that time it was the turn of a certain multitude to provide the Samgha with a meal. They did not get so far as to make (curry with) the peal, but went about in the dining-hall with whole mangoes. The Bhikkhus, fearing to offend, would not accept them.

'Take them, O Bhikkhus, and eat. I allow you, O Bhikkhus, to eat fruit which has become allowable to Sama*n*as in any one of these five ways—when it has been injured by fire[1]—or by sword[2]—or by nails—when it has not yet had any seed in it—and fifthly, when it has no more seed in it[3]. I allow you, O Bhikkhus, to eat fruit which has become allowable to Sama*n*as in any one of these five ways.'

6[4].

1. Now at that time a certain Bhikkhu died of the bite of a snake. They told the matter to the Blessed One.

---

[1] Buddhaghosa gives in the Samanta Pâsâdikâ on the 11th Pâ*k*ittiya the following explanations of these terms. Aggi-pari*g*itan ti agginâ pari*g*ita*m* abhibhûta*m* da*ddh*a*m* phu*tth*an ti attho. The reading pari*g*ita*m* is correct and should be inserted in the text for pari*k*ita*m*.

[2] Sattha-pari*g*itan ti satthena pari*g*ita*m* abhibhûta*m* *kh*inna*m* viddha*m* vâ ti attho. Esa nayo nakha-pari*g*ite (B., loc. cit.).

[3] These last two clauses have already occurred at Mahâvagga VI, 21. The principle of the injunction throughout its five divisions is one and the same—the seed, or the capacity of fructification, must either have never existed, or have passed away, or have been destroyed.

[4] This ancient legend has been expanded into a *G*âtaka story, under the title of Khandha-vatta *G*âtaka, No. 203 in Professor Fausboll's edition (vol. ii, pp. 144–148), in which recur all the verses here given as a snake-charm. The names of the serpents are derived from the ancient mythology, and are not to be supposed to refer to actual breeds of real snakes. Below, *K*ullavagga VI, 2, 5, where a Bhikkhu is bitten by a snake, the simple precaution enjoined is the use of a higher bedstead.

'Now surely, that Bhikkhu, O Bhikkhus, had not let his love flow out over the four royal breeds of serpents! Had he done so, he would not die of the bite of a snake. And which are the four royal breeds of serpents? The Virûpakkhas are a royal breed. The Erâpathas are a royal breed. The *Kh*abyâputtas are a royal breed. The Ka*n*hâgotamakas are a royal breed. Now surely that Bhikkhu, O Bhikkhus, had not let his love flow out over the four royal breeds of serpents! Had he done so, he would not die of the bite of a snake. I allow you, O Bhikkhus, to make use of a safeguard for yourselves for your security and protection, by letting your love flow out over the four royal breeds of serpents. And thus, O Bhikkhus, are you to do so.

'"I love Virûpakkhas, the Erâpathas I love.

'"I love *Kh*abyâputtas, the Ka*n*hâgotamakas I love.

'"I love live things that have no feet, the bipeds too I love.

'"I love four-footed creatures, and things with many feet.

'"Let no footless thing do hurt to me, nor thing that has two feet.

'"Let no four-footed creature hurt, nor thing with many feet.

'"Let all creatures, all things that live, all beings of whatever kind,

'"Let all behold good fortune[1], and let none fall into sin.

[1] This phrase occurs in the passage at Mahâ-parinibbâna Sutta I, 31, by which Buddhaghosa is so much perplexed.

'"Infinite is the Buddha, infinite the Truth, infinite the Order. Finite are creeping things; snakes, scorpions and centipedes, spiders and lizards, rats and mice.

'"Made is my safeguard, made my defence. Let living things retreat,

'"Whilst I revere the Blessed One, the Buddhas seven supreme[1]."'

'I allow you, O Bhikkhus, to let blood[2].'

7.

1. Now at that time a certain Bhikkhu, tormented by distaste (for meditation, &c.), castrated himself[3]. They told this matter to the Blessed One.

'When one thing wanted cutting off, O Bhikkhus, that foolish fellow has cut off another! You are

[1] This is only one of the many passages from which it is evident that in the oldest Buddhism only the seven Buddhas, from Vipassi down to Gotama inclusive, were known by name to the members of the Buddhist community. Compare Rh. D.'s 'Hibbert Lectures, 1881,' p. 142. It is nevertheless probable that, with their ideas as to the infinite number of worlds which had succeeded one another in the past, they considered that the number of previous Buddhas had also been infinite.

[2] This last injunction, which comes in here so tamely, is omitted in the *G*âtaka story, and is merely a hook on which to hang an excuse for introducing this ancient and evidently favourite prescription into the Vinaya. That it is quite out of place is sufficiently evident from the fact that it has already been laid down in identical terms in the Mahâvagga VI, 14, 4, where it is found in its natural connection.

[3] Anabhiratiyâ pî*l*ito attano aṅga*g*âtam *kh*indi. This anabhirati is constantly referred to, and always as the result of falling in love, or in connection with sexual desire.

not, O Bhikkhus, to castrate yourselves. Whoso-ever does so, shall be guilty of a thulla*kk*aya.'

8

1. Now at that time the Se*tth*i of Râ*g*agaha had acquired a block[2] of sandal-wood of the most precious sandal-wood flavour. And the Se*tth*i of Râ*g*agaha thought, 'How would it be if I were to have a bowl carved out of this block of sandal-wood, so that the chips[3] shall remain my property, and I can give the bowl away?' And the Se*tth*i of Râ*g*agaha had a bowl turned out of that block of sandal-wood, and put it in a balance, and had it lifted on to the top of a bamboo[4], and tying that bamboo at the top of a succession of bamboos, he let it be known, saying, 'If any Sama*n*a or Brahman be an Arahat and possessed of Iddhi, let him get down the bowl. It is a gift to him!'

Then Pûra*n*a Kassapa went to the Se*tth*i of Râ*g*agaha, and said to him, 'I, O householder, am

---

[1] A Burmese version of the following legend is translated by Bishop Bigandet in his 'Legend of the Burmese Buddha,' vol. ii, pp. 212–216 (Third Edition).

[2] *K*andana-ga*nth*î uppannâ hotî ti *k*andana-gha*tt*ikâ uppannâ hoti (B.). Compare ga*nth*ikâ at *G*âtaka I, 150=ga*nd*ikâ at ibid. II, 124, and our note below on that word at V, 29, 3.

[3] Lekha*m*. It is clear from V, 9, 2, below, and Buddhaghosa's note there, that likhitu*m* is used in the sense of 'to plane' or 'to adze' wood or metal; and the Sinhalese MSS. read here likha*m* instead of lekha*m*. It cannot be 'to turn,' as the turning lathe is quite a modern invention.

[4] A similar proceeding is related of a Bhikkhu at 24, 1.

an Arahat and possessed of Iddhi. Give me the bowl.'

'If, Sir, you are an Arahat and possessed of Iddhi, let your reverence get down the bowl!'

Then Makkhali Gosâla, and A*g*ita Kesa-kambalî, and Pakudha Ka*kk*âyana, and Sa*ñg*aya Bela*tth*i-putta, and Niga*nth*a Nâta-putta went severally to the Se*tth*i of Râ*g*agaha, [and preferred the same request, and received the same reply.]

Now at that time the venerable Mahâ Moggallâna and the venerable Pi*nd*ola Bhâradvâ*g*a, having dressed themselves early in the morning, went into Râ*g*agaha, duly bowled and robed, for alms. And the venerable Pi*nd*ola Bhâradvâ*g*a said to the venerable Mahâ Moggallâna: 'The venerable Mahâ Moggallâna is both an Arahat and possessed of Iddhi. Go, friend Moggallâna, and fetch down this bowl, for this bowl belongs to thee.'

'The venerable Pi*nd*ola Bhâradvâ*g*a also is both an Arahat and possessed of Iddhi. Go, friend Bhâradvâ*g*a, and fetch down the bowl, for this bowl belongs to thee.'

Then the venerable Pi*nd*ola Bhâradvâ*g*a, rising up in the air, took the bowl, and went thrice round Râ*g*agaha (in the air). And at that time the Se*tth*i of Râ*g*agaha stood in his dwelling-place with his wife and children, and holding up his clasped hands in reverent salutation, he exclaimed, 'May the venerable Bhâradvâ*g*a be pleased to descend upon our dwelling-place.' And the venerable Bhâradvâ*g*a descended into his dwelling-place. Then the Se*tth*i of Râ*g*agaha took the bowl from the hands of the venerable Bhâradvâ*g*a, and filled it with costly food, and presented it to the venerable Bhâradvâ*g*a. And the venerable Bhâradvâ*g*a took the bowl, and departed to his Ârâma.

2. Now the people heard, 'The venerable Pi*nd*ola Bhâradvâ*g*a, they say, has got down the Râ*g*agaha Se*tth*i's bowl.' And those people, with shouts loud and long, followed in the steps of Pi*nd*ola Bhâradvâ*g*a. And the Blessed One heard the shouts loud and long, and on hearing them he asked the venerable Ânanda, 'What now, Ânanda, does this so great shouting mean?'

'The venerable Pi*nd*ola Bhâradvâ*g*a, Lord, has got down the Râ*g*agaha Se*tth*i's bowl; and the people thereof are following in his steps with shouts loud and long.'

Then the Blessed One, on that occasion and in that connection, convened a meeting of the Bhikkhu-Sa*m*gha, and asked Pi*nd*ola Bhâradvâ*g*a, 'Is it true, as they say, that you, Bhâradvâ*g*a, have got down the Râ*g*agaha Se*tth*i's bowl?'

'It is true, Lord.'

The Blessed Buddha rebuked him, saying, 'This is improper, Bhâradvâ*g*a, not according to rule, unsuitable, unworthy of a Sama*n*a, unbecoming, and ought not to be done. How can you, Bhâradvâ*g*a, for the sake of a miserable wooden pot, display before the laity the superhuman quality of your miraculous power of Iddhi? Just, Bhâradvâ*g*a, like a woman who displays herself for the sake of a miserable piece of money[1], have you, for the sake of a miserable

[1] Mâsaka-rûpassa. On the mâsaka, see Rh. D.'s 'Ancient Coins and Measures, &c.,' p. 13. It is evident from the use of the word rûpa here that stamped pieces of money were known in the valley of the Ganges as early as the time when the *K*ulla-

wooden pot displayed before the laity the superhuman quality of your miraculous power of Iddhi. This will not conduce, Bhâradvâ*g*a, either to the conversion of the unconverted, or to the increase of the converted; but rather to those who have not been converted remaining unconverted, and to the turning back of those who have been converted.'

And when he had rebuked him, and had delivered a religious discourse[1], he addressed the Bhikkhus, and said: 'You are not, O Bhikkhus, to display before the laity the superhuman power of Iddhi. Whosoever does so, shall be guilty of a dukka*t*a[2]. Break to pieces, O Bhikkhus, that wooden bowl; and when you have ground it to powder, give it to the Bhikkhus as perfume for their eye ointments[3]. And you are not, O Bhikkhus, to use wooden bowls. Whosoever does so, shall be guilty of a dukka*t*a[4].'

9.

1. Now at that time the *Kh*abbaggiya Bhikkhus used to use bowls of various kinds, made of gold and silver.

The people murmured (&c., as usual, down to) They told this matter to the Blessed One.

'You are not, O Bhikkhus, to use bowls made

vagga was composed. The word occurs also below at *K*ullavagga XII, 1, 1.

[1] See *K*ullavagga I, 1, 2.

[2] Compare the 4th Pârâ*g*ika.

[3] The use of sandal-wood for this purpose is allowed by the closing words of Mahâvagga VI, 11.

[4] This injunction is repeated below in the summary at V, 37.

of gold, or made of silver, or set with jewels, or made of beryl (ve*l*uriya[1]), or made of crystal, or made of copper, or made of glass[2], or made of tin, or made of lead, or made of bronze. Whosoever does so, shall be guilty of a dukka*t*a. I allow you, O Bhikkhus, bowls of two kinds,—those made of iron, and those made of clay.'

2. Now at that time the support at the bottom of the bowls wore out[3].

They told this matter to the Blessed One.

'I allow you, O Bhikkhus, to use circular (pieces of metal) as the supports for your bowls.'

Now at that time the *Kh*abbaggiya Bhikkhus used to have various kinds of circular supports to their bowls,—silver ones, and gold ones.

The people murmured (&c., down to) They told this matter to the Blessed One.

'You are not, O Bhikkhus, to have various kinds of circular supports to your bowls. Whosoever does

---

[1] It is clear from verses 192–196 of the 13th chapter of the Râ*g*a-nigha*n*t*u*, written by Narahari of Kashmîr in the thirteenth century A. D., that at that time Vai*d*ûrya meant 'cat's-eye.' But it is uncertain whether that was the only meaning of the word ve*l*uriya at the time when this passage was composed. (See especially V. 124, p. 25, of Dr. Richard Garbe's edition in his work, 'Die Indischen Mineralien,' Leipzig, 1882.) See also Professor Max Müller's interesting note at p. 266 of his 'What can India teach us?'

[2] Kâ*k*amayo. There was probably no glass in our modern sense of the word when the *K*ullavagga was written. But kâ*k*a is a silicious earth, and some sort of glass-like earthenware may very well have been in use. The phrase has already occurred, together with all the others in this passage, at Mahâvagga V, 8, 3, of foot-coverings, but is omitted in the list at Khudda Sikkhâ V. 10.

[3] Gha*m*sîyati. Literally, 'were rubbed.' See below, § 3, and our note below on V, 9, 2, 4.

so, shall be guilty of a dukka*t*a. I allow you, O Bhikkhus, two kinds of circular supports to your bowls,—tin ones, and lead ones.'

The thick circular supports could not be inserted[1].

They told this matter to the Blessed One.

'I allow you, O Bhikkhus, to shape them[2] (until they get to be the right size to fit in)[3].'

They would not stay in (?)[4].

'I allow you, O Bhikkhus, to split little pieces of crocodiles' teeth (to fit them in with)[5].'

Now at that time the *Kh*abbaggiya Bhikkhus had painted circular linings to the bottoms of their bowls, with painted figures scattered over them, or painted in patches of colour[6], and they used to walk about the streets exhibiting them.

People murmured (&c., down to) They told this matter to the Blessed One.

'You are not, O Bhikkhus, to have painted circular supports to the bottoms of your bowls, covered

---

[1] A*kkh*ûpiyanti. On the use of this word, compare Mahâvagga VIII, 14, 1, where it is used of inserting a slip of cloth in a torn garment.

[2] See our note above on V, 8, 1. Buddhaghosa says here likhitun ti tanu-kara*n*-atthây' eta*m* vutta*m*. The 'shaping' may be by carving, adzing, or planing.

[3] Compare above, V, 8, 1, and see Buddhaghosa's note at p. 316 of the edition of the text.

[4] The reading is corrupt; and therefore this rendering is merely conjectural. See H. O.'s note at p. 316 of his edition of the text.

[5] On these split crocodiles' teeth, see our note above on V, 1, 4.

[6] Rûpakoki*nn*âni bhati-kamma-katâni. Buddhaghosa has nothing on these words. On the second, see below, VI, 2, 7, and H. O.'s note on that passage at p. 321 of the edition of the text. It is most probable that the reading in both passages should be bhatti kamma, 'patchwork,' as further explained in our note below on VI, 2, 7; and we have translated accordingly.

with figures, and painted in patches of colour. Whosoever shall do so, shall be guilty of a dukka*t*a. I allow you, O Bhikkhus, only ordinary linings.'

3. Now at that time the Bhikkhus put away their bowls with water in them, and the bowls were split.

They told this matter to the Blessed One.

'You are not, O Bhikkhus, to put away your bowls with water in them. Whosoever does so, shall be guilty of a dukka*t*a. I enjoin upon you, O Bhikkhus, to dry your bowls in the sunshine[1] before putting them away.'

Now at that time the Bhikkhus dried their bowls in the sunshine, with water in them; and the bowls became evil-smelling.

They told this matter to the Blessed One.

'You are not, O Bhikkhus, to dry your bowls in the sunshine with water in them. Whosoever does so, shall be guilty of a dukka*t*a. I allow you, O Bhikkhus, to empty out the water[2], and then warm the bowls, before you put them away.'

Now at that time the Bhikkhus put their bowls away in a warm place; and the colour of the bowls was spoilt.

They told this matter to the Blessed One.

'You are not, O Bhikkhus, to put your bowls away in a warm place. Whosoever does so, shall be guilty of a dukka*t*a. I allow you, O Bhikkhus, to dry your bowls for a short time in a warm place, and then to put them away.'

---

[1] Otâpetvâ. The word has already occurred in Mahâvagga I, 25, 16. Compare Khudda Sikkhâ V. 6.

[2] Vodaka*m* katvâ. Vodaka*m* bears, of course, the same relation to sa-udaka*m*, used just before, as vagga does to samagga. The expression has occurred already at Mahâvagga I, 25, 13.

4. Now at that time a number of bowls were left in the open air without supports; and the bowls were turned over by a whirlwind[1], and broke.

They told this matter to the Blessed One.

'I allow you, O Bhikkhus, the use of supports for your bowls (when they are left out).'

Now at that time the Bhikkhus put their bowls away at the edge of the sleeping-benches in the verandahs[2], and the bowls fell down and were broken.

They told this matter to the Blessed One.

'You are not, O Bhikkhus, to put your bowls away on the edge of the sleeping-benches in the verandah. Whosoever does so, shall be guilty of a dukka*t*a.'

Now at that time the Bhikkhus put their bowls away on the edge of the Paribha*nd*a[3], and the bowls fell down and were broken.

They told this matter to the Blessed One.

'You are not, O Bhikkhus, to put your bowls away on the edge of the Paribha*nd*a. Whosoever does so, shall be guilty of a dukka*t*a.'

Now at that time the Bhikkhus turned their bowls upside down[4] on the ground, and the lips wore out.

---

[1] Vâta-ma*nd*alikâya. So also in the next section and in the Bhikkhunî-vibhaṅga, Pâ*k*ittiya 96. The reading at *G*âtaka I, 72 is vâta-ma*nd*ala*m*.

[2] Mi*dh*ante. This word recurs below in VI, 2, 3, where see our note. Buddhaghosa's note is given at p. 317 of the edition of the text. See also Khudda Sikkhâ V. 7.

[3] Used of a house, this probably means a plastered flooring of scented earth or dried cowdung. See *K*ullavagga VI, 17, 1, and Buddhaghosa's note there. On the use of the word in tailoring, see Mahâvagga VII, 1, 5, VIII, 21. Buddhaghosa, loc. cit. (p. 317), uses the expression mattika-paribha*nd*a-katâya-bhûmiyâ.

[4] Nikku*gg*anti. See the use of this word at V, 20, 3.

They told this matter to the Blessed One.

'I allow you, O Bhikkhus, the use of a mat made of grass[1].'

The grass-mat was eaten by white ants.

They told this matter to the Blessed One.

'I allow you, O Bhikkhus, the use of a small cloth[2].'

The small cloth was eaten by the white ants.

They told this matter to the Blessed One.

'I allow you, O Bhikkhus, the use of a raised parapet (?) (on which to put your bowls)[3].'

The bowls fell down from the parapet and were broken.

They told this matter to the Blessed One.

'I allow you, O Bhikkhus, the use of a wicker-work stand[4].'

On the wicker-work stand the bowls wore out.

They told this matter to the Blessed One.

'I allow you, O Bhikkhus, the use of bags to carry your bowls in.'

They had no shoulder-straps[5].

---

[1] Tina-santhârakam. That this word means a mat, and not a layer, of grass is clear from its use at Gâtaka I, 360, and below, V, 11, 3.

[2] Kolaka. The meaning of the word is doubtful, but see Mahâvagga VIII, 18. In the uddâna (at p. 143) the corresponding word is kola. See also below, VI, 3, 1, VI, 19, VI, 20, 2.

[3] Patta-mâlakam. Buddhaghosa says merely, 'It should be made either of bricks or of wood.' He confirms the reading of the text (with l as against Childers's reading mâlako).

[4] Patta-kandolikâ ti mahâ-mukha-kunda-santhânâ bhandakukkhalikâ vukkati (B.). Kandola is a wicker-work basket; see Böhtlingk-Roth, sub voce.

[5] See H. O.'s note on the reading here; and compare the table of contents to this chapter (at p. 143), where the reading amsabaddham confirms the suggested alteration. If there were any

They told this matter to the Blessed One.

'I allow you, O Bhikkhus, the use of a shoulder-strap (by which to carry the bag), or of a piece of string (by which to tie it on).'

5. Now at that time the Bhikkhus hung up their bowls on pins in the walls, or on hooks[1]. The pins or hooks falling down, the bowls were broken.

They told this matter to the Blessed One.

'You are not, O Bhikkhus, to hang your bowls up. Whosoever does so, shall be guilty of a dukka*t*a.'

Now at that time the Bhikkhus put their bowls down on a bed[2], or a chair; and sitting down thoughtlessly[3] they upset them, and the bowls were broken.

They told this matter to the Blessed One.

'You are not, O Bhikkhus, to put your bowls on the bed, or on a chair. Whosoever does so, shall be guilty of a dukka*t*a.'

Now at that time the Bhikkhus kept their bowls on their laps; and rising up thoughtlessly they upset them, and the bowls were broken.

---

further doubt it would be removed on comparing the closing words of Mahâvagga VI, 12, 4, which are identical with the present passage and contain the correct reading. The same remarks apply to other passages, where the same words occur below, V, 11, 5, V, 12, VI, 12, 3.

[1] The use of these appliances is formally allowed at VI, 3, 5.

[2] Mañ*k*a. Compare Rh. D.'s note at p. 277 of the 'Buddhist Birth Stories,' and Khuddha Sikkhâ V. 7.

[3] Sati-sammosâ. The word occurs at Milinda-pa*n*ha (ed. Trenckner), p. 260. It must be connected with mu*tth*a-sati, of which the Buddhist Sanskrit equivalent is mushita-sm*ri*ti*h* (see Kathâ Sarit Sâgara 56, 289). It is evident that Childers's original explanation of mu*tth*a-sati from mû*l*ha was wrong, and that both words must be referred to the root mush, as he points out at p. 618 of his Dictionary.

They told this matter to the Blessed One.

'You are not, O Bhikkhus, to keep your bowls on your laps. Whosoever does so, shall be guilty of a dukka*t*a.'

Now at that time the Bhikkhus put their bowls down on a sunshade; and the sunshade being lifted up by a whirlwind, the bowls rolled over, and were broken.

They told this matter to the Blessed One.

'You are not, O Bhikkhus, to put your bowls down on a sunshade. Whosoever does so, shall be guilty of a dukka*t*a.'

Now at that time the Bhikkhus, when they were holding the bowls in their hands, opened the door[1]. The door springing back the bowls were broken.

They told this matter to the Blessed One.

'You are not, O Bhikkhus, to open the door with your bowls in your hands. Whosoever does so, shall be guilty of a dukka*t*a.'

10.

1. Now at that time the Bhikkhus went on their round for alms, carrying water-jugs made out of gourds[2], or water-pots[3].

[1] Kavâ*t*am pa*n*âmetvâ. The construction of doors is described in detail at V, 14, 3, with reference to the bath-house, and again at VI, 2. That pa*n*âmeti is to open, and not to shut, is clear from VIII, 1, 1, just as pattam pa*n*âmeti at VIII, 5, 2 is to uncover, disclose, the bowl. Compare Khuddha Sikkhâ V. 8.

[2] Tumba-ka*t*âhan ti lâpu-ka*t*âham vu*kk*ati (B.). Tumba is gourd, according to Böhtlingk-Roth. See Khuddha Sikkhâ V. 11.

[3] Gha*t*i-ka*t*âhan ti gha*t*i-kapâlam (B.). The whole section is repeated in the text of each kind of vessel.

People murmured, were shocked, and indignant, saying, 'As the Titthiyas do.'

They told this matter to the Blessed One.

'You are not, O Bhikkhus, to go on your rounds for alms with water-jugs, or pots. Whosoever does so, shall be guilty of a dukkata.'

2. Now at that time a certain Bhikkhu, who had taken upon himself a vow to wear or use nothing except what he could procure from dust-heaps or cemeteries, went on his rounds for alms carrying a bowl made out of a skull. A certain woman saw him, and was afraid, and made an outcry [1], saying, 'O horror! This is surely a devil!'

People murmured, were shocked, and indignant, saying, 'How can the Sakyaputtiya Samanas carry about bowls made out of skulls, as the devil-worshippers [2] do?'

They told this matter to the Blessed One.

'You are not, O Bhikkhus, to use bowls made out of skulls. Whosoever does so, shall be guilty of a dukkata. And you are not, O Bhikkhus, to take a vow to wear or to use nothing except what you procure from dust-heaps or cemeteries. Whosoever does so, shall be guilty of a dukkata.'

3. Now at that time the Bhikkhus carried out odd bits, and bones, and dirty water [3] in their bowls.

People murmured, were shocked, and were indignant, saying, 'The very vessel out of which

---

[1] Vissaram akâsi, on the use of which idiom see the passages quoted below, Kullavagga VIII, 1, 1.

[2] Pisâkillikâ. See below, 27, 5, and Mahâvagga III, 12, 3.

[3] This list recurs in the Old Commentary on the 10th Pâkittiya in the Bhikkhunî-vibhaṅga. As an explanation of vighâsa, Buddhaghosa says here ukkhittodakan ti mukha-vikkhâlanodakam.

these Sakyaputtiya Sama*n*as eat, that they use as a waste-tub!'

They told this matter to the Blessed One.

'You are not, O Bhikkhus, to carry out odd bits, and bones, and dirty water in your bowls. Whosoever does so, shall be guilty of a dukka*t*a. I allow you, O Bhikkhus, the use of a waste-tub[1].'

11.

1. Now at that time the Bhikkhus sewed their robes together after tearing the cloth with their hands[2]; and the robes became jagged.

They told this matter to the Blessed One.

'I allow you, O Bhikkhus, the use of a blade and of a sheath (for the blade) made of felt[3].'

Now at that time a blade with a haft to it[4] had come into the possession of the Samgha.

They told this matter to the Blessed One.

---

[1] Pa*t*iggaho. Slop-basin, waste-tub, 'receptacle' for odd bits. It is so used below at VIII, 4, 4.

[2] Vipâ*t*etvâ. The three MSS. read vippâdetvâ, the same corrected to vipphâdetvâ, and vipphâmetvâ. M for L is a common mistake in Sinhalese MSS., and the correct reading may possibly be vipphâletvâ, if it is not vipphâ*t*etvâ, as suggested in H. O.'s note, vol. v, p. 259.

[3] Namatakan ti satthaka-ve*th*anaka*m* pilotika-kha*nd*a*m* (B.). The word occurs again below at V, 19, 1, V, 27, 1, and X, 10, 4 (where the nuns are forbidden to use it). Namata is felt; and nâmatika-aṅga, the wearing of felt, is inserted by some Sanskrit Buddhist writers in the list of Dhutaṅgas. (Burnouf, Introduction, &c., p. 306.)

[4] Da*nd*a-satthakan ti vippalika*m* vâ a*ññ*a*m* pi vâ ya*m* ki*ñk*i da*nd*a*m* yogetvâ kata-satthaka*m* (B.). Compare da*nd*a-ka*th*ina*m* at V, 11, 3, and da*nd*a-parissâvana*m* at V, 13, 3.

'I allow you, O Bhikkhus, the use of a blade with a haft to it.'

Now at that time the *Kh*abbaggiya Bhikkhus used various kinds of long handles to their blades, made of silver, and made of gold.

People murmured (&c., as usual, down to) They told this matter to the Blessed One.

'You are not, O Bhikkhus, to use various kinds of handles to your blades. Whosoever does so, shall be guilty of a dukka*t*a. I allow you, O Bhikkhus, the use of handles to your blades made of bone, or ivory, or horn, or of the na*l*a reed, or of bamboo, or of hard wood, or of lac, or of the shells of fruit, or of bronze, or of the centre of the chank-shell[1].'

2. Now at that time the Bhikkhus sewed their robes with quills or bits of bamboo rind, and the robes were badly sewn.

They told this matter to the Blessed One.

'I allow you, O Bhikkhus, the use of needles.'

The needles got blunted[2].

'I allow you, O Bhikkhus, the use of a needle-case made of bamboo[3].'

Even in the needle-cases the needles became blunt.

[1] This list is given in the Mahâvagga VI, 12, 1 (where see our notes), as the materials of which ointment-boxes may be made; and below, V, 11, 5, of thimbles.

[2] Ka*nn*akitâ hontî ti malagga-kitâ (B.). Mala may probably here mean 'rust,' if the needles were made of iron. Ka*nn*akitâ, 'spoiled,' is used of plastered walls and the floors of a Vihâra at Mahâvagga I, 25, 15=*K*ullavagga VIII, 1, 3; and pa*m*su-kitâ occurs just below in our present passage. Compare also the note on vika*nn*a*m* in the following section.

[3] Sû*k*i-nâ*l*ika*m*. On these needle-cases compare the Introductory Story to the 20th *G*âtaka. It is Pâ*k*ittiya to have them made of ivory, horn, or bone. (80th Pâ*k*ittiya, but they are there called Sû*k*i-ghara*m*.)

'I allow you, O Bhikkhus, to fill the cases with chunam [1].

Even in the chunam the needles became blunt.

'I allow you, O Bhikkhus, to fill the cases with barley-meal [2].'

Even in the barley-meal the needles became blunt.

'I allow you, O Bhikkhus, the use of powdered stone [3].'

Even in the powdered stone the needles became blunt.

'I allow you, O Bhikkhus, to mix (the powder) with beeswax [4].'

The powder still did not cohere.

'I allow you, O Bhikkhus, to mix sipâtika gum [5] with the powder [6].'

3. Now at that time the Bhikkhus sewed their robes together by planting stakes here and there, and uniting them (with strings). The robes became out of shape [7].'

They told this matter to the Blessed One.

'I allow you, O Bhikkhus, the use of a Kaththina [8],

---

[1] Kinnena kunnena (B.).

[2] Satthuyâ ti halidda-missakena pitthka-kunnena (B.).

[3] Saritakan ti pâsâna-kunnam vukkati (B.).

[4] Madhu-sitthakena sâretun ti madhu-sitthakena makkhetum (B.).

[5] The use of this gum for medicine purposes is allowed at Mahâvagga VI, 7, where see our note. The present use is again mentioned below, V, 27, 1.

[6] Sarita-sibbâtikan ti madhu-sitthaka-pilotikam (B.).

[7] Vikannam hoti. See the note on this expression at Mahâvagga VI, 21, 1. The 'robes' were lengths of cloth, and 'out of shape' (vikannam) must mean either that one side was larger than the other, so that each corner (kanno) was not a right angle, or perhaps that each edge (kanno) was not straight.

[8] What Kaththina may mean in this connection is not exactly

and that you are to sew the robes together after tying down Ka*th*ina-strings here and there.'

They spread out the Ka*th*ina on uneven (ground), and the Ka*th*ina fell to pieces [1].

'You are not, O Bhikkhus, to spread out the Ka*th*ina on uneven (ground). Whosoever does so, shall be guilty of a dukka*t*a.'

They spread out the Ka*th*ina on the ground, and the Ka*th*ina became dirty.

'I allow you, O Bhikkhus, the use of a grass-mat.

The edge of the Ka*th*ina decayed through age.

'I allow you, O Bhikkhus, to strengthen it by a doubling or a binding along the edge [2].

The Ka*th*ina was not large enough [3].

'I allow you, O Bhikkhus, the use of a da*nd*a-

---

clear to us, but it is evidently a sort of framework, or bench, for the tailors to lay out their work upon. Our notes above on the 1st Nissaggiya and on Mahâvagga VII, 1, 3, refer to a different and secondary use of the word in the Ka*th*ina ceremonies—so-called doubtless because the Ka*th*ina-dussa (the supply of cloth to be dyed, sewn, and made up into robes, and distributed, on one and the same day) was to be so sewn with the aid of the Ka*th*ina here referred to. Buddhaghosa says here, Ka*th*inan ti nisse*n*i pi tattha attharita-ka*t*asâraka-kila*ñ**k*ana*m* aññatara*m* pi ka*th*ina*m* vu*kk*ati yâya dupa*tt*a-*k*îvara*m* sibbenti ka*th*ine *k*îvara*m* pi bandhanti. On Dupa*tt*a, see Mahâvagga VIII, 14, 1.

The use of obandhitvâ (in reference to the Ka*th*ina), in opposition to sambandhitvâ (in reference to the mere stakes), is worthy of notice.

[1] Paribhi*gg*ati. Perhaps we should translate, 'did not hold together.' See the last section.

[2] Anuvâta*m* paribha*nd*a*m*. See Mahâvagga VII, 1, 5, VIII, 21, *K*ullavagga V, 9, 4, VI, 17, 1, XI, 1, 14, and our notes there.

[3] Ka*th*ina*m* *n*a ppahotî ti dîghassa bhikkhuno pamâ*n*ena kata*m* ka*th*ina*m* tattha rassassa bhikkhuno *k*îvara*m* patthariyamâna*m* na ppahoti anto yeva hoti (B.).

ka*th*ina[1], of a pidalaka[1], of a ticket, of binding strings, and of binding threads[2]; and that you sew your robes together after binding them therewith.'

The interstices between the threads became irregular in length[3].

'I allow you, O Bhikkhus, the use of little marks (of the leaf of the talipot palm, or such-like things)[4].'

The threads became crooked.

'I allow you, O Bhikkhus, the use of false threads (laid along the cloth to show where it is to be cut or sewn)[5].'

4. Now at that time the Bhikkhus got on to the Ka*th*ina with unwashen feet, or wet feet, or with their shoes on[6], and the Ka*th*ina was soiled.

They told this matter to the Blessed One.

'You are not, O Bhikkhus, to get on to the Ka*th*ina with unwashen feet, or with wet feet, or with your shoes on. Whosoever does so, shall be guilty of a dukka*t*a.'

5. Now at that time the Bhikkhus, when sewing

---

[1] On these terms, which we do not attempt to translate, see Buddhaghosa's notes as quoted by H. O. at p. 317 of the edition of the text. The first seems to be a Ka*th*ina with a cross-bar, but da*nd*a at V, 11, 1, and V, 13, 3, means handle.

[2] Vinandhana-ra*gg*u*m* vinandhana-suttaka*m*. See Buddhaghosa's notes loc. cit., and compare Mahâvagga V, 11.

[3] Visamâ honti ti kâ*k*i khuddakâ honti kâ*k*i mahantâ (B.). Sutta here probably means those threads or strings just referred to by which the stuff was to be tied on to the Ka*th*ina.

[4] Ka*l*imbhaka*m*: so explained by Buddhaghosa, loc. cit.

[5] Mogha-suttaka*m*. Buddhaghosa says, 'the making of a mark with a green thread, as carpenters do on wood with a black thread.' Compare also our notes 2 and 3 on Mahâvagga VII, 1, 5.

[6] The whole section is repeated in the text at length for each of these three cases.

their robes, held the stuff with their fingers, and their fingers were hurt.

They told this matter to the Blessed One.

'I allow you, O Bhikkhus, the use of a thimble[1].'

Now at that time the *Kh*abbaggiya Bhikkhus used various kinds of thimbles,—gold ones, and silver ones.

People murmured, &c. The Bhikkhus heard, &c. They told this matter to the Blessed One.

'You are not, O Bhikkhus, to use various kinds of thimbles. Whosoever does so, shall be guilty of a dukka*t*a. I allow you, O Bhikkhus, thimbles made of bone, or ivory, or horn, or of the na*l*a reed, or of bamboo, or of hard wood, or of lac, or of the shells of fruit, or of bronze, or of the centre of the chank-shell[2].'

Now at that time the needles, and scissors, and thimbles got lost.

They told this matter to the Blessed One.

'I allow you, O Bhikkhus, the use of a box or drawer[3] in the workshop.'

They got crowded together in the workshop box.

They told this matter to the Blessed One.

'I allow you, O Bhikkhus, the use of a thimble bag (to carry the thimbles about in).'

They had no shoulder-strap.

---

[1] Pa*t*iggaho, 'receptacle' for the finger. See our note above on V, 10, 3, where the same word means a waste-tub. For other secondary uses of the word, see *G*âtaka I, 146, II, 9, 26. Buddhaghosa says here, pa*t*iggahan ti aṅguli-kosaka*m*.

[2] So of ointment-boxes, Mahâvagga VII, 12, 1; and of scissors, above, V, 11, 1.

[3] Âsevana-(sic)vitthaka*m* nâma *ya*m kiñ*k*i pâtî-*k*aṅgo*t*akâdi (B.).

They told this matter to the Blessed One.

'I allow you, O Bhikkhus, the use of a shoulder-strap, or of a piece of string, to tie the bags on with[1].'

6[2]. Now at that time the Bhikkhus, when sewing their robes in the open air, were distressed by heat and by cold.

They told this matter to the Blessed One.

'I allow you, O Bhikkhus, the use of a hall or of a shed for the Ka*th*ina.'

The Ka*th*ina hall had too low a basement, and it was inundated with water.

They told this matter to the Blessed One.

'I allow you, O Bhikkhus, to make it with a high basement[3].'

The facing (of the basement) fell in.

'I allow you, O Bhikkhus, to line the basement with facing of three kinds[4]—brick facing, stone facing, or wooden facing.'

They found difficulty in getting up into it.

'I allow you, O Bhikkhus, the use of stairs of three kinds—brick stairs, stone stairs, or wooden stairs.'

As they were going up them they fell off.

'I allow you, O Bhikkhus, the use of a balustrade[5].

---

[1] See our note above on V, 9, 4.

[2] The whole of this paragraph is repeated below, though not in the same order, of the *K*aṅkama or cloister, and of the *G*antâghara, or bath-house. (See V, 14, 2, 3.)

[3] That is, to build it on a raised platform, the technical term for which is *k*aya.

[4] See our note below on V, 14, 3. The whole passage recurs of the lining of a well at V, 16, 2, and of Vihâras themselves at VI, 3, 3.

[5] Âlambana-bâha*m*. At Mahâ-sudassana Sutta I, 59, there is

Straw and plaster fell (from the walls and roof) into the K*a*t*h*ina-hall.

'I allow you, O Bhikkhus, to first cover over (the walls and roof with skins[1]), and then plaster them within and without. (And I allow the use of) whitewash, and blacking, and red colouring[2], and wreath-work, and creeper-work, and bone hooks, and cupboards[3], and bamboos to hang robes on, and strings to hang robes on.'

7. Now at that time the Bhikkhus, when they had sewn the robes together, left the Ka*th*ina as it was, and went away; and the robes were eaten by rats and white ants.

They told this matter to the Blessed One.

'I allow you, O Bhikkhus, to fold up the Ka*th*ina.'

The Ka*th*ina came to pieces.

---

a description of flights of stairs (sopânâ), each of which had thambhâ, evidently posts or banisters; sû*k*iyo, apparently cross-bars let in to these banisters; and u*n*hîsa*m*, either a head-line running along the top of the banisters, or a figure-head at the lower end of such a head-line. (See Rh. D.'s 'Buddhist Suttas,' p. 262.) This and the previous paragraphs are repeated below, V, 14, 2, of the *K*aṅkama.

[1] See Mahâvagga V, 11, where the same technical term (ogumpheti) is used. Buddhaghosa's note is given at p. 317 of the text. See also V, 14, 3, below.

[2] Geruka-parikamma*m*. This reading, and not gerika, is confirmed by VI, 3, 1, VI, 17, 1, where the two previous words also occur. On this mode of preparing walls and floors, see our note below on VI, 20.

[3] Pa*ñk*a-pa*t*ika*m* or -pa*tth*ika*m*, a term of doubtful signification which recurs, together with all the previous words, in the Old Commentary on the 19th Pâ*k*ittiya. Compare pa*ñk*a-prastha in B.R. The word is perhaps however connected with Sanskrit pa*tt*ikâ, as *k*ela-pattikam at V, 21, 2 undoubtedly is. It occurs below, in a similar connection, at VI, 3, 1.

'I allow you, O Bhikkhus, to fold up the Ka*th*ina in a cow-hide (?)[1].'

The Ka*th*ina got uncovered.

'I allow you, O Bhikkhus, the use of strings to tie it up with.'

Now at that time the Bhikkhus went away, putting the Ka*th*ina up against the wall or a pillar; and the Ka*th*ina, falling over, was broken.

They told this matter to the Blessed One.

'I allow you, O Bhikkhus, to hang it on a stake of the wall, or on a hook[2].'

12.

1. Now the Blessed One, when he had stayed at Râ*g*agaha as long as he thought fit, set out on his journey toward Vesâlî[3].

Now at that time the Bhikkhus went along, carrying their needles and scissors and drugs in their bowls.

They told this matter to the Blessed One.

'I allow you, O Bhikkhus, the use of a bag to carry the drugs in[4].'

---

[1] Go-gha*m*sikâya. Compare pâda-gha*m*sani at 22. 1; and on the use of sa*m*harati in a similar connection, see VI, 2, 7.

[2] Nâga-dante. See the note on Mallaka at *K*ullavagga V, 1, 4.

[3] This is merely introduced to show that the following rules or privileges in this and the next chapter (§§ 1, 2) were to be in force when the Bhikkhus were on a journey.

[4] Neither here nor in V, 11, 5 are we to understand that the needles and scissors are to be carried in bags. They are mentioned in both passages merely to show the inconvenience of having no separate receptacles for the thimbles and the drugs.

They had no shoulder-strap.

'I allow you, O Bhikkhus, the use of a shoulder-strap[1], or of a string to tie the bags on with.'

Now at that time a certain Bhikkhu tied his sandals on to his girdle, and then entered the village for alms[2]. A certain Upâsaka, when saluting that Bhikkhu, knocked up against the sandals with his head. The Bhikkhu was annoyed; and when he had returned to the Ârâma, he told this matter to the Bhikkhus. They told this matter to the Blessed One.

'I allow you, O Bhikkhus, the use of a bag to carry your sandals in.'

They had no shoulder-strap.

'I allow you, O Bhikkhus, the use of a shoulder-strap, or of a string to tie the bags on with.'

13.

1. Now at that time the water as they went along could not be drunk without breaking the rules[3], as they had no strainers.

They told this matter to the Blessed One.

'I allow you, O Bhikkhus, the use of a strainer.'

The little cloth (that was used for a strainer) was not sufficient (to filter enough water for the whole party).

---

[1] See the note on V, 9, 4.

[2] He would require the sandals only when he came, in his journey, to rough places; not on the smooth, well-trodden, village paths.

[3] The rule, that is, against destroying the life of living things.

'I allow you, O Bhikkhus, the use of a strainer fixed on to a ladle[1].'

Still the little cloth was not sufficient for the purpose.

'I allow you, O Bhikkhus, the use of a regulation water-pot[2].'

2. Now at that time two Bhikkhus were travelling along the high-road in the Kosala country. One of the Bhikkhus was guilty of some transgression. The other one said to him, 'Do not, my friend, do such a thing. It is not becoming.' The first one bore a grudge against him[3]. Afterwards the other Bhikkhu, being tormented with thirst, said to the Bhikkhu who bore the grudge, 'Give me, friend, your strainer. I am going to drink some water.' The Bhikkhu who bore the grudge would not give it to him. The other Bhikkhu died of thirst[4]. Then that Bhikkhu, when he had arrived at the Ârâma, told this matter to the Bhikkhus.

---

[1] Ka*t*a*kkh*u-parissâvana*m* nâma tîsu da*nd*akesu vinandhitvâ kata*m* (B.).

[2] Dhamma-karaka*m*. Doubtless a water-pot with a strainer so fixed into it that a quantity of water could be filtered quickly. The word occurs at Mahâva*m*sa, p. 90, and below, VI, 21, 3.

[3] So tasmi*m* upanandhi. The Introductory Story in the Sutta-vibhaṅga on the 36th Pâ*k*ittiya is, so far, word for word the same as this section. Buddhaghosa there explains upanandhi by *g*anita-upanâho. See vol. iv, p. 359, of H. O.'s edition of the Vinaya Pi*t*aka. The Introductory Story to the 31st *G*âtaka is also based on a similar incident, and there the corresponding expression is vivâda*m* aka*m*su. (Fausböll's *G*âtaka, vol. i, p. 198.)

[4] In the *G*âtaka commentary this tragic result of the refusal is absent. The Bhikkhu who has no strainer merely drinks without straining. (Rh. D.'s 'Buddhist Birth Stories,' vol. i, p. 278.)

'What then, Sir? when asked for your strainer, would you not lend it?'

'It is even so, Sirs.'

Those Bhikkhus who were moderate were annoyed and vexed, and murmured, saying, 'How can a Bhikkhu, when asked for his strainer, refuse to lend it?' And they told this matter to the Blessed One.

Then the Blessed One on that occasion and in that connection (&c., as usual, see for instance in *K*ullavagga I, 1, 2, down to) addressed the Bhikkhus, and said:

'A Bhikkhu who is on a journey is not, O Bhikkhus, to refuse to lend his strainer, when he is asked for it. Whosoever does so, shall be guilty of a dukka*t*a. And (a Bhikkhu who is) not provided with a strainer, O Bhikkhus, is not to undertake a journey. Whosoever does so, shall be guilty of a dukka*t*a. If there be no strainer nor regulation water-pot, the corner of the upper robe is to be adopted[1] for the purpose of straining before drinking.'

3. Now the Blessed One, journeying straight on, arrived in due course at Vesâlî. And there at Vesâlî the Blessed One lodged in the Mahâvana, in the Kû*t*âgâra Hall.

Now at that time the Bhikkhus were engaged in building[2]; and the strainer did not act[3].

---

[1] Adhi*tth*âtabbo, that is, the Bhikkhu is to determine in his mind that that part of his robe is a strainer for the time.

[2] Navakamma*m* karonti. On the use of this and allied idioms, see *G*âtaka I, 92, line 22; *K*ullavagga I, 18, 1, VI, 5, 2; Bhikkhunî-vibhaṅga, Pârâ*g*ika I, 1; Indian Antiquary XI, 29; Senart's Ka*kk*âyana, p. 189.

[3] Na sammati, which is curious. For 'did not suffice,' the standing expression would be na ppahoti.

They told this matter to the Blessed One.

'I allow, O Bhikkhus, the use of a double strainer[1].'

The double strainer did not act.

'I allow, O Bhikkhus, the use of a filter[2].'

Now at that time the Bhikkhus were troubled[3] by mosquitoes.

They told this matter to the Blessed One.

'I allow, O Bhikkhus, the use of mosquito curtains[4].'

14.

1. Now at that time at Vesâlî a regular service of sweet food had been established, the laity taking the duty in turns. The Bhikkhus, eating the sweet food, became very sick with superfluity of humors in their body[5].

Now *G*îvaka Komârabha*kk*a went to Vesâlî on

---

[1] Da*nd*a-parissâvana*m*. Apparently a long box, both ends of which strain the water, which is poured into the middle by means of a pipe (da*nd*aka). Buddhaghosa says, Da*nd*a-parisâvanan ti (sic; only one s) ra*g*anakâna*m* khâra-parisâvana*m* viya *k*atusu pâdesu baddha-nise*n*ikâya sâ*l*aka*m* bandhitvâ ma*ggh*e da*n*-*d*ake udaka*m* âsiñ*k*itabba*m*. Tam ubhohi ko*tth*âsehi pûretvâ parisâvati. Compare da*nd*a atthaka*m* and da*nd*a-kathina*m*, above, V, 11, 1, 3.

[2] Ottharaka*m* nâma ya*m* udake ottharitvâ gha*t*akena udaka*m* ga*n*hanti. Ta*m* hi *k*atusu da*nd*akesu vettha*m* bandhitvâ sabbe pariyante udakato mo*k*etvâ ma*ggh*e ottharitvâ gha*t*ena udaka*m* ga*n*hanti (B.).

[3] Ubbâ*lh*â. See Mahâvagga III, 9, 1–4, and *G*âtaka I, 300.

[4] Makasa-ku*t*ikâ ti *k*îvara-ku*t*ikâ (B.). Literally, a 'mosquito hut,' the walls of which are to be of cloth.

[5] Abhisannakâyâ ti semhâdi-dos'-ussanna-kâyâ (B.). This word has already occurred at Mahâvagga VI, 14, 7, where Buddhaghosa's explanation is much the same. See also Mahâvagga VIII, 1, 30.

some business or other. And on seeing the Bhikkhus very sick with superfluity of humors, he went up to where the Blessed One was; and when he had come there, he saluted the Blessed One and took his seat on one side. And when so seated he said to the Blessed One: 'The Bhikkhus, Lord, are now very sick with superfluity of humors. It would be well if the Blessed One were to prescribe, Lord, for the Bhikkhus the use of the cloister[1] and of the bath-room[2]. Thus will the Bhikkhus become convalescent.'

Then the Blessed One instructed, and aroused, and incited, and gladdened *G*îvaka Komârabha*kk*a with religious discourse. And *G*îvaka Komârabha*kk*a, so instructed, and incited, and aroused, and gladdened with religious discourse, arose from his seat and saluted the Blessed One, and keeping him on his right hand as he passed him, departed thence. And the Blessed One, on that occasion and in that connection, convened an assembly of the Bhikkhu-sa*m*gha, and addressed the Bhikkhus, and said, 'I

---

[1] *K*a*n*kama. A straight piece of ground cleared and levelled for the purpose of walking up and down upon for exercise and meditation. See our note on this word at Mahâvagga V, 1, 14.

[2] *G*antâghara. See our note above on Mahâvagga I, 25, 12. It was not ordinarily used for cold baths, which were taken in the rivers or tanks, but for a kind of hot-water bath, or perhaps steam bath, the exact mode of taking or administering which is not as yet certain. Several Bhikkhus took the bath at the same time, but it is not likely that they got into the water (though the expression uttarati is used, loc. cit., of their leaving the bath), as they scarcely would have made vessels large enough to contain a man. It rather seems that they sat on stools close to a large fire, and had water poured over them. The use of this kind of bath is forbidden to the Bhikkhunîs at *K*ullavagga X, 27, 4.

prescribe, O Bhikkhus, the use of the cloister and of the bath-room.'

2. Now at that time the Bhikkhus walked up and down on a cloister on uneven ground; and their feet were hurt.

They told this matter to the Blessed One.

'I allow you, O Bhikkhus, to make it level.'

The cloister had too low a basement, and was inundated with water [1].

They told this matter to the Blessed One.

'I allow you, O Bhikkhus, to make it with a high basement.'

The facing of the basement fell in [2].

'I allow you, O Bhikkhus, the use of facing of three kinds—brick facing, stone facing, and wooden facing.'

They found difficulty in getting up into it.

'I allow you, O Bhikkhus, the use of stairs of three kinds—brick stairs, stone stairs, and wooden stairs.'

As they were going up them, they fell off.

'I allow you, O Bhikkhus, the use of a balustrade.'

Now at that time the Bhikkhus, when walking up and down in the cloister, fell down.

They told this matter to the Blessed One.

'I allow you, O Bhikkhus, to provide a railing [3] for the cloister.'

---

[1] All the following paragraphs are the same as above, V, 11, 6, where see our notes.

[2] As we have pointed out above, in our note on Mahâvagga V, 1, 14, it is not probable that the *K*aṅkama at first had a roof and stairs and balustrade. These were later improvements.

[3] Vedikâ. See Mahâ-sudassana Sutta I, 60, and Rh. D.'s note there ('Buddhist Suttas,' p. 262), and below, VI, 2, 2.

Now at that time the Bhikkhus, when walking up and down in the open air, were distressed by heat and by cold.

They told this matter to the Blessed One.

'I allow you, O Bhikkhus, the use of a hall for the cloister [1].'

Straw and plaster fell (from the walls and roof) into the cloister-hall.

'I allow you, O Bhikkhus, to first cover over (the walls and roof with skins), and then plaster them. (And I allow the use of) whitewash, and blacking, and red colouring, and wreath-work, and creeper-work, and bone hooks, and cupboards, and bamboos to hang robes on, and strings to hang robes on.'

3. [The whole of the above, from the basement down to the balustrade, is repeated of the hot-bath house.]

The bath house had no door.

'I allow you, O Bhikkhus, the use of a door, with door-posts and lintel [2], with hollows like a mortar (for the door to revolve in [3]), with projections to

---

[1] *K*aṅkamana-sâlâ, already referred to at Mahâvagga III, 5.

[2] Pi*tth*a-sa*m*ghâ*t*a*m*. See Childers under saṅghâ*t*a, and the Samanta Pâsâdikâ on the 19th Pâ*k*ittiya. Kavâ*t*a-pi*tth*a occurs in Mahâvagga I, 25, 15, and in the Samanta Pâsâdikâ on Pâ*k*ittiya 19 (compare upari-pi*tth*iti at *K*ullavagga VIII, 1, 1), and this and the two following phrases below, VI, 2, 1. Buddhaghosa has nothing on them, either here or there; and they were probably therefore in quite common use even in his day. The whole of this paragraph recurs below, VI, 3, 7.

[3] Udukkhalika*m*. Presumably the door had no hinges, but the upper and lower ends of one side projected into hollows prepared for them in the lintel and the threshold. This suggestion is confirmed by the connection in which these words are used at VI, 2, 1.

revolve in those hollows[1], with rings on the door for the bolt to work along in[2], with a block of wood fixed unto the edge of the door-post and containing a cavity for the bolt to go into (called the monkey's head[3]), with a pin[4] (to secure the bolt by), with a connecting bolt[5], with a key-hole[6], with a hole for the string with which the door can be closed, and with a string for that purpose[7].'

---

[1] Uttara-pâsaka*m*. See the last note. Pâsaka recurs also in the next but one. Compare aggala-pâsaga in Âyâraṅga Sutta II, 1, 5, 2.

[2] Aggala-va*tt*i nâma dvâra-bâhâye samappamâ*n*o yeva aggalatthambho vu*kk*ati yattha tîni *k*attâri *kh*iddâni katvâ sû*k*iyo denti (B.).

[3] Kapi-sîsaka*m* nâma dvâra-bâha*m* vi*ggh*itva tattha pavesito aggala-pâsako vu*kk*ati (B.). The word recurs in the Mahâparinibbâna Sutta V, 32, where it is said of Ânanda that he kapisîsaka*m* âlambitvâ a*tth*âsi, just as in the Mahâ-sudassana Sutta II, 24 it is said of the queen under similar circumstances that she dvâra-bâha*m* âlambitvâ a*tth*âsi. Buddhaghosa's commentary on the word in the former of these two passages is given by Rh. D. in his note at p. 95 of the 'Buddhist Suttas.'

[4] Sû*k*ikâ ti tattha (that is, kapi-sîsake) ma*ggh*e *kh*idda*m* katvâ pavesitâ (B.). Apparently a pin to pass through the monkey's head so as to secure the bolt in its place after it has been shot into the cavity. See the next note and below, VI, 2, 1.

[5] Gha*t*ikâ ti upari-yo*g*itâ (B.). At *G*âtaka I, 360 (compare *K*ullavagga IX, 1, 2), we are told of a man who dvârâni pidahanto sabba-dvâresu sû*k*igha*t*ikâdayo datvâ tala*m* (sic, query tâla*m*) abhiruhitvâ tattha pi dvâram pidahitvâ nisîdi. As the principal bolt was probably called aggala (unless that were the name for the whole machinery), this was some smaller bolt. And in *K*ullavagga VIII, 1, 1 an instance is given of a man undoing the bolt (gha*t*ikam ugghâ*t*etvâ) of an uninhabited vihâra, such as is referred to in VI, 2, 1.

[6] Tâla*kkh*idda*m*. See the end of VI, 2, 1, and Childers under the word tâ*l*o. Buddhaghosa says nothing. The word tâla occurs in the last note.

[7] Âviñ*kh*ana-*kkh*iddam âviñ*kh*ana-ra*gg*um. These are said in VI, 2, 1 to be necessary because the door could not be put

The lower part of the wattle and daub wall[1] of the bath-room decayed (through damp).

They told this matter to the Blessed One.

'I allow you, O Bhikkhus, to face round the lower half of the wall (with bricks[2]).'

The bath-room had no chimney[3].

'I allow you, O Bhikkhus, the use of a chimney.'

Now at that time the Bhikkhus made a fire-place in the middle of a small bath-room, and there was no room to get to (the bath).

'I allow you, O Bhikkhus, to make the fire-place at one side of a small bath-room, and in the middle of a large one[4].'

The fire in the bath-room scorched their faces.

'I allow you, O Bhikkhus, the use of clay to spread over your faces[5].'

They moistened the clay in their hands.

'I allow you, O Bhikkhus, the use of a trough to moisten the clay in[6].'

---

to, and doubtless have the meaning above assigned to them. Âviñki (or âviṅgi?) at Sutta-vibhaṅga, Saṁghâdisesa II, 4, 9, means he drew towards himself; and Âviñkanâ (âviṅganâ?), ibid. II, 2, 2, is used as an equivalent of âkaddhanâ, which is much the same thing.

[1] Kudda-pâdo. Compare Rh. D.'s note on Mahâ-parinibbâna Sutta V, 41. The phrase recurs below of Vihâras at VI, 3, 4.

[2] Mandalikam kâtun ti nîka-vatthukam kinitum (B.). Kinâti is the technical word for laying bricks one above another; the comment therefore means 'to line or face the lower part with bricks.' (Compare pokkharaniyo itthikâhi kinitum at Mahâ-sudassana Sutta I, 58; Rh. D.'s 'Buddhist Suttas,' p. 262, 'to face the ponds with bricks or tiles;' and on facing a well below, V, 16, 2.)

[3] Dhûma-nettan ti dhûma-nikkhamana-khiddam (B.). The word is used of a surgical instrument at Mahâvagga VI, 13, 2.

[4] A similar paragraph occurs below, VI, 3, 3, of Vihâras.

[5] Mukha-mattikam. See our note 4 on Mahâvagga I, 25, 12.

[6] Mattikâ-donikam. See the last words of V, 16, 2.

The clay had a bad smell.

'I allow you, O Bhikkhus, to scent it.'

The fire in the bath-room scorched their bodies.

'I allow you, O Bhikkhus, to have water poured over you.'

They poured the water out of dishes and alms-bowls.

'I allow you, O Bhikkhus, a stand for the water, and saucers[1] to pour it from.'

A bath-room with a thatched roof did not produce perspiration.

'I allow you, O Bhikkhus, to cover the roof of the bath-room (with skins[2]), and to plaster it within and without.'

The bath-room became swampy.

'I allow you, O Bhikkhus, to lay the floor with flooring of three kinds—brick flooring, stone flooring, and wooden flooring.'

It still became swampy.

'I allow you, O Bhikkhus, to wash the floor.'

The water settled on the floor.

'I allow you, O Bhikkhus, the use of a drain to carry off the water[3].'

Now at that time the Bhikkhus sat in the bath-room on the ground, and they had pins and needles in their limbs[4].

---

[1] Sarâvaka*m*. See Mahâvagga VI, 12, 1, and *G*âtaka, vol. i, p. 8.

[2] Ogumphetvâ. See above, V, 11, 6, and our note there.

[3] Udaka-niddhamana*m*. See *G*âtaka I, 175, 409, 425, 489, in which passages an entrance to, or an exit from, a palace or a city is effected respectively niddhamana-mukhena, niddhamana-dvârena, niddhamanena, and niddhamana-maggena. Our phrase here recurs below, V, 35, 4.

[4] Gattâni ka*nd*uvanti. Gattâni is nominative, not accusative. Compare Mahâvagga VI, 14, 5, where ka*nd*uvati is used in the neuter sense. ('The sore was irritable.')

'I allow you, O Bhikkhus, the use of stools for the bath-room.'

Now at that time the bath-room had no enclosure.

'I allow you, O Bhikkhus, to enclose it with three kinds of enclosures—brick walls, and stone walls, and wooden fences.'

4. There was no antechamber[1] (in which the water could be kept).

'I allow you, O Bhikkhus, to have an antechamber.'

The basement of the antechamber was too low, and it was inundated with water [and so on, as in 11. 6, and in the last section down to the end of the description of the door, followed by the closing words of 11. 6 and of § 2 from 'straw and plaster fell, &c.,' down to 'cupboards[2]'].

5. The cell[3] became swampy.

'I allow you, O Bhikkhus, to spread gravel[4] over it.'

---

[1] Ko*tth*ako. This word means a room without a window; and it is used either of 1. 'a room over a gateway,' or 2. 'a room used as a store-room.' (Compare Mahâvagga III, 5, 6, 9; *K*ullavagga IV, 4, 6, 7, VI, 3, 7, 9, VI, 4, 10, IX, 1, 2; and *G*âtaka I, 179, 227, 230, II, 168.) The whole of this paragraph recurs below, V, 35, 4, of the ko*tth*aka to a privy; and the two passages taken together show that an entrance room or passage, a porch or antechamber, is meant, in which the water was kept ready for use. For that reason this particular kind of ko*tth*aka is elsewhere called, in both connections, udaka-ko*tth*aka (Mahâvagga VI, 14, 3, of the bath-room—where see Buddhaghosa's note quoted in our 'Vinaya Texts,' vol. ii, p. 57—and Dhammapada, p. 103, of the privy). Buddhaghosa explains it here by dvâra-ko*tth*ako; and it occurs again below, VIII, 8, 2, in the same sense.

[2] The last two items in § 2 are supplied for this case also in the next chapter but one.

[3] Parive*n*a is doubtless here, and below at VIII, 8, 2 in the same connection, a cell used as a cooling-room, after the steam bath. Buddhaghosa says nothing here, but gives a note below, V, 35, 4.

[4] Marumba. This word occurs in a description of different kinds of earths in the Old Commentary on the 10th Pâ*k*ittiya

They did not succeed in getting any[1].

'I allow you, O Bhikkhus, to flag it with stone.'

The water settled on the floor.

'I allow you, O Bhikkhus, to have a drain to it.'

15.

1. Now at that time the Bhikkhus, when naked[2] saluted one another, and received salutes; did service to one another, and received services; gave to one another, and accepted; ate, both hard food and soft; tasted; and drank.

They told this matter to the Blessed One.

'A man, O Bhikkhus, when naked, is not to give salutations, nor receive them; is not to do services, nor to accept them[3]; is not to give, nor to receive; is not to eat either hard or soft; is not to taste; is not to drink. Whosoever does so, shall be guilty of a dukka*t*a.'

16.

1. Now at that time the Bhikkhus in the bathroom put the robes down on the ground, and the robes became dirty.

(Sutta-vibhaṅga, Pâ*k*ittiya X, 2, 1); and in a similar connection at Dîpava*m*sa XIX, 2. Also below, V, 35, 4, VI, 3, 8.

[1] Na pariyâpu*n*anti. See the use of this phrase at *K*ullavagga V, 5, 2.

[2] That is, while in the *G*antâghara, which explains the otherwise inexplicable fact of this chapter being inserted here instead of at the commencement of 16. 2.

[3] In Mahâvagga I, 25, 13, services are to be rendered to a Bhikkhu who is in the bath. This is permitted by 16. 2 below.

They told this matter to the Blessed One.

'I allow you, O Bhikkhus, the use of a bamboo to hang your robes on, and of a string to hang your robes on[1].'

When rain fell, it fell over the robes.

'I allow you, O Bhikkhus, to have a hall to the bath-room.'

The basement of the bath-room hall was too low [&c., as in 11. 6; 14. 2 as to basement, roof-facing, stairs, and balustrade, followed by the closing words of 11. 6 and 14. 2, down to the end].

2. Now at that time the Bhikkhus were afraid[2] to do service to one another, both when in the bath-room and in the water.

They told this matter to the Blessed One.

'I allow you, O Bhikkhus, three kinds of coverings—the covering of the bath-room, the covering of the water, and the covering by clothes[3].'

Now at that time there was no water in the bath-room.

They told this matter to the Blessed One.

'I allow, O Bhikkhus, a well.'

The facing of the well fell in[4].

'I allow you, O Bhikkhus, to line the well with

---

[1] So also above, 11. 6 (at the end), and 14. 2 (at the end).

[2] On account of the rule laid down in chapter 15.

[3] This rule abrogates that laid down in chapter 15, so far as regards bathing and shampooing. Buddhaghosa says accordingly, Tisso pa*t*i*kkh*âdayo ti. Ettha *g*antâghara-pa*t*i*kkh*âdi *k*a udaka-pa*t*i*kkh*âdi *k*a parikamma*m* karontass' eva va*tt*ati, sesesu abhivâdanâdisu na va*tt*ati. Vattha-pa*t*i*kkh*âdi sabba-kammesu va*tt*ati.

[4] Kûla*m* lu*gg*ati. (The reading is not without doubt.) Compare Palu*gg*ati. The same expression occurs below, V, 17, 2; and lu*gg*ati at Mahâvagga VIII, 21, 1.

facings of three kinds[1]—brick facing, stone facing, and wooden facing.'

[Then follow the paragraphs as to the high basement, the facing of the roof, the stairs, and the balustrade, as in 11. 6; 14. 2; and above, § 1[2].]

Now at that time the Bhikkhus drew water with jungle-rope[3], or with their waistbands.

'I allow you, O Bhikkhus, the use of a string rope to draw water with.'

Their hands were hurt (by the rope).

'I allow you, O Bhikkhus, the use of a long pole balanced as a lever[4], of a bullock machine[5], or of a wheel and axle[6].'

---

[1] *K*initu*m* tayo *k*aye. See our note 4 above on V, 14, 3, and the passages there quoted. The whole passage occurs V, 11, 6.

[2] All this refers doubtless to the kind of shed or portico to be erected over the well. (See below.) One would expect that the formal licence for such a ma*n*d*apa would have been inserted here in due course as above, 11. 6, for the Ka*th*ina-sâlâ.

[3] This is the usual Anglo-Indian term for the creepers so commonly used for such purposes. The Pâli word is vallikâ, which occurs in a different sense at V, 2, 1.

[4] Tulâ. This is the ordinary and simple machine, so common in all countries where irrigation is carried on, for raising water from canals or from shallow wells. Buddhaghosa says here: Tulân ti pa*nn*ikâna*m* viya udaka-abbhâhana-tulâ. Pa*nn*ika is 'florist' (see *G*âtaka I, 411, II, 180). Abbhâhana must be wrong (see Sutta Nipâta III, 8, 8); possibly abbhâvâhana is the correct reading.

[5] The name of this machine is spelt differently in the MSS. (karaka*t*aṅka the Sinhalese MS., and karaka*d*aka the Burmese MSS.), and the reading is doubtful. Buddhaghosa says: Dakadaka*t*ako (sic! In the next note but two the same MS. reads ka*t*adaka*t*ake) vu*kk*ati go*n*e vâ yogetvâ hatthehi vâ gahetvâ dî-ha-varattâdîhi âka*ddh*ana-yanta*m*. We can only say negatively the word can have nothing to do either with karka*t*aka, a hook e form of a crab's claw; or with kara-ka*nt*aka, finger-nail.

*K*akkava*tt*aka*m*, on which Buddhaghosa has the unintelli- note arahatta(!)-gha*t*i-yanta*m*.

A number of pots were broken.

'I allow you, O Bhikkhus, water-vessels [1] of three kinds—brass pots, wooden pots, and skins [2].'

Now at that time the Bhikkhus, when drawing water in the open air, suffered from heat and cold.

'I allow you, O Bhikkhus, to build a shed over the well [3].'

Straw and plaster fell into the building over the well.

'I allow you, O Bhikkhus, to cover the shed with skins, and to plaster it within and without; and I allow the use of whitewash, blacking, red-colouring, wreath work, creeper work, cupboards, bamboos to hang robes on, and strings to hang robes on.'

The well was uncovered, and it was littered over with grass, and plaster, and dirt.

'I allow you, O Bhikkhus, a lid [4] to the well.'

Water-vessels were found wanting.

'I allow you, O Bhikkhus, the use of troughs [5] and basons.'

---

[1] Vârake. The spelling of this word in Childers's Dictionary (varâko) is a misprint. Both the passages he quotes read vârako. Other water-vessels, besides these three, are allowed by the closing rule of this chapter.

[2] *K*amma-kha*nd*a*m* nâma tûlâya vâ ka*t*adaka*t*ake vâ yo*g*etabba*m* *k*amma-bhâ*g*ana*m* (B.). The rendering adopted by Childers from Turnour (Mahâva*m*sa, p. 3) is therefore incorrect.

[3] The following passage has already occurred above, V, 11, 6 and V, 14, 3.

[4] Apidhâna*m*. See Mahâvagga VI, 12, 2.

[5] Udaka-do*n*i*m*. At *G*âtaka I, 450, such a do*n*i is said to have been made out of the trunk of a tree. Compare the use of mattikâ-do*n*ika*m* at V, 14, 3.

17.

1. Now at that time the Bhikkhus used to bathe anywhere all over the Ârâma, and the Ârâma became muddy.

They told this matter to the Blessed One.

'I allow you, O Bhikkhus, a pool (at the entrance to the Ârâma).'

The pool was public, and the Bhikkhus were ashamed to bathe in it.

'I allow you, O Bhikkhus, to surround it with enclosures of three kinds—brick walls, stone walls, and wooden fences[1].'

The pool became muddy.

'I allow you, O Bhikkhus, to flag it with three kinds of flooring—brick flooring, stone flooring, or wooden flooring.'

The water settled.

'I allow you, O Bhikkhus, a drain.'

Now at that time the Bhikkhus' limbs became cold.

They told this matter to the Blessed One.

'I allow you, O Bhikkhus, to make use of a towel[2], and to wipe the water off with a cloth.'

2. Now at that time a certain Upâsaka was desirous of making a tank for the use of the Sa*m*gha.

They told this matter to the Blessed One.

'I allow you, O Bhikkhus, a tank.'

The sides of the tank fell in[3].

---

[1] So also the closing words of V, 14, 3.

[2] Udaka-puñ*kh*ani. This is also mentioned in the Old Commentary on the 86th Pâ*k*ittiya. The verb recurs in the same sense below, VI, 3, 1.

[3] Kûlam lu*gg*ati. See V, 16, 2.

'I allow you, O Bhikkhus, to line the tank with facing of three kinds—brick facing, stone facing, and wooden facing.'

They found difficulty[1] in getting into it.

'I allow you, O Bhikkhus, flights of stairs of three kinds—brick steps, stone steps, and wooden steps.'

While going up them, they fell down.

'I allow you, O Bhikkhus, a balustrade.'

The water in the tank became stale.

'I allow you, O Bhikkhus, the use of pipes to lay on the water[2], and to drain the water off[3].'

Now at that time a certain Bhikkhu was desirous of erecting a bath-room with a nillekha[4] roof for the use of the Saṃgha.

They told this matter to the Blessed One.

'I allow you, O Bhikkhus, a bath-room with such a roof to it.'

18.

1. Now at that time the *Kh*abbaggiya Bhikkhus separated themselves from the mats on which they sat down for four months[5].

They told this matter to the Blessed One.

'You are not, O Bhikkhus, to separate yourselves for four months from the mats on which you sit

[1] Vihaññanti. See V, 11, 6.

[2] Udakâyatikan ti udakassa âgamana-mattikam (B.). Compare âyataka at IX, 1, 3.

[3] See above our note on V, 14, 3.

[4] Nillekha-gantâgharam nâma âviddha-pakkha-pâsakam vu*kk*ati. Gopânasînam upari-ma*nd*ale pakkha-pâsake *th*apetvâ kata-kû*t*a-*kkh*adanass' etam nâmam (B.).

[5] Compare the 2nd Nissaggiya.

down. Whosoever does so, shall be guilty of a dukka*t*a.'

Now at that time the *Kh*abbaggiya Bhikkhus lay down to sleep on beds scattered over with flowers.

People who came on a visit to the Vihâras saw it, and murmured, &c., saying, 'Like those who still live in the pleasures of the world.'

They told this matter to the Blessed One.

'You are not, O Bhikkhus, to sleep on beds scattered over with flowers. Whosoever does so, shall be guilty of a dukka*t*a.'

Now at that time people came to the Ârâma, bringing perfumes and garlands. The Bhikkhus, fearing to offend, would not accept them.

They told this matter to the Blessed One.

'I allow you, O Bhikkhus, to accept the perfume, and to apply it to the door for a space of five finger-breadths[1]; and to accept the flowers, and put them on one side in the Vihâra.'

19.

1. Now at that time a sheath of felt[2] had come into the possession of the Sa*m*gha.

They told this matter to the Blessed One.

'I allow you, O Bhikkhus, a sheath.'

The Bhikkhus considered whether a sheath was a thing which each one might keep for himself, or a thing which ought to be handed over from time to time by one Bhikkhu to another.'

[1] Kavâ*t*e pañ*k*aṅgulika*m* dâtu*m*, on which Buddhaghosa has no note. This measure occurs in *G*âtaka I, 166, 192; Fausböll's 'Five *G*âtakas' 6; and Mahâva*m*sa, p. 193.

[2] Namataka*m*. See V, 11, 1.

'A sheath, O Bhikkhus, is neither to be appropriated nor to be handed over[1].'

Now at that time the *Kh*abbaggiya Bhikkhus used to eat lying on decorated divans.

People murmured, &c. . . . . saying, 'Like those still living in the pleasures of the world.'

They told this matter to the Blessed One.

'You are not, O Bhikkhus, to eat lying on decorated divans[2]. Whosoever does so, shall be guilty of a dukka*t*a.'

Now at that time a certain Bhikkhu was sick, and when eating he was not able to hold his bowl in his hand.

They told this matter to the Blessed One.

'I allow, O Bhikkhus, the use of a stand for the bowl[3].'

Now at that time the *Kh*abbaggiya Bhikkhus used to eat out of one dish, to drink out of one vessel, and to lie on one bed, one coverlet, or one mat[4].

The people murmured, &c. . . . .

They told this matter to the Blessed One.

---

[1] Na adhi*tth*âtabba*m* na vikappetabba*m*. That is, it is always to be kept as common property of the Sa*m*gha (Sa*m*ghika). See Mahâvagga VIII, 20, 2, where the same expressions occur.

[2] Âsittakûpadhâna*m* nâma tamba-lohena vâ ragatena vâ katâya pe*l*âya (MS. belâya) eta*m* adhiva*k*ana*m*. The use of an ubhato-lohitakûpadhâna*m* is condemned, among other things of a like kind, in the Ma*ggh*ima Sîla, § 5 (Rh. D.'s 'Buddhist Suttas,' p. 193), and above, Mahâvagga V, 10, 2.

[3] Ma*l*orikâ ti da*nd*âdhârako vu*kk*ati. Ya*tth*i-âdhâraka-pa*nn*â-dhâraka-pa*kkh*ita-pi*tth*âni pi etth' eva pavi*tth*âni. Âdhâraka-sa*m*-khepana-gamanato hi pa*tth*âya *kh*idda*m* viddha*m* pi aviddha*m* pi va*tt*ati yeva (B.).

[4] All these words have already occurred above at *K*ullavagga I, 13, 1. 'Sitting on one seat' is there added to the list.

'You are not, O Bhikkhus, [to do any of these things.] Whosoever does so, shall be guilty of a dukka*t*a.'

20.

1. Now at that time Va*ddh*a the Li*kkh*avi was a friend of the Bhikkhus who were followers of Mettiya and Bhumma*g*aka[1]. Now Va*ddh*a the Li*kkh*avi went up to the place where those Bhikkhus were, and on arriving there he said to them, My salutation to you, Sirs!' When he had thus spoken, the Bhikkhus who were followers of Mettiya and Bhumma*g*aka gave him no reply. And a second and a third time [he said the same words, and still received no reply].

'Wherein have I offended you, Sirs? Why do you give me no reply?'

'Therein, that you, friend, sit contented while we are being molested by Dabba the Mallian.'

'But what, Sirs, can I do?'

'If you wished it, friend, to-day even would the Blessed One expel Dabba the Mallian.

'But what shall I do, Sirs? What is that it is in my power to do?'

'Come then, friend Va*ddh*a. Do you go up to the place where the Blessed One is, and when you have come there, say as follows: "This, Lord, is neither fit nor becoming that the very quarter of the heavens which ought to be safe, secure, and free from danger,

[1] These are two of the *Kh*abbaggiya Bhikkhus; and the evil deeds of the followers form the subject of *K*ullavagga IV, 4, 5 and following sections. Our sections 1, 2 are nearly the same as §§ 8, 9 there.

that from that very quarter should arise danger, calamity, and distress—that where one ought to expect a calm, that just there one should meet a gale! Methinks the very water has taken fire! My wife has been defiled by Dabba the Mallian!"'

2. 'Very well, Sirs!' said Va*ddh*a the Li*kkh*avi, accepting the word of the followers of Mettiya and Bhummagaka. And he went up to the Blessed One [and spake even as he had been directed].

Then the Blessed One, on that occasion and in that connection, convened a meeting of the Bhikkhu-sa*m*gha, and asked the venerable Dabba the Mallian:

'Are you conscious[1], Dabba, of having done such a thing as this Va*ddh*a says?'

'As my Lord, the Blessed One, knows.'

[And a second, and a third time, the Blessed One asked the same question, and received the same reply.]

'The Dabbas, O Dabba, do not thus repudiate. If you have done it, say so. If you have not done it, say you have not.'

'Since I was born, Lord, I cannot call to mind that I have practised sexual intercourse, even in a dream, much less when I was awake!'

3. Then the Blessed One addressed the Bhikkhus, and said: 'Let then the Sa*m*gha, O Bhikkhus, turn the bowl down[2] in respect of *Vaddha* the Li*kkh*avi,

[1] See the note above on IV, 4, 9.

[2] Patta*m* nikku*gg*atu. This phrase is used in the ordinary signification above, V, 9, 4. It is characteristic of the mildness of early Buddhism that this should be the only penalty imposed upon a layman. Compare H. O.'s remarks in his 'Buddha, sein Leben, seine Lehre, seine Gemeinde,' pp. 391–393. The house of such a layman becomes then an ago*k*aro, an 'unlawful resort.' (*K*ulla-vagga VIII, 1, 2.)

and make him incapable of granting an alms to the Sa*m*gha [1].

'There are eight things, O Bhikkhus, which when they characterise an Upâsaka, the bowl is to be turned down in respect of him;—when he goes about to bring loss of gifts on the Bhikkhus, when he goes about to bring harm to the Bhikkhus, when he goes about to cause the Bhikkhus to want a place of residence, when he reviles or slanders the Bhikkhus, when he causes divisions between Bhikkhus and Bhikkhus;—when he speaks in dispraise of the Buddha;—when he speaks in dispraise of the Dhamma;—when he speaks in dispraise of the Sa*m*gha. I allow you, O Bhikkhus, to turn down the bowl in respect of an Upâsaka who is characterised by these eight things [2].'

4. 'And thus, O Bhikkhus, is the bowl to be turned down. Some able and discreet Bhikkhu is to lay the matter before the Sa*m*gha, saying,

[1] Asambhoga*m* sa*m*ghena karotu. This phrase is used in regard to a Bhikkhu at *K*ullavagga I, 25, 1, as the distinctive mark of the Act of Suspension (Ukkhepaniya-kamma), and there means 'depriving him of his right to eat and dwell with the other Bhikkhus.' Sambhoge anâpatti at Mahâvagga I, 79, 2 (at the end), means that it is not an offence for the Bhikkhus to eat and dwell together with a guilty Bhikkhu under certain conditions there specified. As an Upâsaka never, under any circumstances, either eats or dwells together with the Bhikkhus (in Pâ*k*ittiya 5 the reference is to sâma*n*eras), the meaning here must be to make him one who has no dealings with the Sa*m*gha, to withdraw his privilege of providing food or lodging for the Sa*m*gha. The sabho*g*ana*m* kula*m* in the 43rd Pâ*k*ittiya has probably nothing to do with this.

[2] When a Bhikkhu behaves towards the laity in any one of the first five of these eight ways the Pa*t*isâra*n*iya-kamma is to be carried out against him—that is to say, he has to ask pardon of the layman against whom he has offended. See I, 20. The whole eight recur below, § 6.

'"Let the venerable Sa*m*gha hear me. Va*ddh*a the Li*kkh*avi has brought a groundless charge against the venerable Dabba the Mallian of a breach of morality. If the time seems meet to the Sa*m*gha, let the Sa*m*gha turn down the bowl as respects Va*ddh*a the Li*kkh*avi, and make him as one who has no dealings with the Sa*m*gha.

'"This is the motion (*ñ*atti).

'"Va*ddh*a the Li*kkh*avi has brought a groundless charge against Dabba the Mallian of a breach of morality. The Sa*m*gha turns down the bowl as respects Va*ddh*a the Li*kkh*avi, and makes him as one who has no dealings with the Sa*m*gha. Whosoever of the venerable ones approves of the bowl being turned down as regards Va*ddh*a the Li*kkh*avi, and of making him as one who has no dealings with the Sa*m*gha, let him keep silence. Whosoever approves not thereof, let him speak.

'"The bowl is turned down by the Sa*m*gha as regards Va*ddh*a the Li*kkh*avi, he is as one who has no dealings with the Sa*m*gha. The Sa*m*gha approves thereof. Therefore is it silent. Thus do I understand."'

5. Then the venerable Ânanda, having dressed himself early in the morning, went, duly bowled and robed, to the residence of Va*ddh*a the Li*kkh*avi. And when he had come there he spake to Va*ddh*a the Li*kkh*avi, and said: 'The bowl, friend Va*ddh*a, has been turned down by the Sa*m*gha as regards you, and you are as one who has no dealings with the Sa*m*gha.' And Va*ddh*a the Li*kkh*avi, on hearing that saying, immediately[1] fainted and fell.

[1] Literally, 'on that very spot.'

Then the friends and companions of Va*dd*h*a the Li*kk*h*avi, and his relatives of one blood with him, said to him: 'It is enough, friend Va*dd*h*a. Weep not, neither lament. We will reconcile[1] the Blessed One to you, and the Order of Bhikkhus.'

And Va*dd*h*a the Li*kk*h*avi, with his wife and his children, and with his friends and companions, and with his relatives of one blood with him, went up, with wet garments and with streaming hair, to the place where the Blessed One was; and when he had come there, he cast himself down with his head at the feet of the Blessed One, and said: 'Sin has overcome me, Lord—even according to my weakness, according to my folly, according to my unrighteousness—in that without ground I brought a charge against Dabba the Mallian of a breach of morality. In respect thereof may my Lord the Blessed One accept the confession I make of my sin in its sinfulness[2], to the end that I may in future restrain myself therefrom[3].'

'Verily, O friend Va*dd*h*a, sin hath overcome you—even according to your weakness, and according to your folly, and according to your unrighteousness—in that you brought without ground against Dabba the Mallian a charge of breach of morality. But since you, O friend Va*dd*h*a, look upon your sin as sin, and make amends for it as is meet, we do accept at your hands your confession of it. For this, O friend Va*dd*h*a, is the advantage of

[1] This is precisely the expression made use of in the converse case, when a Bhikkhu has offended against the laity. See I, 22, 3.

[2] A*kk*aya*m* a*kk*ayato pa*t*iga*n*hâtu. See the parallel passages in Mahâvagga IX, 1, 9; *K*ullavagga VII, 3, 6, &c.

[3] Âyati*m* sa*m*varâya. So also above of an offending Bhikkhu, IV, 14, 30.

the discipline of the noble one, that he who looks upon his sin as sin, and makes amends for it as is meet, he becomes able in future to restrain himself therefrom[1].'

6. Then the Blessed One addressed the Bhikkhus, and said: 'Let then the Sa*m*gha turn up the bowl again as regards Va*ddh*a the Li*kkh*avi, and make him as one who has dealings with the Sa*m*gha.

'There are eight things, O Bhikkhus, which when they characterise an Upâsaka the bowl should be turned up again as regards him;—when he goes not about to bring loss of gifts on the Bhikkhus, when he goes not about to bring harm to the Bhikkhus, when he goes not about to cause the Bhikkhus to want a place of residence, when he reviles or slanders not the Bhikkhus, when he causes not divisions between Bhikkhus and Bhikkhus;—when he speaks not in dispraise of the Buddha;—when he speaks not in dispraise of the Dhamma;—when he speaks not in dispraise of the Sa*m*gha.

7. 'And thus, O Bhikkhus, is the bowl to be turned up[2]. That Va*ddh*a the Li*kkh*avi should go before the Sa*m*gha, with his upper robe arranged over one shoulder[3], and squatting down, and raising

[1] Sa*m*vara*m* âpa*gg*ati. Compare the use of vikappa*m* âpa*gg*eyya in the 8th Nissaggiya.

[2] The following paragraphs are precisely the same as those in which the revocation of the Ta*gg*aniya-kamma is described in the reverse case of a Bhikkhu, above, I, 8.

[3] Eka*m*sa*m* uttarâsaṅga*m* karitvâ. Unless these words have been introduced by mistake from the corresponding passage in I, 8 (which is not probable), they show that the uttarâsaṅga (on which see the note on Mahâvagga VIII, 13, 4) was also worn by laymen. But this is the only passage known to

his hands with the palms joined together, should speak as follows:

'"The bowl has been turned down against me, Sirs, by the Sa*m*gha, and I am become as one having no dealings with the Sa*m*gha. I am conducting myself, Sirs, aright in accordance thereto, and am broken in spirit[1], and I seek for release; and I request the Sa*m*gha for a turning up again of the bowl."

'And a second time he is to prefer the same request, and a third time he is to prefer the same request in the same words.

'Then some discreet and able Bhikkhu should lay the matter before the Sa*m*gha, saying,

'"Let the venerable Sa*m*gha hear me. The bowl has been turned down by the Sa*m*gha against Va*ddh*a the Li*kkh*avi, and he is conducting himself aright in accordance thereto, and is broken in spirit, and seeks for release, and requests the Sa*m*gha for a turning up again of the bowl. If the time seems meet to the Sa*m*gha, let the Sa*m*gha turn up the bowl again as regards Va*ddh*a the Li*kkh*avi, and make him as one who has dealings with the Sa*m*gha.

'"This is the motion (*ñ*atti).

'"Let the venerable Sa*m*gha hear me. The bowl has been turned down (&c., as before), and he is conducting himself (&c., as before), and he requests the Sa*m*gha (&c., as before). The Sa*m*gha turns up again the bowl as regards Va*ddh*a the Li*kkh*avi, and makes him as one who has dealings with the

---

us in the earlier literature in which such a use of it is mentioned or implied. Compare Rh. D.'s note on the 'Book of the Great Decease,' VI, 26.

[1] Loma*m* pâtemi. See the note on *K*ullavagga I, 6, 1.

Sa*m*gha. Whosoever of the venerable ones approves thereof, let him keep silence; whosoever approves not thereof, let him speak.

'"The bowl is turned up again by the Sa*m*gha as regards Va*ddh*a the Li*kkh*avi, and he is as one who has dealings with the Sa*m*gha. The Sa*m*gha approves thereof. Therefore is it silent. Thus do I understand."'

21.

1. Now the Blessed One, when he had stayed at Vesâlî as long as he thought fit, set out on his journey toward Bhaggâ[1]. And journeying straight on he arrived in due course at Bhaggâ. And there at Bhaggâ the Blessed One resided on the Dragon's Hill, in the hermitage in the Bhesaka*l*â Wood[2].

Now at that time Bodhi the king's son's mansion, which was called Kokanada, had just been finished, and had not as yet been used[3] by Sama*n*a, or by Brâhman, or by any human being. And Bodhi the king's son gave command to the young Brahman, the son of the Sañ*g*ika woman[4], saying, 'Come

[1] Bhaggesu. Compare Buddhaghosa's note on a similar plural at Mahâ-parinibbâna Sutta III, 5, quoted in Rh. D.'s 'Buddhist Suttas from the Pâli,' p. 24.

[2] This place is also mentioned in the Sutta-vibhaṅga on the 55th and 56th Sekhiyas.

[3] Ana*ggh*âvuttho, literally, no doubt, 'dwelt in.' But it is clear that the meal afterwards taken in it by the Buddha was supposed to be the dedication, so to say, or the house-warming, after which it was a*ggh*âvuttho.

[4] On this habit of naming people after the family or tribal (not the personal) name of their mothers, see Rh. D.'s note in his 'Buddhist Suttas,' p. 1.

now, my friend Sañ*g*ikâ-putta, go thou to the place where the Blessed One is, and when you have come there, bow down in salutation at his feet on my behalf, and enquire in my name whether he is free from sickness and suffering, and is in the enjoyment of ease and comfort and vigorous health, saying, "Bodhi the king's son, Lord, bows down in salutation at thy feet, and enquires [as I have said][1], and asks: 'May my Lord the Blessed One consent to take his to-morrow's meal with Bodhi the king's son, together with the Sa*m*gha of Bhikkhus.'"'

'Even so, Sir!' said the young Brahman Sañ*g*ikâ-putta, in assent to Bodhi the king's son. And he went up to the place where the Blessed One was, and when he had come there he exchanged with the Blessed One the greetings and compliments of friendship and civility. And when he had done so, he took his seat on one side, and so seated he [delivered to him the message even as the king's son had commanded]. And the Blessed One gave, by silence, his consent.

2. And when the young Brahman Sañ*g*ikâ-putta had perceived that the Blessed One had consented, he arose from his seat, and went up to the place where Bodhi the king's son was. And when he had come there, he said to him: 'We have spoken, Sir, in your behalf to that venerable Gotama, saying (&c., as before), and have received the consent of the Sama*n*a Gotama.'

Then Bodhi the king's son made ready at the end

---

[1] So far this conversation is the stock phrase for a message from a royal personage to the Buddha. See 'Book of the Great Decease,' I, 2 (Rh. D.'s 'Buddhist Suttas,' p. 2).

of that night sweet food, both hard and soft; and had the mansion Kokanada spread over with white cloths even unto the last planks in the flight of steps (at the entrance)[1]; and gave command to the young Brahman Sañgikâ-putta, saying, 'Come now, my friend Sañgikâ-putta, go thou up to the place where the Blessed One is; and when you have come there, announce the time, saying, "The meal, Lord, is ready, and the time has come."'

'Even so, Lord,' said Sañgikâ-putta in assent [and went to the Blessed One and announced accordingly].

Now the Blessed One, having dressed himself early in the morning, went, duly bowled and robed, to Bodhi the king's son's mansion. And Bodhi the king's son stood at that time at the portico over the outer door to welcome the Blessed One. And he saw the Blessed One coming from afar; and on seeing him he went forth thence to meet him, and when he had saluted the Blessed One, he returned again to the mansion Kokanada.

Now the Blessed One stopped at the last plank on the flight of steps at the entrance. And Bodhi the king's son said to the Blessed One, 'May my Lord the Blessed One walk over the cloths. May the Happy One walk over the cloths, that the same may be to me for a long time for a weal and for a joy.'

And when he had thus spoken, the Blessed One remained silent. And a second time he [preferred the same request in the same words with the same

[1] Sopâna-ka*l*iṅgarâ. Compare the Sanskrit Ka*d*aṅkara (also written ka*d*aṅgara). The correct reading is doubtless *l*, not l.

result]. And a third time he [preferred the same request]. Then the Blessed One looked round at the venerable Ânanda.

And the venerable Ânanda said to Bodhi the king's son, 'Let them gather up, O prince, these cloths. The Blessed One will not walk on a strip of cloth (laid down for ceremonial purposes)[1]. The Tathâgata has mercy even on the meanest thing.'

3. Then Bodhi the king's son had the cloths gathered up, and spread out a seat on the top of Kokanada. And the Blessed One ascended up into Kokanada, and sat down on the seat spread out there with the Sa*m*gha of Bhikkhus. And Bodhi the king's son satisfied the Bhikkhu-sa*m*gha with the Buddha at their head with the sweet food, both hard and soft, waiting upon them with his own hand[2]. And when the Blessed One had cleansed his bowl and his hands, he (Bodhi) took his seat on one side. And the Blessed One instructed, and roused, and incited, and gladdened him thus sitting with religious discourse. And when he had been thus instructed, and roused, and incited, and gladdened

[1] *K*ela-pattikâ ti *k*ela-santhara*m*, says Buddhaghosa. See pa*tt*ikâ in Childers, and compare pa*ñk*a-pa*tth*ika*m* at V, 11, 6. *K*ela is not merely ordinary cloth; it is cloth regarded as a means of giving a decorative or festive appearance to a house by spreading canopies, &c. See *G*âtaka I, 178, and Mahâ-parinibbâna Sutta VI, 26 (p. 64). On such festive occasions the whole house (or the Ma*nd*apa erected in special honour of the guest) is covered with lengths of clean cotton cloth—the same as are otherwise used for ordinary apparel—white being the colour signifying peculiar respect. It is such lengths of cloth so used honoris causâ that are called *k*ela-pattikâ. Compare Rh. D.'s note in 'Buddhist Suttas,' p. 122.

[2] See the note above on Mahâvagga I, 8, 4.

with religious discourse, Bodhi the king's son rose from his seat and departed thence.

Then the Blessed One, on that occasion and in that connection, convened an assembly of the Bhikkhu-sa*m*gha, and after he had delivered a religious discourse, he addressed the Bhikkhus and said:

'You are not, O Bhikkhus, to walk upon cloth laid down (for ceremonial purposes). Whosoever does so, shall be guilty of a dukka*t*a.'

4. Now at that time a certain woman who had had a miscarriage, and had invited the Bhikkhus, and spread cloths in their honour, said to them, 'Step, Sirs, over the cloth.'

The Bhikkhus, fearing to offend, would not do so.

'Step, Sirs, over the cloth, for good luck's sake.'

The Bhikkhus, fearing to offend, would not do so.

Then that woman murmured, was annoyed, and was indignant, saying, 'How can their reverences refuse to step over the cloth when they are asked to do so for good luck's sake?'

The Bhikkhus heard of that woman's murmuring, and being annoyed, and indignant. And they told this matter to the Blessed One.

'I allow you, O Bhikkhus, when asked to do so for the sake of good luck to laymen, to step over cloth laid down for ceremonial purposes.'

Now at the time the Bhikkhus were afraid to step on to a mat to be used for wiping the feet[1].

They told this matter to the Blessed One.

---

[1] Dhota-pâdaka.

'I allow you, O Bhikkhus, to step on to a mat to be used for wiping the feet.'

Here ends the second Portion[1] for Recitation.

22.

1. Now when the Blessed One had remained at Bhaggâ as long as he thought fit, he set out on his journey towards Sâvatthi. And journeying straight on he arrived in due course at Sâvatthi, and there, at Sâvatthi, he stayed in the *G*etavana, in the Ârâma of Anâtha-pi*nd*ika.

Now Visâkhâ the mother of Migâra, bringing small jars[2], and earthenware foot-scrubbers[3], and brooms, went up to the place where the Blessed One was; and when she had come there, she saluted the Blessed One, and took her seat on one side. And so sitting, Visâkhâ the mother of Migâra said to the Blessed One, 'May the Blessed One accept these things at my hands, that that may be to me for long for a blessing and a joy.' And the Blessed One accepted the small jars and the brooms; but the Blessed One did not accept the earthenware foot-scrubbers.

[1] There is no mention in the text of where the first such Portion (Bhâ*n*avâra) ends. There is also no division into Bhâ*n*avâras in the previous books of the *K*ullavagga.

[2] Gha*t*aka*m*. At *G*âtaka I, 32 this word seems to mean the capital of a pillar. We have taken it as the diminutive of gha*t*a, especially as Buddhaghosa says nothing; but this is doubtful.

[3] Kataka*m*. To the note quoted at p. 318 of the text, which shows that this is a kind of foot-rubber, Buddhaghosa adds that this article is forbidden bâhulikânuyogattâ. This injunction is repeated below at V, 37, where kataka is mentioned as a kind of earthenware.

Then the Blessed One instructed (&c., as usual, see 21. 2, down to) she departed thence. And the Blessed One, on that occasion and in that connection, after having delivered a religious discourse, addressed the Bhikkhus, and said:

'I allow you, O Bhikkhus, small jars and brooms. You are not, O Bhikkhus, to make use of earthenware foot-scrubbers. Whosoever does so, shall be guilty of a dukka*t*a. I allow you, O Bhikkhus, three kinds of things to rub the feet with—to wit, sandstone[1], gravel[1], and sea-foam[2].'

2. [A similar paragraph ending]

'I allow you, O Bhikkhus, the use of fans and flower-stands[3].'

23.

1. Now at that time a mosquito-fan had come into the possession of the Sa*m*gha.

They told this matter to the Blessed One.

'I allow you, O Bhikkhus, the use of mosquito-fans.'

A châmara (a tail of the Bos Gruniens or Tibetan ox, mounted on a stick, to be used by

[1] Sakkharâ and ka*th*ala, the exact distinction between which two terms is not stated.

[2] Samudda-phe*n*aka. By this name are designated the bones of the cuttle-fish which, when cast up by the waves on the seashore, are not unlike petrified foam, and have actually been introduced from the East into use in Europe as a kind of rough natural soap; and are now sold for that purpose in most chemists' shops in England (compare Meerschaum). The same word is found in later Sanskrit works.

[3] Tâlava*nt*a*m*. See *G*âtaka I, 26, 5 (at the end); and compare tâlava*nt*aka*m* below, V, 29, 4.

an attendant to whisk off flies) had come into the possession of the Sa*m*gha.

They told this matter to the Blessed One.

'You are not, O Bhikkhus, to make use of a châmara. Whosoever does so, shall be guilty of a dukka*t*a[1]. I allow, O Bhikkhus, three kinds of fly-whisks—those made of bark, those made of Usîra-grass, and those made of peacocks' tails[2].'

2. [Similar paragraph ending]

'I allow you, O Bhikkhus, the use of sun-shades[3].'

Now at that time the *Kh*abbaggiyas went about with sun-shades up. And at that time a certain Upâsaka went to a garden with a number of men who were followers of the Â*g*îvakas (naked ascetics). And those followers of the Â*g*îvakas saw the *Kh*abbaggiya Bhikkhus coming along in the distance with sun-shades held over them; and on seeing them, they said to that Upâsaka:

'Are these, Sir, the men whom you reverence coming along, like lords of the treasury, there with sun-shades held over them?'

'No, Sirs. These are not Bhikkhus; they are Paribbâ*g*akas (wandering mendicants).'

So they made a bet whether they were Bhikkhus or not. And when that Upâsaka recognised them, when they came up, he murmured, was annoyed, and was indignant, saying, 'How can their reverences go about with sun-shades held over them?'

The Bhikkhus heard of that Upâsaka's thus mur-

---

[1] Probably because this, like a white umbrella, was considered an appanage of royalty.

[2] Mora-piñ*kh*a. This word is spelt piñ*g*a by Childers, and by Fausböll, *G*âtaka I, 38, 207.

[3] See the note at the end of the chapter.

muring, &c. And those Bhikkhus told the matter to the Blessed One.

'Is it true, O Bhikkhus, as they say?'

'It is true, Lord.'

The Blessed Buddha rebuked them, saying (&c., as usual, see I, 1, 2, 3). And when he had rebuked them, and had delivered a religious discourse, he addressed the Bhikkhus, and said:

'You are not, O Bhikkhus, to have sun-shades held over you. Whosoever does so, shall be guilty of a dukka*t*a.'

3. Now at that time a certain Bhikkhu was sick, and without a sun-shade (being held over him) he was ill at ease.

They told this matter to the Blessed One.

'I allow, O Bhikkhus, a sun-shade for the sick.'

Now at that time the Bhikkhus, thinking, 'It is for the sick only that sun-shades have been allowed by the Blessed One, and not for those who are not sick,' were afraid to use sun-shades in the Ârâma, or in the precincts of the Ârâma.

They told this matter to the Blessed One.

'I allow, O Bhikkhus, either a sick man, or one who is not sick, to have a sun-shade held over him either in the Ârâma, or in the precincts of the Ârâma[1].'

---

[1] There is an ambiguity, either in the use of the word *kh*atta, or in the use of the verb dhâreti, or both, running through this chapter. As a matter of fact, the Bhikkhus now use sun-shades (usually those made of paper in China) of the same shape as the umbrellas now used in England; and they make no distinction as to the place in which they use them. But there is another shape for shades, to be carried by a dependant walking behind the person to be shaded, in which the handle is fastened to the rim at the side of, and not in the middle underneath that part of it which

24.

1. Now at that time a certain Bhikkhu tied his bowl with a string, and suspending it on a staff[1], went after noon out of a certain village gate. The people calling out, 'There goes a thief; his sword is glistening,' fell upon him, and seized him. But on récognising him, they let him go. That Bhikkhu, returning to the Ârâma, told this matter to the Bhikkhus.

'What then, Sir, did you carry a staff with a string to it?'

'It is even so, Sirs.'

Those Bhikkhus who were moderate murmured (&c., as usual, see I, 1, 2, 3) . . . . told the Blessed One . . . . he addressed the Bhikkhus, and said:

'You are not, O Bhikkhus, to carry a staff with a string to it. Whosoever does so, shall be guilty of a dukka*t*a.'

2. Now at that time a certain Bhikkhu was sick, and he could not wander about without a staff.

They told this matter to the Blessed One.

---

actually keeps off the sun. Both kinds are figured on the most ancient Buddhist sculptures. The Old Commentary on the corresponding rule for the nuns (Bhikkhunî-vibhaṅga, Pâ*k*ittiya LXXXIV, 2, 1) says that sun-shades are either white, or made of matting, or made of leaves (doubtless of the talipot palm); and it adds that they are either ma*nd*ala-baddha*m* or salâka-baddha*m*, which apparently refers to these two ways in which the handle was joined on to the shading-part. In the 57th Sekhiya (compare also the 23rd and the 67th), and in *K*ullavagga VIII, 1, 1, will be found rules of etiquette which show that it was a sign of courtesy or of respect to put down a sun-shade.

[1] See the similar phraseology at V, 8, 1. On u*tt*itvâ, compare o*dd*eti.

'I allow you, O Bhikkhus, to give to a sick Bhikkhu the permission (license) to use a staff. And thus, O Bhikkhus, should it be given. That sick Bhikkhu, O Bhikkhus, should go up to the Sa*m*gha [here follow the words of a Kammavâ*k*â, precisely as in V, 20, 7].'

3. [Similar paragraphs ending with Kammavâ*k*âs for license to lift the bowl with a string, and with both a staff and a string.]

25.

1. Now at that time a certain Bhikkhu was a ruminator[1], and he, continually ruminating, used to chew the cud.

The Bhikkhus murmured, were annoyed, and were indignant, saying, 'This Bhikkhu eats food out of hours[2].' And they told this matter to the Blessed One.

'This Bhikkhu, O Bhikkhus, has but lately fallen from the condition of being an ox. I allow, O Bhikkhus, to a ruminator the chew of the cud. But nothing, O Bhikkhus, brought from the door of the mouth to the outside thereof is to be so chewed[3]. Whosoever does so, shall be dealt with according to the law[4].'

26.

1. Now at that time a certain multitude had

[1] Romanthaka.

[2] Which is against the rule laid down in the 27th Pâ*k*ittiya.

[3] That would be a breach of the 30th Pâ*k*ittiya.

[4] That is, according to the 27th, 28th, or 30th Pâ*k*ittiya.

arranged for the privilege of supplying food to the Sa*m*gha, and in the dining-hall many fragments of rice were allowed to fall.

The people murmured, were annoyed, and were indignant, saying, 'How can the Sakya-puttiya Sama*n*as, when food is being given to them, take it so carelessly. Each single ball of rice is the result of hundredfold labour!'

The Bhikkhus heard of the people thus murmuring, &c., and they told the matter to the Blessed One.

'I allow you, O Bhikkhus, whatever thing falls when it is being given to you, yourselves to pick it up and eat it. That has been presented, O Bhikkhus, by the givers.'

27.

1. Now at that time a certain Bhikkhu went on his round for alms with long finger-nails. A certain woman, seeing him, said to that Bhikkhu: 'Come along, Sir, and have connection with me.'

'Nay, Sister, that is not becoming.'

'If you do not, Sir, I will at once scratch[1] my limbs with my own nails, and will make as if I were angry, saying, "This Bhikkhu has ill-treated me."'

'Settle that with yourself, Sister.'

That woman did as she had said, and people running up seized that Bhikkhu. Then they saw skin and blood on the woman's nails; and on seeing that, they let the Bhikkhu go, saying, 'This is the

[1] On vilikhati, compare VI, 20.

work of the woman herself. The Bhikkhu has not done it.'

Then that Bhikkhu, returning to the Ârâma, told the matter to the Bhikkhus.

'What then, Sir, do you wear long nails?'

'It is even so, Sirs.'

The Bhikkhus who were moderate murmured (&c. . . . .) told the matter to the Blessed One.

'You are not, O Bhikkhus, to wear long nails. Whosoever does so, shall be guilty of a dukka*t*a.'

2. Now at that time the Bhikkhus tore off their nails with the nails, bit them off with their teeth, or rubbed them down against the wall; and their fingers were hurt.

They told this matter to the Blessed One.

'I allow you, O Bhikkhus, nail-cutters.'

They cut their nails down to the blood, and their fingers were hurt.

'I allow you, O Bhikkhus, to cut your nails according to the length of the flesh.'

Now at that time the *Kh*abbaggiya Bhikkhus had all the twenty nails (on their hands and feet) polished.

People murmured, &c., saying, 'Like those who still live in the pleasures of the world.'

They told this matter to the Blessed One.

'You are not, O Bhikkhus, to have the twenty nails polished. I allow you, O Bhikkhus, to remove the dirt only.'

3. Now at that time the Bhikkhus' hair grew long.

They told this matter to the Blessed One.

'Are the Bhikkhus able, O Bhikkhus, to remove one another's hair?'

'They are, Lord.'

Then the Blessed One, on that occasion and in that connection, after he had delivered a religious discourse, addressed the Bhikkhus, and said:

'I allow you, O Bhikkhus, the use of razors, of a hone to sharpen the razors on, of powder prepared with Sipâ*t*ika-gum to prevent them rusting[1], of a sheath to hold them in[2], and of all the apparatus of a barber[3].'

4. Now at that time the *Kh*abbaggiya Bhikkhus wore (&c., as usual, down to)

'You are not, O Bhikkhus, to have your beards cut (by barbers)[4], nor to let them grow long, nor to wear them long on the chin like a goat's beard[5], nor so cut that they have four corners[6], nor to cut off the hair growing on your breast[7], nor to cut the hair on your bellies into figures[8], nor to wear whiskers[9], nor to remove the hair from your private parts[10]. Whosoever does so, shall be guilty of a dukka*t*a.'

---

[1] Khura-sipâ*t*ika*m*. See the notes on V, 11, 2, and Buddhaghosa's note at p. 319 of the text.

[2] Namataka*m*. See above, V, 11, 1, and V, 19, 1.

[3] Khura-bha*nd*a*m*. Compare Mahâvagga VI, 37.

[4] Massu*m* kappâpentî ti kattariyâ massu*m* *kh*edâpenti (B.). On Kattari (a knife), see *G*âtaka I, 223. It is clear from the first words of the next section that Buddhaghosa's explanation here is not quite accurate.

[5] Go-lomikan ti hanukamhi dîgha*m* katvâ *th*apita*m* e*l*akamassu*m* vu*kk*ati (B.).

[6] *K*aturassan ti *k*atu-kona*m* (B.).

[7] Parimukhan ti ure loma-sa*m*hara*n*a*m* (B.).

[8] A*ddh*arûka*m*. See the various readings and Buddhaghosa's note at p. 319 of the text.

[9] Dâ*th*ika*m*. It is the Sanskrit dâ*dh*ikâ or da*m*sh*t*rikâ; and occurs at *G*âtaka I, 305.

[10] On the corresponding rule in the Bhikkhunî-vibhaṅga, the 2nd Pâ*k*ittiya, the Old Commentary has sambâdho nâma ubho upaka*kkh*akâ mutta-kara*n*a*m*.

Now at that time a certain Bhikkhu had a fistula[1], and the ointment would not stick to it.

They told this matter to the Blessed One.

'I allow you, O Bhikkhus, on account of disease, to remove the hair from the private parts.'

5. Now at that time the *Kh*abbaggiya Bhikkhus (&c., as before, down to)

'You are not, O Bhikkhus, to have your hair cut off with a knife[2]. Whosoever does so, shall be guilty of a dukka*t*a.'

Now at that time a certain Bhikkhu had a sore on his head, and the hair could not be removed with a razor.

They told this matter to the Blessed One.

'I allow you, O Bhikkhus, on account of disease, to have your hair cut off with a knife.'

Now at that time the Bhikkhus wore the hair in their nostrils long.

People murmured, &c., saying, 'Like the devil-worshippers[3].'

They told this matter to the Blessed One.

'You are not, O Bhikkhus, to wear the hair in your nostrils long. Whosoever does so, shall be guilty of a dukka*t*a.'

Now at that time the Bhikkhus had the hair in their nostrils pulled out with a potsherd[4], or with beeswax; and their nostrils were hurt.

---

[1] Compare Mahâvagga VI, 22, 2.

[2] Kattarikâyâ ti ga*nd*a-rudhi-(sic MS.)-sîsa-rog'-âbâdha-pa*k*-*k*ayâ va*tt*ati, which is simply a repetition of the next paragraph, is all that Buddhaghosa here says. See note above on § 4.

[3] Pisâ*k*illikâ. So also V, 10, 2, of carrying a skull about; and Mahâvagga III, 12, 3, of living in the hollow of a tree.

[4] Sakkharikâ, said at Mahâvagga VI, 14, 5 to be used as a lancet.

They told this matter to the Blessed One.

'I allow you, O Bhikkhus, the use of pincers[1].'

Now at that time the *Kh*abbaggiya Bhikkhus (&c., as before, ending with)

'You are not, O Bhikkhus, to have the white hairs pulled out (off your heads). Whosoever does so, shall be guilty of a dukka*t*a.'

6. Now at that time a certain Bhikkhu's ears were stopped with the wax.

They told this matter to the Blessed One.

'I allow you, O Bhikkhus, the use of an instrument to remove the wax from the ear[2].'

[Then a paragraph as to the substances of which it may be made, word for word, as in Mahâvagga VI, 6, 21; 12, 3; *K*ullavagga V, 5, 2; 29, 2, &c.]

28.

1. Now at that time the *Kh*abbaggiya Bhikkhus laid up much store of brass ware and copper ware.

People who came on a visit to the Vihâras, seeing it, murmured, &c., saying, 'Like those who spread out copper (for sale)[3].'

They told this matter to the Blessed One.

'You are not, O Bhikkhus, to lay up much store of brass ware and copper ware. Whosoever does so, shall be guilty of a dukka*t*a[4].'

---

[1] Sa*n*d*â*sa. So at *G*âtaka I, 138, 4, a barber pulls out a white hair from the king's head, suva*nn*a-sa*nd*âsena.

[2] This license is repeated in the next chapter.

[3] Ka*m*sa-pattharikâ tî ka*m*sa-bha*nd*a-vâ*n*i*g*â (B.).

[4] They might have all kinds of brass ware, except certain articles, according to chapter 37 below.

2. Now at that time the Bhikkhus were afraid to use boxes to put eye-ointment in[1], and little flat sticks to lay it on with[2], and instruments for removing wax from the ear[3], and handles (for razors, staves, &c.)[4].

They told this matter to the Blessed One.

'I allow you, O Bhikkhus, the use of these things.'

Now at that time the *Kh*abbaggiya Bhikkhus sat down lolling up against their waist-cloths (arranged as a cushion)[5], and the edges of the waist-cloths wore out[6].

They told this matter to the Blessed One.

'You are not, O Bhikkhus, to lcll in this way. Whosoever does so, shall be guilty of a dukka*t*a.'

Now at that time a certain Bhikkhu was sick, and without some handicraft[7] he was ill at ease.

---

[1] Añ*g*ani*m*. The use of these has been already allowed at Mahâvagga VI, 12, 1, 2, 4.

[2] In the text read añ*g*ana-salâka*m*, on which see Mahâvagga VI, 12, 3, 4.

[3] Already allowed in the last chapter.

[4] Bandhana-mattan ti vâsi-kattara-ya*tth*i-âdîna*m* vâ bandhana-matta*m* (B.). It is clear from this note, and the repetition of the pi in the text, that we have to do here with a special object, and not a mere qualification of the other three.

[5] Sa*m*ghâ*t*i-pallatthikâya nisîditvâ. See IV, 4, 7 at the end, and the Old Commentary on the 26th Sekhiya. Childers translates it as if it were the same as ukku*t*ika*m* nisîditvâ; but it must be different from it as that was allowed and constantly practised.

[6] Pa*tt*â lu*gg*anti. So read (not pattâ as in the text) in accordance with our note 3 on Mahâvagga VIII, 21, 1. The second word occurs also above, V, 16, 2; 17, 2. From this passage here it is probable that a*tth*a-pâdaka at Mahâvagga VIII, 21, means a stool.

[7] Âyoga*m*. Compare the Sutta-vibhaṅga, Pâ*k*ittiya LXXXVIII, 2, 2; *G*âtaka III, 447, 6.

They told this matter to the Blessed One.

'I allow you, O Bhikkhus, the use of a loom, and of shuttles, strings, tickets, and all the apparatus belonging to a loom.'

29.

1. Now at that time a certain Bhikkhu ent the village for alms without a girdle on, and in .. highway[1] his waist-cloth fell down[2]. The people made an outcry, and that Bhikkhu was abashed.

On his return to the Ârâma, that Bhikkhu told this matter to the Bhikkhus, and the Bhikkhus told it to the Blessed One.

'You are not, O Bhikkhus, to enter the village without a girdle on. Whosoever does so, shall be guilty of a dukka*t*a. I allow, O Bhikkhus, a girdle[3].'

2. Now at that time the *Kh*abbaggiya Bhikkhus wore (&c., as usual, ending with)

'You are not, O Bhikkhus, to wear special girdles[4]—those made of many strings plaited to-

---

[1] Rathiyâya. The Old Commentary on the Bhikkhunî-vibhaṅga, Pâ*k*ittiya XIV, says, Rathiyâ ti ra*kkh*â. The word recurs, ibid., Pâ*k*ittiya LXXXVI, XCVI (the last of which is nearly the same as our passage here). For the more usual form rathikâ, see *K*ullavagga X, 12.

[2] Pabhassittha. Compare Sutta-vibhaṅga, Pâ*k*ittiya LXXXIII, 1, 2. It is from the root bhrams, not bhâs.

[3] The use of this has already been enjoined at Mahâvagga I, 25, 9, 10. It was to be tied on round the waist, over the waist-cloth, to keep it in its place.

[4] It is curious that ka*t*i-suttaka*m*, a kind of girdle which would seem properly to belong here, has been included in a former list of forbidden articles at V, 2, 1.

gether[1], those made like the head of a water-snake[2], girdles with tambourines on them[3], girdles with beads on (or with ornaments hanging from them)[4]. Whosoever does so, shall be guilty of a dukka*t*a. I allow you, O Bhikkhus, girdles of two kinds—those made of strips of cloth, and those . . . .[5]'

The borders of the girdles decayed through age.

'I allow, O Bhikkhus, an edging of brighter material[6] and strengthening at the ends[7].'

The end of the girdle where the knot was tied decayed through age[8].

'I allow, O Bhikkhus, a buckle[9].'

[A paragraph on the substances of which it may be made, as usual, see Mahâvagga VI, 12, 3; *K*ulla-

---

[1] Kalâbuka*m*. See Buddhaghosa's note at p. 319 of the text, and compare Böhtlingk-Roth under kalâpa, kalâpaka.

[2] De*dd*ubhaka*m* nâma udaka-sappi-sisa-sadisa*m* (B.). De*d*-*d*ubha corresponds to the later Sanskrit du*nd*ubha, an older form of which is dundubha.

[3] Mura*g*a, literally, 'tambourines;' but see Buddhaghosa's note, loc. cit.

[4] Maddavîna*m* nâma pâmaṅga-sa*nth*âna*m* (B.). On pâmaṅga, see our note at *K*ullavagga V, 2, 1.

[5] Sûkarantaka*m*. See Buddhaghosa's note at p. 319 of the text. We do not venture to translate the term.

[6] Sobha*n*am nâma ve*tth*etvâ mukha-va*tt*i-sibhana*m* (B.). In the Ma*ggh*ima Sîla, § 3, sobha*n*akam or sobha*n*a-kara*n*am (so Rh. D.'s MS.) is a kind of game or show.

[7] Gu*n*aka*m* nâma mudika(? muddhika)-san*th*ânena sibbana*m* (B.). Clough, under gu*n*a, gives inter alia, 1. fastening; 2. a plant of the fibres of which bow-strings are made; 3. bow-string.

[8] Pavananto ti pâsanto (B.).

[9] Vidho. But both the reading and the explanation are uncertain, and Buddhaghosa says nothing. The word occurs also, and apparently in the same sense, in the Old Commentary on the 86th Pâ*k*ittiya.

vagga V, 5, 2, &c., adding at the end 'and made of string.']

3. Now at the time the venerable Ânanda went into the village for alms with light garments on[1]; and his garments were blown up by a whirlwind.

The venerable Ânanda, on returning to the Ârâma, told this matter to the Bhikkhus; and the Bhikkhus told this matter to the Blessed One.

'I allow, O Bhikkhus, a block[2] (to be used as a weight) or a chain[3].'

[Similar paragraph to that just above as to the substances of which the block may be made.]

Now at that time the Bhikkhus fastened the block or the chain immediately on to their robes; and the robes gave way.

They told this matter to the Blessed One.

'I allow, O Bhikkhus, a piece of phalaka cloth[4] to attach the block or the chain to.'

They fastened the phalaka cloth for the block or the chain on to the edge of the robe; and the corner came open[5].

---

[1] Sa*m*ghâ*t*iyo in the plural must mean garments and not waist-cloths only. See the parallel passage in the Bhikkhunî-vibhaṅga, Pâ*k*ittiya XCVI.

[2] Ga*nt*hikam. The use of this article is referred to in VIII, 4, 3, and at Dhammapada, p. 372. That ga*nt*hi means a block, usually of wood, is clear from the use of dhamma-ga*nt*hika*m* at *G*âtaka I, 150 (spelt ga*nd*ika however at II, 124), compared with ga*nt*hi (block of sandal-wood) above, V, 8, 1. The word occurs also in the Old Commentary on the 86th Pâ*k*ittiya.

[3] Pâsaka*m*, which does not correspond to Sanskrit prâsaka here, but to pâ*s*aka = pâ*s*a (Böhtlingk-Roth give inter alia, 'Sahl oder Leiste am Anfange eines Gewebes'). Compare pâsanta in Buddhaghosa on ma*kkh*avâ*l*aka*m* in the next section.

[4] See our note on this word at Mahâvagga VIII, 28, 2.

[5] That is, perhaps, the weight dragged the robe to one side and the legs were visible through the opening.

They told this matter to the Blessed One.

'I allow you, O Bhikkhus, to fasten the phalaka cloth for the block on the edge of the robe, and to fasten the phalaka cloth for the chain seven or eight finger-breadths up the robe.'

4. Now at that time the *Kh*abbaggiya Bhikkhus wore (&c., as usual, ending with)

'You are not, O Bhikkhus, to wear your under garments arranged as laymen do, nor arranged with appendages like elephant-trunks[1], nor arranged like fishing-nets[2], nor arranged with four corners showing[3], nor arranged like flower-stands[4], nor arranged like rows of jewelry[5]. Whosoever does so, shall be guilty of a dukka*t*a.'

[Similar paragraph, ending]

'You are not, O Bhikkhus, to wear your upper[6]

---

[1] Hatthi-so*nd*aka*m* nâma nâbhi-mûlato hatthi-so*nd*a-sa*nth*ânam olambaka*m* katvâ nivattha*m*, ko*l*ika-itthîna*m* nivâsana*m* viya (B.).

[2] Ma*kkh*a-vâ*l*aka*m* nâma ekato dasanta*m* ekato pâsantam olambitvâ nivattha*m* (B.).

[3] *K*atu-ka*nn*aka*m* upari dve he*tth*ato dve eva*m* *k*attâro ka*nn*e dassetvâ nivattha*m* (B.).

[4] Tâla-va*nt*aka*m* nâma tâlava*nt*'-âkârena sâ*t*aka*m* olambitvâ nivâsana*m* (B.). See our note on tâlava*nt*a above, V, 22, 2, and on âma*l*aka-va*nt*ika-pî*th*a*m* below, VI, 2, 4.

[5] Sata-vallika*m* nâma dîgha-sâtaka*m* aneka-kkhattu*m* obhañgitvâ ova*tt*ika*m* karontena nivattha*m* vâ, padakkhi*n*a-passesu vâ nirantara*m* valiyo dassetvâ nivattha*m*. Sa*k*e pana *g*â*n*uto pa*tth*âya eko vâ dve vâ valiyo paññâyanti, va*tt*ati (B.). Compare vallikâ and ova*tt*ika*m* at V, 2, 1. Buddhaghosa's second explanation would be possible if the reading were sata-valika*m*, and is probably only a pis aller, due to the difficulty of the first, which we have adopted doubtfully.

[6] Pârupati as opposed to nivâseti above. Compare Dhammapada, pp. 114, 376; *G*âtaka, vol. i, p. 57, line 16.

garments as the laymen do. Whosoever does so, shall be guilty of a dukka*t*a.'

5. [Similar paragraph, ending]

'You are not, O Bhikkhus, to wear your under garments[1] as the king's porters do[1]. Whosoever does so, shall be guilty of a dukka*t*a.'

30.

1. Now at that time the *Kh*abbaggiya Bhikkhus carried a double pingo (a yoke over the shoulders with the weight to be carried on both sides).

People murmured, &c., saying, 'Like the king's porters[2].'

They told this matter to the Blessed One.

'You are not, O Bhikkhus, to carry a double pingo. Whosoever does so, shall be guilty of a dukka*t*a. I allow you, O Bhikkhus, to carry a single pingo, a pingo for two bearers[3], and to carry weights on your head, or your shoulders, or against your hips[4], and suspended over your backs.'

31.

1. Now at that time the Bhikkhus did not use tooth-sticks[5], and their mouths got a bad odour.

[1] Sa*m*velliya*m* nivâsetabba*m* See Buddhaghosa's note at p. 319 of the text.

[2] Mu*nd*a-va*tt*i or -ve*tth*i. See the note from the Samanta Pâsâdikâ at p. 319 of the text.

[3] Antarâ-kâ*g*a*m* nâma ma*ggh*e laggetvâ dvihi vahitabba*m* bhâra*m* (B.).

[4] That is held round by the arm, and resting against the side of the hips. Women in India commonly carry their children so, the children sitting on the hip, with one leg in front and one behind.

[5] Danta-ka*tth*a*m*, not 'tooth-brushes,' as Childers translates.

They told this matter to the Blessed One.

'There are these five disadvantages, O Bhikkhus, in not using tooth-sticks—it is bad for the eyes[1]—the mouth becomes bad-smelling—the passages by which the flavours of the food pass are not pure—bile and phlegm get into[2] the food—and the food does not taste well[3] to him (who does not use them). These are the five disadvantages, O Bhikkhus, in not using tooth-sticks.'

'There are five advantages, O Bhikkhus, (&c., the converse of the last).'

'I allow you, O Bhikkhus, tooth-sticks.'

2. Now at that time the *Kh*abbaggiya Bhikkhus used long tooth-sticks; and even struck the Sâma*n*eras with them.

They told this matter to the Blessed One.

'You are not, O Bhikkhus, to use long tooth-

Mechanical skill had not advanced so far in those days; and we hear nothing of brushes of any kind (see above, V, 2, 3, as to hair-dressing). The 'tooth-sticks' were bits of sweet-smelling wood or root, or creeper (see *G*âtaka I, 80; Mahâva*m*sa, p. 23), the ends of which were to be masticated as a dentifrice, not rubbed on the teeth. After using them the mouth was rinsed out with water; and so in all other passages in the Khandhakas where they are mentioned (always in reference to the duty of providing them), it is in connection with the bringing of water for that purpose.

[1] This has of course nothing to do with keeping the teeth white and beautiful; that was not the purpose which the tooth-sticks were designed to effect. There seems to have been really some idea that the use of them was good for the eye-sight. So Buddhaghosa says here, a*k*akkhussan ti *k*akkhûna*m* hita*m* ma hoti, pari-hâ*n*i*m* *g*aneti, quite in accordance with the Sanskrit *k*akshushya. The words recur below, VI, 2, 2, in the same sense.

[2] Pariyonandhanti. Literally, 'envelope,' 'cover.'

[3] Na *kkh*âdeti. This is a different word from *kh*âdeti, 'to cover. It is *kh*ad No. 2 in Böhtlingk-Roth.

sticks. Whosoever does so, shall be guilty of a dukka*t*a. I allow you, O Bhikkhus, tooth-sticks up to eight finger-breadths in length. And Sâma*n*eras are not to be struck with them. Whosoever does so, shall be guilty of a dukka*t*a.'

Now at that time a certain Bhikkhu, when using too short a tooth-stick, got it stuck in his throat.

They told this matter to the Blessed One.

'You are not, O Bhikkhus, to use too short a tooth-stick. Whosoever does so, shall be guilty of a dukka*t*a. I allow you, O Bhikkhus, tooth-sticks four finger-breadths long at the least.'

32.

1. Now at that time the *Kh*abbaggiya Bhikkhus set the woods on fire.

People murmured, &c., saying, 'Like the charcoal burners.'

They told this matter to the Blessed One.

'You are not, O Bhikkhus, to set woods on fire. Whosoever does so, shall be guilty of a dukka*t*a.'

Now at that time the Vihâras were hidden under masses of grass[1], and when the woods were set on fire the Vihâras were burnt. The Bhikkhus, fearing to offend, would not make a counter-fire for their own protection.

They told this matter to the Blessed One.

'I allow you, O Bhikkhus, when the woods are

[1] Ti*n*a-gahanâ. Not covered with thatch, the word for which is ti*n*a-*kkh*adanâ. See V, 11, 6; V, 14, 3, &c.

on fire to make a counter-fire[1], and thus afford yourselves protection.'

2. Now at that time the *Kh*abbaggiya Bhikkhus climbed up trees, and jumped from tree to tree.

People murmured, &c., saying, 'Like monkeys.'

They told this matter to the Blessed One.

'You are not, O Bhikkhus, to climb up trees. Whosoever does so, shall be guilty of a dukka*t*a.'

Now at that time, when a certain Bhikkhu in the Kosala country was going to Sâvatthi, an elephant pursued him on the way. And that Bhikkhu, when he had run up to the foot of a tree, fearing to offend, did not climb up. The elephant passed on another way.

That Bhikkhu, on arriving at Sâvatthi, told this matter to the Bhikkhus (and the Bhikkhus told this matter to the Blessed One[2]).

'I allow you, O Bhikkhus, when there shall be something to be done to ascend a tree to the height of a man; and in cases of misfortune as high as you like.'

33.

1. Now at that time there were two brothers, Bhikkhus, by name Yame*l*u and Tekula[3], Brâh-

---

[1] Pa*t*aggi*m* dâtu*m*. See the story at *G*âtaka I, 212, and foll.

[2] Omitted in the text.

[3] Yame*l*utekulâ. It is possible that this compound should be dissolved into Yame*l*a and Utekula. Compare the word Yame*l*e at verse 35 of the Uddâna (which stands where a nominative should stand, judging by the form of the other words in the Uddâna). A comma has there been omitted by misprint after Yame*l*e.

mans by birth, excelling in speech, excelling in pronunciation. These went up to the place where the Blessed One was, and when they had come there, they saluted the Blessed One, and took their seats on one side. And so sitting those Bhikkhus spake to the Blessed One thus:

'At the present time, Lord, Bhikkhus, differing in name, differing in lineage, differing in birth, differing in family, have gone forth (from the world). These corrupt the word of the Buddhas by (repeating it in) their own dialect. Let us, Lord, put the word of the Buddhas into (Sanskrit) verse[1].'

'How can you, O foolish ones, speak thus, saying, "Let us, Lord, put the word of the Buddhas into verse?" This will not conduce, O foolish ones, either to the conversion of the unconverted, or to the increase of the converted; but rather to those who have not been converted being not converted, and to the turning back of those who have been converted.'

And when the Blessed One had rebuked those Bhikkhus, and had delivered a religious discourse[2], he addressed the Bhikkhus, and said:

---

[1] We think that in these words (*kh*andaso âropema) there does lie a reference to the earlier Sanskrit. And this especially for four reasons: firstly, this is required by the antithesis to 'their own dialect;' secondly, the use of the word *kh*andasi in Pâ*n*ini, where it always means precisely 'in the Veda-dialect,' requires it; thirdly, it is difficult to understand otherwise the mention of 'Brâhmans by birth;' and fourthly, this is in accordance with the traditional interpretation of the passage handed down among the Bhikkhus. Buddhaghosa says, *kh*andaso âropemâ ti Veda*m* viya sakka*t*a-bhâsâya vâ*k*anâ-magga*m* âropema. Sakka*t*a is of course Sa*m*skr*i*ta.

[2] See the substance intended at *K*ullavagga I, 1, 3.

'You are not, O Bhikkhus, to put the word of the Buddhas into (Sanskrit) verse. Whosoever does so, shall be guilty of a dukka*t*a. I allow you, O Bhikkhus, to learn the word of the Buddhas each in his own dialect[1].'

2. Now at that time the *Kh*abbaggiya Bhikkhus learnt the Lokâyata system[2].

People murmured, &c., saying, 'Like those who still enjoy the pleasures of the world!'

The Bhikkhus heard of the people thus murmuring; and those Bhikkhus told the matter to the Blessed One.

'Now can a man who holds the Lokâyata as valuable reach up, O Bhikkhus, to the full advantage of, or attain to full growth in, to full breadth in this doctrine and discipline[3]?'

'This cannot be, Lord.'

'Or can a man who holds this doctrine and discipline to be valuable learn the Lokâyata system?'

---

[1] On the historical conclusions which may be drawn from this tradition, see H. O.'s introduction to the text of the Mahâvagga, pp. xlix and following.

[2] This is mentioned also in the Assalâyana Sutta (at the beginning), and in the same terms in the Milinda Pa*n*ha, p. 10, as one of the branches of learning distinctive of well-educated Brâhmans. It is condemned among other 'low arts' in the very ancient Mahâ Sîla, § 5. (See Rh. D.'s 'Buddhist Suttas from the Pâli,' p. 199, and his note on the age of this work, ibid. p. 188.) Among later works, the Nepalese Buddhists refer to it as one of the things with which a Bodhisattva will not condescend to occupy himself (Lotus of the Good Law, ch. xiii, Burnouf's version, p. 168), and in which good disciples will take no pleasure (ibid. p. 280). Buddhaghosa has a note on the passage in the Mahâ Sila (quoted by Childers sub voce), which shows that it was understood in his time to be, or rather to have been, a system of casuistry.

[3] So also in the *K*etokhila Sutta 2 (translated in Rh. D.'s 'Buddhist Suttas from the Pâli,' p. 223).

'This cannot be, Lord.'

'You are not, O Bhikkhus, to learn the Lokâyata system. Whosoever does so, shall be guilty of a dukka*t*a.'

Now at that time the *Kh*abbaggiya Bhikkhus taught the Lokâyata system.

People murmured, &c., saying, 'Like those still enjoying the pleasures of the world!'

They told this matter to the Blessed One.

'You are not, O Bhikkhus, to teach the Lokâyata system. Whosoever does so, shall be guilty of a dukka*t*a.'

[Similar paragraphs to the last, ending]

'You are not, O Bhikkhus, to learn—to teach—the low arts[1] (of divination, spells, omens, astrology, sacrifices to gods, witchcraft, and quackery).'

3. Now at that time the Blessed One when, surrounded by a great assembly, he was preaching the Dhamma, sneezed. The Bhikkhus raised a great and mighty shout, 'Long life to our Lord the Blessed One! Long life to the Happy One!' and by the sound thereof the discourse was interrupted. Then the Blessed One said to the Bhikkhus:

'Now if when a man has sneezed, O Bhikkhus, some one says, "Long life to you," can he live or die on that account?'

'Not so, Lord.'

[1] Tira*kkh*âna-vi*gg*â. Literally, 'brutish, or beastly, wisdom.' These are set out in full in the seven sections of the Mahâ Sîla (translated in Rh. D.'s 'Buddhist Suttas from the Pâli,' pp. 196–200). As noticed above, the Lokâyata system is there mentioned (§ 5) as one of them. Learning or teaching these things are forbidden in almost identical terms to the Bhikkhunîs in the Bhikkhunî-vibhaṅga, Pâ*k*ittiyas XLIX and L.

'You are not, O Bhikkhus, when one has sneezed, to call out, "Long life to you." Whosoever does so, shall be guilty of a dukka*t*a[1].'

Now at that time people said to the Bhikkhus when they sneezed, 'Long life to your reverence!' and the Bhikkhus, fearing to offend, gave no reply. The people murmured, were annoyed, and were indignant, saying, 'How can the Sakya-puttiya Sama*n*as omit to reply when people say, "Long life to your reverence?"'

They told this matter to the Blessed One.

'Laymen, O Bhikkhus, are given to lucky phrases[2]. I allow you, O Bhikkhus, to reply, "May you live long!" to laymen who say to you, "Long life to your reverence!"'

34.

1. Now at that time the Blessed One when, surrounded by a great assembly, he was preaching the Dhamma, was seated. And a certain Bhikkhu, who had eaten onions, sat down apart, thinking, Let not the Bhikkhus be annoyed[3]!'

The Blessed One saw that Bhikkhu sitting apart; and on seeing him, he said to the Bhikkhus, 'Why now, O Bhikkhus, is that Bhikkhu seated apart?'

'This Bhikkhu, Lord, has eaten onions, and has

---

[1] This story forms the Introductory Story also to the Gagga *G*âtaka (No. 155 in Fausböll's edition). On the superstition here condemned, see Dr. Morris's remarks in the 'Contemporary Review' for May, 1881.

[2] Gihî bhikkhave mañgalikâ.

[3] Vyâbâhi*m*su is for vyâbâdhi*m*su. See p. 320 of the edition of the text.

seated himself apart in order not to annoy the Bhikkhus.'

'But ought, O Bhikkhus, anything to be eaten, that will cause the eater to keep away from such a preaching of the Dhamma as this?'

'No, indeed, Lord.'

'You are not, O Bhikkhus, to eat onions. Whosoever does so, shall be guilty of a dukka*t*a[1].'

2. Now at that time the venerable Sâriputta had wind in his stomach. And the venerable Mahâ Moggallâna went up to the place where the venerable Sâriputta was, and when he had come there, he said to the venerable Sâriputta:

'How did you formerly, friend Sâriputta, get relief, when you had wind in the stomach?'

'By eating onions, my friend[2].'

They told this matter to the Blessed One.

'I allow you, O Bhikkhus, to eat onions on account of disease.'

35.

1. Now at that time the Bhikkhus made water here and there in the Ârâma, and the Ârâma was defiled.

They told this matter to the Blessed One.

'I allow you, O Bhikkhus, to make water at one side (of the Ârâma).'

---

[1] There is a similar rule for the Bhikkhunîs in the Bhikkhunî-vibhaṅga, Pâ*k*ittiya I. So also onions are mentioned among the things a *G*ain Bhikkhu may not accept (Âyâraṅga Sutta II, 1, 8, 13).

[2] It is gruel of various kinds that is prescribed for this malady in Mahâvagga VI, 16, 3–17, 2.

The Ârâma became offensive. . . .

[The rest of this chapter is scarcely translateable. It records in like manner the various sanitary difficulties which arose from the living together of a number of Bhikkhus. Each such difficulty is quite solemnly said to have been reported to the Blessed One, and he is said to have found a way out of it. The result of the whole is, that the building of privies is enjoined, and all the contrivances, such as seats, doors, steps, plastering, &c., already mentioned with respect to the bath-room, above, V, 14, are here repeated verbatim[1].]

36.

Now at that time the *Kh*abbaggiya Bhikkhus followed evil practices such as these—they used to plant [&c., word for word as in the long list at I, 13, 1, 2, down to the end].

They told this matter to the Blessed One.

'You are not, O Bhikkhus, to follow manifold evil practices. Whosoever does so, shall be dealt with according to the law.'

37.

1. Now at the time when the venerable Kassapa of Uruve*l*a went forth (from the world), much property in brass and wood and earthenware came into the possession of the Sa*m*gha[2]. And the

[1] For some of the details, compare Mahâvagga V, 8, 3, and Mahâvagga I, 25, 19=*K*ullavagga VIII, 1, 5, and *K*ullavagga VIII, 9 and 10.

[2] See Mahâvagga I, 20, 19–21.

Bhikkhus thought, 'What kinds of brass ware—of wooden things—of earthenware [1]—has the Blessed One allowed, and what kinds has he not allowed?'

They told this matter to the Blessed One.

Then the Blessed One, on that occasion and in that connection, when he had delivered a religious discourse, addressed the Bhikkhus, and said:

'I allow you, O Bhikkhus, all kinds of brass ware, except weapons [2]—all kinds of wooden things, except divans [3], and long-armed chairs [3], and bowls [4], and shoes [5],—and all kinds of earthenware, except katakas [6], and large earthen vessels to be used as huts to live in [7].'

Here ends the Fifth Khandhaka, on minor details.

---

[1] See *K*ullavagga VIII, 3, 1.

[2] Pahara*n*attha*m* kata*m* pahara*n*î ti vu*kk*ati. Yassa kassa *k*i âvudha-sa*m*ghâtass' eta*m* adhivâ*k*ana*m* (B.).

[3] See Mahâvagga V, 10, 4, 5.

[4] See *K*ullavagga V, 8, 2.

[5] See Mahâvagga V, 6, 4.

[6] On this word see our note above at V, 22, 1.

[7] This is the only one of the things here mentioned not referred to in previous rules. Buddhaghosa says, Kumbha-kârikâ ti Dhaniyass' eva sabba-mattikâmaya-ku*t*i vu*kk*ati. The story of Dhaniya is given in the text of the Vinaya, vol. iii, pp. 42 and following.

SIXTH KHANDHAKA.

On Dwellings and Furniture.

1.

1. Now at that time the Blessed Buddha[1] was staying at Râgagaha in the Veluvana, in the Kalandaka Nivâpa[2]. And at that time no permission had been given to the Bhikkhus by the Blessed One with respect to dwellings. So the Bhikkhus dwelt now here, now there—in the woods, at the foot of trees, on hill-sides, in grottoes, in mountain caves, in cemeteries, in forests, in open plains, and in heaps of straw. And at early morn they came in from this place or from that place—from the woods (&c., as before) decorous in their walking and turning, in their looking on or looking round, in stretching out their arms or in drawing them back, with eyes cast down, and dignified in deportment[3].

2. Now at that time the Setthi of Râgagaha went at early morn to his garden. And the Setthi of

[1] Our readers will have noticed that the phrase at the beginning of each Khandhaka is 'the Blessed Buddha,' and not merely 'the Blessed One.' It recurs besides only in the constantly-repeated paragraph 'The Blessed Buddha rebuked them, saying, &c.' (see, for instance, Kullavagga I, 1, 2, where the connection is given in full).

[2] Compare the note on Mahâvagga III, 1, 1.

[3] So also Mahâvagga I, 23, 2, and frequently in the Suttas.

Râgagaha saw those Bhikkhus coming in from this place and from that place, from the woods (&c., as in § 1, down to the end), and on seeing them he took pleasure therein[1]. And the Se*tth*i of Râgagaha went up to those Bhikkhus, and said to them:

'If, Sirs, I were to have dwellings erected for you, would you take up your abode in those dwellings?'

'Not so, O householder. Dwellings have not been allowed by the Blessed One.'

'Then, Sirs, ask the Blessed One about it, and let me know.'

'Very well, O householder,' said they, in assent to the Se*tth*i of Râ*g*agaha. And they went up to the Blessed One, and saluted him, and took their seats on one side. And when they were so seated, they said to the Blessed One:

'The Se*tth*i of Râ*g*agaha, Lord, wishes to have dwellings erected for us. What, Lord, should be done?'

Then the Blessed One, on that occasion and in that connection, when he had delivered a religious discourse, addressed the Bhikkhus, and said:

'I allow you, O Bhikkhus, abodes of five kinds—Vihâras, A*ddh*ayogas, storied dwellings, attics, caves[2].'

3. Then those Bhikkhus went up to the Se*tth*i of Râ*g*agaha, and said to him: 'The Blessed One, Sir, has allowed us dwellings; do, therefore, what seemeth to thee good.' And the Se*tth*i of Râ*g*agaha had sixty dwelling-places put up in one day.

---

[1] So also of Bimbisâra in the *G*âtaka Commentary, I, 66.

[2] Buddhaghosa's note on these pa*ñk*a le*n*âni has already been given in our note above, Mahâvagga I, 30, 4.

4. And when the Se*tth*i of Râ*g*agaha had completed those sixty dwelling-places, he went up to the place where the Blessed One was, and [invited him and the Bhikkhu Sa*m*gha for the morrow's meal; and so on, as usual[1], down to the time when, after the meal, the Se*tth*i] said to the Blessed One:

'I have had, Lord, these sixty dwelling-places made for the sake of merit, and for the sake of heaven. What am I to do, Lord, with respect to them?'

'Then, O householder, dedicate[2] these sixty dwelling-places to the Sa*m*gha of the four directions, whether now present, or hereafter to arrive.'

'Even so, Lord!' said the Se*tth*i of Râ*g*agaha, in assent to the Blessed One, and he dedicated those sixty dwelling-places to the use of the Sa*m*gha of the four directions whether present or to come[3].'

5. Then the Blessed One gave thanks to the Se*tth*i of Râ*g*agaha in these verses[4]:

'1. Cold he wards off and heat, so also beasts of prey,
And creeping things and gnats, and rains in the wet season.
And when the dreaded heated winds arise, they are kept off.

---

[1] See, for instance, Mahâvagga VI, 30, or *K*ullavagga V, 27.

[2] Literally, 'establish' (pa*t*i*tth*âpehi).

[3] This formula of dedication has been constantly found in rock-inscriptions in India and Ceylon over the ancient cave-dwellings of Buddhist hermits. See Rh. D. in the 'Indian Antiquary' for May, 1872.

[4] The following verses recur below at VI, 9, 2; and also in that connection in the *G*âtaka Commentary, I, 93.

2. To give Vihâras to the Samgha, wherein in safety and in peace
To meditate and think at ease, the Buddha calls the best of gifts.

3. Let then the able man, regarding his own weal,
Have pleasant monasteries built, and lodge there learned men [1].

4. Let him with cheerful mind give food to them, and drink,
Raiment, and dwelling-places, to the upright in heart.

5. Then shall they preach to him the Truth—
The Truth dispelling every grief—
Which Truth when here that man perceives
He sins no more, and dies away [2]!'

And when the Blessed One had given thanks to the Se*tth*i of Râ*g*agaha in these verses, he rose from his seat, and departed thence.

2.

1. And the people heard, saying, 'Vihâras have been allowed by the Blessed One.' And they built Vihâras zealously. Those Vihâras had no doors [3], and snakes, scorpions, and centipedes got in.

[1] This verse forms the subject of one of the 'Questions of Milinda' (ed. Trenckner, p. 211).

[2] The above verses may have stood originally in a different context from that in which they have been handed down, as the opening phrase sîta*m* pa*t*ihanti would be more intelligible if the word vihâro occurred in the immediately preceding clause.

[3] Kavâ*t*a. This is the special word for door. Dvâra often roughly translated door, is not really 'door,' but 'door-' or 'gateway,' with special reference to the aperture and not to that by which the aperture could be closed. The latter word is also

They told this matter to the Blessed One.

'I allow, O Bhikkhus, a door[1].'

They made holes in the wall, and tied the door on with string or with creepers, These were eaten by mice and white ants; and when the things by which the doors had been tied on had been eaten away, the doors fell.

They told this matter to the Blessed One.

'I allow, O Bhikkhus, door-posts and lintel, hollow like a mortar, for the door to revolve in, and projections to the door for it to revolve on.'

The doors would not come to.

'I allow, O Bhikkhus, a hole to pass a string through with which to pull the door to, and a string for that purpose.'

The doors could not be made fast[2].

'I allow, O Bhikkhus, rings on the door for the bolt to work along in, blocks of wood fixed to the edge of the door-post and containing a cavity for the bolt to go into, a pin to secure the bolt by, and a bolt.'

Now at that time the Bhikkhus were not able to open the door.

They told this matter to the Blessed One.

---

different from 'door,' in that it is never used for the entrance into an inner chamber. It is always the outer entrance (and the entrance at the front as distinguished from the entrance at the back) of a house, or one of the principal entrances to a walled town or village. See, for instance, Pâkittiya XIX; Kullavagga VIII, 5, 1, VIII, 8, 1; Gâtaka I, 63, 114, 346, 361, II, 63, 140.

[1] On this and the following details, compare V, 14, 3, and the notes there.

[2] Thakiyanti: literally, 'covered, or stopped, up.' The same word is used at Kullavagga VIII, 1, 5, of closing up the lattices mentioned in the next section (VI, 2, 2).

'I allow, O Bhikkhus, key-holes, and keys of three kinds—bronze keys, and keys of hard wood, and keys of horn.'

When anybody unlocked them[1], and entered, the Vihâras became unprotected.

They told this matter to the Blessed One.

'I allow, O Bhikkhus, a yantaka, and a pin to it[2].'

2. Now at that time the Vihâras were thatched; and in the cold season they were cold, and in the hot season hot.

They told this matter to the Blessed One.

'I allow you, O Bhikkhus, to cover them (with skins)[3], and to plaster them within and without.'

Now at that time the Vihâras had no windows, and they were bad for the eyes, and had a disagreeable odour.

They told this matter to the Blessed One.

'I allow, O Bhikkhus, windows of three kinds—windows made with railings[4], windows made with network[5], and windows made with slips of wood[6].'

---

[1] Ugghâ*t*etvâ, an expression used in VIII, 1, 1 of undoing the bolt (gha*t*ikâ) just referred to.

[2] Yantaka*m* sû*k*ika*m*, which is the only expression here used which has not already occurred above at V, 14, 3. Buddhaghosa says, Yantaka-sû*k*ikan ti ettha ya*m* ya*m* *g*ânâti ta*m* ta*m* yantaka*m*. Tassa vivara-sû*k*ika*m* kuñ*k*ika*m* kâtu*m* va*tt*ati.

[3] See the note at V, 14, 3.

[4] Vedikâ-vâtapâna*m* nâma *k*etiye vedikâ-sadisa*m* (B.). See our note on vedikâ above, V, 14, 2. These windows or lattices are mentioned in *K*ullavagga VIII, 1, 5; Mahâvagga I, 25, 18.

[5] *G*âla-vâtapâna*m* nâma *g*âlaka-baddha*m* (B.). *G*âlam, literally 'net,' is given as a word for 'window' at Abhidhânappadîpikâ, verse 216. The expression probably corresponds to our 'lattice,' and does not mean that an actual net was used. Compare the Anglo-Indian 'jalousie.'

[6] Salâka-vâtapâna*m* nâma thambhaka-vâtapâna*m* (B.). Pos-

Squirrels and bats[1] entered through the opening for the window.

'I allow, O Bhikkhus, window-blinds (or curtains)[2].'

The squirrels and bats still got in through the interstices between the blind (and the wall).

'I allow, O Bhikkhus, shutters, and rolls or bags (to fill up interstices with)[3].

3. Now at that time the Bhikkhus slept on the floor, and both their limbs and their robes became dirty.

They told this matter to the Blessed One.

'I allow, O Bhikkhus, mats made of grass.'

The mats were eaten by mice and white ants.

'I allow, O Bhikkhus, a solid bench or divan (built up against the wall of a room, or under the verandah against the outside wall of the house)[4].

---

sibly this means with slips of wood arranged horizontally as in our venetian blinds.

[1] Vagguliyo. This habit of the bat and its harmlessness are referred to in Milinda Pa*n*ha, p. 404. Compare the Sanskrit valgulî.

[2] *K*akkalikan ti. Ettha *k*olaka-pâda-puñ*kh*ana*m* bandhitu*m* anu*g*ânâmî ti attho (B.). The word *k*akkali occurs below, VI, 19, probably in the sense here meant.

[3] Vâtapâna-bhisî ti vâtapâna-pamâ*n*ena bhisi*m* katvâ bandhitu*m* anu*g*ânâmî ti attho (B.). Probably like the sand-bags used in England to keep out draughts. On the use of the word in other connections, see our note on Mahâvagga VIII, 13, 1, and the Old Commentary on Pâ*k*ittiya XIV (where five kinds are named) with the Kankhâ-vitara*n*î on the last passage quoted by Minayeff, p. 86.

[4] Mi*dh*im. See the note on V, 9, 4. Native huts in Ceylon always have such solid benches (of brick or mud covered with plaster) built up against the wall under the verandah: and they are commonly used as sleeping-places for the unmarried males

On the solid bench their limbs ached.

'I allow, O Bhikkhus, bedsteads made of laths of split bamboo [1].'

Now at that time a bier-like masâraka [2] bedstead—a masâraka chair—a bier-like bundikâbaddha [3] bedstead—a bundikâbaddha chair—a bier-like kulîra-pâdaka [4] bedstead—a kulîra-pâdaka chair—a bier-like âha*kk*a-pâdaka [5] bedstead—an âha*kk*a-pâdaka chair—had come into the possession of the Sa*m*gha.

---

in the house. Waska*d*uwa Subhûti has this in his mind in the explanation he gives in English of vedikâ (Abhidhâna-ppadîpikâ, verse 222), though he applies it to the wrong word.

[1] Bidala-ma*ñk*aka*m* nâma vetta-ma*ñk*a*m*, ve*l*u-vilîvâhi vâ vîta*m* (B.). The word occurs in the *G*âtaka Commentary I, 9, lines 26, 34. Compare the Sanskrit bidala and vidala.

[2] Masârako, on which Buddhaghosa says nothing here; but on the Old Commentary to the 14th Pâ*k*ittiya, where all the four words in this paragraph also occur, he has the following note (see Minayeff, p. 68): Masârako ti ma*ñk*a-pâde vi*ggh*itvâ tattha a*t*aniyo pavesetvâ kato—just the opposite therefore of âha*kk*a-pâdako below. On a*t*ani, compare our note to the 87th Pâ*k*ittiya. The four names recur, of chairs only, in the Old Commentary on the 87th and 88th Pâ*k*ittiyas.

[3] Buddhaghosa, loc. cit., says, Bundikâbaddho ti a*t*anîhi ma*ñk*a-pâde *dam*sâpetvâ pallaṅka-sa*m*khepena kato. The first word, bundika, may mean a small bolt.

[4] Kulîra-pâdako ti assa-me*nd*âdîna*m* pâda-sadisehi pâdakehi kato: yo vâ pana ko*k*i vaṅka-pâdako aya*m* kulîra-pâdako (B. loc. cit.). A bedstead or chair with curved or carved legs, especially when carved to represent animals' feet. Kulîra is a crab.

[5] Âha*kk*a-pâdako ti. Aya*m* pana âha*kk*a-pâdako nâma ma*ñk*o aṅge vi*ggh*itvâ kato hotîti eva*m* parato pâliya*m* yeva vutto. Tasmâ a*t*aniyo vi*ggh*itvâ tattha pâda-sikha*m* pavesetvâ upari â*n*im datvâ kata-ma*ñk*o âha*kk*a-pâdako ti veditabbo (B. loc. cit.). This is in agreement with the Old Commentary on the 18th Pâ*k*ittiya in which this word already occurs. Compare âha*kk*a in the Âyâranga Sûya II, 1, 1, 2, II, 1, 10, 6.

They told this matter (in each case) to the Blessed One.

'I allow you, O Bhikkhus, (each of these things).'

4. Now at that time a rectangular chair[1]—an arm-chair[2]—a sofa[3]—a sofa with arms to it[4]—a state chair[5]—a cushioned chair[6]—a chair raised on a pedestal[7]—a chair with many legs[8]—a board (to recline on)[9]—a cane-bottomed chair[10]—a straw-bottomed chair—had come into the possession of the Sa*m*gha.

They told this matter (in each case) to the Blessed One.

'I allow you, O Bhikkhus, (each of these things).'

---

[1] Âsandiko. Buddhaghosa says, Âsandako (sic) ti *k*aturassa-pî*th*a*m* vu*kk*ati. An âsandi (cushioned chair) is forbidden at Mahâvagga V, 10, 4.

[2] U*kk*aka*m* pi âsandikan ti va*k*anato ekato-bhâgena dîgha-pî*th*am eva hi a*tth*aṅgula-pâdaka*m* va*tt*ati (B.).

[3] Sattaṅgo nâma tîsu disâsu apassaya*m* katvâ mañ*k*o (B.). On apassaya*m*, compare note 9.

[4] U*kk*ako pi sattaṅgo. Compare note 2.

[5] Bhadda-pî*th*an ti vetta-maya*m* pîtha*m* vu*kk*ati (B.). We follow Böhtlingk-Roth sub voce bhadra-pî*th*a.

[6] Pî*th*ikâ ti pilotika-baddha*m* pîtham eva (B.). Childers says 'bench, stool.' Compare Sanskrit pî*th*aka (in the addenda to the Petersburg Dictionary).

[7] E*l*aka-pâdaka-pî*th*a*m* nâma dâru-pa*tt*ikâya upari pâde *th*apetvâ bho*g*ana-phalaka*m* viya kata-pî*th*a*m* vu*kk*ati (B.).

[8] Âma*l*aka-va*n*t*i*ka-pî*th*a*m* nâma âma*l*akâkârena yo*g*ita*m* bahu-pâda-pî*th*am (B.). Compare tâlava*n*t*a at V, 22, 2, and tâla-va*n*t*aka at V, 29, 4.

[9] Phalaka*m*. Compare apassena-phalaka*m* at Mahâvagga I, 25, 12, and below, *K*ullavagga VI, 20, 2.

[10] Ko*kk*ha*m* nâma vâkamaya*m* vâ usîramaya*m* vâ muñ*g*a-maya*m* vâ babba*g*amaya*m* vâ anto sa*m*ve*th*etvâ baddha*m* hoti, says the Old Commentary on the 14th Pâ*k*ittiya. Buddhaghosa gives here the same explanation, omitting vâka.

5. Now at that time the *Kh*abbaggiya Bhikkhus slept on lofty beds.

People coming on a visit to the Vihâra, when they saw them, murmured, &c., saying, 'Like those who still live in the pleasure of the world.'

They told this matter to the Blessed One.

'You are not, O Bhikkhus, to sleep on lofty beds. Whosoever does so, shall be guilty of a dukka*t*a[1].'

Now at that time a certain Bhikkhu, when sleeping on a low couch, was bitten by a snake[2].

They told this matter to the Blessed One.

'I allow you, O Bhikkhus, supports to your bedsteads[3].'

Now at that time the *Kh*abbaggiya Bhikkhus used lofty supports to their bedsteads, and rocked themselves with these bedstead supports, backwards and forwards[4].

'You are not, O Bhikkhus, to use lofty supports to your bedsteads. Whosoever does so, shall be guilty of a dukka*t*a. I allow you such supports up to eight inches in length.'

6. Now at that time a quantity of string had come into the possession of the Sa*m*gha.

They told this matter to the Blessed One.

'I allow you, O Bhikkhus, to weave (a texture of string across) the bedstead.'

Much string was taken up by (passing it round) the sides of the bedstead.

---

[1] Compare the 8th *K*ûla Sîla (Rh. D.'s 'Buddhist Suttas,' p. 191).

[2] Compare *K*ullavagga V, 6.

[3] Mañ*k*a-pa*t*ipâdaka*m* mentioned in Mahâvagga I, 25, 16.

[4] Pavedhenti. The reading is doubtful, but the suggestion at p. 321 of the text must be withdrawn.

'I allow you, O Bhikkhus, to pierce the sides of the bedstead, and thus to weave the string across and across[1].'

A cloth had come into their possession.

'I allow you, O Bhikkhus, to use it as a carpet[2].'

A mattress stuffed with cotton[3] had come into their possession.

'I allow you, O Bhikkhus, to comb out the cotton, and make the cotton up into pillows[4] if it be of any of these three kinds—cotton produced on trees, cotton produced on creepers, cotton produced from Po*t*aki-grass.'

Now at that time the *Kh*abbaggiya Bhikkhus made use of pillows half the size of a man's body.

People who came on a visit to the Vihâras murmured, &c., on seeing this, saying, 'Like those who still enjoy the pleasures of the world.'

---

[1] A*tth*apadaka*m* vetu*m*. Buddhaghosa says nothing, either here or at Mahâvagga VIII, 21, where the word also occurs. A*tth*apada-*tth*âpana at *G*âtaka II, 5, 14, is a mode of dressing the hair, probably in broad plaits crossing each other so as to resemble the squares of a chessboard.

[2] Or 'rug.' *K*ilimikâ ti nâma parikammakatâya bhûmiyâ *kh*avi-sa*m*rakkhanatthâya atthara*n*a*m* vu*kk*ati (B.). It is probably the same word as, or connected with, *k*imilikâ, used by Buddhaghosa in note 5 on Mahâvagga VII, 1, 5, and explained by him (in Minayeff, p. 87, line 5) as tâla-pa*nn*âdîhi katâ. Both words are possibly diminutives of *k*ola, and it is not improbable that the reading should be *k*ilimikâ in both cases, as Buddhaghosa so spells the word again in his note below on VI, 2, 7.

[3] Tûlikâ. This is undoubtedly what is meant to be forbidden in § 5 of the Ma*gg*hima Sîla, although Grimblot, 'Sept Suttas Palis,' p. 9, reads kulika*m*. See Mahâvagga V, 10, 4.

[4] Compare IV, 4, 4, VIII, 1, 3, where such pillows are mentioned among the ordinary belongings of a Vihâra. The present rule is repeated below in VI, 14.

They told this matter to the Blessed One.

'You are not, O Bhikkhus, to make use of pillows half the size of a man's body. Whosoever does so, shall be guilty of a dukka*t*a. I allow you, O Bhikkhus, to have pillows the size of a man's head.'

7. Now at that time there was a festival on a high place[1] at Râ*g*agaha. The people provided for the use of high officials bolsters stuffed with wool, or cotton cloth, or bark, or grass, or leaves. When the festival had been held they tore open the covers of skin and carried them off. And the Bhikkhus saw much wool, and cotton cloth, and bark, and grass, and leaves thrown away on the spot where the festival had been held; and on seeing this, they told the matter to the Blessed One.

'I allow, O Bhikkhus, bolsters[2] of five kinds—those stuffed with wool, or cotton cloth, or bark, or grass, or talipot leaves.'

Now at that time a bed coverlet had come into the possession of the Sa*m*gha.

They told this matter to the Blessed One.

'I allow you, O Bhikkhus, to cover a bolster with it.'

Now at that time the Bhikkhus folded up bed bolsters on to chairs[3], and chair bolsters on to bedsteads, and the bolsters came to pieces.

They told this matter to the Blessed One.

'I allow you, O Bhikkhus, chairs and bedsteads covered (with upholstered cushions to fit them).'

---

[1] Giragga-samag*g*o. See our note above on V, 2, 6.

[2] Bhisi. See the note on this word at Mahâvagga VIII, 13, 1.

[3] Buddhaghosa says here ma*ñk*a-bhisi*m* pî*th*e sa*m*harantî ti ma*ñk*a-pî*th*e attharanti attharanatthâya harantî ti yu*gg*ati (B.). On this use of sa*m*harati compare above, V, 11, 7.

They covered the bedsteads and chairs without putting a cloth beneath them[1], and the stuffing came out from below.

'I allow you, O Bhikkhus, first to spread out a cloth under the bedsteads or chairs, and then to upholster them.'

They tore off the coverings[2], and took them away.

'I allow you, O Bhikkhus, to bespatter (the coverings with dye)[3].'

They still took them away.

'I allow you, O Bhikkhus, to use coverings coloured in patches[4].'

They still took them away.

'I allow you, O Bhikkhus, to colour the coverings in patches only the size of a man's hand[5].'

---

[1] Ullokam akaritvâ hetthâ *k*ilimikam adatvâ (B.). The word occurs again at Mahâvagga I, 25, 15 = *K*ullavagga VIII, 1, 3, where cobwebs are to be removed with a cloth (ullokâ !).

[2] *Kh*avi*m*; but perhaps not necessarily of leather. See the commencement of this section.

[3] So that the coverings would be useless for other purposes. The Pâli word is positu*m*, which Buddhaghosa explains thus—hesitun ti (so the Berlin MS.) ra*g*anena vâ haliddhâya vâ upari pusitâni dâtu*m*. The word is evidently connected not with the root push, but with the roots p*ri*sh and prush, 'to bespatter;' and is the same as phositun at Mahâvagga VI, 14, 5, which is probably the better reading of the two.

[4] Bhatti-kamma*m*. The meaning is doubtful, because the reading is uncertain. Buddhaghosa says, Bhitti-kamman ti (sic) bhisi-*kh*aviyâ upari bhitti-kamma*m*. The word is probably analogous in formation to our English 'patchwork,' though the 'patches' are not of pieces of different coloured stuffs, but of bits of different colour spread over the same stuff, and whatever its meaning, it is probably the same word as bhati-kamma at V, 9, 2.

[5] Again both reading and interpretation are open to question. Hattha-bhittin ti pa*ñk*angula-bhitti*m* is all that Buddhaghosa

3.

1. Now at that time the sleeping-rooms of the Titthiyas were whitewashed, the floors of their rooms were coloured black, and the walls coloured with red chalk [1]. Much people went to look at their sleeping-rooms.

They told this matter to the Blessed One.

'I allow, O Bhikkhus, the use in your Vihâras of whitewash, black colouring, and red colouring.'

Now at that time the whitewash would not lie on to the rough walls.

They told this matter to the Blessed One.

'I allow you, O Bhikkhus, to apply the husks of grain made up into little balls; and when you have thus removed the unevenness with your hands [2], to lay on the whitewash.'

The whitewash would not adhere.

They told this matter to the Blessed One.

'I allow you, O Bhikkhus, to apply soft clay; and when you have thus removed the unevenness with your hands [2], to lay on the whitewash.'

(Still) the whitewash would not adhere.

'I allow you, O Bhikkhus, the use of slime [3] (of trees) or of paste [4].'

---

says; and we have followed in our translation the reading of the Sinhalese MS. (see p. 321 of the edition of the text), which brings the word into connection with the preceding phrase.

[1] See V, 11, 6, where all these words recur.

[2] Pâ*n*ikâya. Buddhaghosa says nothing.

[3] Ikkâsa, on which we have nothing to add to Buddhaghosa's note at p. 321 of the edition of the text. It recurs below again in this section.

[4] Pi*tth*a-maddan ti pi*tth*a-khala*m* (B.). Compare the Sanskrit m*ri*d.

Now at that time the colouring matter of red chalk would not lie on the rough walls.

They told this matter to the Blessed One.

'I allow you, O Bhikkhus, to apply the husks of grain made up into little balls; and when you have thus removed the unevenness with your hands, to lay on the colouring matter of red chalk.'

The red colour would not adhere.

'I allow you, O Bhikkhus, to apply clay mixed with the red powder which adheres to the grain of rice under the husks[1]; and when you have so taken off the unevenness with your hands to lay on the red colouring matter.'

Still the red colouring matter would not adhere.

'I allow you, O Bhikkhus, the use of a paste made of mustard seed[2], and of oil of beeswax[3].'

It lay on the wall too thickly in great drops[4].

'I allow you, O Bhikkhus, to wipe it down with a cloth[5].'

Now at that time the black colouring matter did not lie on the rough ground.

'I allow you, O Bhikkhus, to apply husks of grain

---

[1] Kundaka-mattikan ti ku*nd*aka-missaka-mattika*m* (B.). Compare ku*nd*aka-pûva*m* in the *G*âtaka Commentary I, 423 (cakes made of flour mixed with this powder).

[2] Sâsapa-ku*tt*an ti sâsapa-pi*tth*am. The word has occurred already at Mahâvagga VI, 14, 5, where the reading is ku*tt*a instead of ku*dd*a given in the text here. The latter should be altered in accordance with that passage, and with Buddhaghosa here.

[3] Sittha-telakan ti vilîna-madhu-sitthaka*m* (B.). It is mentioned as used for hair-oil at *K*ullavagga V, 2, 3.

[4] A*kk*ussanna*m* hotî ti bindu*m* bindu*m* hutvâ ti*tth*ati, says Buddhaghosa.

[5] *K*olakena pa*kk*uddharitu*m*. Buddhaghosa says pa*kk*utharitun ti muñ*k*itu*m* ; but compare for the right form V, 17, 1.

made up into little balls; and when you have thus removed the unevenness with your hands, to lay on the black colouring matter.'

The black colouring matter would not adhere.

They told this matter to the Blessed One.

'I allow you, O Bhikkhus, to apply clay mixed with (the excrement of) earth-worms[1]; and when you have thus removed the unevenness with your hands, to lay on the black colouring matter.'

Still the black colouring matter would not adhere.

They told this matter to the Blessed One.

'I allow you, O Bhikkhus, the use of slime and astringent liquid[2].'

2. Now at that time the *Kh*abbaggiya Bhikkhus had imaginative drawings[3] painted on their Vihâras—figures of men, and figures of women.

People, when they saw them on going to visit the Vihâras, murmured, &c., saying, 'Like those who still enjoy the pleasures of the world.'

They told this matter to the Blessed One.

'You are not, O Bhikkhus, to have imaginative drawings painted—figures of men, and figures of

---

[1] Ga*nd*u-mattikan ti ga*nd*uppâda-gûtha-mattika*m* (B.).

[2] Kasâvan ti âmalaka-hari*t*akâna*m* kasâva*m* (B.). Compare Mahâvagga VI, 4.

[3] Pa*t*ibhâna-*k*itta*m*. The Bhikkhunîs were forbidden by the 41st Pâ*k*ittiya of the Bhikkhunî-vibhaṅga to go and see such paintings. (Sutta-vibhaṅga II, 298, where a picture gallery, *K*ittâgâra, belonging to King Pasenadi of Kosala, is mentioned.) We are not quite sure of the connotation of the term, which appears to imply some reproach. Perhaps it means 'suggestive.' Figures as such were not forbidden; and remains of statues and bas reliefs erected in the Vihâras, illustrative of every-day life, have been found in great numbers. In the introductory story to the 26th Pâ*k*ittiya it certainly means 'indecent.'

women. Whosoever does so, shall be guilty of a dukka*t*a. I allow you, O Bhikkhus, representations of wreaths and creepers and bone hooks and cupboards[1].'

3. Now at that time the Vihâras had too low a basement (&c., as in V, 11, 6 as to roofing, stairs, and balustrade).

Now at that time the Vihâras were crowded with people[2]. The Bhikkhus were ashamed to lie down to sleep.

'I allow you, O Bhikkhus, the use of curtains.'

They lifted up the curtains and looked in.

They told this matter to the Blessed One.

'I allow you, O Bhikkhus, to put up a lath and plaster wall half the height of the Vihâra.'

They looked on from over this half-wall.

'I allow you, O Bhikkhus, to make inner chambers of three kinds—chambers in shape like a palankeen[3], chambers in shape like a quart measure[4], and chambers on an upper storey[5].'

---

[1] All these words occur above at V, 11, 6, and V, 14, 4. The meaning of the two last is very doubtful. Perhaps it is intended that these should occupy the space on the walls instead of any ornamentation.

[2] Âlakamandâ, literally, 'like Kuvera's city in heaven.' Buddhaghosa tells us why. Â*l*akamandâ ti ekaṅganâ manussâbhikin*n*â. Âkin*n*a-yakkhâ, corresponding to this last word, recurs in the standing description of Â*l*akamandâ at Mahâ-parinibbâna Sutta V, 43 = Mahâ Sudassana Sutta I, 3. The name of the city is spelt in both those passages with *l* not l.

[3] Sivikâ-gabbho ti *k*aturassa-gabbho says Buddhaghosa.

[4] Nâ*l*ikâ-gabbho ti vitthârato dvigu*n*a-tigu*n*-âyâmo dîgha-gabbho (B.). That na*l*ikâ is used like nâ*l*i for a bushel measure follows from a comparison of *G*âtaka I, 124, last lines, with I, 126, line 3.

[5] Hammiya-gabbho ti âkâsa-tale ku*t*âgâra-gabbho muda*nd*a-

Now at that time the Bhikkhus made inner chambers in the middle of small Vihâras, and there was no room to move about in.

They told this matter to the Blessed One.

'I allow you, O Bhikkhus, to make the inner chambers at one side of small Vihâras, and in the middle of large ones [1].'

4. Now at that time the lower part of the lath and plaster wall of the Vihâra decayed.

They told this matter to the Blessed One.

'I allow you, O Bhikkhus, buttresses of timber [2].'

Rain leaked through on to the lath and plaster wall of the Vihâra [3].

'I allow you, O Bhikkhus, a protecting arrangement [4] and cement [5].'

Now at that time a snake fell from the roof on to the back of a certain Bhikkhu. He was terrified, and made an outcry [6]. The Bhikkhus, running up, said to that Bhikkhu: 'Why, Sir, do you make an outcry?' Then that Bhikkhu told the matter to

---

*kkh*adana-gabbho vâ (B.). Compare our note on Mahâvagga I, 30, 4.

[1] There is a similar injunction at V, 14, 3, with respect to fire-places in bath-rooms.

[2] Kulanka-pâdaka*m*. See Buddhaghosa's note at p. 321 of the edition of the text. The remedy here is different from that provided in the similar case, at V, 14, 3, with respect to bath-houses.

[3] On the use of ovassati compare V, 16, 1, and VIII, 3, 3.

[4] Parittâna-ki*t*ikan ti tassa parittânattha*m* ki*t*ika*m* is all that Buddhaghosa says. Compare the end of § 5.

[5] Uddha-sudhan ti va*kkh*aka-gomayena *k*a *kh*arikâya *k*a saddhi*m* maddita-matika*m* (B.).

[6] Vissara*m* akâsi. See the note on *K*ullavagga VIII, 1, 1, where the whole incident is similar.

the Bhikkhus, and they told the matter to the Blessed One.

'I allow you, O Bhikkhus, a ceiling-cloth.'

5. Now at that time the Bhikkhus hung their bags at the feet of the bedsteads, and at the feet of the chairs; and they were gnawed by the mice and white ants.

They told this matter to the Blessed One.

'I allow you, O Bhikkhus, pins in the wall, and bone hooks[1].'

Now at that time the Bhikkhus laid aside their robes on the bedsteads and on the chairs, and the robes were torn.

They told this matter to the Blessed One.

'I allow you, O Bhikkhus, bamboos to hang your robes on, and strings to hang your robes on[2].'

Now at that time the Vihâras had no verandahs, and no defences[3].

They told this matter to the Blessed One.

'I allow you, O Bhikkhus, verandahs[4], covered terraces[5], inner verandahs[6], and over-hanging eaves[7].'

---

[1] The use of these has been already referred to at V, 9, 5.

[2] These have already been allowed in *K*ullavagga V, 11, 6, and V, 14, 3. The license under the present rule extends only to their use in Vihâras.

[3] Apa*t*issaranâ, which must have some special, technical, meaning unknown to us. Buddhaghosa says nothing.

[4] Âlindo nâma pamukha*m* vu*kk*ati (B.). Compare Abhidhâna-ppadîpikâ, verse 218.

[5] Paghana*m* nâma ya*m* nikkhamantâ *k*a pavisantâ *k*a pâdehi hananti. Tassa vihâra-dvâre ubhato ku*tt*am (?) niharitvâ kata-padesass' eta*m* adhiva*k*ana*m*. Paghânan ti pi vu*kk*ati (B.).

[6] Paku*tt*an ti ma*ggh*e gabbhassa samantâ pariyâgâro vu*kk*ati. Paku*t*an ti pi pâ*th*o (B.).

[7] Osarako ti anâ*l*indake vihâre va*m*sa*m* datvâ tato da*nd*ake

The verandahs were too public; and the Bhikkhus were ashamed to lie down in them to sleep.

'I allow you, O Bhikkhus, an arrangement in form of a curtain that can be drawn aside[1], or an arrangement in form of a moveable screen[2].'

6. Now at that time the Bhikkhus, when taking their midday meal in the open air, were troubled by cold and heat.

They told this matter to the Blessed One.

'I allow you, O Bhikkhus, a Service Hall.'

The Service Hall had too low a basement (&c., as in V, 11, 6, down to the end).

Now at that time the Bhikkhus spread their robes out on the ground in the open air, and they became dirty.

'I allow, O Bhikkhus, bamboos to hang robes on, and strings to hang robes in, in the open air.

7. The water became warm.

'I allow, O Bhikkhus, a water-room and a water-shed.'

The water-room had too low a basement (&c., as in V, 11, 6, down to the end).

There were no vessels for the water.

'I allow, O Bhikkhus, chank shells and saucers for the water.'

8. Now at that time the Vihâras had no fence round them.

'I allow you, O Bhikkhus, to enclose them with

osâretvâ katam *kh*adana-pamukham (B.). At *G*âtaka III, 446, it is said of a dying man 'nîharitvâ osârake nipa*gg*âpesum.'

[1] Samsarana-ki*t*iko nâma *k*akkala-yutto ki*t*iko (B.). *K*akkala should be compared with *k*akkhalikâ at VI, 2, 2, and *k*akkhali at VI, 19.

[2] Ugghâ*t*ana-ki*t*iko, on which Buddhaghosa says nothing.

ramparts (Pâkâra) of three kinds—brick walls, stone walls, and wooden fences.'

There was no store-room [1].

'I allow, O Bhikkhus, a store-room.'

The store-room had too low a basement, and it was flooded with water.

'I allow you, O Bhikkhus, to make it with a high basement.'

The store-room had no door.

'I allow, O Bhikkhus, a door; with door-posts and lintel, with hollows like a mortar for the door to revolve in, with projections to revolve in those hollows, with rings on the door for the bolt to work along in, with a block of wood fixed into the edge of the door-post, and containing a cavity for the bolt to go into (called the Monkey's Head), with a pin to secure the bolt by, with a connecting bolt, with a key-hole, with a hole for a string with which the door may be closed, and with a string for that purpose [2].'

Grass and plaster fell from the store-room.

'I allow you, O Bhikkhus (&c., as in V, 14, 4, down to the end of V, 14, 5, as to roofing, flooring, drains, &c.).'

9. Now at that time the Bhikkhus made fire-places here and there in the Parive*n*a, and the Parive*n*a was covered with the remains of the fires [3].

---

[1] Ko*tth*aka. See our note above on V, 14, 4, as to the various allied meanings of this word. Perhaps 'gateway' should be chosen as the rendering here, as it clearly must be in the closely allied passage in the next section but one (§ 10). As the chamber supposed always to be built over the gateway could be used as a store-room, the difference is not very essential.

[2] The whole as above in V, 14, 3, where see the note.

[3] Uklâpo. On this use of the word compare *K*ullavagga VIII, 1, 3.

They told this matter to the Blessed One.

'I allow you, O Bhikkhus, to make a separate room for the fire at one side.'

The fire-room had too low a basement (&c., as in V, 11, 6, as to flooring, stairs, and balustrade, followed by the paragraph as to the door, and the facing, as in V, 14, 3, &c.).

10. Now at that time the Ârâmas had no fences to them, and goats and cattle injured the plantations[1].

They told this matter to the Blessed One.

'I allow you, O Bhikkhus, to surround them with fencing of three kinds—bamboo fences, thorn fences, and ditches.'

There was no gateway (ko*tth*aka), and goats and cattle, even so, injured the plantations.

'I allow, O Bhikkhus, a gateway, with gates made of stakes interlaced with thorny brakes[2], with fences (across the gateway) made of the akka plant[3], with ornamental screen-work over the gateway[4], and with bars.'

[Then the paragraphs allowing the roofing, &c., of this ko*tth*aka as in V, 11, 6, and drains for the Ârâma, as in V, 14, 3.]

11. Now at that time Seniya Bimbisâra, the king of Magadha, wanted to build a pâsâda[5] (residence),

---

[1] Uparope. Compare Uparopaka at *G*âtaka II, 345.

[2] Apesiyam. See p. 321 of the edition of the text, reading of course ka*nth*aka.

[3] Akkavâ*t*a, on which Buddhaghosa says nothing. A kind of dress made from the stalks of the akka plant is mentioned in Mahâvagga VIII, 28, 2.

[4] Tosa*n*a, which is the ornamental erection over a gateway of which such excellent examples in stone have been found at the Sânchi and Bharhut Topes.

[5] The exact meaning of the word Pâsâda at the time when this

covered with cement and clay, for the use of the Sa*m*gha. And it occurred to the Bhikkhus, 'What kind of roof now has been allowed by the Blessed One, and what kind of roof has not been allowed?'

They told this matter to the Blessed One.

'I allow, O Bhikkhus, roofing of five kinds—brick roofing, stone roofing, cement roofing, straw roofing, and roofing of leaves.'

End of the First Bhâ*n*avâra (or Portion for Recitation).

4.

1. Now at that time the householder Anâtha Pi*nd*ika was the husband of the sister of the Râ*g*agaha Se*tth*i. And Anâtha Pi*nd*ika the householder went to Râ*g*agaha on some business or other. Now at that time the Sa*m*gha, with the Buddha at its head, had been bidden by the Se*tth*i of Râ*g*agaha for the morrow's meal. And the Se*tth*i of Râ*g*agaha gave command to his slaves and work-people, saying, 'So get up at early morn, my men, and cook congey, and cook rice, and prepare curries, and prepare delicacies[1]!'

book was written has not yet been precisely ascertained. In later times it meant a building of several storeys, each successive storey being smaller in superficial area than the one immediately beneath it. Compare the Mahâ-loha-pâsâda so often mentioned in the Mahâva*m*sa (pp. 161–257), the stone pillars of the lowest stories of which are still one of the sights of Anurâdhapura.

[1] Uttari-bhaṅga*m*. Childers sub voce uttari is in doubt what the meaning of this phrase is. It is no longer uncertain that the word means 'delicacy' of some sort. Whether the term was more

And it occurred to Anâtha Pi*nd*ika the householder, 'Now formerly this householder was wont, when I arrived, to lay aside all other business, and exchange the greetings of courtesy with me; but now he appears excited, and is giving orders to his slaves and work-people. How can it be? Is he taking in marriage, or is he giving in marriage, or has he set a great sacrifice on foot, or has he invited the Mâgadhan Seniya Bimbisâra, together with his retinue, for to-morrow's meal?'

2. Now when the Se*tth*i of Râ*g*agaha had given commandment to his slaves and his work-people, he went up to the place where Anâtha Pi*nd*ika the householder was, and exchanged with him the greetings of courtesy, and took his seat on one side. And when he was so seated, Anâtha Pi*nd*ika the householder [told him the thoughts that had passed through his mind].

'I am neither taking nor giving in marriage, O householder' (was the reply), 'nor have I invited the Mâgadhan Seniya Bimbisâra to to-morrow's meal. But a great sacrifice I have set on foot, for the Sa*m*gha, with the Buddha at its head, has been invited for to-morrow's meal at my house.'

'Did you, O householder, say "the Buddha?"'

'Yes, it was "the Buddha" that I said.'

precise, and denoted some particular delicacy or not, is still doubtful. Compare the passages quoted in our note above on Mahâvagga VI, 14, 3 (adding *G*âtaka I, 186, and *K*ullavagga IV, 4, 5, VIII, 4, 4), which show that it was eaten with boiled rice or congey; is mentioned along with ghee and oil; and could be made from the flesh (or other parts) of a sucking-pig. If it were not for the latter circumstance (*G*âtaka I, 197) it might well be pickles or chutney.

[And thrice the same question was put, and the same reply was given.]

'Hard is it, O householder, to meet even with the mere expression in the world—the news, that is, of "a Buddha, a Buddha[1]." Would it be possible for us, at this very time, to go and visit that Blessed One, the Arahat, the very Buddha[2]?'

'It is not now, O householder, the proper time to pay a visit to the Blessed One; but early on the morrow you shall go and visit him.'

Then Anâtha Pi*nd*ika, pondering of the visit he was about to pay, lay down to sleep with his thoughts so bent upon the Buddha that thrice in the night he arose, thinking the daylight had appeared.

3. And Anâtha Pi*nd*ika the householder went up to the gate leading to the Sîtavana, and celestial beings opened the gate. And as he emerged from the city, the light disappeared and a thick darkness arose, and fear and trembling and consternation sprang up within him, so that a longing came upon him to turn back again from that spot. But Sîvaka the Yakkha, himself the while invisible, caused a sound to be heard, saying:

'A hundred elephants, a hundred steeds, a hundred chariots with mules[3],

'A hundred thousand virgins with their jewelled earrings on,—

---

[1] 'Much more so with the reality' is to be understood. Compare Mahâ-parinibbâna Sutta VI, 63 (at the end).

[2] On this rendering of Sammâ-sambuddha*m*, see Rh. D.'s 'Hibbert Lectures,' pp. 145–147.

[3] Assatari. Compare va*kkh*atarî at Mahâvagga V, 9, 1, 3. The word recurs below at VII, 2, 5.

'These are not worth, O householder, the sixteenth portion of one single stride.

'Go on, go on, O householder! Advance, and not retreat, shall profit thee.'

Then the darkness disappeared before Anâtha Pi*nd*ika the householder, and a bright light arose, and the fear and trembling and consternation that had sprung upon within him were appeased.

[And a second and a third time the same thing happened, and the same words were heard, and with the same result.]

4. And Anâtha Pi*nd*ika the householder arrived at the Sîtavana; and at that time the Blessed One, who had arisen at early dawn, was walking up and down (meditating) in the open air. And the Blessed One saw Anâtha Pi*nd*ika the householder when he was coming from afar; and the Blessed One left the place where he had been walking up and down, and sat himself down on the seat put out for him. And when he was so seated, he addressed Anâtha Pi*nd*ika the householder, and said:

'Come hither, Sudatta!'

Then Anâtha Pi*nd*ika, glad and happy at the thought that the Blessed One had addressed him by his name, went up to the place where the Blessed One was, and bowed down before him, falling at his feet, and said:

'I trust my lord the Blessed One has slept in peace!'

'He ever sleeps in peace, the Arahat who is free[1],

[1] Brâhma*n*o parinibbuto. To translate the first of these words by 'Brahman' would mislead English readers. It is constantly used in early Buddhist texts for Arahat. On the use of

'Who is not touched by lusts, but calm and free from sin[1],

'Has broken all the bars (to freedom of the mind)[2], has quenched the anguish in his heart,

'Has fixed peace in his mind, and peaceful, sleeps in peace[3].'

5[4]. Then the Blessed One discoursed to Anâtha Pi*nd*ika the householder in due order; that is to say, he spake to him of giving, of righteousness, of heaven, of the danger, the vanity, and the defilement of lusts, and of the advantages of renunciation. And when the Blessed One saw that Anâtha Pi*nd*ika the householder had become prepared, softened, unprejudiced, and upraised and believing in heart, then he proclaimed that which is the special doctrine of the Buddhas; that is to say, Suffering, its Origin, its Cessation, and the Path. And just as a clean cloth from which all stain has been washed away will readily take the dye, just even so did Anâtha

---

parinibbuto not in the sense of 'dead,' but of a living man in the sense of 'spiritually free,' compare Dhammapada, verse 89; Sutta Nipâta II, 13, 1, 12, III, 12, 35; and Mahâ-parinibbâna Sutta IV, 3.

[1] Nirûpadhi, i.e. free from Kâma, Kilesa, and Kamma.

[2] Sabbâ âsattiyo *kh*etvâ. Having cut or broken all the âsatti's (from the root sa*ñ*g, to hang), the things which hang on to and burden a man in his spiritual progress. Compare the figure of speech at *G*âtaka I, 5 (âsatta*m* ku*n*apa*m* *kh*addetvâ). Buddhaghosa says sabbâ âsattiyo *kh*etvâ ti . . . . hadaye daratha*m* *k*itte kilesa-daratha*m* *g*inetvâ.

[3] Vineyya and appuya are no doubt gerunds. In a corresponding passage of the Aṅguttara Nikâya the Phayre MS. reads appeyya, which smoothes over a difficulty at the expense of the better reading.

[4] The following section is in identical terms with Mahâvagga I, 7, 5, 10, V, 1, 9, 10, VI, 26, 8, 9.

Pi*nd*ika the householder obtain, even while sitting there, the pure and spotless Eye of the Truth; (that is to say, the knowledge that) whatsoever has a beginning, in that is inherent also the necessity of dissolution. Thus did Anâtha Pi*nd*ika the householder see, and master, and understand, and penetrate the Truth; and he overcame uncertainty, and dispelled all doubts, and gained full knowledge, becoming dependent upon no one else for his knowledge of the doctrine of the Teacher. And he addressed the Blessed One, and said:

'Most excellent, Lord (are the words of thy mouth), most excellent! Just as if a man were to set up that which is thrown down, or were to reveal that which is hidden away, or were to point out the right road to him who has gone astray, or were to bring a light into the darkness so that those who had eyes could see external forms—just even so, Lord, has the Truth been made known to me, in many a figure, by the Blessed One. And I, even I, betake myself, Lord, to the Blessed One as my refuge, to the Truth, and to the Order. May the Blessed One accept me as a disciple, as one who, from this day forth as long as life endures, has taken his refuge in him. And may the Blessed One consent to accept at my hand the to-morrow's meal for himself and for his Order of Bhikkhus.'

Then the Blessed One, by silence, granted his consent. And when Anâtha Pi*nd*ika the householder perceived that his request had been granted, he rose from his seat, and bowed down before the Blessed One, and keeping him on his right hand as he passed him, he departed thence.

6. Now the Se*tth*i of Râ*g*agaha heard that the

Order of Bhikkhus which has the Buddha at its head had been invited by Anâtha Pi*nd*ika the householder for the morrow's meal. And the Se*tth*i of Râ*g*agaha said to Anâtha Pi*nd*ika the householder: 'They say, O householder, that you have invited the Bhikkhu-sa*m*gha, with the Buddha at its head, for the morrow's meal, and you are but a stranger here. I will provide the means[1], O householder, for you to provide the Order of Bhikkhus, which has the Buddha at its head, with food.'

'It is not necessary, O householder; I have means sufficient for the purpose.'

[And the townsman of Râ*g*agaha[2], and Seniya Bimbisâra the Râ*g*a of Magadha, made the same offer in the same words, and received the same reply.]

7. Then Anâtha Pi*nd*ika the householder, when the night was far spent, made ready in the house of the Se*tth*i of Râ*g*agaha sweet food both hard and soft, and had the time announced to the Blessed One, saying, 'The time, Lord, has come; and the meal is ready.'

And the Blessed One, when he had dressed himself in the early morning, went duly bowled and

---

[1] Veyyâyika*m* formed from vyaya, expenditure. Veyyâyikan ti vayakara*n*a*m* vu*kk*ati (B.).

[2] Râ*g*agahako negamo. This person has been already mentioned, and there also in intimate connection with the Se*tth*i of Râ*g*agaha, in the Mahâvagga VIII, 1, 2, 16. It is tolerably clear from the connection that this is no ordinary citizen, but one holding a distinct and semi-official position. In this respect the word is an exact parallel to its neighbour the Se*tth*i. For instances of the word in its more general sense, see Ka*kk*âyana (ed. Senart), p. 219, and Dâ*th*âva*m*sa III, 3.

robed to the house of the Se*tth*i of Râ*g*agaha, and sat down there on the seat spread out for him, together with the Order of Bhikkhus. And Anâtha Pi*nd*ika the householder offered to the Order of Bhikkhus which had the Buddha at its head the sweet food both hard and soft, waiting upon them with his own hand[1]. And when the Blessed One had finished his meal, and had cleansed his hands and his bowl, Anâtha Pi*nd*ika took his seat on one side; and, so seated, he said to the Blessed One: 'May the Blessed One consent to spend the rainy season of Was at Sâvatthi, together with the Order of Bhikkhus.'

'The Tathâgatas, O householder, take pleasure in solitude.'

'I understand, O Blessed One; I understand, O Happy One' (was the reply)[2].

Then the Blessed One, after he had instructed and aroused and incited and gladdened Anâtha Pi*nd*ika the householder with religious discourse, arose from his seat, and departed thence.

8. Now at that time Anâtha Pi*nd*ika the householder had many friends and large acquaintance, and his word was held of weight[3]. When he had

---

[1] Compare the note on Mahâvagga I, 8, 4.

[2] Aññâta*m* bhagavâ aññâta*m* sugatâ ti. The first word is the standing expression used when the Buddha or a Thera has signified a request, not in so many words, but in some phrase from which the request may be implied, and the person addressed desires to express that he has perceived the intended implication. Compare Dîpava*m*sa XIV, 65, XV, 5.

[3] Âdeyyavâ*k*o ti tassa va*k*ana*m* bahu*g*anâ mânetabba*m* maññantî ti attho (B.). In Puggala III, 11, we have the phrase tassa va*k*ana*m* âdheyya*m* ga*kkh*ati, which the commentary explains by hadaye âdhâtabba*m* *th*apitabba*m*.

brought the business he had in hand at Râ*g*agaha to its conclusion, he set out towards Sâvatthi; and on the way he gave orders to people, saying, 'Build dwellings, my good men, and make rest-houses ready, and prepare gifts. A Buddha has appeared in the world, and that Blessed One has been invited by me, and by this road will he come.' And those people [did all even as they were commanded].

And when Anâtha Pi*nd*ika the householder had arrived at Sâvatthi, he examined all the region round about it, saying[1], 'Where now shall I fix the place for the Blessed One to stay in, not too far from the town and not too near, convenient for going and for coming, easily accessible for all who wish to visit him, by day not too crowded, by night not exposed to too much noise and alarm, protected from the wind[2], hidden from men, well fitted for a retired life?'

9. And Anâtha Pi*nd*ika the householder saw that the garden of *G*eta the Kumâra had [all these advantages]. And when he saw that, he went to *G*eta the Kumâra, and said to him, 'Sir, let me have your garden to make an Ârâma on it.'

'It is not, Sir, for sale, even for (a sum so great that the pieces of money would be sufficient to cover it if they were) laid side by side.'

'I take, Sir, the garden at the price.'

'No, O householder, there was no bargain meant[3].'

---

[1] The following speech is identical with that put into Bimbisâra's mouth on choosing the Ve*l*uvana, above Mahâvagga I, 22, 16, 17.

[2] Viganavâta*m*, of which neither the reading nor the meaning is certain. See the various forms given from the commentaries in the notes on the text of the passage in the Mahâvagga, loc. cit.

[3] Na gahito: literally, 'it is not taken.'

Then they asked the lords of justice whether a bargain of sale had been made or not. And the lords decided thus: 'The Ârâma is taken, Sir, at the price which you fixed.'

And Anâtha Pi*nd*ika the householder had gold brought down in carts, and covered the *G*etavana with (pieces) laid side by side[1].

10. Now the gold that he had brought down the first time did not suffice (after the rest of the garden was covered) to cover one small space close by the gateway. So Anâtha Pi*nd*ika the householder told his servants to go back and fetch more gold, saying he would cover that piece also.

Then thought *G*eta the Kumâra, 'This can be no ordinary matter[2], for which this householder is ready to lavish so much gold!' And he said to Anâtha Pi*nd*ika the householder, 'It is enough, O householder. You need not have that space covered. Let me have that space, and it shall be my gift.'

Then Anâtha Pi*nd*ika the householder thought[3], 'This *G*eta the Kumâra is a very distinguished and illustrious person. Great would be the efficacy of the adherence of so well known a man as he to this doctrine and discipline.' And he gave up that

[1] It is evident from the illustration of this story on a bas relief at the Bharhut Tope that these pieces of money were supposed to be square, not round. See Cunningham's 'The Stûpa of Bharhut,' Plate No. LVII and pp. 84–86.

[2] Na oraka*m* bhavissati. Compare Mahâvagga I, 9, 1, and the commencement of our next chapter below. The idiom recurs in VII, 3, 3.

[3] The following phrase is identical with that put into the mouth of Ânanda, at Mahâvagga VI, 36, 3, with respect to Roga the Malla. In the text here there is a slight misprint; the full-stop after *ñ*âtamanusso should be struck out.

space to *G*eta the Kumâra. And *G*eta the Prince erected thereon a gateway, with a room over it.

And Anâtha Pi*nd*ika the householder built[1] dwelling-rooms, and retiring-rooms, and store-rooms (over the gateways), and service halls, and halls with fire-places in them, and storehouses (outside the Vihâra)[2], and closets, and cloisters, and halls for exercise, and wells, and sheds for the well[3], and bath-rooms, and halls attached to the bath-rooms, and ponds, and open-roofed sheds[4].

5.

1. Now when the Blessed One had stayed at Râ*g*agaha as long as he thought fit, he set out towards Vesâlî; and journeying straight on he in due course arrived there. And there at Vesâlî the Blessed One stayed in the peak-roofed hall at the Mahâvana.

Now at that time the people were zealously engaged in putting up new buildings (for the use of the Order)[5], and as zealously provided with the

---

[1] With the following list should be compared the list of things that laymen build for themselves given in Mahâvagga III, 5, 7.

[2] Kappiya-ku*t*iyo. See Mahâvagga VI, 33.

[3] Udapâna-sâlâyo. See above, V, 16, 2.

[4] Ma*nd*ape. See Mahâvagga VIII, 7, 1, and above, *K*ullavagga VI, 3, 7.

[5] Navakamma*m* karonti. This idiom always connotes buildings for the use of the Order. See the passages quoted in our note on *K*ullavagga I, 18, 1. If the buildings were for the Bhikkhus, then a Bhikkhu, if for the Bhikkhunîs, then a Bhikkhunî, was appointed to superintend the works in order to ensure the

requisite clothes, and food, and lodging, and medicine for the sick, all such Bhikkhus as superintended their work.

Now a certain poor tailor thought, 'This can be no every-day matter on which the people are so zealously engaged. Let me too set to work on a new building.' And that poor tailor himself kneaded the clay, and laid the bricks, and raised the walls. But by his want of experience the laying was out of line and the wall fell down. And a second and a third time he [repeated his work, and with the same result].

2. Then that poor tailor murmured, was annoyed, and became indignant, saying, 'These Sakyaputtiya Sama*n*as exhort and teach those men who provide them with the requisite clothes, food, lodging, and medicine, and superintend their buildings for them. But I am poor, and no one exhorts or teaches me, or helps me in my building!'

The Bhikkhus heard him so murmuring, and told the matter to the Blessed One. Then the Blessed One on that occasion and in that connection made a religious discourse, and gave command to the Bhikkhus, saying, 'I permit you, O Bhikkhus, to give new buildings in course of erection (for the use of the Order) in charge (to a Bhikkhu who shall superintend[1] the work). And the Bhikkhu who

---

buildings being in accordance with the rules of the Order as to size, form, and object of the various apartments.

The buildings referred to in this section are no doubt intended to be the same as those referred to in *K*ullavagga V, 13, 3.

[1] Navakamma*m* dâtu*m*. For the works which ought not to be included, and for those which might be lawfully included in this term, see below, *K*ullavagga VI, 17. Hence the overseer is called navakammika.

is overseer shall zealously exert himself to the end that the work on the Vihâra may be brought to a rapid conclusion, and shall afterwards cause repairs to be executed wherever the buildings have become broken or worn out[1].

3. 'And thus, O Bhikkhus, is the work to be given in charge. In the first place a Bhikkhu is to be asked (whether he will undertake the duty). When he has been asked, some able and discreet Bhikkhu is to lay the matter before the Sa*m*gha, saying, "Let the venerable Sa*m*gha hear me. If the time seems meet to the Sa*m*gha, let the Sa*m*gha give in charge to such and such a Bhikkhu the Vihâra of such and such a householder as a navakamma*m*. This is the motion (*ñ*atti). Let the venerable Sa*m*gha hear me. The Sa*m*gha hereby gives in charge . . . . (&c., as before). Whosoever of the venerable ones approves thereof, let him keep silence; whosoever approves not thereof, let him speak. The Sa*m*gha has given in charge . . . . (&c., as before). Therefore is it silent. Thus do I understand."'

6[2].

1. Now when the Blessed One had stayed as long as he thought fit at Vesâlî he set out towards Sâvatthi.

---

[1] Kha*nd*an ti bhinnokâso: phullan ti phalitokâso (B.). The expression recurs below at VI, 17, 1.

[2] The incident related in the following chapter is identical with the 37th *G*âtaka (including the Introductory Story there given) already translated by Rh. D. in the 'Buddhist Birth Stories,' pp. 310-314.

Now at that time the pupils of the *Kh*abbaggiya Bhikkhus went on in front of the Bhikkhu-sa*m*gha which had the Buddha at its head, and occupied the rooms, and occupied the sleeping-places, saying, 'This will do for our superiors (upa*ggh*âyas), this for our teachers (â*k*ariyas), this for ourselves.' And the venerable Sâriputta who had followed after the Bhikkhu-sa*m*gha which had the Buddha at its head since all the rooms and all the sleeping-places had been occupied, found no place to sleep in, and took his seat at the foot of a certain tree.

Now the Blessed One, at early dawn, after he had risen, coughed. The venerable Sâriputta coughed also.

'Who is this?' (said the Blessed One.)

'It is I, Lord; Sâriputta.'

'How do you come to be sitting here, Sâriputta?'

Then the venerable Sâriputta told the matter to the Blessed One.

2. Then the Blessed One on that occasion and in that connection convened a meeting of the Bhikkhu-sa*m*gha, and asked, 'Is it true, as I have been told, O Bhikkhus, that the pupils of the *Kh*abbaggiya Bhikkhus have (acted in this way)?'

'It is true, Lord.'

Then the Blessed One rebuked them, saying (as usual, see *K*ullavagga I, 1, 2, 3), and he said to the Bhikkhus, 'Who is it, O Bhikkhus, who is worthy of the best seat, and the best water, and the best food?'

Some of the Bhikkhus said, 'One who belonged to a Kshatriya family before he entered the Order.' Others of the Bhikkhus said, 'One who belonged to a Brahman family before he entered the Order.' Others again said, 'One who belonged to a Gahapati[1] family before he entered the Order—one versed in the Suttas—one versed in the Rules of the Order—an expounder of the Dhamma[2]—one who has attained the first, second, third, fourth *Gh*âna—one who has entered the first, second, third Path—an Arahat—one who has the threefold wisdom[3]—one who has the six powers[4].'

3. Then the Blessed One addressed the Bhikkhus, and said, 'Long ago, O Bhikkhus, there was a great banyan tree on the lower slopes of the Himâlaya range; and near it there dwelt three friends—a partridge, a monkey, and an elephant. And they dwelt together without mutual reverence, confidence, and courtesy[5]. Then, O Bhikkhus, it occurred to those friends, "Come now, let us find out which of us is the elder by birth; and let us agree to honour and reverence and esteem and support him, and by his counsels let us abide." So, Bhikkhus, the partridge and the monkey asked the elephant,

'"How far back can you, friend, remember?"

'"Friends! when I was little I used to walk over

---

[1] On this mention of gahapati as the name of a caste or rank, compare the passage in the Tevi*gg*a Sutta I, 47 = Sâma*ññ*aphala Sutta, p. 133 (translated by Rh. D. in 'Buddhist Suttas from the Pâli,' S. B. E. vol. xi, p. 187), where the word is opposed to a*ññ*atarasmi*m* kule pa*kk*âgâto.

[2] Dhamma is here possibly already used in the special sense to which the term Abhidhamma was afterwards applied. So Pu*nn*a, who in the Aṅguttara Nikâya I, 14, is called the chief of the expounders of the Dhamma (compare Dîpava*m*sa IV, 4), says of himself in the Apadâna abhidhammanaya*ññ*o 'ha*m*.

[3] Tevi*gg*o. See Rh. D.'s remarks in 'Buddhist Suttas,' pp. 161, 162.

[4] This list contains one or two terms which are omitted in the *G*âtaka introduction.

[5] These terms recur at Mahâvagga I, 25, 6.

this banyan tree, keeping it between my thighs, and its topmost twig brushed against my stomach. So far back, friends, can I remember."

'Then, O Bhikkhus, the partridge and the elephant asked the monkey [the same question],

'"Friends! when I was little, sitting once on the ground, I gnawed at the then topmost twig of this banyan. So far back can I remember."

'Then, O Bhikkhus, the monkey and the elephant asked the partridge [the same question],

'"Friends! there was formerly a lofty banyan tree in yonder open space. One day after eating one of its fruits, I voided the seed here; and from that this banyan tree grew up. So I must be older than either of you."

'Thereupon, O Bhikkhus, the elephant and the monkey said to the partridge, "You, friend, are the oldest of us all. Henceforth we will honour and reverence and esteem and support you, and by your counsels will we abide."

'Thenceforth, O Bhikkhus, the partridge kept the monkey and the elephant in obedience to the Five Precepts, and observed them also himself. And dwelling together in mutual reverence, confidence, and courtesy, at the dissolution of the body after death they were reborn unto a happy state in heaven. And this (perfect life of theirs) became known as "the good life of the partridge [1]."

'Tis those who reverence the old
That are the men who Dhamma know,

---

[1] Tittiriya*m* brahma*k*ariya*m*. It is quite possible that a covert sarcasm is here intended to be understood against the Taittirîya Brahmans.

Worthy of praise while in this life
And happy in the life to come.

4. 'So that, O Bhikkhus, since even animals can live together in mutual reverence, confidence, and courtesy, so much more, O Bhikkhus, should you so let your light shine forth[1] that you, who have left the world to follow so well taught a doctrine and discipline, may be seen to dwell in like manner together.' And when he had delivered a religious discourse (as in I, 1, 3), he said to the Bhikkhus:

'I enjoin upon you, O Bhikkhus, that paying of reverence, rising up in reverence, salutation, proper respect, and apportionment of the best seat and water and food, shall be according to seniority. But property belonging to the Sa*m*gha shall not be exclusively appropriated according to seniority[2]. Whosoever does so, shall be guilty of a dukka*t*a.

5. 'These ten, O Bhikkhus, are not to be saluted —a Bhikkhu afterwards admitted unto the higher grade of the Order by one previously admitted—a person not admitted—a senior Bhikkhu when he belongs to a different community, and does not speak according to the Dhamma—a woman[3]—a eunuch[4]—a Bhikkhu who has been placed under probation[5]—one who, having been so placed, is

[1] Ta*m* sobhetha ya*m* . . . . On this idiom compare Mahâvagga X, 2, 20.

[2] Compare chapter 7 and also chapter 12. It would seem from these passages that the prohibition to reserve exclusively according to seniority the use of property belonging to the whole Sa*m*gha was held to imply that the temporary use of it was to go according to seniority. Compare X, 18.

[3] See *K*ullavagga X, 3.

[4] Compare Mahâvagga I, 61, 2.

[5] See *K*ullavagga II, 1, 2.

liable to be thrown back to the beginning of his probationary term[1]—one who is liable to have a penance (Mânatta) imposed upon him—one who is undergoing a penance—one who, so undergoing a penance, is fit to be rehabilitated.

'And these three, O Bhikkhus, ought to be saluted—one previously admitted into the higher grade of the Order by one afterwards admitted—the senior in a different community when he speaks according to the Dhamma—and, O Bhikkhus, throughout the worlds of men and gods, of Mâras and of Brahmas, by all creatures Sama*n*as and Brâhmans, gods and men, the Arahat Sammâsambuddha.'

7.

1. Now at that time people provided arbours (ma*nd*apas), and couches, and room for the use of the Sa*m*gha. And the pupils of the *Kh*abbaggiya Bhikkhus, saying, 'It has been laid down by the Blessed One that that which pertains (wholly) to the Sa*m*gha shall be used according to seniority, but not that which is given only for the temporary use of the Sa*m*gha,' went on in front of the Sa*m*gha and occupied the ma*nd*apas, and occupied the couches, and occupied the room, saying, 'This shall be for our superiors, and this for our teachers, and this for ourselves.'

And Sâriputta (&c., as in last chapter, §§ 1, 2, down to) Then the Blessed One rebuked them, &c., and said to the Bhikkhus, 'Even that which has been set aside only for the temporary use of

[1] See *K*ullavagga III, 14.

the Sa*m*gha is not, O Bhikkhus, to be reserved for exclusive use according to seniority.'

8.

1. Now at that time people arranged in the eating-rooms, or in the interior courtyards of their houses, lofty and large couches, such as [here follows the list of things forbidden in Mahâvagga V, 10, 4]. The Bhikkhus, fearing to offend, would not sit down upon them.

They told this thing to the Blessed One.

'I allow you, O Bhikkhus, to sit down on seats arranged by laymen—excepting three, (that is to say) large cushions, divans, mattresses [1]—but not to lie down upon them.'

Now at that time people put in the eating-rooms, or in the courtyards, stuffed couches and stuffed chairs. The Bhikkhus, fearing to offend, would not sit down on them.

They told this matter to the Blessed One.

'I allow you, O Bhikkhus, to sit down on any [such] things arranged by laymen, but not to lie down upon them [2].'

9.

1. Now the Blessed One, proceeding on his journey, arrived in due course at Sâvatthi; and there,

[1] These are Nos. 1, 2, and 7 in the list just referred to, and may be kept if treated in the way laid down in VI, 14, 2 below.

[2] This rule has already occurred in identical terms at Mahâvagga V, 11. Probably both here and there the word such, which we have here added in brackets, is to be understood.

at Sâvatthi, the Blessed One stayed in the *G*etavana, the park of Anâtha Pi*nd*ika. Then Anâtha Pi*nd*ika the householder [invited the Blessed One for the morrow's meal, and when the meal was over, he said to the Blessed One [1]]:

'What, Lord, shall I do with regard to the *G*etavana?'

'You may dedicate it, O householder, to the use of the Sa*m*gha of the four directions [2] either now here present, or hereafter to arrive.'

'Even so, Lord,' said Anâtha Pi*nd*ika the householder in assent to the Blessed One, and he did so.

2. Then the Blessed One gave thanks to Anâtha Pi*nd*ika the householder in these verses. [Here follow the same verses as were used above in VI, 1, 5 on the presentation of the *G*etavana [3].]

10.

1. Now at that time it had been settled that a certain high official at court, a follower of the Â*g*îvakas, should provide the day's meal for the Sa*m*gha. And the venerable Upananda the Sâkyan, coming late, but before the meal was over, made the Bhikkhu next (junior to him in seniority [4]) get

---

[1] The usual terms are here followed throughout: see, for instance, above, VI, 4, 6, 7.

[2] That is 'of all the world.' See our note above on Mahâvagga VIII, 27, 5, where the phrase has already occurred.

[3] The verses are quoted in the account of Anâtha Pi*nd*ika's gift given in the *G*âtaka commentary (Fausböll I, 93; Rh. D.'s 'Buddhist Birth Stories,' I, 131).

[4] Ânantarika*m*; perhaps 'the Bhikkhu (who happened to be)

up out of his seat; and the dining-hall was thrown into confusion.

Then that minister became indignant, murmured, and was annoyed: 'How can the Sakyaputtiya Samanas behave so! Is it not then lawful for any one, unless he have been seated, to eat as much as he requires?'

And the Bhikkhus heard him murmuring, &c. And they told the matter to the Blessed One.

'Is it true as they say, &c.?'

'It is true, Lord.'

Then the Blessed One rebuked him, &c., and he said to the Bhikkhus, 'A Bhikkhu is not, O Bhikkhus, to be made to get up out of his seat before the meal is over. Whosoever does so, shall be guilty of a dukkata. And if any one causes another to get up, and be then invited to partake of the meal, he shall be ordered to go and fetch water. If he shall thus receive the place, it is well; if not, the other one shall first complete his swallowing of the rice, and shall then give up the place to his senior. But in no case, O Bhikkhus, do I say that a place properly belonging to a senior Bhikkhu is to be taken (by a junior). Whosoever does so, shall be guilty of a dukkata[1].'

2. Now at that time the *Kh*abbaggiya Bhikkhus made sick Bhikkhus get up (from their seats). The sick men said, 'We cannot, Sirs, get up; for we are sick.'

'We insist upon your getting up,' said they; and

next (to him).' The text reads anantarikam, which is a misprint. Compare Mahâvagga IX, 4, 8, and *K*ullavagga VII, 3, 9, VIII, 4, 1.

[1] Compare the rule for Bhikkhunîs at X, 18.

seizing them, and pulling them up, they let them go as they were standing. The sick men, as soon as they were let go, fell down.

They told this matter to the Blessed One.

'A sick man, O Bhikkhus, is not to be made to get up. Whosoever does so, shall be guilty of a dukka*t*a.'

Now at that time the *Kh*abbaggiya Bhikkhus, saying, 'We are sick, and cannot be turned out,' took possession of the best sleeping-places.

They told this matter to the Blessed One.

'I enjoin, O Bhikkhus, that you allot to sick Bhikkhus suitable sleeping-places.'

Now at that time the *Kh*abbaggiya Bhikkhus, on pretext of some slight indisposition[1], took exclusive possession of sleeping-places.

They told this matter to the Blessed One.

'You are not, O Bhikkhus, to do so. Whosoever does so, shall be guilty of a dukka*t*a.'

11[2].

1. Now at that time the Sattarasa-vaggiya Bhikkhus made ready a certain large Vihâra in the neighbourhood[3], with the intention of dwelling in it. And when the *Kh*abbaggiya Bhikkhus saw what they were doing, they said: 'These venerable ones, the Sattarasa-vaggiya Bhikkhus, are

---

[1] Lesakappenâ ti appakena sîsâbâdhâdimattena (B.).

[2] The story in this section forms also the introductory story to the 17th Pâ*k*ittiya.

[3] Pa*kk*antima*m*; perhaps 'in the border-country.' Compare pa*kk*anta*m* nagara*m*, a frontier fort at Dhammapada, p. 56.

getting a Vihâra ready; come, let us turn them out.' Some of them said: 'Let us stay here[1] whilst they get it ready, and turn them out when it is prepared.' So the *Kh*abbaggiya Bhikkhus said to the Sattarasa-vaggiyas: 'Depart, Sirs; the Vihâra has fallen unto us.'

'Why did you not, Sirs, say so sooner; and we would have got some other one ready?'

'Is not, then, this Vihâra the common property of the Sa*m*gha?'

'Yes, Sirs; that is so.'

'Then depart, Sirs; for the Vihâra has fallen unto us.'

'It is large, Sirs, this Vihâra. You can dwell in it, and we as well.'

Then, full of anger and displeasure, they repeated, 'Depart, Sirs; this Vihâra has fallen unto us.' And seizing them by the throat, they cast them out. And the others, being ejected, wept.

The Bhikkhus asked, 'Why, Sirs, do you weep?'

Then they told them; and the moderate Bhikkhus murmured, &c., and told the matter to the Blessed One.

'Is it true, as they say, &c.?'

'It is true, Lord.'

Then he rebuked them; and when he had delivered a religious discourse, he said to the Bhikkhus:

'A Bhikkhu is not, O Bhikkhus, to be cast out of a Vihâra, the common property of the Sa*m*gha, in anger and vexation. Whosoever does so, shall

---

[1] Âgametha yâva. Compare the introductory story to the 46th Pâ*k*ittiya.

be dealt with according to the law[1]. I allow you, O Bhikkhus, to allot the lodging-places (common to the Sa*m*gha to those who have need of them)[2].'

2. Now the Bhikkhus thought, 'How then shall the lodging-places be allotted?'

They told this matter to the Blessed One.

'I allow you, O Bhikkhus, to appoint as an apportioner of lodging-places a Bhikkhu possessed of these five qualifications—one who does not walk in partiality, who does not walk in malice, who does not walk in stupidity, who does not walk in fear (and so on, as in Khandhaka IV, chapter 10, down to the end of the Kammavâ*k*â).'

3. Now the apportioners of lodging-places thought, 'How then ought the lodging-places to be apportioned?'

They told this matter to the Blessed One.

'I allow you, O Bhikkhus, in the first place to count the Bhikkhus, then to count the sleeping-places, then to apportion accordingly[3].'

When apportioning according to the number of sleeping-places, some remained unallotted[4].

---

[1] That is, under the 17th Pâ*k*ittiya.

[2] Senâsanam gâhetu*m*. Buddhaghosa has nothing on this idiom, but its meaning is sufficiently clear from the connection.

[3] Seyyaggena gâhetu*m*. Buddhaghosa has no special explanation of agga here, but in his explanation of the passage says that this is to be so done that each Bhikkhu receives room for a couch (mañ*k*a*tth*âna*m*). Agga must here be agra, to which Böhtlingk-Roth give, from Indian lexicographers, the subsidiary meaning of 'multitude.' So below in XII, 1, 1, the Va*gg*iputtakas divide money amongst themselves bhikkhu-aggena, 'according to the number of the Bhikkhus.' Seyyâ is here used in the same meaning as that in which senâsana is used throughout the rest of this chapter and the next. See VIII, 1, 4.

[4] Ussâdiyi*m*su. Buddhaghosa says ussârayi*m*sû ti mañ-

'I allow you, O Bhikkhus, to apportion according to the number of apartments (Vihâras).'

When so apportioning, some apartments (Vihâras) remained unallotted.

'I allow you, O Bhikkhus, to apportion according to the number of buildings (Parive*n*as)[1].'

When so apportioning, some buildings (Parive*n*as) remained unallotted.

'I allow you, O Bhikkhus, to give a supplementary share to each Bhikkhu[2].'

When more than one share had been allotted, another Bhikkhu arrived.

'In that case a share need not be allotted to him, if the Bhikkhus do not wish to do so[3].'

Now at that time they allotted sleeping-places to a Bhikkhu who was then staying outside the boundary (of the district in which the building was situate)[4].

They told this matter to the Blessed One.

---

*ka*ṭṭ*h*ânâni atirekâni ahesu*m*. His reading is in a copy of his work in Burmese characters, and is supported, both here and in Pâ*k*ittiya XLVI, 2, where the word recurs, by a Burmese copy of the text. The Sinhalese reading is the correct one, but one may compare the idiom *g*ana*m*, or parisa*m*, ussâreti at Mahâvagga VIII, 1, 22, and *G*âtaka I, 419, 434. So at IX, 1, 3, 4, the reading ussâreti given in the text is corrected at p. 363 into ussâdeti, in accordance with the reading of the Sinhalese MS.

[1] The relation of the Vihâra to the Parive*n*a is here curious. In the later language parive*n*a means 'cells.' Here it evidently includes several vihâras.

[2] Anubhâgan ti puna apara*m* pi bhâga*m* dâtu*m* (B.).

[3] Na akâmâ is used here in a sense precisely parallel to that in which it occurs at Mahâvagga VII, 24, 4. See the passages quoted in our note there.

[4] Nissîme *th*itassa. See on this phrase above, Mahâvagga VII, 1, 5, and VIII, 2, 3. It is repeated below, VI, 17, 2.

'You are not, O Bhikkhus, to [do so]. Whosoever does so, shall be guilty of a dukka*t*a.'

Now at that time the Bhikkhus, after the lodging-places had been allotted, kept them to the exclusion of others for all time.

They told this matter to the Blessed One.

'You are not, O Bhikkhus, to do so. Whosoever does so, shall be guilty of a dukka*t*a. I allow you to retain them for the three months of the rainy, but not for the dry season.'

4. Then the Bhikkhus thought, 'What is (it now that constitutes) an allotment of lodging-places?'

They told this matter to the Blessed One.

'There are these three allotments of lodging-places, O Bhikkhus,—the earlier, the later, and the intermediate. The earlier is to be held on the day after the full moon of Âsâ*lh*a (June—July); the later, a month after that full moon[1]; the intermediate (literally that which involves a giving up during the intervening time) is held on the day after the Pavâra*n*â ceremony, with reference to the rainy season of the following year. These, O Bhikkhus, are the three allotments of lodging-places.'

Here ends the Second Portion for Recitation.

12.

1. Now the venerable Upananda the Sâkyan, after having had a lodging allotted to him in

[1] These first two dates are the days on which the earlier and the later Vassa begins. See Mahâvagga III, 2.

Sâvatthi, went to a certain country-place where a community of the Sa*m*gha resided, and there also had a lodging allotted to him. Then the Bhikkhus there thought, 'Now this brother, Upananda the Sâkyan, is a maker of strife, quarrelsome, a maker of disputes, given to idle talk, a raiser of legal questions in the Sa*m*gha[1]. If he should spend the rainy season here, then shall we all dwell in discomfort. Come, let us question him.' And they asked the venerable Upananda the Sâkyan:

'Have not you, friend Upananda, had a lodging allotted to you in Sâvatthi?'

'That is so, Sirs.'

'What then do you, friend Upananda, being one, yet take exclusive possession of two (lodging-places)?'

'Well, I do now, Sirs, set (the lodging) here free, and take the one there.'

Those Bhikkhus who were moderate murmured, &c., and they told the matter to the Blessed One.

Then the Blessed One, on that occasion and in that connection, convened a meeting of the Bhikkhu-sa*m*gha, and asked the venerable Upananda the Sâkyan:

'Is it true, Upananda, that you, being one, have taken possession of two places?'

'It is true, Lord.'

Then the Blessed One rebuked him, saying, 'How can you, O foolish one, do such a thing? What you took there, O foolish one, has been lost here; what you took here, has been lost there[2]. Thus, O

[1] These are the acts which render a Bhikkhu liable to the Tagganiya Kamma. See *K*ullavagga I, 1, 1.

[2] That is, by taking a lodging here you ipso facto renounced

foolish one, you are deprived of both.' And when he had delivered a religious discourse, he said to the Bhikkhus:

'One man is not, O Bhikkhus, to take two lodging-places. Whosoever does so, shall be guilty of a dukka*t*a.'

13.

1. Now at that time the Blessed One spake in many a figure concerning the Vinaya, speaking in praise of the Vinaya, in praise of learning the Vinaya, and again and again in reference thereto in praise of the venerable Upâli. Then said the Bhikkhus: 'The Blessed One speaks (&c., down to) Upâli. Come, let us learn the Vinaya under the venerable Upâli.' And many Bhikkhus, senior and junior, and of medium standing, went to learn the Vinaya under the venerable Upâli. The venerable Upâli taught them standing, out of reverence for the senior Bhikkhus, and the senior Bhikkhus heard him standing, out of reverence for the law; and thereby both the senior Bhikkhus grew weary, and the venerable Upâli.

They told this matter to the Blessed One.

'I allow, O Bhikkhus, a junior Bhikkhu, when giving instruction, to sit on a seat of equal height, or higher, out of reverence for the law; and a senior Bhikkhu, when receiving instruction, to sit on a seat

your right to a lodging there, and by taking one there you ipso facto renounced your right to get one here.

of equal height, or lower, out of reverence for the law[1].'

2. Now at that time a number of Bhikkhus stood around Upâli, waiting for seats[2]; and they grew weary.

They told this matter to the Blessed One.

'I allow you, O Bhikkhus, to sit down together with brethren entitled to sit on seats of equal height.'

Then the Bhikkhus thought, 'How many of us are entitled to sit on seats of equal height?'

They told this matter to the Blessed One.

'I allow you, O Bhikkhus, to sit on the same seat with those who are within three years of one another in seniority.'

Now at that time a number of Bhikkhus, entitled to sit on the same seat, sat down on a couch, and broke the couch down; or sat down on a chair, and broke the chair down.

'I allow, O Bhikkhus, the use of a couch, or a chair, for three persons.'

Even when three sat on the couch, or chair, it broke.

'I allow, O Bhikkhus, two to sit on a couch or a chair.'

Now at that time Bhikkhus who were not entitled to seats of equal height, were afraid they would offend if they sat together on a long seat.

They told this matter to the Blessed One.

---

[1] Compare the fifteen rules of a similar character, Sekhiyas 57–72, and especially No. 69.

[2] Onlookers apparently, not strictly learners. On the force of pa*t*imâneti, compare the Bhikkhunî-vibhaṅga, Pârâgika I, 1, and *G*âtaka II, 423.

'I allow you, O Bhikkhus, to sit together on a long seat with others not entitled to sit on seats of equal height, unless they are women, or eunuchs, or hermaphrodites.'

Then the Bhikkhus thought, 'What is the limit of length which is included under the term "long seat?"'

'I allow the term "long seat" to be used, O Bhikkhus, of any seat long enough to accommodate three persons.'

14.

1. Now at that time Visâkhâ the mother of Migâra was anxious to have a storeyed building (pâsâda), with a verandah (âlinda) to it, supported on pillars with capitals of elephant heads[1], built for the use of the Samgha. Then the Bhikkhus thought, 'Of things which appertain to a storeyed building, which has been permitted by the Blessed One, and which not[2]?'

They told this matter to the Blessed One.

[1] Hatthi-nakhakam, 'supported on the frontal globes (kumbhe) of elephants,' says Buddhaghosa.

[2] On the meaning of paribhoga here compare VI, 18, 1. The doubt here expressed is curious, as a storeyed building (pâsâda) is one of the five kinds of abodes (lenâni) specially sanctioned by Mahâvagga I, 30, 4, and Kullavagga VI, 1, 2; and a verandah (âlinda) has been also authorised by Kullavagga VI, 3, 5. No doubt the special point here is as to the carved pillars: but, even so, that this rule should be thus separated from the other rules as to buildings, in the commencement of this book (VI, 1–4), is a proof of the unsystematic way in which the Khandhakas have been put together. Even the final redaction which we have now before us contains much similar evidence of the gradual growth of these rules. See note 3 on the next paragraph.

'I allow, O Bhikkhus, the use of all appurtenances to a storeyed building.'

Now at that time the grandmother of Pasenadi of Kosala had died, and many unauthorised things had come into the hands of the Sa*m*gha, such as couches, divans (&c., as in chapter 8 above, and Mahâvagga V, 10, 4).

They told this matter to the Blessed One.

'I allow you, O Bhikkhus, to use the stuffed couches (âsandi) after having broken off the legs[1], and the divans (pallaṅka) after having removed the hair, and to comb out the cotton of the mattresses and make pillows of it[2], and to use all the rest as floor covering[3].'

15.

1. Now at that time the Bhikkhus who dwelt in a certain country residence, not far from Sâvatthi, were worried by having constantly to provide sleeping accommodation for travelling Bhikkhus who came in (from country-places). And those Bhikkhus

---

[1] Compare the 87th Pâ*k*ittiya.

[2] This rule has already been given in VI, 2, 6.

[3] It is distinctly laid down without any reservation in Mahâvagga V, 10, 5 (in the paragraph erroneously numbered V, 10, 4 in vol. ii, p. 28, of the present work), that the use of any of these things is a dukka*t*a offence. That this relaxation of that rule should be inserted only here, looks very much like an after-thought, even though the former passage merely refers to the use of these things as seats. This is more especially noteworthy from the fact mentioned in the last note.

The rules as to new rugs or mats to be used for sitting upon, are contained in the 11th to the 15th Nissaggiya Pâ*k*ittiyas.

thought: '[This being so,] let us hand over all the sleeping accommodation which is the property of the Sa*m*gha to one (of us), and let us use it as belonging to him.' And they [did so[1]].

Then the incoming Bhikkhus said to them: 'Prepare, Sirs, sleeping accommodation for us.'

'There are no beds, Sirs, belonging to the Sa*m*gha. We have given them all away to one of us.'

'What, Sirs? Have you then made away with property belonging to the Sa*m*gha?'

'That is so, Sirs.'

The moderate Bhikkhus murmured, &c., and told this matter to the Blessed One.

'Is it true, O Bhikkhus, as they say, that Bhikkhus make away with Sa*m*gha property?'

'It is true, Lord.'

2. Then the Blessed One rebuked them, &c., and said to the Bhikkhus: 'These five things, O Bhikkhus, are untransferable; and are not to be disposed of either by the Sa*m*gha, or by a company of two or three Bhikkhus (a Ga*n*a), or by a single individual. And what are the five? A park (Ârâma), or the site for a park—this is the first untransferable thing, that cannot be disposed of by the Sa*m*gha, or by a Ga*n*a, or by an individual. If it be disposed of, such disposal is void; and whosoever has disposed of it, is guilty of a thulla*kk*aya. A Vihâra, or the site for a Vihâra—this is the second, &c. (as before). A bed, or a chair, or a bolster, or a pillow—this is the third, &c. A brass vessel, or a brass jar, or a brass pot, or a brass vase, or a razor, or an axe, or a

[1] This is a direct infringement of the 82nd Pâ*k*ittiya, which forbids property dedicated to the Sa*m*gha being diverted to the use of any individual.

hatchet, or a hoe, or a spade—this is the fourth, &c. Creepers, or bamboos, or mu*ñg*a, or babba*g*a grass, or common grass, or clay, or things made of wood, or crockery—this is the fifth, &c. (as before, down to) thulla*kk*aya.'

16.

1. Now when the Blessed One had dwelt at Sâvatthi as long as he thought fit, he went on on his journey towards the Ki*t*â Hill with a great multitude of Bhikkhus—to wit, with about five hundred Bhikkhus, besides Sâriputta and Moggallâna.

And the Bhikkhus who were followers of Assa*g*i and Punabbasu[1] hearing the news, said one to another, 'Come, Sirs; let us divide all the sleeping accommodation belonging to the Sa*m*gha. Sâriputta and Moggallâna are men of sinful desires, and are under the influence of sinful desires. We will not provide sleeping-places for them.' And they did so.

Now the Blessed One, proceeding on his journey, arrived at the Ki*t*â Hill. And he addressed a number of Bhikkhus, saying, 'Do you go, O Bhikkhus, to the followers of Assa*g*i and Punabbasu, and say: "The Blessed One, Sirs, has arrived with a large number of Bhikkhus—to wit, with about five hundred Bhikkhus, besides Sâriputta and Moggallâna. Make ready sleeping-places, Sirs, for the Blessed One, and for the Bhikkhu-sa*m*gha, and for Sâriputta and Moggallâna."'

[1] On these Bhikkhus and their relations with Sâriputta and Moggallâna, see above, *K*ullavagga I, 13–16.

'Even so, Lord,' said those Bhikkhus in assent to the Blessed One; and they did so.

'There is no sleeping accommodation belonging to the Samgha. We have divided it all' (was the reply). 'The Blessed One, Sirs, is welcome: and he may stay in whatever Vihâra he chooses. But Sâriputta and Moggallâna are men of sinful desires, and under the influence thereof; for them we will provide no sleeping-places.'

2. 'What then, Sirs? Have you divided sleeping accommodation that is the property of the Samgha?'

'That is so, Sirs.'

The moderate Bhikkhus murmured, &c. (down to) The Blessed One said to the Bhikkhus:

'These five things, O Bhikkhus, are unapportionable, and are not to be divided either by the Samgha, or by a Gana, or by an individual. If divided, the division is void; and whosoever does so, shall be guilty of a thullakkaya. And what are the five (&c., as in VI, 15, 2)[1]?'

17.

1. Now when the Blessed One had remained at the Kitâ Hill as long as he thought fit, he proceeded on his journey towards Âlavî; and in due course he arrived at Âlavî, and there, at Âlavî, the Blessed One stayed at the Aggâlava Shrine.

Now at that time the Bhikkhus of Âlavî[2] used to

[1] These expressions 'untransferable' (avissaggiyâni) and 'unapportionable' (avebhangiyâni) have already occurred above at Mahâvagga VIII, 27, 5.

[2] The Bhikkhus of Âlavî are frequently mentioned in connection

give new building operations in charge (to one or other of their number)[1], such as the following[2]: when some clay or earth had merely to be put aside in heaps, when a wall had merely to be re-plastered, when a door had merely to be made, when the socket for a bolt had merely to be made, when some joinery-work had merely to be done to a window, when some whitewashing merely had to be done, or some black colouring laid on, or some red colouring[3], or some roofing-work, or some joinery, or a bar had to be fixed to a door[4], when breaches or decay had merely to be repaired[5], or the flooring to be re-plastered[6]; and they assigned this office to one another for terms of twenty or thirty years, or

---

with offences in relation to the navakammam. See, for instance, Pârâgika III, 5, 30.

[1] For the rule authorising such giving in charge in general cases, see above, VI, 5.

[2] For most of the following technical terms in building, see our notes above on *K*ullavagga V, 11, and V, 1, 2.

[3] See our note on this phrase above, V, 11, 6.

[4] Ga*n*d*ikâdhâna-mattenâ ti dvâra-bâhânam upari-kapo*l*a-ga*nd*ika-yogana-mattena (B.). Ga*nd*i is used in this sense at *G*âtaka I, 237. Compare the use of Dhamma-ga*nd*ikâ, 'block of execution,' at *G*âtaka I, 150, II, 124. The word ga*nd*ikâ occurs also at *G*âtaka I, 474 (last line), in the sense of 'bunch:' but it is there probably a misprint; for Oldenberg, in the parallel passage at Bhikkhunî-vibhaṅga, Pâ*k*ittiya I, 1, reads bha*nd*ike. That the two words are easily confused in Burmese writing is shown by the fact that the Berlin (Burmese) copy of Buddhaghosa reads here also bha*nd*ikâdhâna-mattenâ ti, &c., and again afterwards bha*nd*ika.

[5] See our note on this phrase above, VI, 5, 2.

[6] Paribha*nd*a-kara*n*a-mattenâ ti gomaya-paribha*nd*a-kasâva-parikara*n*a-mattena (B.). The very same expression is used in a wholly doubtful sense, and of some process of tailoring, in Mahâvagga VII, 1, 5.

for life; or they gave in charge a completely finished Vihâra to a Bhikkhu for such time as should elapse till the smoke rose (from the funeral pyre on which his body should be burnt[1]).

The moderate Bhikkhus murmured, &c. (as usual, down to) The Blessed One said to the Bhikkhus:

'You are not, O Bhikkhus, to confer the office of building overseer when clay has merely to be put aside in heaps .... (&c., as before, down to) body shall be burnt. Whosoever shall so confer it, shall be guilty of a dukka*t*a. I allow you, O Bhikkhus, to give a Vihâra not yet begun, or not yet finished[2], in charge as a new building. And with reference to the work on a small Vihâra, it may be given in charge as a navakamma for a period of five or six years, that on an A*ddh*ayoga for a period of seven or eight years, that on a large Vihâra or a Pâsâda for ten or twelve years.'

2. Now at that time the Bhikkhus gave the whole of a Vihâra as a navakamma (to one Bhikkhu to superintend)—or two Vihâras to one Bhikkhu—or the Bhikkhu who had taken the work in charge got another (Bhikkhu to live there and take charge for him)—or the Bhikkhu who had taken in charge a

---

[1] Dhûmakâlikan ti ida*m* yâv' assa *k*itaka-dhûmo na pa*ññ*âyatîti tâva aya*m* vihâro etass' evâ ti eva*m* dhûma-kâle apaloketvâ kata-pariyosita*m* vihâra*m* denti (B.). The word recurs below, applied to sikkhâpada*m*, in XI, 1, 9.

[2] Vippakatan ti ettha vippakato nâma yâva gopânasiyo na ârohanti. Gopânasîsu pana âru*l*hâsu bahukato nâma hoti: tasmâ tato pa*tth*âya na dâtabbo (B.). The use of bahukato is noteworthy, for in the only other passage where we have found the word (Mahâvagga VI, 36, 2), it has a totally different application. There is possibly a misreading in the one MS. available. (? pakato.)

building belonging to the Sa*m*gha kept exclusive possession of it—or the Bhikkhus gave work in charge to one not at that time within the boundary[1]—or Bhikkhus who had once taken charge kept exclusive possession for all time.

They told [each of] these matters to the Blessed One.

'You are not, O Bhikkhus, to do [any one of these things]. Whosoever does, he is guilty of a dukka*t*a. And the Bhikkhu in charge may take one good sleeping-place into his exclusive possession for the three months of the rainy, but not during the dry season.'

3. Now at that time Bhikkhus who had taken charge of building operations left the place [or otherwise became incompetent in one or other of the twenty and three ways set out in the next paragraph[2]].

They told this matter to the Blessed One.

'In case that occurs, O Bhikkhus, as soon as he has taken charge, or before the building has been completed, let the office be given to another lest there should be loss to the Sa*m*gha. In case the building has been completed, O Bhikkhus, if he then leaves the place, it (the office and its privileges) is still his—if he then returns to the world, or dies, or admits that he is a sâma*n*era, or that he has abandoned the precepts, or that he has become guilty of an extreme offence, the Sa*m*gha

---

[1] See above, VI, 11, 3.

[2] See Mahâvagga II, 22, 3, and II, 36, 1-3. In the latter of these two passages the three cases are omitted. In Mahâvagga IX, 4, 2, and 8, the whole 23 are given.

becomes the owner[1]—if he then admits that he is mad, or that his mind is unhinged, or that he is afflicted with bodily pain, or that he has been suspended for his refusal to acknowledge an offence, or to atone for an offence, or to renounce a sinful doctrine, it (the office and its privileges) is still his—if he then admits that he is a eunuch, or that he has furtively attached himself to the Sa*m*gha, or that he has gone over to the Titthiyas, or that he is an animal, or that he has murdered his mother, or his father, or an Arahat, or that he has violated a Bhikkhunî, or that he has caused a schism in the Sa*m*gha, or that he has shed (a Buddha's) blood, or that he is an hermaphrodite, then the Sa*m*gha becomes the owner.'

18.

1. Now at that time the Bhikkhus made use elsewhere of beds which were appurtenances[2] to the Vihâra of a certain lay-disciple (upâsaka).

Then that upâsaka murmured, &c.

They told the matter to the Blessed One.

'Things appurtenant to one place are not, O Bhikkhus, to be used in another. Whosoever does so, shall be guilty of a dukka*t*a.'

Now at that time the Bhikkhus, fearing to offend if they took (things to sit upon) even into the

[1] That is, the navakammiko loses his privileges (his lien on the best sleeping-place, &c.).

[2] Vihâra-paribhoga*m*. 'Meant for use only in that Vihâra.' Compare above, VI, 14, 1.

Uposatha Hall, or the meeting-place, sat on the ground; and their legs and robes got soiled.

They told the matter to the Blessed One.

'I allow you, O Bhikkhus, to take things away for a certain time only[1].'

Now at that time a large Vihâra belonging to the Sa*m*gha went to ruin[2]. The Bhikkhus, fearing to offend, did not take the bedding in it away.

They told this matter to the Blessed One.

'I allow you, O Bhikkhus, to take away things in order to save them from destruction.'

19.

1. Now at that time there was a very valuable rug, and a very valuable piece of cloth, among the bedding furniture belonging to the Sa*m*gha.

They told this matter to the Blessed One[3].

'I allow you, O Bhikkhus, to barter either of these things in order to increase the stock of legally permissible furniture[4].'

Now at that time the Sa*m*gha had received a

---

[1] Tâvakâlika*m*. The word occurs in *G*âtaka I, 121, 393 (on which see Rh. D. in 'Buddhist Birth Stories,' p. 170, and 'Buddhist Suttas,' p. 241), in Buddhaghosa's notes on Mahâvagga VII, 5, 1 (above, II, 154, note 7), in the Bhikkhunî-vibhaṅga, Pâ*k*ittiya XXV, 2, and in *K*ullavagga X, 16, 1.

[2] Sa*m*ghassa vihâro udriyati. The whole phrase has already occurred at Mahâvagga III, 8.

[3] Because such things were forbidden by Mahâvagga V, 10, 4, though kambala is not there specially mentioned.

[4] Phâtikammatthâyâ ti va*ddh*ikammatthâyâ ti. Vaddhikammatthâya phâtikamma*m*·*k*' ettha samaka*m* vâ atireka*m* vâ agghanaka*m* mañ*k*a-pî*th*âdi-senâsanam eva va*tt*ati (B.).

bear-skin, and a *k*akkali[1] rug, and a *k*olaka cloth[2].

They told this matter to the Blessed One.

'I allow you, O Bhikkhus, to use them as mats to wipe your feet on[3].'

20.

1. Now at that time the Bhikkhus walked over the mats used for sleeping upon with unwashen or wet feet, or with their sandals on; and the matting was soiled.

They told these matters to the Blessed One.

'You are not, O Bhikkhus, to do so. Whosoever does, shall be guilty of a dukka*t*a[4].'

2. Now at that time the Bhikkhus spat on the newly prepared floor[5], and the colour was spoilt.

---

[1] According to VI, 2, 2, and VI, 3, 5, this could also be used as a screen or curtain over the space in a wall left for a window.

[2] According to Mahâvagga VIII, 18, this might be used to wipe faces with; and according to *K*ullavagga V, 9, 4, VI, 19, to place crockery or furniture on. The word *k*ola means simply cotton cloth, but it is clear from these passages that *k*olaka has some special connotation.

[3] Not to sit upon.

[4] With this should be compared the other rule in Mahâvagga V, 6, 1, according to which the Bhikkhus were to wear sandals when getting upon bedsteads or chairs, lest these should become soiled. The two passages are parallel in wording throughout.

[5] Parikammakatâya. The floors were of earth, not of wood, and were restored from time to time by fresh clay or dry cowdung being laid down, and then covered with a whitewash, in which sometimes black or red (geruka) was mixed. See above, V, 11, 6; VI, 3, 1; 17, 1; 27. From the parallel passage at Mahâvagga I, 25, 15, and *K*ullavagga VIII, 3, 1, it would seem that the red colouring was used rather for walls, and the black one for floors.

They told this matter to the Blessed One.

'You are not, O Bhikkhus, to do so. Whosoever does, shall be guilty of a dukka*t*a. I allow, O Bhikkhus, the use of a spittoon.'

Now at that time the legs of the bedsteads and chairs made scratches on the newly prepared floor.

They told this matter to the Blessed One.

'I allow you, O Bhikkhus, to cover it up with floor-cloth.'

Now at that time the Bhikkhus leant up against the newly prepared walls[1], and the colouring was spoilt.

They told this thing to the Blessed One.

'You are not, O Bhikkhus, to do so. Whosoever does, shall be guilty of a dukka*t*a. I allow you, O Bhikkhus, the use of a board to lean up against[2].'

The board scratched the floor at the bottom, and ruined the wall at the top.

'I allow you, O Bhikkhus, to cover it at the top and bottom with cloth.'

Now at that time, fearing to offend, they would not lie down on places over which it was permissible to walk with washen feet[3].

---

[1] The walls were no doubt usually made with 'wattle and daub;' that is, sticks with clay between the interstices. This was treated from time to time like the flooring (see last note).

[2] Apassena-phalaka*m*. This article of furniture is mentioned, with the spittoon, in Mahâvagga I, 25, 15, 16, and in the parallel passage at *K*ullavagga VIII, 1, 3. We have rendered it in the Mahâvagga by 'board to recline on.' Compare the use of apassaya*m* in Buddhaghosa's note on *K*ullavagga VI, 2, 4 (above, p. 153, note 3) of an arm-chair or sofa.

[3] Dhotapâdakâ ti dhotapâdakâ hutvâ dhotehi pâdehi akkamitabba*tth*âne nipa*gg*itu*m* kukku*kk*âyanti. Dhotapâdake ti pi pâ*th*o. Dhotehi pâdehi akkamitabba*tth*ânass' eva eta*m* adhiva*k*ana*m* (B.).

They told this matter to the Blessed One.

'I allow you, O Bhikkhus, to lie down in such a place when you have spread something over it.'

21.

1. Now when the Blessed One had remained at Â*l*avî as long as he thought fit, he set out on his journey towards Râ*g*agaha. And proceeding straight on, he arrived in due course at Râ*g*agaha. And there, at Râ*g*agaha, the Blessed One stayed at the Ve*l*uvana in the Kalandaka Nivâpa.

Now at that time there was a scarcity of food at Râ*g*agaha[1]. The people were unable to provide food for the (whole) Sa*m*gha; and they were desirous of providing food[2] (to be sent to the Vihâra) for the use of a special Bhikkhu (designated by the donor)[3], or for special Bhikkhus invited (by the donor in his own house)[4], or for (single Bhikkhus) appointed by ticket (issued by the Sa*m*gha)[5], or of providing food during a fortnight[6], or on Uposatha

[1] Other special rules for times of scarcity will be found at Mahâvagga VI, 17, 7; 18, 4; 19, 2; 20, 4 (repealed for times of plenty in VI, 32). Compare also Pârâ*g*ika IV, 1, 1.

[2] The above modes of receiving food (instead of collecting in a bowl morsels of food given in alms) are the dispensations allowed by Mahâvagga I, 30, 4.

[3] Uddesa-bhatta*m* *k*âtu*m*. Compare the story of Upananda at Mahâvagga VI, 19, 1.

[4] Nimantana*m* kâtu*m*. The word is only used in this special technical sense. Compare the whole story of *K*ulla-panthaka at *G*âtaka I, 116, and especially the last line.

[5] Salâka-bhatta*m* *k*âtu*m*. See especially above, *K*ullavagga IV, 9; IV, 10.

[6] Pakkhika*m* kâtu*m*. Both Childers sub voce and Frankfurter

days (that is, on the last days of each fortnight) or on the first days of each fortnight.

They told this matter to the Blessed One.

'I allow you, O Bhikkhus, each of three ways of obtaining food.'

Now at that time the *Kh*abbaggiya Bhikkhus having received good food for themselves, gave over the worse food (which they had also received) to the other Bhikkhus.

They told this matter to the Blessed One.

'I allow you, O Bhikkhus, to appoint as apportioner of rations [1] a Bhikkhu who is possessed of the following five qualifications—(&c., as in IV, 9, down to the end of the Kammavâ*k*â).'

Now the Bhikkhus who were apportioners of rations, thought: 'How then are the rations to be apportioned?'

They told this matter to the Blessed One.

'I allow you, O Bhikkhus, to apportion them by arranging the food in small heaps, and fastening tickets or marks upon them [2].'

2. Now at that time the Sa*m*gha had no dis-

('Pali Handbook,' p. 165), in interpreting the passage at Mahâvagga I, 30, 4, take this to mean a feast given on the eighth day of the month. But paksha is the half-month. The expression much more probably means, therefore, to provide food either during the whole of a half-month for one or more specially invited Bhikkhus, or for a larger number on any one day of the half-month to be chosen by the Sa*m*gha.

[1] Compare above, *K*ullavagga IV, 4, 1.

[2] Buddhaghosa says, Salâkâya vâ pa*t*ikâya vâ upanibandhitvâ opu*ññ*h*i*tvâ uddisitun ti va*k*anato rukkhasâramayâya salâkâya vâ ve*l*uvilivatâlapa*nn*âdinayâya pa*t*ikâya vâ asukassa nâma salâkabhattan ti eva*m* akkharâni upanibandhitvâ pa*kkh*iya*m* vâ *k*îvarabhoge vâ katvâ sabbâ salâkâyo omu*ñkh*itvâ [sic] punappuna*m* he*tth*â-vasena â*l*oletvâ . . . dâtabbâ.

tributor of lodging-places—no overseer of stores—no receiver of robes—no distributor of robes, of congey, or of fruits—and no distributor of dry foods, and through not being distributed it went bad.

They told each of these matters[1] to the Blessed One.

'I allow you, O Bhikkhus, to appoint as distributor of lodging-places, &c., a Bhikkhu who has (&c., as in § 1, down to the end of the Kammavâkâ, inserting throughout the appropriate variations in the fifth qualification).

3. Now at that time articles of trifling value had accumulated in the storehouse of the Samgha.

They told this matter to the Blessed One.

'I allow you, O Bhikkhus, to appoint as disposer of trifles a Bhikkhu who has (&c., as before, down to the end of the Kammavâkâ). Each separate needle, and pair of scissors, and pair of sandals, and girdle, and pair of braces, and filtering cloth, and regulation strainer[2], and plait[3], and half-plait[3], and gusset[3], and half-gusset[3], and binding[4], and braiding[4], is to be given away. If the Samgha has any ghee, or oil, or honey, or molasses, he is to give it away for personal consumption only, and if it be wanted, he is to give it a second and a third time[5].'

---

[1] There is another officer (âsana-paññâpaka) mentioned at Kullavagga XII, 2, 7, whose omission from the list here is worthy of notice.

[2] Dhamma-karako. See V, 13, 1.

[3] On these words, see Mahâvagga VIII, 12, 2.

[4] On these two words, see Mahâvagga VIII, 1, 5.

[5] These things were to be used only as medicines, according to Mahâvagga VI, 1, 1–5, where butter is also added. That would be under the charge of the distributor of dry foods (§ 2), as if kept it would go bad. According to VI, 15, 10, none of these five

Now at that time the Sa*m*gha had no receiver of under-garments [1], or of bowls,—no superintendent of those who kept the grounds in order (the Ârâmikas), and the Ârâmikas not being looked after, the necessary work was not done,—no superintendent of sâma*n*eras, and the sâma*n*eras not being looked after did not perform their duties.

They told each of these matters to the Blessed One.

'I allow you, O Bhikkhus, to appoint as receiver of under-garments, &c., a Bhikkhu who has (&c., as before, down to the end of the Kammavâ*k*â).'

End of the Sixth Khandhaka, on Sleeping Arrangements, &c.

---

kinds of medicine were to be kept for a period exceeding seven days, but that was a rule that was not very probable to be strictly followed.

[1] Sâ*t*iya; no doubt the same as is spelt elsewhere sâ*t*ikâ or sâ*t*akâ, and is used for such purposes as bathing in.

SEVENTH KHANDHAKA.

Dissensions in the Order.

1[1].

1. Now at that time the Blessed One was staying at Anupiyâ[2]. Anupiyâ is a town belonging to the Mallas[3]. Now at that time the most distinguished of the young men of the Sâkya clan had renounced the world in imitation of the Blessed One.

Now there were two brothers, Mahânâma the Sâkyan, and Anuruddha the Sâkyan. Anuruddha the Sâkyan was delicately nurtured; and he had three storeyed residences, one for the cold season, one for the hot season, and one for the season of the rains[4]. During the four months spent in the

[1] With the whole of the following story compare the, in many respects, fuller account given by the commentator on the Dhammapada (Fausböll, pp. 139 and following).

[2] This was the spot where Gotama spent the first week after his renunciation of the world, before he went on to Râ*g*agaha (Rh. D.'s 'Buddhist Birth Stories,' I, 87). Professor Fausböll there (*G*âtaka I, 65) reads Anûpiya*m*, but all his MSS. have the ŭ short. It is noteworthy that in our text the locative is formed as if the word were feminine, though the neuter form is used for the nominative.

[3] The more usual mode of adding this description in similar passages at the commencement of all the Suttas would lead us to expect here Mallâna*m* nigame.

[4] Compare Mahâvagga I, 7, 1, where the same thing is said of Yasa.

residence for the season of the rains, he was waited upon by women performing music[1], and came not down from the upper storey of his residence.

Then Mahânâma the Sâkyan thought: 'Now the most distinguished of the young men of the Sâkya clan have already renounced the world in imitation of the Blessed One, but from our own family no one has gone forth from the household life into the houseless state. Let therefore either I, or Anuruddha, renounce the world.' And he went to Anuruddha the Sâkyan, and said [so to him, adding], 'Either therefore do you go forth, or I will do so.'

'I am delicate. It is impossible for me to go forth from the household life into the houseless state. Do you do so.'

2. 'But come now, O beloved Anuruddha, I will tell you what is incident to the household life. First, you have to get your fields ploughed. When that is done, you have to get them sown. When that is done, you have to get the water led down over them. When that is done, you have to get the water led off again. When that is done, you have to get the weeds pulled up[2]. When that is done, you have to get the crop reaped. When that is done, you have to get the crop carried away. When that is done, you have to get it arranged

[1] Nippurisehi turiyehi. That Childers's rendering, 'without men, without people,' is inadequate is clear from the context at the passage which he quotes from *G*âtaka I, 53.

[2] Ni*dd*âpeti. Buddhaghosa says, 'Pull up the weeds' (ti*n*âni). The word occurs also at *G*âtaka I, 215, where there is a similar list of farming operations, which, though smaller, contains one or two items not given here.

into bundles. When that is done, you have to get it trodden out[1]. When that is done, you have to get the straw picked out. When that is done, you have to get all the chaff removed. When that is done, you have to get it winnowed. When that is done, you have to get the harvest garnered[2]. When that is done, you have to do just the same the next year, and the same all over again the year after that.

'The work is never over: one sees not the end of one's labours. O! when shall our work be over? When shall we see the end of our labours? When shall we, still possessing and retaining the pleasures of our five senses, yet dwell at rest? Yes! the work, beloved Anuruddha, is never over; no end appears to our labours. Even when our fathers and forefathers had completed their time[3], even then was their work unfinished.'

'Then do you take thought for the household duties. I will go forth from the household life into the houseless state.'

And Anuruddha the Sâkyan went to his mother, and said to her: 'I want, mother, to go forth from the household life into the houseless state. Grant me thy permission to do so.'

And when he had thus spoken, his mother replied

---

[1] Maddâpeti. There is mention of threshing (prati-han) already in the Vedas. See the passages collected by Zimmer, 'Altindisches Leben,' p. 238. But treading out is even still a very common, if not the more usual, process throughout India and Ceylon.

[2] Atiharâpeti. See Milinda Pañha, p. 66. The simple verb occurs also in a similar connection in the Bhikkhunî-vibhaṅga in the introductory story to Pâ*k*ittiya VII.

[3] That is, had died.

to Anuruddha the Sâkyan, and said: 'You two, O beloved Anuruddha, are my two only sons, near and dear to me, in whom I find no evil. Through death I shall some day, against my will, be separated from you; but how can I be willing, whilst you are still alive, that you should go forth from the household life into the houseless state?'

[And a second time Anuruddha the Sâkyan made the same request, and received the same reply. And a third time Anuruddha the Sâkyan made the same request to his mother.]

3. Now at that time Bhaddiya the Sâkya Râ*g*a held rule over the Sâkyas; and he was a friend of Anuruddha the Sâkyan's. And the mother of Anuruddha the Sâkyan, thinking that that being so, the Râ*g*a would not be able to renounce the world, said to her son: 'If, beloved Anuruddha, Bhaddiya the Sâkyan Râ*g*a will renounce the world, thou also mayest go forth into the houseless state.'

Then Anuruddha the Sâkyan went to Bhaddiya the Sâkyan Râ*g*a, and said to him: 'My renunciation of the world, dear friend, is being obstructed by thee.'

'Then let that obstruction, dear friend, be removed. Even with thee will I[1]—renounce thou the world according to thy wish.'

'Come, dear friend, let us both renounce the world together!'

---

[1] Aha*m* tayâ. Buddhaghosa explains that the Râ*g*a is beginning to say that he will go with his friend. But a desire for the glory of sovereignty comes over his heart, and he leaves the sentence unfinished. (The Pâli is given in the notes on the text, p. 323.)

'I am not capable, dear friend, of giving up the household life. Whatsoever else you can ask of me, that I will do[1]. Do you go forth (alone).'

'My mother, dear friend, has told me that if thou dost so, I may. And thou hast even now declared "If thy renunciation be obstructed by me, then let that obstruction be removed. Even with thee will I—renounce thou the world, according to thy wish." Come, then, dear friend, let us both renounce the world.'

Now at that time men were speakers of truth, and keepers of their word which they had pledged. And Bhaddiya the Sâkya Râ*g*a said to Anuruddha the Sâkyan: 'Wait, my friend, for seven years. At the end of seven years we will renounce the world together.'

'Seven years are too long, dear friend. I am not able to wait for seven years.'

[And the same offer was made successively of six years and so on down to one year, of seven months and so on down to one month, and even of a fortnight, and still there was ever the same reply. At last the Râ*g*a said,]

'Wait, my friend, for seven days, whilst I hand over the kingdom to my sons and my brothers.'

'Seven days is not too long. I will wait thus far' (was the reply).

4. So Bhaddiya the Sâkya Râ*g*a, and Anuruddha, and Ânanda, and Bhagu, and Kimbila, and Devadatta—just as they had so often previously gone

[1] Tyâha*m*. See Dr. Morris's remarks on this elision in his introduction to the *K*ariyâ Pi*t*aka (Pâli Text Society, 1882), where he makes it equal to tad aha*m*. This seems to us open to question, at least in this passage, where it may possibly stand for te aha*m*.

out to the pleasure-ground with fourfold array—even so did they now go out with fourfold array, and Upâli the barber went with them, making seven in all.

And when they had gone some distance, they sent their retinue back, and crossed over into the neighbouring district, and took off their fine things, and wrapped them in their robes, and made a bundle of them, and said to Upâli the barber: 'Do you now, good Upâli, turn back. These things will be sufficient for you to live upon.'

But as he was going back, Upâli the barber thought: 'The Sâkyas are fierce. They will think that these young men have been brought by me to destruction, and they will slay me. But since now these young men of the Sâkya clan can go forth from the household life into the houseless state, why indeed should not I?' And he let down the bundle (from his back), and hung the bundle on a tree, saying, 'Let whoso finds it, take it, as a gift,' and returned to the place where the young Sâkyans were.

And the Sâkya youths saw him coming from afar, and on seeing, they said to him: 'What have you come back for, good Upâli?'

Then he told them [what he had thought, and what he had done with the bundle, and why he was returned].

'Thou hast done well, good Upâli (was the reply), in that thou didst not return; for the Sâkyas are fierce, and might have killed thee.'

And they took Upâli the barber with them to the place where the Blessed One was. And on arriving there, they bowed down before the Blessed One, and took their seats on one side. And so seated they said to the Blessed One: 'We Sâkyas, Lord, are haughty. And this Upâli the barber has long been an attendant, Lord, upon us. May the Blessed One admit him to the Order before us, so that we may render him respect and reverence, and bow down with outstretched hands before him (as our senior), and thus shall the Sâkya pride be humbled in us Sâkyans[1].'

Then the Blessed One received first Upâli the barber, and afterwards those young men of the Sâkya clan, into the ranks of the Order. And the venerable Bhaddiya, before that rainy season was over, became master of the Threefold Wisdom[2], and the venerable Anuruddha acquired the Heavenly Vision[3], and the venerable Ânanda realised the effect of having entered upon the Stream[4], and Devadatta attained to that kind of Iddhi which is attainable even by those who have not entered upon the Excellent Way[5].

---

[1] This reputation of the Sâkya family for pride is referred to in *G*âtaka I, 88, 89.

[2] Tisso vi*gg*â, see Rh. D.'s remarks at pp. 161, 162 of 'Buddhist Suttas from the Pâli' (S. B. E., vol. xi). They are probably here the three vi*gg*as referred to in the Sutta-vibhaṅga, Pârâ*g*ika I, 1, 6–8, as the second of those is the Heavenly Vision, here mentioned in the next clause.

[3] Dibba*k*akkhu, a full description of the details of which will be found in the stock paragraph translated by Rh. D. in 'Buddhist Suttas from the Pâli' (S. B. E., vol. xi, pp. 216–218).

[4] Sotâpattiphala; that is, he became free from the delusion of self (sakkâyadi*tth*i), from doubt (vi*k*iki*kkh*â), and from dependence upon ceremonies or works (sîlabbata-parâmâsa). See Rh. D.'s manual, 'Buddhism,' pp. 108–110.

[5] Pothu*gg*anikâ iddhi. What this may be is unknown to us. A fourfold Iddhi is described in detail in the stock passage

5[1]. Now at that time the venerable Bhaddiya, who had retired into the forest to the foot of a tree, into solitude, gave utterance over and over again to this ecstatic exclamation: 'O happiness! O happiness!' And a number of Bhikkhus went up to the place where the Blessed One was, and bowed down before him, and took their seats on one side. And, so seated, they [told the Blessed One of this], and added, 'For a certainty, Lord, the venerable Bhaddiya is not contented as he lives the life of purity; but rather it is when calling to mind the happiness of his former sovranty that he gives vent to this saying.'

Then the Blessed One addressed a certain Bhikkhu, and said: 'Do you go, O Bhikkhu, and in my name call Bhaddiya the Bhikkhu, saying, "The Teacher, venerable Bhaddiya, is calling for you."'

'Even so, Lord,' said that Bhikkhu, in assent to the Blessed One. And he went to Bhaddiya, and called him [in those words].

6. 'Very well,' said the venerable Bhaddiya, in

translated by Rh. D. in 'Buddhist Suttas from the Pâli,' S. B. E., vol. xi, p. 214, and the fourfold Iddhi of the ideal king in the similar passage, loc. cit., pp. 259–261. The Iddhi here referred to may be the former of these two, though that list does not include the power ascribed to Devadatta in the next chapter. At *G*âtaka I, 140, the expression of our text here is replaced by *gh*âna, though the account there is otherwise the same.

It is worthy of notice that Devadatta, though a Bhikkhu, is not honoured with the standing epithet, 'venerable,' always used of the other members of the Order, even when they are represented to have been of bad character.

[1] The following incident, with a summary of the preceding sections, forms the introductory story to the 10th *G*âtaka (Rh. D.'s 'Buddhist Birth Stories,' i. pp. 190–193). The legend may have first arisen as an explanation of the name Bhaddiya, which means 'the fortunate one.'

assent to that Bhikkhu; and he came to the Blessed One, and bowed down before him, and took his seat on one side. And when he was so seated, the Blessed One said to the venerable Bhaddiya:

'Is it true, as they say, that you Bhaddiya, when retired into the forest to the foot of a tree, into solitude, have given utterance over and over again to this ecstatic exclamation, "O happiness! O happiness!" What circumstance was it, O Bhaddiya, that you had in your mind when you acted thus?'

'Formerly, Lord, when I was a king, I had a guard completely provided both within and without my private apartments, both within and without the town, and within the (borders of my) country. Yet though, Lord, I was thus guarded and protected, I was fearful, anxious, distrustful, and alarmed. But now, Lord, even when in the forest, at the foot of a tree, in solitude, I am without fear or anxiety, trustful and not alarmed; I dwell at ease, subdued[1], secure[2], with mind as peaceful as an antelope's[3]. It was when calling this fact to mind, Lord, that I gave utterance over and over again to that cry, "O happiness! O happiness!"'

Then the Blessed One, on hearing that, gave utterance at that time to this song:

---

[1] Pannalomo. See our note 2 on Kullavagga I, 6, 1 (above, vol. ii, p. 339).

[2] Paradavutto. This is the reading of the Sinhalese MS., and is the correct one. See Oldenberg's note at p. 363 of the edition of the text. Our translation is conjectural.

[3] Migabhûtena *k*etasâ. The meaning of miga in this phrase is not certain; and the figure may be drawn from the careless mind of any animal in its natural state. We have not noticed the idiom elsewhere; but compare the converse figure, bhantamiga-sappa*t*ibhâgo sâsane anabhirato, at *G*âtaka I, 303, 6.

'The man who harbours no harsh thoughts within him,
Who cares not whether things are thus or thus,
His state of joy, freedom from grief or care,
The very gods obtain not to behold!'

2.

1. Now when the Blessed One had stayed at Anupiyâ as long as he thought fit, he set out on his journey towards Kosambî. And journeying straight on he arrived in due course at Kosambî, and there, at Kosambî, he stayed at the Ghosita Ârâma.

Now the following thought occurred to Devadatta, when he had retired into solitude, and was plunged in meditation: 'Whom now[1] can I so gain over that, he being well pleased with me, much gain and honour may result to me?' And it occurred to him, 'Now this prince A*g*âtasattu is young, and has a lucky future before him. Let me then gain him over; and he being well pleased with me, much gain and honour will result.'

Then Devadatta folded up his sleeping-mat, and set out, fully bowled and robed, for Râ*g*agaha; and in due course he arrived at Râ*g*agaha. Then he laid aside his own form, and took upon himself the form of a child clad in a girdle of snakes, and appeared on the lap of prince A*g*âtasattu[2]. Then was

[1] In the text, for kin nu read ka*m* nu.

[2] This taking upon oneself another shape is not one of the powers of Iddhi included in the first list referred to at note 5, p. 230.

prince A*g*âtasattu terrified, and startled, and anxious, and alarmed.

And Devadatta said to prince A*g*âtasattu, 'Are you afraid of me, O prince?'

'Yes, I am. Who are you?'

'I am Devadatta.'

'If you, Sir, are really the worthy Devadatta, be good enough to appear in your own shape.'

Then Devadatta, laying aside the form of the child, appeared there before prince A*g*âtasattu with his inner and outer robes on, and with his bowl in his hand. And prince A*g*âtasattu was well pleased with Devadatta by reason of this marvel of Iddhi, and morning and evening he used to go in five hundred chariots to wait upon him, and food was brought and laid before him in five hundred dishes.

Then there arose in Devadatta's mind, possessed and vanquished by gain and hospitality and fame[1], some such thought as this: 'It is I who ought to lead the Bhikkhu-sa*m*gha.' And as the idea rose up within him, (that moment) was Devadatta deprived of that his power of Iddhi.

2. Now at that time a Koliyan, by name Kakudha, who had been (as Bhikkhu) the attendant on Moggallâna, had just died, and had appeared again in a certain spiritual body[2], possessed of a personality as large as two or three of the common rice-fields of a Mâgadha village, and yet so constituted[3] that he was

---

[1] Compare Mahâvagga V, 1, 22, on this expression. Also below, § 5.

[2] Aññatara*m* manomaya*m* kâya*m* upapanno. Perhaps 'in a mode of existence in which his body was changeable at will.' (See Childers, sub voce manomayo.)

[3] Attabhâvo. See IX, 1, 3.

not in the way either of himself or of others[1]. And this celestial being, Kakudha, went to the venerable Moggallâna, and bowed down before him, and took his stand on one side. And so standing, he told the venerable Moggallâna [of the thought that had arisen in Devadatta's mind, and of the result thereof]. And when he had told him, he bowed down before the venerable Moggallâna, and keeping him on his right side as he passed him, he vanished away.

And the venerable Moggallâna went to the place where the Blessed One was, and told him [the whole matter][2].

'What then, Moggallâna, have you so penetrated the mind of that celestial being Kakudha, that you know that whatsoever he speaks, that will be accordingly, and not otherwise[3]?'

'I have, Lord.'

'Keep that saying, Moggallâna, secret; keep that saying secret. Even now that foolish man will himself make himself known.

3[4]. 'There are, Moggallâna, these five kinds of teachers now existing in the world. What are the five?

'In the first place, Moggallâna, there is one kind of teacher whose conduct not being pure, he yet

---

[1] Vyâbâdheti. He could occupy the same space as other beings without incommoding them. The word occurs in the same sense in the passage quoted from Buddhaghosa in Rh. D.'s note 1 on the Mahâ-parinibbâna Sutta V, 10, but originally occurring in the Aṅguttara Nikâya.

[2] The last paragraph is here repeated in the text.

[3] On the use here of *ketasâ keto parikka*, compare Mahâ-parinibbâna Sutta I, 16, 17.

[4] The following two sections are repeated below, VII, 3, 10, to all the Bhikkhus.

gives out that he is a person of pure conduct, one whose conduct is pure, and innocent, and without stain. His disciples know that that is so, but they think, "If we announce the fact to the laity, he will not like it. And how can we conduct ourselves towards him in a way that is displeasing to him? And besides he is honoured with gifts of the requisite clothing, food, lodging, and medicine for the sick. He will sooner or later become known by that which he himself will do." Such a teacher, Moggallâna, do his disciples protect in respect of his own conduct. And being as he is, he expects[1] to be protected by his disciples in respect of his own conduct.

4. 'Again, Moggallâna,' &c. [as before, putting successively 'mode of livelihood,' 'preaching of the Dhamma,' 'system of exposition,' &c., 'insight arising from knowledge,' for 'conduct']. 'These, Moggallâna, are the five kinds of teachers now existing in the world. But I being pure in conduct, mode of livelihood, preaching of the Dhamma, system of exposition, and insight arising from knowledge, give out that I am so, that I am pure, innocent, and without stain in all these things. And neither do my disciples protect me in respect of my own conduct, nor do I expect them to do so.'

5. Now when the Blessed One had remained at Kosambî as long as he thought fit, he set out on his journey towards Râ*g*agaha. And journeying straight on, he arrived in due course at Râ*g*agaha; and there, at Râ*g*agaha, he stayed at the Ve*l*uvana in the Kalandaka Nivâpa.

[1] Pa*kk*âsi*m*sati. Perhaps this word here means 'he requires, needs.'

And a number of Bhikkhus went to the Blessed One, and bowed down before him, and took their seats on one side. And when so seated, they said to the Blessed One: 'Prince A*g*âtasattu is in the habit of going morning and evening with five hundred carts to wait upon Devadatta, and food is brought and laid before him in five hundred dishes.'

'Envy not, O Bhikkhus, the gain and hospitality and fame of Devadatta. So long, O Bhikkhus, as A*g*âtasattu [so waits upon him and gives him alms] so long may we expect Devadatta not to prosper, but to decline in virtuous qualities [1]. Just, O Bhikkhus, as if you were to burst a gall (bladder) [2] before the nose of a fierce dog, the dog would thereby become so much the fiercer, just so long, O Bhikkhus (&c., as before). To his own hurt, O Bhikkhus, has this gain, hospitality, and fame come to Devadatta, to his own destruction. Just, O Bhikkhus, as a plantain, or a bamboo, or a reed gives fruit to its own hurt and its own destruction [3], just so to his own hurt (&c., as before). Just as a young she-mule conceives to her own hurt and her own destruction [4], just so, O Bhikkhus, to his own hurt has this gain, &c., come to Devadatta.

'Its fruit destroys the plantain-tree; its fruit the bamboo and the reed.

---

[1] This phrase runs in the same mould as the one so constantly repeated at the commencement of the Mahâ-parinibbâna Sutta (I, §§ 4–11).

[2] Pitta*m* bhindeyyu*m*. Literally, 'should break a gall.'

[3] These three plants die after producing fruit.

[4] Because she would die if she did. On assatarî, compare above, VI, 4, 3, and our note there.

'Honour destroys the evil man, just as its foal destroys the young she-mule.'

Here endeth the First Portion for Recitation.

3.

1. Now at that time the Blessed One was seated preaching the Dhamma, and surrounded by a great multitude, including the king and his retinue. And Devadatta rose from his seat, and arranging his upper robe over one shoulder, stretched out his joined hands to the Blessed One, and said to the Blessed One:

'The Blessed One, Lord, is now grown aged, he is old and stricken in years, he has accomplished a long journey, and his term of life is nearly run[1]. Let the Blessed One now dwell at ease in the enjoyment of happiness reached even in this world. Let the Blessed One give up the Bhikkhu-sa*m*gha to me, I will be its leader.'

'Thou hast said enough, Devadatta. Desire not to be the leader of the Bhikkhu-sa*m*gha.'

[And a second time Devadatta made the same request, and received the same reply. And a third time Devadatta made the same request.]

'I would not give over the Bhikkhu-sa*m*gha, Devadatta, even to Sâriputta and Moggallâna.

---

[1] This string of epithets recurs in Pârâ*g*ika I, 1, 2, of old and venerable Brâhmans.

How much less, then, to so vile and evil-living a person as you[1].'

Then Devadatta thought: 'Before the king and his retinue the Blessed One denies me, calling me "evil-living," and exalts Sâriputta and Moggallâna.' And, angry and displeased, he bowed down before the Blessed One, and keeping him on his right hand as he passed him, he departed thence.

This was the first time that Devadatta bore malice against the Blessed One.

2. And the Blessed One said to the Bhikkhus, 'Let then the Sa*m*gha, O Bhikkhus, carry out against Devadatta the Act of Proclamation[2] in Râ*g*agaha, to the effect that whereas the nature of Devadatta used to be of one kind it is now of another kind, and that whatsoever he shall do, either bodily or verbally, in that neither shall the Buddha be recognised, nor the Dhamma, nor the Sa*m*gha, but only Devadatta.

'And thus, O Bhikkhus, shall the Act be carried out. Some discreet and able Bhikkhu (&c.,

---

[1] In the text read *kh*avassa khe*l*âpakassa. On the first word, compare V, 2, 8. For the second the Dhammapada commentator (Fausböll, p. 143) reads, as does the Sinhalese MS. in our passage, khe*l*âsika. Buddhaghosa, explaining it, says, 'In this passage (we should recollect) that those who obtain the requisites (of a Bhikkhu) by an evil mode of life are said by the Noble Ones to be like unto spittle. The Blessed One calls him khe*l*âpaka (to express that) he eats, (that is, 'gains a living) in sin like that.' (For the Pâli, see the edition of the text, p. 323, where the comma after khe*l*asadisâ should be before it.)

[2] Pakâsaniya-kamma*m*. This is not one of the regular official acts of the Sa*m*gha, as described in *K*ullavagga I, and is only mentioned in this passage. It is not referred to by the Dhammapada commentator.

in the same form as in I, 1, 4, down to the end of the Kammavâkâ).'

And the Blessed One said to the venerable Sâriputta, 'Do you then, Sâriputta, proclaim Devadatta throughout Râgagaha.'

'In former times, Lord, I have sung the praises of Devadatta in Râgagaha, saying, "Great is the power (Iddhi) of the son of Godhi! Great is the might of the son of Godhi!" How can I now proclaim him throughout Râgagaha?'

'Was it not truth that you spoke, Sâriputta, when you [so] sang his praises?'

'Yea, Lord!'

'Even so, Sâriputta, do you now, speaking the truth, proclaim Devadatta throughout Râgagaha.'

'Even so, Lord,' said Sâriputta, in assent to the Blessed One.

3. And the Blessed One said to the Bhikkhus: 'Let then the Samgha appoint Sâriputta to the office of proclaiming Devadatta throughout Râgagaha to the effect (&c., as before, § 2). And thus, O Bhikkhus, should he be appointed. First, Sâriputta should be asked, &c. (as usual in official appointments[1], down to the end of the Kammavâkâ).'

Then Sâriputta, being so appointed, entered Râgagaha with a number of Bhikkhus, and proclaimed Devadatta accordingly. And thereupon those people who were unbelievers, and without devotion or insight, spake thus: 'They are jealous, these Sakyaputtiya Samanas! They are jealous of the gain and hospitality that fall to Devadatta!' But those who were believers, full of devotion, able, and gifted with in-

[1] See, for instance, I, 22, 2.

sight, spake thus: 'This cannot be any ordinary affair[1], in that the Blessed One has had Devadatta proclaimed throughout Râ*g*agaha!'

4. And Devadatta went to A*g*âtasattu the prince, and said to him: 'In former days, prince, people were long-lived, but now their term of life is short. It is quite possible, therefore, that you may complete your time while you are still a prince. So do you, prince, kill your father, and become the Râ*g*a; and I will kill the Blessed One, and become the Buddha.'

And prince A*g*âtasattu thought, 'This worthy Devadatta has great powers and might; he will know (what is right).' And fastening a dagger[2] against his thigh, he entered with violence and at an unusual hour[3], though fearful, anxious, excited, and alarmed, the royal chamber. And when the ministers who were in attendance in the private chamber saw that, they seized him. And when, on searching him, they found the dagger fastened on his thigh, they asked him:

'What were you going to do, O prince?'

'I wanted to kill my father.'

'Who incited you to this?'

'The worthy Devadatta.'

Then some of the ministers advised 'The prince should be slain, and Devadatta, and all the Bhikkhus.' Others of them advised 'The Bhikkhus ought not to be slain, for they have done no wrong;

[1] Na oraka*m* bhavissati. See Mahâvagga I, 9, 1, and *K*ullavagga VI, 4, 10, and our note on the latter passage.

[2] Potthanika*m*. This word has already occurred at Mahâvagga VI, 23, 3.

[3] Divâdivassa. See the use of this word at *G*âtaka II, 1.

but only the prince and Devadatta.' Others of them again said, 'Neither should the prince be slain, nor Devadatta, nor the Bhikkhus. But the king should be told of this, and we should do as the king shall command.'

5. So these ministers, taking the prince with them, went to the Râ*g*a of Magadha, to Seniya Bimbisâra, and told him what had happened.

'What advice, my friends, did the ministers give?'

[When they had told him all (as before) he said]: 'What, my friends, can the Buddha, or the Sa*m*gha, or the Dhamma have to do with this? Has not the Blessed One had a proclamation already made throughout Râ*g*agaha concerning Devadatta, to the effect that whereas his nature used to be of one kind, it is now of another; and that whatsoever he shall do, either bodily or verbally, in that shall neither the Buddha, nor the Dhamma, nor the Sa*m*gha be required, but only Devadatta?'

Then those ministers who had advised that the prince and Devadatta and all the Bhikkhus should be slain, them he made incapable (of ever again holding office). And those ministers who had advised that the prince should be slain, and Devadatta, them he degraded to lower offices. But those ministers who had advised that neither should the prince be slain, nor Devadatta, nor the Bhikkhus, but that the king should be informed of it, and his command be followed, them he advanced to high positions.

And the Râ*g*a of Magadha, Seniya Bimbisâra, said to prince A*g*âtasattu: 'Why did you want to kill me, O prince?'

'I wanted a kingdom, O king!'

'If you then want a kingdom, O prince, let this kingdom be thine!' And he handed over the kingdom to Agâtasattu the prince [1].

6. Then Devadatta went to prince [2] Agâtasattu, and said, 'Give such orders, O king, to your men that I may deprive the Samana Gotama of life.' And Agâtasattu the prince gave orders to his men: 'Whatsoever the worthy Devadatta tells you, that do!'

Then to one man Devadatta gave command: 'Go, my friend, the Samana Gotama is staying at such and such a place. Kill him, and come back by this path.' Then on that path he placed other two men, telling them, 'Whatever man you see coming alone along this path, kill him, and return by that path.' Then on that path he placed other four men [and so on up to sixteen men]

7. And that man took his sword and shield, and hung his bow and quiver at his back, and went to the place where the Blessed One was, and when at some little distance from the Blessed One, being

[1] The early literature already mentions that Agâtasattu eventually killed his father. (See, for instance, Sâmañña-phala Sutta, p. 154.) Bigandet I, 261 (3rd edition) adds that the mode adopted was by starving him to death in prison.

[2] The Buddhist writers being so especially careful in their accurate use of titles, it is particularly noteworthy that Agâtasattu is here called prince (kumâra) and not king (râga). It is almost impossible to avoid the conclusion that this paragraph stood originally in some other connection; and that the events it describes must then have been supposed to have taken place before Agâtasattu actually became king. That the Dhammapada commentator says here (Fausböll, p. 143) tasmim (that is, Agâtasattu) ragge patitthite, is no evidence the other way; for that account is either taken from this, or depends ultimately upon it.

terrified, anxious, excited, and alarmed, he stood stark still and stiff[1].

On the Blessed One seeing him so, he said to the man: 'Come hither, friend, don't be afraid.'

Then that man laid aside his sword and his shield, took off his bow and his quiver, and went up to the Blessed One; and falling at his feet, he said to the Blessed One: 'Transgression, Lord, has overcome me even according to my folly, my stupidity, and my unrighteousness, in that I have come hither with evil and with murderous intent. May the Blessed One accept the confession I make of my sin in its sinfulness, to the end that in future I may restrain myself therefrom!'

'Verily, my friend, transgression has overcome thee [&c., down to] intent. But since you, my friend, look upon your sin as sin, and duly make amends for it, we do accept (your confession of) it. For this, O friend, is progress in the discipline of the Noble One, that he who has seen his sin to be sin makes amends for it as is meet, and becomes able in future to restrain himself therefrom[2].'

Then the Blessed One discoursed to that man in due order, that is to say (&c., as usual in conversions[3], down to) May the Blessed One accept me as a disciple, as one who, from this day forth as long as life endures, has taken his refuge in him.

And the Blessed One said to the man: 'Do not, my friend, leave me by that path. Go by this path,' and so dismissed him by another way.

[1] Patthaddha; that is, prastabdha. See Sutta-vibhaṅga, Pârâ*g*ika I, 10, 17, 21.

[2] This confession and acceptance are in a standing form, which occurs, for instance, at Mahâvagga IX, 1, 9; *K*ullavagga V, 20, 5.

[3] See, for instance, *K*ullavagga VI, 4, 5.

8. But the two men thought, 'Where now can that man be who was to come alone? He is delaying long.' And as they were going to meet him, they caught sight of the Blessed One sitting at the foot of a certain tree. On seeing him they went up to the place where he was, and saluted him, and took their seats on one side. To them also the Blessed One discoursed, [and they were converted as the other man had been, and he sent them back by another way. And the same thing occurred as to the four, and the eight, and the sixteen men [1].]

9. And the one man returned to Devadatta, and said to him: 'I cannot, Lord, deprive the Blessed One of life. Great is the power (Iddhi [2]) and might of the Blessed One.'

'That will do, friend. You need not do so. I will slay the Blessed One myself.'

Now at that time the Blessed One was walking up and down (meditating) in the shade below [3] the mountain called the Vulture's Peak. And Devadatta climbed up the Vulture's Peak, and hurled down a mighty rock with the intention of depriving the Blessed One of life. But two mountain peaks came together and stopped that rock, and only a splinter [4] falling from it made the foot of the Blessed One to bleed [5].

---

[1] The last two paragraphs of § 7 are repeated in full in the text in each case.

[2] The Iddhi here must be the power of religious persuasion.

[3] Pa*kkh*âyâya*m*. See Mahâvagga V, 1, 5, and Mahâ-parinibbâna Sutta II, 31 (p. 22 of the text).

[4] Papatikâ. In the text, by a misprint, this and the preceding word have been joined together.

[5] Pâde ruhiram uppâdesi, where ruhira is equal to lohita.

Then the Blessed One, looking upwards, said to Devadatta: 'Great, O foolish one, is the demerit you have brought forth for yourself[1], in that with evil and murderous intent you have caused the blood of the Tathâgata to flow.'

And the Blessed One said to the Bhikkhus: 'This is the first time that Devadatta has heaped up (against himself) a Karma which will work out its effect in the immediate future[2], in that with evil and murderous intent he has caused the blood of the Tathâgata to flow.'

10. And the Bhikkhus having heard that Devadatta was compassing the death of the Blessed One, walked round and round the Vihâra, making recitation in high and loud tones, for a protection and guard to the Blessed One. On hearing that noise the Blessed One asked the venerable Ânanda what it was. And when Ânanda [told him], the Blessed One said: 'Then, Ânanda, call the Bhikkhus in my

---

It is so used at *G*âtaka II, 275, in the Milinda Pañha, p. 125, and in the account of the present incident in the Dhammapada commentary (p. 144). In Mahâvagga I, 67, where it is said that one who has shed (a Buddha's) blood cannot be received into the Order, the expression is lohita*m* uppâdeti: and in numerous passages elsewhere it is added that such a lohituppâdako becomes ipso facto discharged from one or other of the duties and privileges of a member of the Order, just as if he had thrown off the robes.

[1] Pasûta*m*. By a misprint the text has pasuta*m*. Compare the end of § 16 below.

[2] Ânantarika-kamma*m*. That is, that will work out its effect, (not in the next birth, as is the case of all other Karma,) but immediately, in the present life. There are five such deeds (see Childers, sub voce pa*ñk*°, and Milinda Pañha, p. 25). The Bodisats, according to *G*âtaka I, 45 (verse 256), are free from such sins.

name, saying, "The Teacher sends for the venerable ones."'

And he [did so], and they came, and saluted the Blessed One, and took their seats on one side. And when they were so seated, the Blessed One said to the Bhikkhus: 'This, O Bhikkhus, is an impossible thing, and one that cannot occur, that one should deprive a Tathâgata of life by violence. The Tathâgatas, O Bhikkhus, are extinguished (in death) in due and natural course.

'There are, O Bhikkhus, these five kinds of teachers now living in the world (&c., as in VII, 2, 3, 4, down to the end). And this, O Bhikkhus, is an impossible thing, and one that cannot occur, that a Tathâgata should be slain by any act set on foot by any one besides himself. The Tathâgatas, O Bhikkhus, are extinguished (in death) in due course (of nature). Go, therefore, O Bhikkhus, each one to his Vihâra, for the Tathâgatas require no protection.'

11. Now at that time there was at Râ*g*agaha an elephant named Nâlâgiri, fierce, and a manslayer. And Devadatta went into Râ*g*agaha, and to the elephant stables, and said to the elephant-keepers[1]: 'I, my friends, am a relative of the râ*g*a's, and am able to advance a man occupying a low position to a high position, and to order increase of rations or of pay. Therefore, my friends, when the Sama*n*a Gotama shall have arrived at this carriage-road[2], then loose the elephant Nâlâgiri, and let him go down the road.'

[1] Hatthi-bha*nd*e. See the note on Mahâvagga VI, 37, 2.

[2] Ra*kkh*am; that is, rathyâm. Compare *G*âtaka I, 346, and the Old Commentary on the Bhikkhunî-vibhaṅga, Pâ*k*ittiya VII.

'Even so, Sir,' said those elephant-keepers in assent to Devadatta.

And when the Blessed One early in the morning had dressed himself, he entered Râ*g*agaha duly bowled and robed, and with a number of Bhikkhus, for alms; and he entered upon that road. On seeing him the elephant-keepers loosed Nâlâgiri, and let it go down the road. And the elephant saw the Blessed One coming from the distance; and as soon as it saw him, it rushed towards the Blessed One with uplifted trunk, and with its tail and ears erect.

When those Bhikkhus saw the elephant Nâlâgiri coming in the distance, they said to the Blessed One: 'This elephant, Lord, Nâlâgiri, is fierce, and a manslayer, and it has got into this road. Let the Blessed One, Lord, turn back: let the Happy One turn back.'

'Come on, O Bhikkhus. Be not alarmed. There is, O Bhikkhus, no possibility [&c., as in last section, down to the end].'

[And a second and a third time the Bhikkhus made the same appeal, and received the same reply.]

12. Then at that time the people climbed up on to the upper storeys of the houses, and on to the balconies, and on to the roofs. And those of them who were unbelievers and without faith or insight, said, 'Truly the countenance of the great Sama*n*a is beautiful; but the elephant will do him a hurt[1].' But those who were believers, full of

[1] The setting of this paragraph is parallel to § 3 above in this chapter; the speech of the unbelievers is the same as that of the *Ga*t*ilas* at Mahâvagga I, 15, 4.

devotion, able, and gifted with insight, said, ''Twill be long e'er the elephant can fight a fight with the elephant (of men)!'

And the Blessed One caused the sense of his love to pervade the elephant Nâlâgiri[1]; and the elephant, touched by the sense of his love, put down his trunk, and went up to the place where the Blessed One was, and stood still before him. And the Blessed One, stroking the elephant's forehead with his right hand, addressed him in these stanzas:

'Touch not, O elephant, the elephant of men; for sad, O elephant, is such attack[2],

'For no bliss is there, O elephant, when he is passed from hence, for him who strikes the elephant of men.

'Be not then mad, and neither be thou careless[3], for the careless enter not into a state of bliss,

'Rather do thou thyself so act, that to a state of bliss thou mayest go.'

And Nâlâgiri the elephant took up with his trunk the dust from off the feet of the Blessed One, and sprinkled it over its head, and retired, bowing backwards the while it gazed upon the Blessed One.

And Nâlâgiri the elephant returned to the elephant stables, and stood in its appointed place, and

---

[1] Mettena *k*ittena phari; literally, 'he suffused him with loving heart.' Compare Rh. D.'s 'Buddhist Birth Stories,' i. p. 112.

[2] In nâgamâsado the m is inserted for euphony. See the instances given by Kuhn, 'Beiträge zur Pâli-grammatik,' p. 63. Many others might be added; siva-m-a*ñg*ase, *G*âtaka, vol. i, verse 27; samana-m-a*k*ala, Childers sub voce, &c. Compare the curious use of âsâdeti at *K*ullavagga I, 27.

[3] A play on the words is here lost in English (mâ mado mâ *k*a pamâdo).

became once more the tame Nâlâgiri. And at that time the people sung these verses:

'They can be tamed by sticks, and goads, and whips,
'But the great Sage has tamed this elephant without a weapon or a stick.'

13. The people were angry, murmured, and became indignant, saying, 'How wicked is this Devadatta, and how wretched[1], in that he can go about to slay the Samana Gotama, who is so mighty and so powerful.' And the gain and honour of Devadatta fell off, while that of the Blessed One increased.

[2] Now at that time, when the gain and honour of Devadatta had fallen off, he went, surrounded by Bhikkhus, to people's houses, appealing for alms[3].

The people were angry, murmured, and became indignant, saying, 'How can the Sakyaputtiya Samanas live on food that they ask for at people's houses? Who is not fond of well-cooked food? Who does not like sweet things?'

The Bhikkhus heard (&c., down to) the Blessed One said to the Bhikkhus: 'Therefore do I lay down this rule, O Bhikkhus, for the Bhikkhus that

---

[1] Alakkhiko ti ettha na lakkhetîti alakkhiko na gânâtîti attho. Apâkata-kammam karomîti na gânâtîti na lakkhitabbo ti alakkhano passitabbo ti attho (B.). We venture to differ from both of these explanations, and to follow rather the derivation of the word, and the meaning of the corresponding Sanskrit term alakshmîka.

[2] From here down to the 'decision' is identical with the introductory story in the Sutta-vibhanga to the 32nd Pâkittiya,—a rule the previous existence of which is implied in the decision given here.

[3] Viññâpeti is continually used in the Sutta-vibhanga in this sense, and even occurs already in the Pâtimokkha, Pâkittiya 39.

(not more than) three shall enjoy an alms (together) at people's houses—and this for the sake of three reasons; (to wit) for the restraint of the evil-minded, and for the ease of the good [1], lest those who have evil desires should, in reliance upon a particular party (among the Bhikkhus), break up the Sa*m*gha [2], and (lastly) out of compassion for the laity [3]. (A Bhikkhu) who shall enjoy an alms in parties of more than three, shall be dealt with according to law [4].'

14 [5]. Now Devadatta went to the place where Kokâlika, and Ka*t*amoraka-tissaka, and the son of Kha*nd*a-devî and Samudda-datta were, and said to them, 'Come, Sirs, let us stir up a division in the Sama*n*a Gotama's Sa*m*gha, and in the body of his adherents [6].'

When he had thus spoken, Kokâlika said to Devadatta, 'The Sama*n*a Gotama, Sir, is mighty and powerful. How can we [do such a thing]?'

'Come, Sirs, let us go to the Sama*n*a Gotama, and make the following five demands, saying,

---

[1] This whole phrase recurs in Sutta-vibhaṅga, Pârâ*g*ika I, 5, 11, and in the Aṅguttara Nikâya II, 17, 2. In the latter passage Dr. Morris reads dummaññûna*m*; see his note at pp. 127, 128. But the Sanskrit Buddhist vocabulary Vyutpatti (teste Böhtlingk-Roth, s. v. maṅku) authorises the use of dummaṅku.

[2] So the Aṅguttara, loc. cit., has, in the same connection, gihîna*m* anukampâya pâpi*kkh*âna*m* pakkhupa*kkh*edâya.

[3] See last note. The idea is here, of course, lest any particular layman should be burdened by providing for many Bhikkhus.

[4] That is, under the 32nd Pâ*k*ittiya, on which rule the Sutta-vibhaṅga explains the phrase ga*n*a-bho*g*ana.

[5] Sections 14, 15, and the greater part of 16 recur, word for word, as the introductory story to the 10th Sa*m*ghâdisesa.

[6] In *k*akka-bheda*m* the first word no doubt connotes 'kingdom, lordship,' as in dhamma-*k*akka, *k*akkavatti, &c.

"The Blessed One, Lord, has declared in many a figure the advantages of the man who wishes for little, who is easy to satisfy in the matter of support and nourishment, who has eradicated evil from his mind, has quelled his passions, and is full of faith, of reverence, and of the exercise of zeal[1]. The following five things, Lord, conduce to such a condition[2] It would be good, Lord, if the Bhikkhus should be, their lives long, dwellers in the woods—if whosoever goes to the neighbourhood of a village should thereby commit an offence. It would be good if they should, their lives long, beg for alms—if whosoever should accept an invitation, should thereby commit an offence. It would be good if they should clothe themselves, their lives long, in cast-off rags—if whosoever should accept a gift of robes from a layman[3], should thereby commit an offence. It would be good if they should dwell, their lives long, under the trees[4]—if whosoever should (sleep) under a roof, should thereby commit an offence. It would be good if they should, their lives long, abstain from fish[5]—if whosoever should

[1] This is part of the standing 'religious discourse' so often ascribed to the Buddha in the Vinaya texts, and given at full in the *K*ullavagga I, 1-3.

[2] It was on precisely the same reasoning that a certain Bhikkhu in Mahâvagga VIII, 28, 1, endeavoured to get the Buddha to convert to the rejection of all clothing.

[3] At Mahâvagga VIII, 1, 35, it is laid down that a Bhikkhu may either dress in cast-off rags, or accept robes from a layman, according as he likes.

[4] This dwelling under trees is expressly forbidden, as regards the season of the rains, in Mahâvagga III, 12, 5.

[5] The rule of the Order is merely that no one may knowingly eat fish which he has seen or heard or suspected to have been caught for that purpose. See Mahâvagga VI, 31, 14.

eat fish, should thereby commit an offence." The Sama*n*a Gotama will not grant these things. Then will we gain over the people by means thereof.'

'Yes; it may be possible so to stir up divisions in the Sa*m*gha, and in the party of the Sama*n*a Gotama. For the people believe in rough measures.'

15. And Devadatta went to the Blessed One, surrounded by his friends, and made these demands [in the words just set out].

'No, Devadatta. Whosoever wishes to do so, let him dwell in the woods; whosoever wishes to do so, let him dwell in the neighbourhood of a village. Whosoever wishes to do so, let him beg for alms; whosoever wishes to do so, let him accept invitations from the laity. Whosoever wishes to do so, let him dress in rags; whosoever wishes to do so, let him receive gifts of robes from laymen. Sleeping under trees has been allowed by me, Devadatta, for eight months in the year; and the eating of fish that is pure in the three points—to wit, that the eater has not seen, or heard, or suspected that it has been caught for that purpose.'

And Devadatta, pleased and delighted that the Blessed One had refused the five demands, arose from his seat, and keeping him on his right hand as he passed him, departed thence with his friends. And he entered into Râ*g*agaha, and urged his view upon the people by means thereof, saying, 'Such and such things did we ask, Sirs, of the Sama*n*a Gotama. He would not allow them, but we live in accordance with them.'

16. Then those of the people who were unbelievers, and without reverence or insight, said, 'These Sakyaputtiya Sama*n*as have eradicated evil

from their minds, and have quelled their passions, while on the other hand the Sama*n*a Gotama is luxurious, and his mind dwells on abundance[1].' But those of the people who were believers, and full of reverence and insight, were indignant, became vexed, and murmured, saying, 'How can Devadatta go about to stir up division in the Sa*m*gha of the Blessed One, and in the party that is subject to him.'

The Bhikkhus, hearing them so murmuring, told the matter to the Blessed One.

'Is it true, O Devadatta, as they say, that thou goest about to stir up division in the Sa*m*gha, and in the body of my adherents?'

'It is true, Lord.'

'(Thou hast gone far) enough, Devadatta. Let not a division in the Sa*m*gha seem good to thee[2]; —grievous is such division. Whosoever, O Devadatta, breaks up the Sa*m*gha, when it is at peace, he gives birth to a fault (the effect of) which endures for a kalpa[3], and for a kalpa is he boiled in niraya. But whosoever, O Devadatta, makes peace in the Sa*m*gha, when it has been divided, he gives birth to the highest merit, and for a kalpa is he happy in heaven[4]. Thou hast gone far enough,

[1] Bâhulliko bâhullâya *k*eteti. Both these expressions occur above in Mahâvagga VI, 15, 9, 10, and elsewhere (see, for instance, the introductory stories to *G*âtaka, Nos. 6 and 32) as the standing expression for the opposite of the state of mind in which a good Bhikkhu ought to live.

[2] Mâ te ru*kk*i sa*m*ghabhedo. For the connotation of this phrase, compare below, VII, 4, 4.

[3] Kappa*tth*ika*m* kibbisa*m*. At *G*âtaka I, 172, 213, 215. Prof. Fausböll reads kappa*tth*iya. In saying that the fault itself (kibbisa*m*) is to endure for a kalpa, the meaning of course is that its effects on the Karma will endure so long.

[4] Either the text has here preserved (as in other cases elsewhere)

Devadatta. Let not a division in the Sa*m*gha, O Devadatta, seem good to thee. Grievous, O Devadatta, is such division.'

17. Now the venerable Ânanda, having dressed himself early in the morning, went duly bowled and robed into Râ*g*agaha for alms. And Devadatta saw the venerable Ânanda proceeding through Râ*g*agaha for alms. On seeing that he went up to the venerable Ânanda, and said to him: 'At once, from this day forth, friend Ânanda, I intend to perform Uposatha, and to carry out the formal proceedings of the Order, without either the Blessed One or the Bhikkhu-sa*m*gha.'

And when the venerable Ânanda had gone through Râ*g*agaha for alms, and had returned from his rounds, and had finished his meal, he went to the Blessed One, and bowed down before him, and took his seat on one side. And when he was so seated, he told the Blessed One [what Devadatta had said, and added], 'This very day, Lord, Devadatta will break up the Sa*m*gha.'

Then the Blessed One, when he heard that, gave utterance at that time to this expression of strong emotion:

'Easy is a good act to the good, a good act is hard to the wicked;

'Easy is evil to the evil, but evil is hard for the Noble Ones to do.

Here ends the Second Portion for Recitation.

---

the fragments of earlier verses, or the poetical forms of the verses below at VII, 5, 4, have crept into the prose here, where we should otherwise expect sagge and niraye.

4.

1. Now Devadatta on that day, which was Uposatha day, arose from his seat, and gave out voting-tickets[1], saying, 'We went, Sirs, to the Samana Gotama and asked for the Five Points, saying—(&c., as above in VII, 3, 14 and 15). These the Samana Gotama will not allow; but we live in accordance therewith. Whosoever of the venerable ones approves of the Five Things, let him take a ticket.'

Now at that time there were five hundred Bhikkhus, Vesâliyans, and belonging to the Vaggian clan[2], who had but recently joined the Order, and were ignorant of what he had in hand[3]. These took the voting-tickets, believing [the Five Points to be according to] the Dhamma, and the Vinaya, and the teaching of the Master. And Devadatta, having thus created a division in the Samgha, went out to the hill Gayâ-sîsa, taking those five hundred Bhikkhus with him.

Then Sâriputta and Moggallâna went to the Blessed One, and bowed down before him, and took their seats on one side. And when they were so seated, Sâriputta said to the Blessed One: 'Deva-

[1] It may be noticed that Devadatta here takes upon himself the office of a salâka-gâhâpako without having been appointed to it in the manner required by the rule laid down in Kullavagga IV, 9 and 10. On the process to be followed when voting with tickets, see IV, 4, 26.

[2] So it is the Vaggians from Vesâlî who are represented, below XII, 1, 1, to have put forward those Ten Points which gave rise to the Council and the schism at Vesâlî a hundred years after the Buddha's death.

[3] Apakataññuno.

datta, Lord, has gone forth to Gayâ-sîsa, taking five hundred Bhikkhus with him.'

'Verily, Sâriputta and Moggallâna, there must be a feeling of kindness towards those young Bhikkhus among you both. Go therefore, both of you, before they have fallen into entire destruction.'

'Even so, Lord,' said Sâriputta and Moggallâna, in assent to the Blessed One. And rising from their seats, they bowed down before him, and keeping him on their right hand as they passed him, they set out for Gayâ-sîsa.

Then at that time a certain Bhikkhu, standing not far from the Blessed One, began to weep. And the Blessed One said to him: 'Why, O Bhikkhu, dost thou weep?'

'Those, Lord, who are the Blessed One's chief disciples, Sâriputta and Moggallâna, even they have gone to Devadatta's side, approving the Dhamma of Devadattà.'

'That, O Bhikkhu, would be impossible, that Sâriputta and Moggallâna should approve his teaching. They are gone only to gain those Bhikkhus over again[1].'

2. Now at that time Devadatta, surrounded by a great number of adherents, was seated, preaching the Dhamma. And when he saw from afar Sâriputta and Moggallâna coming towards him, he said to the Bhikkhus: 'See, O Bhikkhus, how well preached must be my doctrine, in that even the two chief disciples of the Sama*n*a Gotama—Sâriputta

[1] Bhikkhu-sa*ññ*attiyâ. The phrase occurs above at IV, 14, 26, and below XII, 2, 8, and corresponds to the expression *ganam* sa*ññ*âpeti (above, VII, 3, 14), used of Devadatta's trying to gain the people over to his views.

and Moggallâna—are coming to join me, being pleased with my Dhamma.'

When he had thus spoken Kokâlika said to Devadatta: 'O venerable Devadatta, trust not Sâriputta and Moggallâna, for they are inclined towards evil, and under the influence of evil desires.'

'Nay, my friend, let us bid them welcome since they take pleasure in my teaching (Dhamma).'

And Devadatta invited Sâriputta to share his own seat, saying, 'Come, friend Sâriputta. Sit thou here!'

'Nay (there is no need of that),' said Sâriputta; and taking another seat, he sat down on one side. And Devadatta instructed and incited and aroused and gladdened the Bhikkhus far into the night with religious discourse; and then made request to Sâriputta, saying, 'The assembly, friend Sâriputta, is still alert and sleepless. Will you, friend Sâriputta, be so good as to think of some religious discourse to address to the Bhikkhus[1]? My back is tired, and I would stretch myself a little.'

'Even so, friend,' said the venerable Sâriputta, in assent to Devadatta. And Devadatta spread his waist-cloth folded in four on the ground, and lay down on his right side. And in a moment even sleep overcame him who was tired, and had lost his presence of mind and his self-consciousness[2].

3. Then the venerable Sâriputta taught and exhorted the Bhikkhus in a religious discourse touching the marvels of preaching, and the venerable

[1] Pa*t*ibhâtu ta*m* bhikkhûna*m* dhammî kathâ. See our note above on Mahâvagga V, 13, 9.

[2] Compare Mahâvagga VIII, 16 = Sutta-vibhaṅga, Sa*m*ghâdisesa I, 2, 1.

Moggallâna taught and exhorted the Bhikkhus in a religious discourse touching the marvels of Iddhi. And whilst they were being so taught and exhorted those Bhikkhus obtained the pure and spotless Eye of the Truth [1]—(that is, the knowledge that) whatsoever has a beginning, in that is inherent also the necessity of dissolution. Then the venerable Sâriputta addressed the Bhikkhus, and said: 'Let us go, my friends, to the Blessed One's side. Whosoever approves of his doctrine (Dhamma), let him come.'

And Sâriputta and Moggallâna went back to the Ve*l*uvana, taking those five hundred Bhikkhus with them. But Kokâlika awoke Devadatta, and said: 'Arise, friend Devadatta! Your Bhikkhus have been led away by Sâriputta and Moggallâna. Did I not tell you, Devadatta, not to trust Sâriputta and Moggallâna, in that they were inclined towards evil, and were under the influence of evil desires?'

Then hot blood came forth from Devadatta's mouth [2].

4. But Sâriputta and Moggallâna went to the place where the Blessed One was, and bowed down before him, and took their seats on one side. And when they were so seated, Sâriputta said to the Blessed One:

'It were well, Lord, that Bhikkhus who have turned aside to schism should be received afresh into the higher grade of the Order.'

'Nay, Sâriputta, let not the reordination of schis-

---

[1] This expression is the standing one in conversions; see, for instance, Mahâvagga I, 7, 6; *K*ullavagga VI, 4, 5, VII, 3, 6.

[2] The later legends preserved in Spence Hardy and Bigandet say that Devadatta died on the spot.

matical Bhikkhus seem good to thee. But rather cause such Bhikkhus to confess that they have committed a thulla*kk*aya offence. And how, Sâriputta, did Devadatta treat you?'

'When Devadatta, Lord, had instructed and aroused and incited and gladdened the Bhikkhus far into the night with religious discourse, he then made request to me, saying, "The assembly, friend Sâriputta, is still alert and sleepless. Will you, friend Sâriputta, think of some religious discourse to address to the Bhikkhus? My back is tired, and I would stretch myself a little." This, Lord, was the way in which Devadatta behaved to me.'

5. Then the Blessed One addressed the Bhikkhus, and said: 'Once upon a time, O Bhikkhus, there was a great pond in a forest region. Some elephants dwelt beside it; and they, plunging into the pond, plucked with their trunks the edible stalks of the lotus plants, washed them till they were quite clean[1], masticated them[2] without any dirt, and so eat them up. And that produced in them both beauty and strength, and by reason thereof they neither went down into death, nor into any sorrow like unto death. Now among those great elephants, O Bhikkhus, there were young elephant calves, who also, in imitation of those others, plunged into that pond, and plucked with their trunks the edible stalks of the lotus plants; but they did not wash them till they were clean, but masticated them, dirt and all, and so eat them up. And that produced in them

[1] The last three lines have occurred word for word in Mahâvagga VI, 20, 2.

[2] Sa*m*khâditvâ. Compare the use of this word at *G*âtaka I, 507.

neither beauty nor strength; and by reason thereof they went down into death, and into sorrows like unto death. Just so, O Bhikkhus, will Devadatta die who, poor creature, is emulating me.

'Like the elephant calf who eateth mud in imitation of the great beast[1]

That shakes the earth, and eats the lotus plant, and watches through the night among the waters[2]—

So will he, poor creature, die that emulateth me.'

6. 'A Bhikkhu who is possessed of eight qualifications is worthy, O Bhikkhus, to do the work of an emissary. And what are the eight? The Bhikkhu, O Bhikkhus, must be able to hear and to make others listen, able to learn, able to bear in mind, able to discern and to make others discern, skilful to deal with friends and foes, and no maker of quarrels. These are the eight qualifications of which when a Bhikkhu is possessed, he is worthy, O Bhikkhus, to do the work of an emissary.

'Sâriputta, O Bhikkhus, being possessed of eight qualifications, is worthy to do the work of an emissary. What are the eight (&c., as in last paragraph)?

'He who on entering a company that is violent of speech,

---

[1] Mahâ-varâha. At Abhidhânappadîpikâ, verse 1115, varâha is said to mean 'elephant' as well as 'boar;' and so here Buddhaghosa says Mahâ-varâhassa mahâ-nâgassa. As this explanation possibly rests only on such passages as the present, we have chosen an ambiguous rendering.

[2] Nadîsu *g*aggato ti. Ettha so kira hatthi-nâgo sâya*n*hasamaya*m* ta*m* nadî-nâmaka*m* pokkhara*n*i*m* ogâhetvâ kilanto sabbaratti*m* vîtinâmesi *g*âlika*m* karoti. Tena vutta*m* nadîsu *g*aggato ti (B.).

Fears not, forgoes no word, disguises not his message,
Is unambiguous in what he says, and being questioned angers not,
Of such is surely the Bhikkhu worthy to go on a mission [1].'

7. 'Devadatta, O Bhikkhus, being overcome, his mind being taken up by eight evil conditions [2], is irretrievably (doomed to) remain for a Kalpa in states of suffering and woe [3]. And what are the eight? He is overcome, his mind is taken up by gain, by want of gain, by fame, by want of fame, by honour, by want of honour, by his having wicked desires, and by his having wicked friends. These, O Bhikkhus, are the eight evil conditions by which Devadatta being overcome, and his mind being taken up, he is irretrievably (doomed to) remain for a Kalpa in states of suffering and woe.

'It would be well, O Bhikkhus, that Bhikkhus should continue in complete ascendancy over any gain or loss, any fame or the reverse, any honour or

[1] On these lines compare some similar expressions at Mahâvagga X, 6, 3.

[2] Asaddhamma. It is very difficult to find a proper rendering for this expression. Dhamma here means, no doubt, 'quality,' 'condition' (as it does in the title of the Sanskrit work Saddharmapu*nd*arîka, unhappily rendered by Burnouf, 'Lotus de la bonne loi'). But the details of the various particulars suggest rather the rendering 'surrounding occurrences' or 'matters,' for they are objective, external, and not (or only incidentally and secondarily) subjective, internal.

[3] Âpâyiko nerayiko. 'Liable to re-birth in apâya and in niraya.' Of these the former includes the latter, and also the states of being an animal, a disembodied ghost (peta), or an asura. Hell, though a convenient, is a misleading translation of the latter of the two words, for the reasons given by Rh. D. on Mahâ-parinibbâna Sutta I, 23. All the expressions used here recur below at VII, 5, 4.

dishonour, any evil longing or evil friendship, that may accrue to them. And for what reason[1]? For as much, O Bhikkhus, that bad influences (âsavas) arise, full of vexation and distress[2], to one who is not continuing in complete ascendancy over each of these eight things, but to one, who is so continuing, such influences arise not. This is the reason, O Bhikkhus, why it would be well (&c., as before). Let us then, O Bhikkhus, continue in complete ascendancy over any gain or loss, any fame or the reverse, any honour or dishonour, any evil longing or evil friendship, that may accrue to us. And thus, O Bhikkhus, should you train yourselves.

'There are three evil conditions, O Bhikkhus, by which Devadatta being overcome, and his mind being taken up, he is irretrievably doomed to remain for a Kalpa in states of suffering and woe. And what are the three? His having wicked desires, and his having wicked friends, and his having come to a stop on his way (to Nirvâ*n*a or Arahatship) because he had already attained to some lesser thing[3]. These are the three (&c., as before).'

---

[1] Kim (read kam) atthavasa*m* pa*t*i*kk*a. So also above, Mahâvagga VIII, 15, 7; *K*ullavagga VII, 1, 6, and in the Mahâ-parinibbâna Sutta V, 28, and Dhammapada, verse 289. The whole of the previous sentence is here repeated in the text.

[2] Vighâta-pari*l*âhâ. This is a standing epithet of the Âsavas, recurring, for instance, many times in the Sabbâsava Sutta, §§ 18–37 (Rh. D.'s 'Buddhist Suttas,' pp. 302 and following). The word 'influence,' here chosen as a rendering for âsava, is suggested by Dr. Morris as being similar, both in its derivation and in the history of its meaning, to the Pâli one. The principal objection against it is that it has never acquired the bad connotation of âsava, and requires, therefore, to be supplemented by some epithet.

[3] Oramattakena visesâdhigamena antarâ vosânam âpâdi. On this phrase, which recurs in full in the Mahâ-parinib-

8. "Verily! let no wicked desire whatever arise within you!
Know rather from this what is the outcome thereof.
'Known was he as wise, reputed to be trained;
Aglow with glory did Devadatta stand' (thus have I heard).
He gave himself to vanity, to attacking[1] the Tathâgata:
He fell into the Avîki hell, guarded fourfold and terrible[2].
The injurer of the good, of the man who does no wrong,
Him sin pervades, the man of cruel heart, and void of love.
Though one should think the ocean to befoul with but one poison pot,
Yet could he not befoul it, for awful[3] is the sea, and great;
Just so though one should injure the Tathâgata by words,—

bâna Sutta I, 7, see Buddhaghosa's note there, quoted by Rh. D., 'Buddhist Suttas,' p. 7. The 'lesser thing' here referred to is doubtless the pothuggaṇikâ iddhi mentioned above in § 4.

[1] Anukinno âsagganam. On the former of these two words the passages at Dîpavamsa I, 18, and Gâtaka I, 20 (verse 126), and below, VII, 5, 2 = Mahâvagga X, 5, 4, may be referred to. The latter seems to bear the same relation to âsâdana, 'attack,' as vikubbana does to vikarana. Buddhaghosa's notes (text, p. 325) presuppose different readings of both words.

[2] 'Guarded fourfold' is katudvâram, that is, 'having gates and the ramparts (through which they pass) on all four sides.' On the general sentiment of these stanzas, and especially of this line, compare the Kokâliya Sutta in the Sutta Nipâta (III, 10).

[3] Bhasmâ is explained by Buddhaghosa as equal to bhayânako.

That perfect one, that peaceful heart,—against him
the words would not avail.
Let the wise Bhikkhu make a friend of, and resort
to him
By following whose way he will come to the end of
griefs!"

5.

1. Now the venerable Upâli went up to the Blessed One, and bowed down before him, and took his seat on one side. And when he was so seated, the venerable Upâli said to the Blessed One: 'The expressions, Lord, "disunion in the Sa*m*gha," and "schism in the Sa*m*gha," are used[1]. How much, Lord, goes to make disunion and not schism in the Sa*m*gha, and how much goes to make both disunion and schism in the Sa*m*gha?'

'If one is on one side, Upâli, and two on the other side, and a fourth makes a formal proposition, and gives them voting-tickets, saying, "This is according to the Dhamma, and according to the Vinaya, and according to the teaching of the Master. Take this (ticket) and give your sanction to this (opinion)"—then this, Upâli, is disunion in the Sa*m*gha, and not schism.

'If, Upâli, two are on one side, and other two are on the other side, and a fifth . . . . (and so on up to) and an eighth tell them something (&c., as before)—then this, Upâli, is disunion in the Sa*m*gha, and not schism.

'If, Upâli, four are on one side, and other four

[1] Sa*m*gha-râ*g*i and sa*m*gha-bhedo. See Mahâvagga X, 1, 6, where other expressions, not here referred to, are also used.

are on the other side, and a ninth tell them (&c., as before)—then this, Upâli, is both disunion in the Sa*m*gha, and it is schism[1].

'(A separation) of nine, Upâli, or of more than nine, is both disunion in the Sa*m*gha, and it is schism.

'A Bhikkhunî, Upâli, cannot make (one of the requisite number to cause) a schism, though she may help to produce a schism—nor a woman novice, nor a Sâma*n*era, male or female, nor a layman, nor a laywoman. It is only a Bhikkhu who is in full possession of all his privileges, and belongs to the same communion, and is domiciled in the same district[2] who can make (one of the number requisite to form) a schism.'

2. 'There is the expression, Lord, "schism in the Sa*m*gha." How much, Lord, does it require to constitute a schism in the Sa*m*gha?'

'They put forth[3], Upâli, what is not Dhamma as Dhamma (1), or what is Dhamma as not Dhamma (2), or what is not Vinaya as Vinaya (3), or what is Vinaya as not Vinaya (4), or what has not been taught and spoken by the Tathâgata as taught and spoken by him (5), or what has been taught and spoken by the Tathâgata as not taught

---

[1] That is, stated shortly, it requires the breaking up of a body of at the least nine Bhikkhus to make a schism.

[2] Pakatatto samâna-sa*m*vâsako samâna-sîmâya *th*ito. On the two last of these expressions, see our notes on Mahâvagga IX, 4, 8. The first is there wrongly rendered, and should be translated as it is here; see the frequent passages in which the word occurs (e.g. *K*ullavagga I, 5, 1; I, 6, 1; I, 27, 1; II, 1, &c., where we have rendered it shortly 'a regular Bhikkhu').

[3] The first ten of the following list recur word for word in the Aṅguttara Nikâya 1, 11, 1–20 (Adhammâdi-vagga), and the whole eighteen above in the Mahâvagga X, 5, 4, 5.

and spoken by him (6), or what has not been practised by the Tathâgata as practised by him (7), or what has been practised by the Tathâgata as not practised by him (8), or what has not been ordained by the Tathâgata as ordained by him (9), or what has been ordained by the Tathâgata as not ordained by him (10), or what is no offence as an offence (11), or what is an offence as no offence (12), or what is a slight offence to be a grievous offence (13), or what is a grievous offence to be a slight offence (14), or what is (a rule regarding) an offence to which there is an atonement as without atonement (15), or what is (a rule regarding) an offence to which there is no atonement as admitting of atonement (16), or what is a grave offence as not a grave offence (17), or what is not a grave offence as a grave offence (18). In these Eighteen Points they hinder and mislead (their followers)[1], and perform independently Uposatha, and Pavâra*n*â, and (official) acts of the Sa*m*gha. So much, Upâli, does it require to constitute a schism in the Sa*m*gha.'

3. 'There is the expression, Lord, "concord in the Sa*m*gha." What, Lord, does it require to constitute concord in the Sa*m*gha?'

'They put forth, Upâli, what is not Dhamma as not Dhamma' (and so on through the Eighteen Points down to the end).

[2]4. 'To what (result of Karma), Lord, does that

---

[1] Both the exact Pâli form and the interpretation of these terms are uncertain. Buddhaghosa's notes will be found at p. 325 of H. O.'s edition of the text, and most probably we should there read parisa*m* in both cases.

[2] On the whole of the following section, compare above, VII, 3, 16, where much of the phraseology recurs.

man give rise who brings about a schism in the Sa*m*gha when it is in concord?'

'He gives rise, Upâli, to a fault (the result of which) endures for a Kalpa, and for a Kalpa is he boiled in Niraya.'

"He who breaks up the Sa*m*gha is (doomed) to remain for a Kalpa in states of suffering and woe[1].
He who delights in party (strife), and adheres not to the Dhamma, is cut off from Arahatship:
Having broken up the Sa*m*gha when it was at peace he is boiled for a Kalpa in Niraya."

'To what (result of Karma), Lord, does that man give rise who brings about reconciliation in the Sa*m*gha when it has been split up?'

'He gives rise, Upâli, to the highest merit, and for a Kalpa is he happy in heaven.

"Blessed is concord in the Sa*m*gha, and the support of those who are at peace!
He who delights in peace, adhering to the Dhamma, is not cut off from Arahatship:
On reconciling the Sa*m*gha, when it was at strife, he is happy for a Kalpa in heaven."'

5. 'Can it be, Lord, that one who breaks up the Sa*m*gha is irretrievably (doomed) to remain for a Kalpa in states of suffering and woe?'

'Yes, Upâli, that can be.'

'Can it be, Lord, that one who breaks up the Sa*m*gha is not doomed to be reborn in states either of suffering or of woe; that he is not doomed to remain so in such states for a Kalpa; and that he (his position) is not irretrievable?'

'Yes, Upâli, that can be.'

---

[1] On this line see our note above on VII, 4, 7.

'Who then, Lord, [comes under the first head?]'

'In case, Upâli, a Bhikkhu gives out what is not Dhamma as Dhamma, directing his opinion and his approval and his pleasure and his intention[1] (to what he says and does); and in belief that the doctrine (he propounds) is against the Dhamma, and that the schism resulting therefrom would be against the Dhamma[2]; and makes publication thereof[3], giving out tickets, and saying, "Take this (voting-ticket): approve this (opinion)[4]. This is Dhamma; this is Vinaya; this is the teaching of the Master,"—a man, Upâli, who thus divides the Sa*m*gha, is irretrievably doomed to remain for a Kalpa in states of suffering and woe.'

[The above paragraph is then repeated in full, reading successively for 'in belief that the doctrine (he propounds) is against the Dhamma, and the schism resulting therefrom would be against the Dhamma,' each of the following clauses:—

(*b*) . . . in belief that the doctrine is against the Dhamma, but that the schism resulting therefrom would be in accordance with the Dhamma . . .

---

[1] Vinidhâya di*tth*i*m*, vinidhâya khanti*m*, vinidhâya ru*k*i*m*, vinidhâya bhâva*m*. These expressions all recur in the Sutta-vibhaṅga, Pâ*k*ittiya I, 2, 2 and following sections, where the question at issue is whether an erroneous statement is, or is not, a conscious lie. The meaning of the whole is clear, though each of the words is used in a rather uncommon sense. On khanti, compare di*tth*e sute khanti*m* akubbamâno (of the Arahat) at Sutta Nipâta IV, 13, 3, and the standing use of the verb khamati, at the end of the Kammavâ*k*âs.

[2] Bhede adhamma-di*tth*i; literally, 'in the schism (there will be) doctrine that is against the Dhamma.'

[3] Anussâveti, which is here equivalent to the technical 'publication' required in the English law of libel and slander.

[4] See the note above on VII, 4, 1.

(*c*) . . . in belief that the doctrine is against the Dhamma, but in uncertainty whether the schism resulting therefrom would be against the Dhamma or not . . .

(*d*) . . . in belief that the doctrine is in accordance with the Dhamma, but that the schism resulting therefrom would be against the Dhamma . . .

(*e*) . . . in belief that the doctrine is in accordance with the Dhamma, but in uncertainty whether the schism resulting therefrom would be against the Dhamma or not . . .

(*f*) . . . in uncertainty whether the doctrine is against the Dhamma or not, but in the belief that the schism resulting therefrom would be against the Dhamma . . .

(*g*) . . . in uncertainty whether the doctrine is against the Dhamma or not, and in the belief that the schism resulting therefrom would be against the Dhamma . . .

(*h*) . . . in uncertainty whether the doctrine would be against the Dhamma, and in uncertainty whether the schism resulting therefrom would be against the Dhamma or not . . .]

[The whole paragraph is then again repeated, reading successively for 'gives out that which is not Dhamma as Dhamma' each of the Eighteen Points given in full in VII, 5, 2.]

6. 'Who then, Lord, is one who breaks up the Sa*m*gha, and yet is not doomed to be reborn in states either of suffering or of woe; is not doomed to remain in such states for a Kalpa; and is not so doomed that his position is irretrievable?'

'In case, Upâli, a Bhikkhu gives out what is not Dhamma as Dhamma [and so on successively through the whole Eighteen Points] without directing his opinion and his approval and his pleasure and his intention thereto, and in the belief that the doctrine he propounds is in accordance with the Dhamma, and that the schism resulting therefrom would be so too[1].'

Here ends the Third Portion for Recitation.

Here ends the Seventh Khandhaka, on Divisions in the Sa*m*gha.

[1] The sum of the last two sections seems to come to this, that practically such a schism as would have the awful effects set out above in § 4 would be impossible in Buddhism. For not only is a formal putting forward and voting on the false doctrine essential to schism as distinct from mere disagreement, but the offending Bhikkhu must also be quite aware that the doctrine so put forth is wrong, or at least doubtful, and also that the schism resulting from his action will be, or will probably be, disastrous to the Dhamma. In other words, the schism must be brought about by deliberately putting forward a doctrine known to be false, or at least doubtful, or with the express intention or hope of thereby injuring the cause of the Dhamma (that is, of the Truth).

THE EIGHTH KHANDHAKA.

REGULATIONS AS TO THE DUTIES OF THE BHIKKHUS TOWARDS ONE ANOTHER.

1.

1. Now at that time the Blessed One was staying at Sâvatthi, in Anâtha Pi*nd*ika's Ârâma.

Now at that time incoming Bhikkhus entered the Ârâma with their sandals on[1], or with sunshades held up over them[2], or with their heads muffled up[3], or with their upper robe carried in a bundle on their heads[4]; and they washed their feet in the drinking-water; and they did not salute resident Bhikkhus senior to them, nor ask them where they (the incomers) should sleep.

And a certain incoming Bhikkhu undid the bolt[5] of an unoccupied room (Vihâra), and opened the door[6], and so entered by force; and a snake fell

[1] That this was a sign of disrespect is clear from Mahâvagga V, 12, and the 61st and 62nd Sekhiyas.

[2] See our discussion of the sunshade question in the note on *K*ullavagga V, 23, 2.

[3] Ogu*nth*itâ. See the 23rd and the 67th Sekhiyas.

[4] Sîse katvâ. Compare VIII, 6, 3.

[5] Gha*t*ikâ. This word is discussed at *K*ullavagga V, 14, 3.

[6] Such an act has been already guarded against by the rule laid down at the end of *K*ullavagga V, 9, 5, where the same expression is made use of.

on to his back from the lintel above[1], and he was terrified, and made an outcry[2].

The Bhikkhus, running up, asked him why he did so. He told them that matter. Then those Bhikkhus who were moderate in their desires were vexed and indignant, and murmured, saying, 'How can incoming Bhikkhus enter the Ârâma ....? (&c., as before, down to) .... where they should sleep[3].'

They told the matter to the Blessed One (&c., as usual, I, 1, 2, 3, down to) he addressed the Bhikkhus, and said, 'Therefore, O Bhikkhus, do I establish a rule of conduct for incoming Bhikkhus, according to which they ought to behave.

2. 'An incoming Bhikkhu, O Bhikkhus, when he knows he is about to enter an Ârâma, ought to take off his sandals, turn them upside down[4], beat them (to get the dust) off, take them (up again) in his

[1] Upari-pi*tth*ito. On pi*tth*a (which we should possibly read here), as the lintel of a door, see our note above at *K*ullavagga V, 14, 3. It recurs immediately below, VIII, 1, 3.

[2] Vissara*m* akâsi. As Childers, sub voce, expresses doubt as to the meaning of this word, it may be well to note that this phrase occurs above, *K*ullavagga V, 10, 2 and VI, 3, 4, and also in the Bhikkhunî-vibhaṅga, Pâ*k*ittiya LX, and always in the sense here given. The meaning of the allied idiom, vissaro me bhavissati, might be just doubtful as used in a peculiar connection at Bhikkhunî-vibhaṅga, Pârâ*g*ika I, 1, and Sa*m*ghâdisesa III, 3, were it not clear from ibid. Pâ*k*ittiya LXXXVI, that it means simply 'there will be an outcry against me.'

[3] The form of this speech bears very clear testimony to the artificial way in which these introductory stories are put together, for the speech does not arise out of the story. Similar instances are not infrequent. See VIII, 5, 1.

[4] Nî*k*a*m* katvâ. So also at VIII, 6, 2. The word is used below and at Mahâvagga I, 25, 11 and 15 of a bedstead and chair, and below, VIII, 4, 4, of a bowl when it is being washed.

hand, put down his sunshade, uncover his head, arrange his upper robe on his back[1], and then carefully and slowly enter the Ârâma.

'When he enters the Ârâma he ought to notice where the resident Bhikkhus are gone to; and whithersoever they are gone—whether to the service hall, or to the portico (ma*nd*apa), or to the foot of a tree—thither he ought to go, and laying his bowl on one side, and his robe on one side, he ought to take a suitable seat, and sit down.

'He ought to ask as to the drinking-water, and the water for washing[2], which is appropriated to the one use, and which to the other. If he has need of drinking-water, he ought to fetch it and drink. If he has need of water for washing, he ought to fetch it, and wash his feet. In washing his feet he ought to pour the water over them with one hand, and wash them with the other; he ought not to pour the water over them and wash them with one and the same hand.

'He ought to ask for the cloths with which sandals are cleaned, and clean his sandals. In cleaning his sandals he ought first to wipe them with a dry cloth, and afterwards with a wet cloth: and then he ought to wash the cloths, and lay them on one side[3].

---

[1] See the note below on VIII, 8, 2.

[2] On these expressions, compare the note above on *K*ullavagga IV, 4, 4 (at the end), and *K*ullavagga VIII, 1, 5 = Mahâvagga I, 25, 19.

[3] These cloths (*k*olaka*m*) are not specially permitted anywhere in the Khandhakas, as cloths for wiping the face and feet are in Mahâvagga VIII, 18, and *K*ullavagga VI, 19, respectively. The word is used for 'duster' below, VIII, 1, 3, and for 'tinder' at Milinda Pañha, p. 53.

'If the resident Bhikkhu be senior, he ought to be saluted; if junior, he ought to be made to salute (the incomer). The incomer ought to ask as to the lodging-place, which has fallen (to his lot)[1], and whether it is occupied or unoccupied. He ought to ask as to lawful and unlawful resorts[2], and as to what families have been officially declared to be in want[3].

[4]'He ought to ask as to the retiring-places, (where they are), and as to the drinking-water, and as to the water for washing, and as to the staves for walking with, and as to the place for the conferences of the Sa*m*gha, (and as to) the time at which he ought to enter (it) and at which he ought to leave it.

3. 'If the Vihâra be unoccupied, he ought to knock at the door, then to wait a minute, then to undo the bolt, and open the door, and then, still standing outside, to look within.

'If that Vihâra is covered with dust[5], or the beds or chairs are piled one upon another, and the bedding put in a heap on the top of them[6],—then if

---

[1] See the rules as to the division of lodging-places according to the number of applicants at *K*ullavagga VI, 21, 2, and especially VI, 11, 3.

[2] Go*k*aro ago*k*aro. There were some places or families to which the Bhikkhus of a particular residence were not allowed to resort for alms. See the rule as to 'turning down the bowl' with respect to a person at *K*ullavagga V, 20.

[3] Sekha-sammatâni kulâni. See the note on the 3rd Pâ*t*idesaniya.

[4] All the following expressions have occurred together at *K*ullavagga IV, 4, 4, where an example is given of the course of proceeding here laid down. And they are repeated below, VIII, 2, 2.

[5] Ukl̄âpo. Compare *K*ullavagga VI, 3, 9, and below, § 5.

[6] This was the way in which a Bhikkhu, on going away from it,

he can do so he ought to clean up the Vihâra. [1]And when cleaning the Vihâra, he ought to take the floor matting out and put it down on one side, and the supports of the bedsteads[2], and the bolsters[3] and pillows, and the mat which is used as a seat. Putting the bedsteads and chairs down on to the ground, and carefully avoiding scratching (the floor with them) or knocking them up against (the door-posts), he ought to take them outside the door, and put them down on one side. The spittoon and the board to lean up against[4] ought to be taken out, and put down on one side[5].

'If the Vihâra is covered with cobwebs, they should first be removed with a cloth[6]. The casements should be dusted, especially in the corners and joints.

'If the wall which had been plastered and red-washed, or the floor which had been laid (with earth) and black-washed[7], has become dirty in the corners[8], they should be wiped down with a

was to leave his Vihâra. See below, VIII, 3, 2, and on the details of the terms used, see our note below on VIII, 1, 4.

[1] The rest of this section is repeated in full below, VIII, 7, 2.

[2] Pa*t*ipâdakâ. Doubtless the same as forms part of the âha*kk*a-ma*ñk*a mentioned in the 18th Pâ*k*ittiya and above, VI, 2, 5.

[3] Bhisi. See the note on Mahâvagga VIII, 13.

[4] Apassena-phalaka*m*. See the note on *K*ullavagga VI, 20, 2.

[5] All the expressions in this sentence and the next are the same as those used in a similar connection at Mahâvagga I, 25, 15.

[6] Ullokâ. See the note at *K*ullavagga VI, 2, 7, according to which our rendering at Mahâvagga I, 25, 15 should be corrected.

[7] On this mode of preparing walls and floors, see the notes above on *K*ullavagga VI, 20.

[8] Ka*nn*akitâ. See our note above on *K*ullavagga V, 11, 3.

duster[1] that has been first wetted and wrung out. If the floor has not been so prepared, it should be sprinkled over with water and swept[2], lest the Vihâra should be spoilt[3] by dust. The sweepings should be gathered together, and cast aside.

The translation of our present passage at Mahâvagga I, 25, 15, must be corrected accordingly.

[1] *K*olaka. See the note on this word in last section.

[2] Samma*gg*ati is to sweep (not to scrub), as is apparent from Mahâvagga VI, 34, 1.

[3] Ûha*ññ*i. So also at Mahâvagga I, 25, 15. At Mahâvagga I, 49, 4, we should have rendered 'defiled their beds' instead of 'threw their bedding about,' correcting uhananti of the text there into ûhadanti. Ûhan (originally 'to throw up,' 'raise,' &c.) seems, like samûhan, to have acquired the meaning of to destroy, injure, spoil. From this meaning of spoiling, ûhan evidently came to be used for, or confounded in the MS. with, ûhad, 'to defile (with excrement).' So the phrase 'ûhananti pi ummihanti pi' (at Mahâvagga I, 49, 4) exactly corresponds in meaning to 'omuttenti pi ûhadayanti pi' in Dhammapada, p. 283. There are other passages showing the same confusion. (1) The gerund, ûha*kk*a, which occurs in *G*âtaka II, p. 71 ('idâni kho (ahan) ta*m* ûha*kk*a'), is explained by the commentator to mean 'va*kk*an te sîse katva.' (2) ûhanti, in *G*âtaka II, p. 73 ('aggihutta*ñ* *k*a ûhanti, tena bhinnâ kama*nd*alûti'), must mean the same and be = ûhadeti. For the monkey here referred to is said to have been guilty of the following dirty trick:—'ku*nd*ikâ bhindati, aggisâlâya va*kk*a*m* karoti.' (3) mutteti ohaneti at *K*ariyâ Pi*t*aka II, 5, 4, represents u*kk*âra-pasâvam katvâ at *G*âtaka II, 385. In the first of these passages uha*kk*a may well be a copyist's blunder, arising from the similarity of the words, for uha*gg*a. Dr. Morris, to whom we owe the comparison of these passages and the suggested emendation of Mahâvagga I, 49, 4, is rather of opinion that the words were confounded by the writers. For it is not an uncommon thing to find two words, not very remote in form or meaning, confounded together. It is well known that the English word livelihood properly and originally meant 'liveliness,' and has only afterwards replaced the earlier livelode, to which the sense of livelihood properly belongs. And something of this kind

4. 'The floor coverings[1] should be dried in the sun, cleaned, beaten to get the dust out, taken back, and spread out again in the place to which they belonged[2]. The supports of the bed should be dried in the sun, dusted, taken back, and put in the place to which they belonged. The bed (mañ*k*a) and the chairs (pî*th*a) should be aired in the sun, cleaned, beaten to get the dust out, turned upside down, taken back, carefully avoiding scratching them against the floor, or knocking them up against the door-posts, and then put in the place to which they belonged[3]. The bolsters and pillows, and the

---

must have occurred, he thinks, in Pâli in the use of ûhan for ûhad. The past participle ûhata occurs at *K*ullavagga VIII, 10, 3.

[1] Bhummattharana*m*; usually, no doubt, matting of various kinds, but occasionally also skins or rugs of the kinds specially allowed by VI, 14, 2.

[2] Yathâbhâga*m*. The use of this word here constitutes the only variation between our passage and that in the Mahâvagga I, 25 = below, VIII, 7, 2, where it is replaced by yathâ*tth*âne or yathâpaññatta*m*.

[3] This passage throws a welcome light on the meaning of mañ*k*a and pî*th*a: for as they were to be beaten to get the dust out, it is clear that they were upholstered. The mañ*k*a, or bed, must have been a wooden framework, stuffed (probably with cotton), covered at the top with cotton cloth, and made underneath and at the sides of wood. It had no legs fixed to it, but was supported on movable tressels—the pa*t*ipâdakâ. When using it, the sleeper covered it with a mat, or a cotton sheet, and had over him a coverlet of some kind; and these articles, which he would also use if he slept on the ground, constituted, together with the bolster and pillows, the senâsana*m* or bedding,—that is, in the more special and limited use of that term (as, for instance, above, § 3, and perhaps below, 7, 1). In its larger sense the same word is used, putting the part for the whole, for the whole sleeping apparatus, and is nearly equivalent to seyyâyo (so, for instance, in VI, 11 and 12, and below, VIII, 2, 1; 6, 2; and perhaps VIII, 7, 1; whereas the latter term is used in the same connection at VI, 6,

mats used as seats, should be aired in the sun, cleaned, beaten to get the dust out, taken back, and put in the place to which they belonged. The spittoon, and the board for leaning up against, should be put in the sun, dusted, taken back, and put in the place to which they belonged.

[1]5. '(Then the incoming Bhikkhu) should put away his bowl and his robe. In putting away his bowl, he should hold it in one hand while he feels under the bed or the chair with the other, and then put it away; and he should not put it on a part of the floor which has been left bare. In putting away his robe, he should hold it in one hand while he feels along the bamboo or the rope used for hanging robes on with the other; and then hang it up with the border turned away from him, and the fold turned towards him.

[2]'If the winds, bearing dust with them[3], blow from the East, West, North, or South, the window spaces[4] on the side in question should be closed up (with shutters or lattices). If it is cold weather, the lattices should be opened by day, and closed by

---

and VI, 11, 3). Sayana, in VI, 8, is a generic term including bed, couch, sofa, and divan, but probably with special reference to these three latter things used in the day-time.

[1] The following paragraph occurs, word for word, at Mahâvagga I, 25, 11, and below, VIII, 7, 2.

[2] The following paragraph is the same as Mahâvagga I, 25, 18.

[3] Saragâ vâtâ. These are the well-known hot winds (like the sand-bearing simoom that blows from North Africa over Italy), against which modern residents endeavour to protect themselves by the use of 'tats.'

[4] There were, of course, no windows in our modern sense, but only spaces left in the wall to admit light and air, and covered by lattices of three kinds allowed by VI, 2, 2.

night: if it is hot weather, they should be closed by day, and opened by night.

[1] 'If the cell, or the store-room, or the refectory, or the room where the fire is kept, or the privy, is covered with dust, it should be swept out. If there is no drinking-water, or water for washing, they should be provided. If there is no water in the rinsing-pot[2], water should be poured into it.

'This, O Bhikkhus, is the rule of conduct for incoming Bhikkhus, according to which they ought to behave.'

2.

1. Now at that time resident Bhikkhus, on seeing incoming Bhikkhus, did not prepare seats for them, nor provide water and footstools and towels for them to wash their feet, nor go to meet them and take charge of their bowls and their robes, nor ask them whether they wanted drinking-water[3], nor salute such of the incoming Bhikkhus as were their seniors, nor make beds ready for them.

The moderate Bhikkhus murmured, &c., and told the matter to the Blessed One, &c., (down to) he said to the Bhikkhus: 'Therefore, O Bhikkhus,

[1] The following paragraph is the same as Mahâvagga I, 25, 19, and part of it is repeated below, VIII, 10, 3.

[2] Â*k*amana-kumbhi. This formed part of the sanitary apparatus for use in the privy. See above, Mahâvagga V, 8, 3, and below, *K*ullavagga VIII, 9 and 10.

[3] All the above expressions are used at the opening of Mahâvagga IX.

do I establish a rule of conduct for resident Bhikkhus, according to which they ought to behave.

2. 'A resident Bhikkhu, on seeing an incoming Bhikkhu, who is senior to him, ought to make ready a seat for him, provide water and a footstool and a towel for him to wash his feet, go to meet him, and take charge of his robe and his bowl, ask him if he wants water to drink, and if he can (bring himself to do so), he ought to wipe his sandals. In wiping the sandals, they should be first wiped with a dry cloth, then with a wet one, and the cloths ought then to be washed, and put aside.

[1] 'An incoming Bhikkhu ought to be saluted. A bed should be laid for him, saying, "This bed is for you." He should be informed whether (the bedroom) is occupied or not, what are lawful and what are unlawful resorts, and what families have been officially declared to be in want. He should be told where the retiring-places are, and the drinking and washing water, and the staves, and the place for the conferences of the Sa*m*gha, and what is the time when he ought to enter, and ought to leave (it).

3. 'If (the incoming Bhikkhu) be junior to him, then (the resident Bhikkhu), keeping his seat, should tell him where he is to put his bowl and his robe away, and on which mat he is to sit down. The incoming Bhikkhu should be informed where the drinking and washing water are, and the cloths to clean sandals with; he should be allowed to salute the resident Bhikkhu: and he should be told

[1] This paragraph corresponds to the last paragraph of VIII, 1, 2.

where his bed is, saying, "That bed is for you." He should be informed whether (that bedroom) is occupied or not (and so on, as in last paragraph, down to the end).

'This, O Bhikkhus, is the rule of conduct for resident Bhikkhus, according to which they ought to behave.'

3.

1. Now at that time Bhikkhus, about to leave, started without setting the wooden articles and crockery in order, leaving doors and lattices open, and without giving the sleeping-places in charge to any one. The wooden articles and crockery were spoilt, and the sleeping-places were unprotected.

The moderate Bhikkhus murmured, &c. . . . . told the Blessed One, &c. . . . . (down to) He said to the Bhikkhus: 'Therefore, O Bhikkhus, do I establish a rule of conduct for Bhikkhus about to leave, according to which they ought to behave.

2. 'A Bhikkhu about to leave should, O Bhikkhus, put the wooden articles and earthenware in order, close the doorways and lattices, give the sleeping-places in charge[1] (to some one, and only) then set out. If there be no Bhikkhu remaining, a Sâma*n*era should be put in charge. If there be no Sâma*n*era remaining, the attendant who keeps the grounds in order[2] should be put in charge. If

---

[1] Senâsana*m* âpu*kkh*â. Compare the Old Commentary on the 14th and 15th Pâ*k*ittiyas. The lengthening of the last vowel in âpu*kkh*â is noteworthy.

[2] Ârâmiko. In Mahâvagga VI, 15, the king wishing to present a man for this purpose, it is there laid down that the Bhikkhus

there be neither Bhikkhu, nor Sâma*n*era, nor Ârâmika, the bed frame should be laid on four stones[1], the other bed frames put on the top of it, the chairs should be put one on the top of the other, the bedding piled in a bundle on the top, the wooden articles and the earthenware should be put away in order, and the doorways and lattices should be closed[2], and then should be set out.

3. 'If the Vihâra leaks, it should be repaired if he can, or he should exert himself to get the Vihâra roofed. If he should thus succeed, it is good. If not, he should put the bed frame on four stones in that part of the Vihâra which does not leak, and then put the other bed frame (&c., as in last paragraph, to the end). If the whole of the Vihâra leaks, he should if he can take all the bedding to the village, or should exert himself to get it taken there. If he should succeed, it is good. If not, he should lay a bed frame on four stones in the open air, put the others on the top of it, put the chairs one on another, pile the bedding on the top, lay the wooden and earthenware utensils in order by them, and cover the whole up with grass or leaves, so that at least the principal articles of furniture might remain (uninjured)[3]; and (only) then go away.

'This, O Bhikkhus, is the rule of conduct for

may accept him; and at *K*ullavagga VI, 21, 3, a superintendent of such slaves is mentioned as one of the officials of the Order.

[1] This is the usual method still adopted by native servants as a safeguard against white ants, who would eat up into the legs of furniture left standing on the ground.

[2] This arrangement is referred to above at VIII, 1, 3.

[3] Angâni pi seseyyu*m*. See Buddhaghosa's note as appended to the edition of the text (p. 325).

Bhikkhus about to leave, according to which they should behave themselves.'

4.

1. Now at that time the Bhikkhus did not give thanks in the place where a meal was served. People murmured, &c.; the Bhikkhus heard, &c.; the Blessed One on that occasion, &c.[1] said to the Bhikkhus:

'I allow, O Bhikkhus, the giving of thanks.'

Then the Bhikkhus thought, 'By whom should the thanks be given?'

They told this matter to the Blessed One.

'I allow, O Bhikkhus, the elder Bhikkhu (present) to give thanks in the place where a meal is served.'

Now at that time (the turn to provide) the Sa*m*gha with a meal had fallen to a certain company[2]; and the venerable Sâriputta was the senior (Bhikkhu in that) Sa*m*gha. The Bhikkhus, thinking, 'The Blessed One has permitted the senior Bhikkhu to return thanks in the place where a meal is served,' went away, leaving the venerable Sâriputta alone. And the venerable Sâriputta gave thanks to those people, and then came away alone.

The Blessed One saw the venerable Sâriputta coming from the distance; and on seeing him, he said to him: 'Did the meal, then, Sâriputta, pass off well[3]?'

---

[1] For the passages here implied, see I, 1, 2, 3.

[2] Aññatarassa pûgassa. This sentence has already occurred at V, 5, 2.

[3] On this use of iddho, compare ovâdo iddho in the Bhikkhunî-vibhaṅga, Pâ*k*ittiya LVI.

'The meal, Lord, passed off well. But the Bhikkhus went away and left me alone.'

Then the Blessed One, in that connection, having delivered a religious discourse, said to them:

'I allow, O Bhikkhus, four or five of the Bhikkhus, who are senior or next to the seniors, to wait.'

Now at that time a certain elder waited in the dining hall, though he wanted to retire, and through holding himself back, he fainted and fell.

They told this matter to the Blessed One.

'I allow you, O Bhikkhus, if necessity should arise, to leave the hall after informing the Bhikkhu sitting immediately next[1] (to the one who wants to go).'

2. Now at that time the *Kh*abbaggiya Bhikkhus went to the place where a meal was to be served with their under-garments or their robes improperly put on, and not decently attired; and turning aside[2], they pushed on in front of the senior Bhikkhus; and they encroached on (the space intended for) the senior Bhikkhus[3] when taking their seats, and they compelled the junior Bhikkhus to give up their seats to them; and spreading out their upper robes

---

[1] Anantarika*m* bhikkhu*m*. See the note on this phrase at VI, 10, 1. Ânantarika*m* in the text (with long â) is a misprint.

[2] Vokkamma, which is not, as Childers supposes, equal to okkamma with euphonic v, but to vyavakramya or vyutkramya.

[3] Anupakhag*g*a: which is here used, not in the sense it has at IV, 14, 1, but in the sense in which it is used in the 16th and 43rd Pâ*k*ittiyas, in both which passages it is explained by the Old Commentary by anupavisitvâ. This clause and the next occur also at Mahâvaggâ I, 25, 13.

(as mats)[1] they took their seats in the space between the houses[2].

The moderate Bhikkhus murmured, &c. . . . told the Blessed One, &c. . . . he said to the Bhikkhus:

'Therefore, O Bhikkhus, do I establish a rule of conduct for the Bhikkhus at a meal, which they are to observe thereat.

[3] 3. 'When time has been called in the Ârâma, a Bhikkhu should put on his waistcloth so as to cover himself all round from above the navel to below the knees, tie his belt round his waist, fold[4] his upper robes and put them on, fasten the block on[5], wash (his hands), take his alms-bowl, and then slowly and carefully proceed to the village. He is not to turn aside (from the direct route) and push on in front of senior Bhikkhus[6]. He is to go amidst the houses properly clad, with (his limbs) under control, with downcast eye, with (his robes) not tucked up, not laughing, or speaking loudly, not swaying his body or his arms or his head about, not with his arms akimbo, or his robe pulled over his head, and without walking on his heels. And he is to take his

---

[1] Samghâ*t*i*m* ottharitvâ. This use of the Sa*m*ghâ*t*i is referred to at *G*âtaka I, 212, and above, I, 13, 2.

[2] Antaraghare. See Sekhiyas 3–26, repeated in the next section. It is perhaps doubtful whether this word may not mean here (as in Sekhiya 27 = below, § 6) the inner courtyard of a house which is surrounded by buildings; but we follow the interpretation we have adopted, loc. cit.

[3] The following section repeats the Sekhiyas, Nos. 3–26, where see further notes. Much of it recurs below in VIII, 5, 2.

[4] Sagu*n*a*m* katvâ. Compare Mahâvagga I, 25, 9.

[5] Ga*n*th*i*ka*m*. See the note on V, 29, 3. It was to prevent the robe being blown up by the wind. The word occurs again in VIII, 5, 2.

[6] The following sentence is repeated, word for word, below, § 6.

seat amidst the houses properly clad (&c., all as before, down to) not with his arms akimbo, or his robes pulled over his head, and without lolling, and without encroaching on (the space intended for) the senior Bhikkhus, or ejecting the junior Bhikkhus from the seats, or spreading his upper robe out (as a mat).

4. 'When the water is being given out (before the meal), he is to hold his bowl with both hands, receive the water (in it), lower the bowl carefully down to the ground so as to avoid scratching the floor, and then wash it. If there be (a person there) whose duty it is to take away the water (which has been so used), (the Bhikkhu) should lower (his bowl on to the ground) and pour the water into the waste tub[1] without splashing the person in question, nor the Bhikkhus near, nor (his own) robes. If there be no such person, he should lower his bowl on to the earth and pour the water away, without splashing the Bhikkhus near or (his own) robes.

'When the boiled rice is being given out, he should hold his bowl with both hands, and receive the rice in it. Room should be left for the curry. If there is ghee, or oil, or delicacies[2], the senior Bhikkhu should say: "Get an equal quantity for all." The alms (given) are to be accepted with mind alert, paying attention to the bowl, with equal curry, and equally heaped up[3]. And the senior

[1] Paṭiggahe. See the note on V, 10, 3. Avakkâra-pâtî, at Mahâvagga IV, 1, 2 = Kullavagga VIII, 5, 3, seems to have very nearly the same meaning. The whole of this paragraph is repeated below, § 6.

[2] Uttaribhaṅgam. See the note on VI, 4, 1.

[3] On the expressions in this sentence, compare the notes on Sekhiyas 27–32.

Bhikkhu is not to begin to eat until the boiled rice has been served out to all.

[1] 5. 'The alms given are to be eaten with mind alert, paying attention to the bowl, with equal curry, and equally heaped up; without pressing down from the top; without covering up the curry or the condiment with the rice, desiring to make it nicer; an without asking for either rice or curry for the Bhikkhu's own particular use, unless he be sick. Others' bowls are not to be looked at with envious thoughts. The food is not to be rolled up (by the fingers) into balls that are too large, but into round mouthfuls. The door of the mouth is not to be opened till the ball is brought close to it. When eating, the whole hand is not to be put into the mouth. He is not to talk with his mouth full, nor to toss the food into his mouth as he eats, nor to nibble at the balls of food, nor to stuff his cheeks out as he eats, nor to shake (particles of food off) his hands, nor to scatter lumps of rice about, nor to put out his tongue, nor to smack his lips, nor to make a hissing sound as he eats, nor to lick his fingers, or his bowl, or his lips. And the jar containing drinking-water is not to be taken hold of with hands soiled with food.

6. 'The senior Bhikkhu is not to accept water (to rinse out his bowl with) until all Bhikkhus have finished eating. When water is being given out (after the meal . . . . &c., as in the first paragraph of § 4, down to the end). The water that has been used for washing the bowl is not to be thrown with the rinsings in it into the inner court[2].

[1] This paragraph repeats Sekhiyas 31–55, where see our notes.

[2] This is the 57th Sekhiya.

'In returning, the junior Bhikkhus are to go back first, and the senior Bhikkhus after them. Each Bhikkhu is to pass amidst the houses properly clad . . . . (&c., as above, § 3, down to) without walking on his heels.

'This, O Bhikkhus, is the rule of conduct that I establish for Bhikkhus at a meal, which they are to observe thereat.'

Here ends the First Portion for Recitation.

5.

1. Now at that time Bhikkhus who were going on their rounds for alms did so with their under garments or their robes improperly put on, and not decently attired, and they entered dwellings without deliberation, and left them without deliberation, and they entered dwellings roughly, and left them roughly, and they stood at too great a distance or too near, and they stood too long or turned back too soon.

And a certain Bhikkhu, on his round for alms, entered a dwelling without noticing where he was going to, and taking (a doorway) for a house-door he passed into an inner chamber. A woman was lying asleep naked on her back in that chamber; and when the Bhikkhu saw her he went out again, perceiving that that was no house-door, but a chamber. Now the husband of that woman, seeing his wife in that position in the chamber, thought: 'My wife has been defiled by that Bhikkhu.' And he seized him, and beat him.

But the woman, being woke up by the noise, said to the man, 'Why, Sir, are you beating this Bhikkhu?'

'You have been defiled by this Bhikkhu.'

'Not so, Sir. This Bhikkhu has done nothing (said she), and had the Bhikkhu set free.

Then the Bhikkhu, on going to the Ârâma, told the matter to the Bhikkhus . . . . murmured . . . . told the Blessed One . . . . he said to the Bhikkhus:

'Therefore, O Bhikkhus, do I establish a rule of conduct for Bhikkhus going their rounds for alms, which they are to observe therein.

2. 'A Bhikkhu, O Bhikkhus, who intends to go his round for alms, should put on his waistcloth (&c., as in chapter 4, § 3, sentences 1 and 3, down to the end).

'When he enters a dwelling, he should take notice (where he goes, saying to himself), "By this way will I go in, and by this way will I come out." He should not go in, nor come out, roughly. He should not stand too far off, nor too near, nor too long; and he should not turn back too easily.

'As he stands still he should notice where (the people in the house) seem willing or not willing to give (him food). If she lays aside her work, or rises from her seat, or wipes a spoon, or wipes or puts ready a dish, he should stand still, perceiving that she seems willing to give.

'When food is being given to him, he should lift up his robe (Sa*m*ghâ*t*i) with his left hand so as to disclose his bowl[1], take the bowl in both his hands,

[1] The bowl is always carried by the left hand under the robe. On pa*n*âmeti, see the note at V, 9, 5.

and receive the food into it. And he should not look into the face of the woman who is giving the food.

'He should take notice whether she seems willing or not to give curry. If she wipes a spoon, or wipes or puts aside a dish, he should stand still, perceiving that she seems willing to give.

'After the food has been given, he should cover up the bowl with his robe, and turn back slowly and carefully. He should pass through the houses (on his way back) properly clad . . . . (&c., as in § 3, sentence 3, down to the end).

[1] 3. 'He who comes back first from the village, from his round for alms, should make seats ready, and place the water and footstools and towels ready there for washing feet, and clean the waste-tub[2] and put it ready, and put ready water to drink and water for washing.

'He who comes back last from the village, from his round for alms, may eat if there be any food left (from the meal of the other Bhikkhus), if he desires to do so. If he does not desire to do so, he should throw away the leavings on the (ground at a place) which is free from grass, or pour them away into water in which there are no living things. He should put away the water, footstools, and towels used for washing feet, clean the waste-tub and put it away, put away the drinking-water and the water

[1] The following section is, word for word, parallel to Mahâvagga IV, 1, 2-4.

[2] Avakkâra-pâtî. We have had pa/iggaha used just above (VIII, 4, 4) in a very similar sense and connection. The present word occurs also at Mahâvagga IV, 1, 2.

for washing, and sweep the room where the meal was eaten.

'Whosoever sees a pot for drinking-water or for washing-water, or a chamber utensil empty and void, should put it in its proper place. If he is not able to do so single-handed, he should call some one else, and they should put it away with their united effort, and silence should not be broken on that account[1].

'This, O Bhikkhus, is the rule of conduct which I establish for Bhikkhus going their rounds for alms, which they are to observe therein.'

6.

1. Now at that time a number of Bhikkhus dwelt in the woods; and they provided neither drinking-water, nor water for washing, nor fire, nor drill sticks nor tinder (for starting a fire)[2]; nor did they know the stations of the constellations, nor the divisions of the (ten) 'directions' (of the sky).

Thieves went there and said to the Bhikkhus, 'Have you, Sirs, got drinking-water?'

---

[1] Vâ*k*a*m* bhindati. To break silence by speaking. See Mahâvagga IV, 1, 3, where it makes good sense.

[2] Ara*n*i-sahita*m*, on which Buddhaghosa merely says ara*n*i-sahite sati aggi*m* kâtu*m* pi va*tt*ati. In the *G*âtaka Commentary (I, 212, ed. Fausböll) we have the phrase ara*n*i-sahita*m* nîharitvâ aggi*m* karonti. At p. 34 of the Assalâyana Sutta (ed. Pischel) we hear of there being an upper and lower stick to the ara*n*i; and at p. 53 of the Milinda Pañha (ed. Trenckner) we find the same upper and lower sticks, the thong by which to turn the latter, and the piece of rag for tinder mentioned as the constituent parts of this ancient means of producing fire. The expression in the text is probably a collective term for the whole of these.

'No, friends, we have not.'

'Have you, Sirs, got water for washing?'

'No, friends, we have not.'

'Have you, Sirs, got fire?'

'No, friends, we have not.'

'Have you, Sirs, got sticks and tinder for producing fire?'

'No, friends, we have not.'

'With what (constellation is the moon now in) conjunction?'

'That, friends, we do not know.'

'Which direction is this?'

'That, friends, we do not know.'

[On hearing these answers][1], the thieves said, 'These are thieves. These men are no Bhikkhus.' And they beat them, and went away.

The Bhikkhus told this matter to the Bhikkhus. The Bhikkhus told it to the Blessed One. Then the Blessed One, on that occasion and in that connection, after delivering a religious discourse, said to the Bhikkhus:

'Therefore, O Bhikkhus, do I establish a rule of conduct for Bhikkhus dwelling in the woods, according to which they are to behave themselves therein.

2. 'A Bhikkhu, O Bhikkhus, who is dwelling in the woods, should rise betimes, place his bowl in the bag[2], hang it over his shoulder, arrange his upper robe over his back (over both shoulders)[3], get on

[1] They are all repeated in the text.

[2] Thavikâ. This is possibly one of the bags referred to in the permission granted by Mahâvagga VIII, 20, but it was only to be used when the bowl had to be carried a long distance, and not when passing through a village. (See the beginning of the next section.)

[3] *K*îvara*m* khandhe katvâ: either in contradistinction to

his sandals, put the utensils of wood and earthenware in order, close the doorway and lattice, and then leave his lodging-place.

'When he perceives that he is about to enter a village, he should take off his sandals, turn them upside down [1], beat them to get the dust out, put them into a bag, hang it over his shoulder, put on his waistcloth [and so on as laid down for a Bhikkhu entering the village for alms above, VIII, 5, 2, paragraph 1, to the end].

3. 'On leaving a village he should put the bowl into its bag, hang it over his shoulder, roll his robes up, put them on his head [2], get on his sandals, and then go.

'A Bhikkhu living in the woods, O Bhikkhus, should keep drinking-water, and water for washing, and fire, and drill sticks and tinder, and walking staves ready. He should learn the stations (of the moon) in the constellations, either in the whole or in part, and he should know the directions of the sky.

'This, O Bhikkhus, is the rule of conduct that I lay down for Bhikkhus dwelling in the woods, according to which they should behave themselves therein.'

7.

1. Now at that time a number of Bhikkhus carried on robe-making in the open air. The *Kh*abbaggiya Bhikkhus beat their bedding to get

---

eka*m*sa*m* *k*îvara*m* katvâ (on which question there is a great division among modern Buddhists. Compare Rh. D.'s note on the Mahâ-parinibbâna Sutta VI, 47), or possibly 'put it in a roll on his back.'

[1] On this expression, see above, VIII, 1, 2.

[2] See Mahâvagga VIII, 13, 1.

the dust out in the open space[1] to windward of them, and covered the Bhikkhus (who were at work) with dust.

The moderate Bhikkhus murmured, &c. . . . . told the Blessed One, &c. . . . . and he said to the Bhikkhus:

'Therefore, O Bhikkhus, do I establish a rule of conduct for the Bhikkhus in respect of lodging-places, according to which they are to behave themselves in respect thereof.

2. 'In whatever Vihâra he is staying, if that Vihâra is dirty, he should, if he can, make it clean. When cleaning the Vihâra, he should first take out his bowl and his robe and the mat used for sitting upon, and the bolster and pillows, and put them down on one side. Taking the bed-frame down (from its stand), he should carry it out [and so on as in VIII, 1, 2, down to the end][2].

'He should not beat the bedding to get the dust out close to the Bhikkhus, or to the Vihâra, or to the drinking-water, or to the water for washing, or in the open space (in front of the Vihâra) to windward of it or the Bhikkhus, but to leeward.

[1] Aṅgana. This is not 'courtyard,' as Childers renders it, but a part of the Ârâma, immediately in front of the hut or Vihâra, which is kept as an open space, and daily swept. The Sinhalese name for it is midula; there those who sleep in the hut spend the greater part of the day and not even grass is allowed to grow upon it. The term is a very common one, and its meaning is not doubtful. Compare the *G*âtaka book, I, 124, 151, 421; II, 249, 250, 345. Ekaṅgana*m* bhavati, at ibid. I, 53, 12, is to become one open space, as ekaṅgana*m* karoti at II, 357, is to clear a forest, and turn it into an open space.

[2] The order is slightly different, but all the details are the same. The only addition is that in speaking of taking out the floor coverings, he is directed to notice where they lay.

3. 'The floor coverings should be dried in the sun [and so on as in VIII, 1, 4, and 5, to the end, reading "in the place where it stood (or lay)" for "in the place to which it belongs"].

4. 'If he is dwelling in the same Vihâra with an older (Bhikkhu), no recitation should be given, nor examination held, nor exhortation made, nor Dhamma spoken[1] (to a pupil), without leave being asked of the senior. Nor should a lamp be lighted or extinguished, nor the lattices opened or closed, without his leave.

'If he is walking up and down on the same *K*aṅkama with an older (Bhikkhu), then he should turn back at the spot where his senior turns back; and he should not touch his senior even with the corner of his robe.

'This, O Bhikkhus, is the rule of conduct that I lay down for the Bhikkhus in respect of lodging-places, according to which they are to behave themselves therein.'

8.

1. Now at that time the *Kh*abbaggiya Bhikkhus, on being hindered by the senior Bhikkhus in (their use of) the hot bath-room, out of spite piled up a quantity of sticks (in the fireplace), set fire to them, closed up the doorway, and sat down in the doorway. The Bhikkhus, scorched by the heat, and not being allowed a way out, fell down in a faint.

The sober Bhikkhus murmured, &c. . . . told the Blessed One, &c. . . . He said to the Bhik-

[1] All the preceding expressions have occurred at Mahâvagga I, 26, 1; see also 32, 1, and 38, 6.

khus, 'No one, O Bhikkhus, is to [do so]. Whosoever does, shall be guilty of a dukka*t*a.

2. 'Therefore, O Bhikkhus, do I establish a rule of conduct for the Bhikkhus, in respect of the hot bath-room[1], according to which they ought to behave themselves therein.

'Whosoever first enters the bath-room, if ashes have accumulated (in the fireplace) should throw the ashes out. If the hot bath-room, or its prepared flooring, or the cell, or the ante-chamber of the bath, or the cooling-room, or the hall are dirty, they should be swept. The chunam should be pounded, the clay moistened with water, and water poured into the water-jar.

'When entering the hot bath-room, the face should be smeared over with clay, and the person well covered up in front and behind before entering. A seat is not to be taken so as to hustle the senior Bhikkhus, and junior Bhikkhus are not to be ousted from their seats. If possible, shampooing is to be performed for the senior Bhikkhus in the hot bath-room.

'When leaving the hot bath-room, the chair (that has been used to sit on before the fire) should be carried off, and the person well covered up before and behind before leaving. If possible, shampooing is to be performed for the senior Bhikkhus in the water also.

'A bath is not to be taken in front of the senior Bhikkhus, nor above them. One who has bathed

[1] *G*antâghara, not simply bath-room, but room in which hot or steam baths were taken. Most of the following expressions occur in Mahâvagga I, 25, 12, or above at V, 14, 3.

and is getting up out (of the water) is to make way for one who is getting down into the water.

'Whoso comes last out of the hot bath-room is to wash it, if it be dirty; to wash the vessel in which the clay is kept, to put the chairs used in the hot bath-room in order, to extinguish the fire, to close up the doorway, and then come out.

'This, O Bhikkhus, is the rule of conduct which I lay down for the Bhikkhus, in respect of the hot bath-room, according to which they are to behave themselves therein.'

9 and 10.

[These chapters deal with the manner of using the privies, and other sanitary arrangements described in V, 35, where see our note.]

11, 12, 13, and 14.

[These chapters simply repeat, word for word, Mahâvagga I, 25, 14–24; I, 26, 1–11; I, 32, 3; and I, 33 respectively.]

Here ends the Eighth Khandhaka, containing the Rules for Conduct.

NINTH KHANDHAKA.

ON EXCLUSION FROM THE PÂTIMOKKHA CEREMONY.

1.

1. Now at that time the Blessed One was staying at Sâvatthi, in the Eastern Ârâma, the mansion of the mother of Migâra. And at that time, it being Uposatha Day, the Blessed One was seated in the midst of the Bhikkhu-sa*m*gha. And the venerable Ânanda, when the night was far spent, when the first watch was passing away, arose from his seat, arranged his robe over one shoulder, and stretching out his joined hands towards the Blessed One, said to the Blessed One:

'The night, Lord, is far spent. The first watch is passing away. For a long time has the Bhikkhu-sa*m*gha been seated here. Let my lord the Blessed One recite to the Bhikkhus the Pâtimokkha.'

When he had thus spoken, the Blessed One remained silent. And a second time, when the second watch was passing away [he made the same request with the same result]. And a third time, when the third watch had begun, and the dawn was breaking[1] [he made the same request].

'The assembly, Ânanda, is not pure[2].'

---

[1] Nandimukhiyâ rattiyâ ti aru*n*adhata-kâle pîti-mukhâ viya ratti khâyati ten' âha nandimukhiyâ ti (B.). See also our note on this at Mahâvagga VIII, 13, 1.

[2] That is, there is some one present who is disqualified by some

2. Then the venerable Mahâ Moggallâna thought, 'What individual can the Blessed One be referring to in that he says, "The assembly, Ânanda, is not pure."' And the venerable Mahâ Moggallâna considered the whole Bhikkhu-saṁgha, penetrating their minds with his. Then the venerable Mahâ Moggallâna perceived who was that individual,—evil in conduct, wicked in character, of impure and doubtful[1] behaviour, not a Samaṇa though he had taken the vows of one, not a religious student though he had taken the vows of one, foul within, full of cravings, a worthless creature,—who had taken his seat amongst the Bhikkhu-saṁgha. On perceiving which it was, he went up to that individual, and said to him, 'Arise, Sir! The Blessed One has found you out. There can be no communion[2] between you and the Bhikkhus!'

When he had thus spoken, that man kept silence. And a second and a third time the venerable Mahâ Moggallâna addressed to him [the same words, and with the same result]. Then the venerable Mahâ Moggallâna took that man by the arm and made him go out beyond the porch[3], and bolted the door,

fault from taking part in the proceedings, which would therefore be invalid.

[1] Saṁkassara. See the passages quoted by Dr. Morris in the introduction to his edition of the Aṅguttara (pp. viii, ix), though we cannot accept his conclusions. We may add that the Tibetan rendering of Dhammapada 312, given in Rockhill's 'Udâna-varga,' p. 49, from which we might expect some help, throws no light on the exact meaning of the word, the translator contenting himself with an ambiguous phrase.

[2] Saṁvâso. See Mahâvagga I, 79, 2, and Kullavagga.

[3] On these expressions, see the notes above, V, 14, 3, in accordance with which we should read here, in the text sûki, for suki.

and went up to the place where the Blessed One was, and said to him, 'Lord, I have made that man go out. The assembly is now undefiled. May my lord the Blessed One recite the Pâtimokkha to the Bhikkhus.'

'How astonishing and curious a thing it is, Moggallâna, that that foolish fellow should have waited up to the very point when he had to be taken by the arm.'

3. And the Blessed One said to the Bhikkhus: 'There are, O Bhikkhus, in the great ocean, then, eight astonishing and curious qualities, by the constant perception of which the mighty creatures take delight in the great ocean. And what are the eight?

'The great ocean, O Bhikkhus, gets gradually deeper, slope following on slope, hollow succeeding hollow, and the fall is not precipitously abrupt[1]. This is the first [of such qualities][2].

'Again, O Bhikkhus, the great ocean remains of the same nature[3], and passes not beyond the shore. This is the second [of such qualities].

'Again, O Bhikkhus, the great ocean will not brook association with a dead corpse. Whatsoever dead corpse there be in the sea, that will it—and quickly—draw to the shore, and cast it out on the dry ground[4]. This is the third [of such qualities].

'Again, O Bhikkhus, all the great rivers—that is to say, the Gaṅgâ, the Yamunâ, the A*k*iravatî, the

---

[1] Na âyataken' eva. See *K*ullavagga V, 3, 1, and V, 17, 2.

[2] Paragraph 1 is here, and in the succeeding paragraphs, repeated in full.

[3] *Th*ita-dhammo, 'has characteristics which are stable.'

[4] For ussâreti read ussâdeti. See our note on VI, 11, 3.

Sarabhû, and the Mahî—they, when they have fallen into the great ocean, renounce their names and lineage, and are reckoned thenceforth as the great ocean. This is the fourth [of such qualities].

'Again, O Bhikkhus, though all the streams in the world flow on till they reach the great ocean, and all the waters of the sky fall into it, yet does it not thereby seem to be the more empty or more full. This is the fifth [of such qualities].

'Again, O Bhikkhus, the great ocean has only one taste, the taste of salt. This is the sixth [of such qualities].

'Again, O Bhikkhus, the great ocean is full of gems, of gems of various kinds; among which are these gems—that is to say, the pearl, the diamond, the catseye, the chank, rock, coral, silver, gold, the ruby, and the cornelian[1]. This is the seventh [of such qualities].

'Again, O Bhikkhus, the great ocean is the dwelling-place of mighty beings, among which are these—that is to say, the Timi, the Timiṅgala, the Timitimiṅgala, the Asuras, the Nâgas, and the Gandhabbas. There are in the great ocean creatures so constituted that they stretch from one to five hundred leagues[2]. This is the eighth [of such qualities].

4. 'And just in the same way, O Bhikkhus, there are in this doctrine and discipline eight marvellous and wonderful qualities, by the constant perception

[1] On these gems, compare Rh. D.'s note on the Mahâ-sudassana Sutta I, 4, in 'Buddhist Suttas from the Pâli,' pp. 249, 250.

[2] On this belief, compare above, VII, 2, 2, of land creatures, where the same term, attabhâva, is used.

of which the Bhikkhus take delight in this doctrine and discipline. What are the eight?

'Just, O Bhikkhus, as the great ocean gets gradually deeper, slope following on slope, hollow succeeding hollow, and the fall is not precipitately abrupt—just so, O Bhikkhus, in this doctrine and discipline is the training a gradual one, work following on work, and step succeeding step; and there is no sudden attainment to the insight (of Arahatship)[1]. This is the first [of such qualities].

'Just, O Bhikkhus, as the great ocean remains of the same nature, and passes not beyond the shore—just so, O Bhikkhus, is the body of precepts which I have established for those who are hearers of my word, and which they, their lives long, do not pass beyond. This is the second [of such qualities].

'Just, O Bhikkhus, as the great ocean will not brook association with a dead corpse; but whatsoever dead corpse there be in the sea that will it—and quickly—draw to the shore, and cast it out upon the dry land—just so, O Bhikkhus, if there be any individual evil in conduct, wicked in character, of impure and doubtful behaviour, not a Sama*n*a though he have taken the vows of one, not a religious student though he have taken the vows of one, foul within, full of cravings, a worthless creature; with him will the Sa*m*gha brook no association, but quickly, on its meeting together, will it cast him out. And what though that man should himself be seated in the midst of the Bhikkhusa*m*gha, verily, both is he afar off from the Sa*m*gha,

---

[1] Aññâ-pa*t*ivedho. On the use of aññâ, standing alone, in this sense, see the note above on Mahâvagga V, 1, 19.

and the Sa*m*gha from him. This is the third [of such qualities].

'Just, O Bhikkhus, as the great rivers—that is to say, the Gaṅgâ, the Yamunâ, the A*k*iravatî, the Sarabhû, and the Mahî—when they have fallen into the great ocean, renounce their name and lineage and are thenceforth reckoned as the great ocean—just so, O Bhikkhus, do these four castes—the Khattiyas, the Brahmans, the Vessas, and the Suddas—when they have gone forth from the world under the doctrine and discipline proclaimed by the Tathâgata, renounce their names and lineage, and enter into the number of the Sakyaputtiya Sama*n*as. This is the fourth [of such qualities].

'Just, O Bhikkhus, as though all the streams in the world flow on till they reach the great ocean, and all the waters of the sky fall into it, yet does it not seem thereby to be either more empty or more full—just so, O Bhikkhus, though many Bhikkhus pass entirely away in that kind of passing away which leaves not a trace behind, yet does not [the Sa*m*gha] thereby seem to be either more empty or more full. This is the fifth [of such qualities].

'Just, O Bhikkhus, as the great ocean has only one taste, the taste of salt—just so, O Bhikkhus, has this doctrine and discipline only one flavour, the flavour of emancipation. This is the sixth [of such qualities].

'Just, O Bhikkhus, as the great ocean is full of gems, of gems of various kinds—that is to say, the pearl, the diamond, the catseye, the chank, rock, coral, silver, gold, the ruby, and the cornelian—just so, O Bhikkhus, is this doctrine and discipline full of gems, of gems of various kinds, among which are these gems,—that is to say, the four Earnest Meditations, the fourfold Great Struggle, the four Roads to Iddhi, the five Moral Powers, the five Moral Senses, the seven kinds of Wisdom, and the noble eightfold Path. This is the seventh [of such qualities].

'Just, O Bhikkhus, as the great ocean is the dwelling-place of mighty beings, among which are the Timi, the Timiṅgala, the Timitimiṅgala, the Asuras, the Nâgas, and the Gandhabbas; just as there are in the great ocean creatures so constituted that they stretch from one to five hundred leagues—just so, O Bhikkhus, is this doctrine and discipline the resort of mighty beings, among whom are he who has entered the First Path (the converted man, the Sotâpanno) and he who has realised the fruit thereof, he who has entered the Second Path (the Sakadâgâmin) and he who has realised the fruit thereof, he who has entered the Third Path (the Anâgâmin) and he who has realised the fruit thereof, the Arahat, and he who has realised the fruit of Arahatship. This is the eighth [of such qualities].

'These, O Bhikkhus, are the eight marvellous and wonderful qualities in this doctrine and discipline by the constant perception of which the Bhikkhus take delight therein.'

And the Blessed One, on perceiving that matter, gave forth at that time this ecstatic utterance:

'The rain falls heavily on that which is covered, not upon that which is revealed.

'Reveal, therefore, what thou hast concealed, and the rain shall touch thee not [1].'

[1] This enigmatical saying amounts apparently to this: 'As a usual thing, no doubt, the rain falls not on that which is covered

2.

1. Now the Blessed One addressed the Bhikkhus, and said: 'Now henceforth I, O Bhikkhus, will not hold Uposatha, nor recite the Pâtimokkha; let you yourselves, O Bhikkhus, henceforth hold Uposatha and recite the Pâtimokkha. It is, O Bhikkhus, an impossible thing and an inexpedient that the Tathâgata should hold Uposatha and recite the Pâtimokkha before an assembly which is not pure. And the Pâtimokkha, O Bhikkhus, is not to be listened to by one who has committed an offence. Whosoever shall so listen to it, shall be guilty of a dukka*t*a. I allow you, O Bhikkhus, for whomsoever shall listen to the Pâtimokkha at a time when he is guilty, to interdict for him the Pâtimokkha[1].

'And thus, O Bhikkhus, is it to be interdicted. On the day of Uposatha, on the fourteenth or fifteenth day of the month, and at a time when that individual is present, thus shall it be proposed in the midst of the Sa*m*gha:

'"Let the venerable Sa*m*gha hear me. Such and such an individual is guilty of an offence. For him

with a roof; but in morals it is precisely where there is already a fault concealed, unconfessed, that new faults rain in upon him who adds deceit to his fault.' Buddhaghosa says, *Kh*anna*m* ativassatîti âpatti*m* âpa*gg*itvâ pa*t*i*kkh*âdento aññam nava*m* âpatti*m* âpa*gg*atîti idam eta*m* sandhâya vutta*m*. Viva*t*a*m* nâtivassatîti âpatti*m* âpa*gg*itvâ vivaranto aññam n' âpa*gg*atîti ida*m* eta*m* sandhâya vutta*m*.

[1] Pâtimokkha*m* *th*apetu*m*: exactly analogous to pavâra*n*a*m* *th*apetu*m* at Mahâvagga IV, 16, 2. H. O. has already pointed out (in his 'Buddha,' p. 381, note 2) that we have evidently here a later innovation. The whole frame of the Pâtimokkha shows that it was at first intended that a guilty Bhikkhu should confess his offence during the recitation, if he had not done so before.

do I interdict the Pâtimokkha to the effect that it shall not be recited when he is present. The Pâtimokkha is accordingly interdicted." '

3.

1. Now at that time the *Kh*abbaggiya Bhikkhus thinking, 'No one knows that we are guilty,' listened to the Pâtimokkha. The Thera Bhikkhus, who understood the thoughts of other men, told the Bhikkhus, saying, 'Such and such a one, Sirs, and such and such a one, *Kh*abbaggiya Bhikkhus, thinking, "No one knows that we are guilty," are listening to the Pâtimokkha.'

When the *Kh*abbaggiya Bhikkhus heard that, they, thinking 'the good Bhikkhus will (otherwise) first interdict the Pâtimokkha to us,' interdicted the Pâtimokkha to the Bhikkhus who were pure and innocent before (they had time to do so to them), and this without ground and without cause.

Those Bhikkhus who were moderate murmured, &c., ... (as usual, down to) told the matter to the Blessed One.

'Is it true, O Bhikkhus, that the *Kh*abbaggiya Bhikkhus have [acted thus]?'

'It is true, Lord!'

Then he rebuked them, and when he had delivered a religious discourse, he said: 'The Pâtimokkha is not, O Bhikkhus, to be interdicted to pure and innocent Bhikkhus without ground and without cause. Whosoever does so, shall be guilty of a dukka*t*a.

2. 'There is one kind of inhibition of the Pâtimokkha, O Bhikkhus, which is illegal, and one

which is legal. There are two . . . ., three . . . ., four (&c., up to) ten kinds of inhibition of the Pâtimokkha which are illegal, and one, two (&c., up to) ten which are legal.

3. 'Which is the one kind of inhibition of the Pâtimokkha which is illegal? When one inhibits the Pâtimokkha for a breach of morality without ground. This is the one kind, &c.

'And which is the one kind of inhibition of the Pâtimokkha which is legal? When one inhibits the Pâtimokkha for a breach of morality with good ground. This is the one kind, &c.

'And which are the two kinds of inhibition of the Pâtimokkha which are illegal? When one inhibits the Pâtimokkha for a breach of morality, or for an offence against conduct, and each of them without ground. These are the two kinds, &c.

'And which are the two kinds of inhibition of the Pâtimokkha which are legal? When one inhibits the Pâtimokkha for a breach of morality, and for an offence against conduct, and each of them with good ground. These are the two kinds, &c.

'And which are the three kinds, &c.? [as the last two, adding "offence against doctrine."]

'And which are the four kinds, &c.? [as the last, adding "offence against the right mode of livelihood."]

'And which are the five kinds of inhibition of the Pâtimokkha which are illegal? When one inhibits the Pâtimokkha for a Pârâ*g*ika, or for a Sa*m*ghâdisesa, or for a Pâ*k*ittiya, or for a Pâ*t*idesanîya, or for a Dukka*t*a, and each of them without ground. These are the five kinds, &c.

'And which are the five kinds of inhibition of the

Pâtimokkha which are legal? [Same as the last, "with good ground."]

'And which are the six kinds of inhibition of the Pâtimokkha which are illegal? When one inhibits the Pâtimokkha for an offence against morality.... conduct.... doctrine[1].... without ground, the offence being one of omission—when one inhibits the Pâtimokkha for an offence against morality.... conduct.... doctrine.... without ground, the offence being one of commission[2]. These are the six, &c.

'And which are the six kinds of inhibition of the Pâtimokkha which are legal? [Same as the last, "with good ground."]

'And which are the seven kinds of inhibition of the Pâtimokkha which are illegal? When one inhibits the Pâtimokkha for a Pârâ*g*ika, or for a Sa*m*ghâdisesa, or for a Thulla*kk*aya, or for a Pâ*k*ittiya, or for a Pâ*t*idesanîya, or for a Dukka*t*a, or for a Dubbhâsita, and each of them without ground. These are the seven kinds, &c.

'And which are the seven kinds of inhibition of the Pâtimokkha which are legal? [Same as the last, "with good ground."]

'And which are the eight kinds of inhibition of the Pâtimokkha which are illegal? [The same as the six, adding "offence against the right means of livelihood."]

---

[1] The paragraph is repeated in the section full for each of these cases.

[2] Kata.... akatâ.... katâkatâ we have rendered here and below as offence of omission—of commission—of both, as seems imperatively demanded by the context. Buddhaghosa, however, says, Akatâyâ ti tena puggalena sâ vipatti katâ vâ hotu akatâ vâ pâtimokkha-*th*apanakassa sa*ññ*â amûlika-vasena amûlikâ hoti. Katâkatâyâ ti kata*ñ k*a akata*ñ k*a ubhaya*m* gahetvâ vutta*m*.

'And which are the nine kinds of inhibition of the Pâtimokkha which are illegal . . . . legal? [The same as the six, adding for each kind of offence, "the offence being one both of omission and of commission."]

'And which are the ten kinds of inhibition of the Pâtimokkha which are illegal? When (a Bhikkhu) who has been guilty of a Pârâgika is not seated in that assembly[1],—when no discussion is still going on (in the assembly) as to a Pârâgika offence (supposed to have been committed by a Bhikkhu then present),—when (a Bhikkhu) who has abandoned the precepts[2] is not seated in that assembly,—when no discussion is still going on (in the assembly) in respect of (a Bhikkhu then present having been charged with) abandoning the precepts,—when (the person charged) submits himself to the legally prescribed concord (of the assembly)[3], —when (the person charged) does not withdraw his acceptance of the legally prescribed concord (of the assembly)[4],—when no discussion is still going on (in the assembly) in respect of the withdrawal of (any member's) acceptance of the legally (prescribed) concord (of the assembly),—when (the Bhikkhu charged) has not been suspected of an offence against morality, nor seen (to have committed one), nor heard (to have committed one)— . . . . of an offence against conduct — . . . . of an

[1] This and the following phrase are further enlarged upon in § 4 and the following sections.

[2] See our note on Mahâvagga II, 22, 3.

[3] See Mahâvagga X, 5, 13, &c.

[4] Pa*kk*âdîyati. Buddhaghosa says here, pa*kk*âdîyatî ti puna kâtabba*m* kamma*m* pa*kk*âdîyati. Tena ukko*t*anake pâ*k*ittiya*m* âpa*gg*ati.

offence against doctrine. . . . . These are the ten kinds, &c.

'And which are the ten kinds of inhibition of the Pâtimokkha which are legal? [The same as the last, positive instead of negative.]

4. 'And how (can it be legally said that) a Bhikkhu who has been guilty of a Pârâ*g*ika offence is seated in the assembly?

'In case, O Bhikkhus, a Bhikkhu sees that (another) Bhikkhu is incurring a Pârâ*g*ika offence by those means, marks, and signs by which the incurring of a Pârâ*g*ika offence is brought about. Or in case a Bhikkhu does not himself see that (another) Bhikkhu is incurring a Pârâ*g*ika offence, but another Bhikkhu inform the (first-mentioned) Bhikkhu, saying, "Such and such a Bhikkhu, Sir, has been guilty of a Pârâ*g*ika offence." Or in case a Bhikkhu does not himself see that another Bhikkhu is incurring a Pârâ*g*ika offence, but that one himself inform the (first-mentioned) Bhikkhu, saying, "I, Sir, have been guilty of a Pârâ*g*ika offence."

'(In either of these cases), O Bhikkhus, if he seem to do so, the Bhikkhu may, on the ground of what he has seen and heard and suspected, bring forward the following resolution on an Uposatha day, on the fourteenth or fifteenth day of the month, at a time when that individual is present in the midst of the Sa*m*gha: "Let the venerable Sa*m*gha hear me. Such and such an individual has been guilty of a Pârâ*g*ika offence. I interdict for him the Pâtimokkha, to the effect that the Pâtimokkha ought not to be recited at a time when he is present." That is a legal inhibition of the Pâtimokkha.

'If, when the Pâtimokkha has been inhibited for

that Bhikkhu, the assembly should rise on account of any one or other of the Ten Dangers[1]—danger arising from the king, or from thieves, or from fire, or from water, or from human beings, or from non-human beings, or from beasts of prey, or from creeping things, or danger of life, or danger against chastity—the Bhikkhu may, if he desire to do so, bring forward the following resolution, either in that circle of residence or in another circle of residence, at a time when that individual is present in the midst of the assembly: "Let the venerable Sa*m*gha hear me. A discussion had commenced with regard to a Pârâ*g*ika offence of such and such a person, but that matter was not decided. If the time seems meet to the Sa*m*gha, let the Sa*m*gha decide that matter." If he thus succeed, it is well. If not, then on an Uposatha day, on the fourteenth or fifteenth day of the month, at a time when that individual is present in the midst of the Sa*m*gha, let him bring forward the following resolution: "Let the venerable Sa*m*gha hear me. A discussion had commenced with regard to a Pârâ*g*ika offence of such and such a person, but that matter was not decided. I interdict the Pâtimokkha for him to the effect that the Pâtimokkha ought not to be recited at a time when he is present." That is a legal inhibition of the Pâtimokkha.

5. 'And how (can it be legally said that a Bhikkhu) who has abandoned the precepts is seated in the assembly?'

[The same as last, reading 'abandoned the precepts,' &c., for 'Pârâ*g*ika offence,' &c.]

6. 'And how (can it be legally said that the person

[1] See the rule laid down in Mahâvagga II, 15, 4.

charged) does not submit himself to the legally (prescribed) concord (of the assembly)?'

[Same as last, reading 'not submit himself to the legally (prescribed) concord of the assembly,' &c., instead of 'abandon the precepts,' &c.]

7. 'And how (can it be legally said that the person charged) withdraws his acceptance of the legally (established) concord (of the assembly)?'

[Same as last, reading 'withdraws his acceptance,' &c., for 'does not submit,' &c.]

8. 'And how can it be legally said that the person charged has been seen or heard or suspected of having committed an offence against morality . . . . an offence against conduct . . . . an offence against doctrine?'

[Same as § 4, reading 'offence against morality,' &c., for 'Pârâgika offence.']

These are the ten kinds of the inhibition of Pâtimokkha which are legal.

Here ends the First Portion for Recitation.

4.

1. Now the venerable Upâli[1] went up to the Blessed One, and bowed down before him, and took his seat on one side. And when he was so seated, the venerable Upâli said to the Blessed One:

'When a Bhikkhu, Lord, intends to take upon himself the conduct (of any matter that has to be

[1] No doubt in his rôle of a chief of the Vinaya-dharas, as in Mahâvagga IX, 6, &c.

decided)[1], under what conditions should he take the conduct thereof upon himself[2]?'

'A Bhikkhu, Upâli, who intends to take upon himself the conduct of any matter, should take such conduct upon himself under five conditions.

'(In the first place.) A Bhikkhu, Upâli, who intends to take the conduct of any matter upon himself, should thus consider: "The conduct of this matter which I intend to take upon myself, is it now the right time for the taking charge of the conduct thereof, or is it not?" If that Bhikkhu, Upâli, so considering, come to the conclusion that it is not the right time, he should not, Upâli, take charge of it.

'(Secondly.) If that Bhikkhu, Upâli, so considering, come to the conclusion that it is the right time, he should, Upâli, further consider thus: "The conduct of this matter which I intend to take upon myself, is it just, or is it not?" If that Bhikkhu, Upâli, so considering, come to the conclusion that it would not be just, he should not take charge of it.

'(Thirdly.) If that Bhikkhu, Upâli, so considering, come to the conclusion that it would be just, he should, Upâli, further consider thus: "The conduct of this matter which I intend to take upon myself, would it tend to advantage, or would it not?" If that Bhikkhu, Upâli, so considering, come to the conclusion that it would not tend to advantage, he should not, Upâli, take charge of it.

'(Fourthly.) If that Bhikkhu, Upâli, so considering, come to the conclusion that it would tend to

[1] As, for instance, in the last chapter (§§ 4 and following) the Bhikkhu who lays the matter before the Sa*m*gha.

[2] Attâdâna*m* âdîyati, in our explanation of which we follow Buddhaghosa.

profit, he should, Upâli, further consider thus: "While I am taking the conduct of this matter upon myself, shall I find that the Bhikkhus who are my intimates and associates are on my side in accordance with the Dhamma and the Vinaya, or shall I not?" If that Bhikkhu, Upâli, so considering, come to the conclusion that he will not, he should not, Upâli, take charge of it.

'(Fifthly.) If that Bhikkhu, Upâli, so considering, come to the conclusion that he will find them so, he should further, Upâli, consider thus: "Whilst I am taking the conduct of this matter upon myself, will the Sa*m*gha, as a result thereof, fall into strife, quarrel, contention, or dispute, or will there arise a split in the Sa*m*gha, disunion in the Sa*m*gha, diversity of position in the Sa*m*gha, diversity of action in the Sa*m*gha[1]?" If that Bhikkhu, Upâli, so considering, come to the conclusion that that will happen, he should not take charge of it. But if that Bhikkhu, Upâli, thus considering, should come to the conclusion that that will not happen, he should take charge of it. The taking charge of a matter, Upâli, subject to these five conditions, will not give cause to subsequent remorse.'

5.

1. 'When, Lord, a Bhikkhu who takes upon himself to warn another, is about to do so, of how many qualities should he consider whether they are within himself before he does so?'

(a) 'A Bhikkhu who warns another should, Upâli,

[1] This list has occurred above, Mahâvagga X, 1, 6; X, 5, 13; *K*ullavagga VII, 5, 1.

when he is about to do so, consider thus: "Am I pure in the conduct of my body; pure therein without a flaw, without a fleck? Is this quality found in me, or is it not?" If, Upâli, the Bhikkhu is not so, there will be some who will say to him: "Come, now, let your reverence continue still to train yourself in matters relating to the body!"—thus will they say.

(b) 'And further, a Bhikkhu who warns another should, Upâli, when he is about to do so, consider thus: "Am I pure in the conduct of my speech; pure therein without a flaw, without a fleck? Is this quality found in me, or is it not?" If, Upâli, the Bhikkhu is not so, there will be some who will say to him: "Come, now, let your reverence continue still to train yourself in matters relating to speech!"—thus will they say.

(c) 'And further, a Bhikkhu who warns another should, Upâli, consider thus: "Is a kindly mind ever present in me, one without anger against those who are my companions in the religious life? Is this quality found in me, or is it not?" If, Upâli, such a mind is not in that Bhikkhu, there will be some who will say to him: "Come, now, let your reverence continue still to cultivate a friendly feeling towards those who are your companions in the religious life!"—thus will they say.

(d) 'And further, a Bhikkhu who warns another should, Upâli, consider thus: "Am I a man versed in the tradition, a custodian of the tradition, a storehouse of the tradition? Whatsoever truths, lovely in their origin, lovely in their progress, lovely in their consummation, magnify the higher life, both in the spirit and in the letter, and in all its points, in all its perfectness,—in such truths am I well versed, of such am I full, are such laid up in my words, dwelt on in my heart, penetrated throughout through right insight[1]? Is this quality found in me, or is it not?" If that Bhikkhu, Upâli, is not such a man, there will be some who will say to him: "Come, now, let your reverence continue still to learn the faith!"—thus will they say.

(e) 'And further, a Bhikkhu who warns another should, Upâli, consider thus: "Have both the Pâtimokkhas been completely handed down to me in their full extent; have I well divided them, well established them, well investigated them, both Rule by Rule[2], and in every detail? Is this quality found in me, or is it not?" If, Upâli, that is not so, then when he is asked, "Where has this, Sir, been declared by the Blessed One?" he will not be able to explain[3], and there will be some who will say to him: "Come, now, let your reverence continue still to learn the Vinaya!"—thus will they say.

'These are the five qualities, Upâli, of which a Bhikkhu about to warn another should consider before he does so, whether they are within himself or not.'

2. 'When, Lord, a Bhikkhu who takes upon himself to warn another, is about to do so, how many qualities should he call up (establish) within himself before he does so?'

---

[1] On the whole of this and of the next paragraph, which have occurred already above at IV, 14, 19, see our notes there.

[2] That is, 'Sutta by Sutta.' On the whole stock phrase, compare our remarks in p. xviii of the Introduction; and above, Mahâvagga I, 36, 14; *K*ullavagga IV, 14, 19.

[3] Read na sampâyati, in accordance with H.O.'s note at p. 364 of the text.

'A Bhikkhu, Upâli, who is about to warn another, should call up within himself five qualities before he does so, (saying to himself): "At the right time will I speak, not at the wrong time. In truth will I speak, and not in falsehood. Gently will I speak, and not in harshness. To profit will I speak, and not senselessly. In kindly spirit will I speak, and not in anger[1].

'These, Upâli, are the five,' &c.

3. 'In how many ways, Lord, is repentance to be brought home to a Bhikkhu who has wrongfully warned another Bhikkhu?'

'In five ways, Upâli, is repentance to be brought home to a Bhikkhu who has wrongfully warned another Bhikkhu, (that is to say, by saying to him): "At the wrong time did you warn him, Sir, not at the right time: wherein is need of repentance. Untruthfully did you warn him, Sir, and not according to fact: wherein is need of repentance. In harshness did you warn him, Sir, and not gently: wherein is need of repentance. Senselessly did you warn him, Sir, and not in a way redounding to profit: wherein is need of repentance. In anger did you warn him, Sir, and not in kindly spirit: wherein is need of repentance.

'In these five ways, Upâli, should repentance be brought home to a Bhikkhu who has wrongfully warned another Bhikkhu. And why? That no other Bhikkhu may think that warning is to be given not according to fact.'

4. 'In how many ways, Lord, is it to be brought

---

[1] On these phrases, compare the *K*ûla Sîla*m*, translated by Rh. D. in 'Buddhist Suttas,' p. 190.

about that repentance shall not be brought home to a Bhikkhu who has been wrongfully warned?'

'In five ways, Upâli, (that is to say, by saying to him): "At the wrong time, Sir, were you warned, and not at the right time: there is no need of repentance,"' [&c., as in § 3, paragraph 2, with similar alterations.]

5. 'In how many ways, Lord, is the contrary of repentance to be brought home to a Bhikkhu who has rightfully warned another Bhikkhu?'

[The answer is the exact contrary of § 3.]

6. [This section is the contrary of § 5.]

7. 'When, Lord, a Bhikkhu who warns another Bhikkhu, is about to do so, how many things should he call to mind before he does so?'

'Five things, Upâli—to wit: mercy, seeking the good of others, compassion, the giving up of offences, and deference towards the Vinaya. These are the five,' &c.

'And a Bhikkhu, Lord, who is warned, in how many qualities should he keep himself firm?'

'In two things, Upâli—to wit: in truth and in freedom from anger'

Here ends the Ninth Khandhaka, on the Interdiction of the Pâtimokkha.

TENTH KHANDHAKA.

On the Duties of Bhikkhunîs.

1.

1. Now at that time the Blessed Buddha was staying among the Sâkyas in Kapilavatthu, in the Nigrodhârâma. And Mahâ-pagâpatî the Gotamî went to the place where the Blessed One was, and on arriving there, bowed down before the Blessed One, and remained standing on one side. And so standing she spake thus to the Blessed One:

'It would be well, Lord, if women should be allowed to renounce their homes and enter the homeless state under the doctrine and discipline proclaimed by the Tathâgata.'

'Enough, O Gotamî! Let it not please thee that women should be allowed to do so.'

[And a second and a third time did Mahâ-pagâpatî the Gotamî make the same request in the same words, and receive the same reply.]

Then Mahâ-pagâpatî the Gotamî sad and sorrowful for that the Blessed One would not permit women to enter the homeless state, bowed down before the Blessed One, and keeping him on her right hand as she passed him, departed thence weeping and in tears.

2. Now when the Blessed One had remained at Kapilavatthu as long as he thought fit, he set out on his journey towards Vesâlî; and travelling

straight on he in due course arrived thereat. And there at Vesâlî the Blessed One stayed, in the Mahâvana, in the Kû*t*âgâra Hall.

And Mahâ-pa*g*âpatî the Gotamî cut off her hair, and put on orange-coloured robes, and set out, with a number of women of the Sâkya clan, towards Vesâlî; and in due course she arrived at Vesâlî, at the Mahâvana, at the Kû*t*âgâra Hall. And Mahâ-pa*g*âpatî the Gotamî, with swollen feet and covered with dust, sad and sorrowful, weeping and in tears, took her stand outside under the entrance porch.

And the venerable Ânanda saw her so standing there, and on seeing her so, he said to Mahâ-pa*g*âpatî: 'Why standest thou there, outside the porch, with swollen feet and covered with dust, sad and sorrowful, weeping and in tears?'

'Inasmuch, O Ânanda, as the Lord, the Blessed One, does not permit women to renounce their homes and enter the homeless state under the doctrine and discipline proclaimed by the Tathâgata.'

3. Then did the venerable Ânanda go up to the place where the Blessed One was, and bow down before the Blessed One, and take his seat on one side. And, so sitting, the venerable Ânanda said to the Blessed One:

'Behold, Lord, Mahâ-pa*g*âpatî the Gotamî is standing outside under the entrance porch, with swollen feet and covered with dust, sad and sorrowful, weeping and in tears, inasmuch as the Blessed One does not permit women to renounce their homes and enter the homeless state under the doctrine and discipline proclaimed by the Blessed One. It were well, Lord, if women were to have permission granted to them to do as she desires.'

'Enough, Ânanda! Let it not please thee that women should be allowed to do so.'

[And a second and a third time did Ânanda make the same request, in the same words, and receive the same reply.]

Then the venerable Ânanda thought: 'The Blessed One does not give his permission, let me now ask the Blessed One on another ground.' And the venerable Ânanda said to the Blessed One:

'Are women, Lord, capable—when they have gone forth from the household life and entered the homeless state, under the doctrine and discipline proclaimed by the Blessed One—are they capable of realising the fruit of conversion, or of the second Path, or of the third Path, or of Arahatship?'

'They are capable, Ânanda.'

'If then, Lord, they are capable thereof, since Mahâ-pa*g*âpatî the Gotamî has proved herself of great service to the Blessed One, when as aunt and nurse she nourished him and gave him milk, and on the death of his mother suckled the Blessed One at her own breast, it were well, Lord, that women should have permission to go forth from the household life and enter the homeless state, under the doctrine and discipline proclaimed by the Tathâgata [1].'

4. 'If then, Ânanda, Mahâ-pa*g*âpatî the Gotamî take upon herself the Eight Chief Rules [2], let that be reckoned to her as her initiation.'

[3][They are these]: (1) 'A Bhikkhunî, even if of

[1] Ânanda's conduct in this matter was afterwards charged against him as a dukka*t*a. See below, XI, 1, 10.

[2] The A*tth*a Garudhammâ, on which see further our note above on the 21st Pâ*k*ittiya, and below, X, 9.

[3] The whole of the following eight paragraphs recur in the

a hundred years standing, shall make salutation to, shall rise up in the presence of, shall bow down before, and shall perform all proper duties towards a Bhikkhu, if only just initiated. This is a rule to be revered and reverenced, honoured and observed, and her life long never to be transgressed.

(2) 'A Bhikkhunî is not to spend the rainy season (of Was) in a district[1] in which there is no Bhikkhu. This is a rule . . . . never to be transgressed.

(3) 'Every half month a Bhikkhunî is to await from the Bhikkhu-sa*m*gha two things, the asking as to (the date of) the Uposatha ceremony[2], and the (time when the Bhikkhu) will come to give the Exhortation[3]. This is a rule . . . . never to be transgressed.

(4) 'After keeping the rainy season (of Was), the Bhikkhunî is to hold Pavâra*n*â (to enquire whether any fault can be laid to her charge) before both Sa*m*ghas—as well that of Bhikkhus as that of Bhikkhunîs—with respect to three matters, namely, what has been seen, and what has been heard, and what has been suspected[4]. This is a rule . . . . never to be transgressed.

Sutta Vibhaṅga, Pâ*k*ittiya XXI, 3, 1. It is very instructive to notice the curious blunders which the Tibetan writers (translated by Rockhill in his 'Life of the Buddha,' pp. 62, 63) make in the rendering of the difficult technical terms in these Eight Rules.

[1] Âvâsa. Compare *K*ullavagga I, 18, 1, VI, 15, 1, VIII, 1, 2. This rule is the 56th Bhikkhunî Pâ*k*ittiya.

[2] The Bhikkhunîs are to ask two or three days beforehand whether the Uposatha is to be held on the 14th or 15th day of the month, says Buddhaghosa here. Compare also the 59th Bhikkhunî Pâ*k*ittiya, where the whole passage recurs.

[3] Compare the 21st Pâ*k*ittiya, and our note there.

[4] See Mahâvagga IV, 1, 13, 14. This rule is the same as the 57th Bhikkhunî Pâ*k*ittiya. The mode of carrying out this rule is explained in detail below, X, 19.

(5) 'A Bhikkhunî who has been guilty of a serious offence is to undergo the Mânatta discipline towards both the Sa*m*ghas (Bhikkhus and Bhikkhunîs). This is a rule . . . . never to be transgressed.

(6) 'When a Bhikkhunî, as novice, has been trained for two years in the Six Rules[1], she is to ask leave for the upasampadâ initiation from both Sa*m*ghas (as well that of Bhikkhus as that of Bhikkhunîs[2]). This is a rule . . . . never to be transgressed.

(7) 'A Bhikkhunî is on no pretext to revile or abuse a Bhikkhu[3]. This is a rule . . . . never to be transgressed.

(8) 'From henceforth official admonition[4] by Bhikkhunîs of Bhikkhus is forbidden, whereas the official admonition of Bhikkhunîs by Bhikkhus is not forbidden. This is a rule . . . . never to be transgressed.

'If, Ânanda, Mahâ-pa*g*âpatî the Gotamî take upon herself these Eight Chief Rules, let that be reckoned to her as her initiation.'

5. Then the venerable Ânanda, when he had learnt from the Blessed One these Eight Chief Rules, went to Mahâ-pa*g*âpatî the Gotamî and [told her all that the Blessed One had said].

---

[1] *Kh*asu dhammesu. The Six Rules for novices. They are referred to in the Bhikkhunî Vibhaṅga, under Pâ*k*ittiyas LXIII–LXVII.

[2] The actual ordination (upasampadâ) itself is not complete till it has been conferred by Bhikkhus (see the rule at X, 2, 2). The whole proceeding is fully set out below, X, 17. Compare also the 63rd and 64th Bhikkhunî Pâ*k*ittiyas.

[3] This is the 52nd Bhikkhunî Pâ*k*ittiya.

[4] Va*k*ana-patho. That is, literally, speech. But the reference is, no doubt, to the various kinds of official admonitions given in detail in chapter 20 below.

'Just, Ânanda, as a man or a woman, when young and of tender years, accustomed to adorn himself, would, when he had bathed his head, receive with both hands a garland of lotus flowers, or of jasmine flowers, or of atimuttaka flowers, and place it on the top of his head; even so do I, Ânanda, take upon me these Eight Chief Rules, never to be transgressed my life long.'

6. Then the venerable Ânanda returned to the Blessed One, and bowed down before him, and took his seat on one side. And, so sitting, the venerable Ânanda said to the Blessed One: 'Mahâ-pa*g*âpatî the Gotamî, Lord, has taken upon herself the Eight Chief Rules, the aunt of the Blessed One has received the upasampadâ initiation.'

'If, Ânanda, women had not received permission to go out from the household life and enter the homeless state, under the doctrine and discipline proclaimed by the Tathâgata, then would the pure religion, Ânanda, have lasted long, the good law would have stood fast for a thousand years. But since, Ânanda, women have now received that permission, the pure religion, Ânanda, will not now last so long, the good law will now stand fast for only five hundred years. Just, Ânanda, as houses in which there are many women[1] and but few men are easily violated[2] by robber burglars[3]; just so, Ânanda, under

[1] Bahutthikâni. The context shows that we are to understand itthi and not attha. Compare Rockhill's 'Life of the Buddha,' p. 61.

[2] Suppadha*m*siyâni. Compare Bhikkhunî Vibhaṅga, Sa*m*ghâdisesa III, 1, 2, and see also *K*ullavagga VII, 5, 4.

[3] *K*orehi kumbatthenakehi; on which Buddhaghosa has the following note:—Kumbathenakehi ti kumbhe dîpa*m* *g*âletvâ ena âlokena paraghare bha*nd*a*m* vi*k*initvâ thenaka*k*orehi.

whatever doctrine and discipline women are allowed to go out from the household life into the homeless state, that religion will not last long. And just, Ânanda, as when the disease called mildew falls upon a field of rice in fine condition, that field of rice does not continue long; just so, Ânanda, under whatsoever doctrine and discipline women are allowed to go forth from the household life into the homeless state, that religion will not last long. And just, Ânanda, as when the disease called blight falls upon a field of sugar-cane in good condition, that field of sugar-cane does not continue long; just so, Ânanda, under whatsoever doctrine and discipline women are allowed to go forth from the household life into the homeless state, that religion does not last long. And just, Ânanda, as a man would in anticipation build an embankment to a great reservoir, beyond which the water should not overpass; just even so, Ânanda, have I in anticipation laid down these Eight Chief Rules for the Bhikkhunîs, their life long not to be overpassed.'

Here end the Eight Chief Rules for the Bhikkhunîs.

2.

1. Now Mahâ-pagâpatî the Gotamî went up to the place where the Blessed One was, and bowed down before him, and stood respectfully on one side. And, so standing, Mahâ-pagâpatî the Gotamî spake thus to the Blessed One: 'What course, Lord,

should I pursue towards these women of the Sâkya clan?'

Then the Blessed One taught Mahâ-pa*g*âpatî the Gotamî and incited her, and aroused her, and gladdened her with religious discourse; and she, so taught, incited, aroused, and gladdened, bowed down before the Blessed One, and keeping him on her right hand as she passed him, she departed thence.

Then the Blessed One, in that connexion, delivered a religious discourse, and said to the Bhikkhus, 'I allow Bhikkhunîs, O Bhikkhus, to receive the upasampadâ initiation from Bhikkhus[1].'

2. Now those Bhikkhunîs said to Mahâ-pa*g*âpatî the Gotamî: 'Neither have you received the upasampadâ initiation, nor have we; for it has thus been laid down by the Blessed One: "Bhikkhunîs are to be initiated by Bhikkhus."'

Then Mahâ-pa*g*âpatî the Gotamî went to the venerable Ânanda, and [repeated their words to him]. And the venerable Ânanda went to the Blessed One, and [repeated them to him].

'In that moment, Ânanda, when Mahâ-pa*g*âpatî the Gotamî took upon herself the Eight Chief Rules, that was to her as the upasampadâ initiation.'

3.

1. Now Mahâ-pa*g*âpatî the Gotamî went up to the place where the venerable Ânanda was, and bowed down before him, and stood respectfully on one side.

[1] Compare the 6th Garudhamma above, X, 1, 4.

And, so standing, Mahâ-pa*g*âpatî the Gotamî said to the venerable Ânanda: 'One thing, Ânanda, would I ask of the Blessed One. It were well, Sir, if the Blessed One would allow the making of salutations, the rising up in presence of another, the paying of reverence, and the performance of proper duties one towards another, to take place as between both Bhikkhus and Bhikkhunîs (equally) according to seniority.'

And the venerable Ânanda went to the Blessed One [and repeated her words to him].

'This is impossible, Ânanda, and unallowable, that I should so order. Even those others, Ânanda, teachers of ill doctrine, allow not such conduct towards women; how much less, then, can the Tathâgata allow it?'

And the Blessed One, on that occasion, having delivered a religious discourse, addressed the Bhikkhus, and said: 'You are not, O Bhikkhus, to bow down before women, to rise up in their presence, to stretch out your joined hands towards them, nor to perform towards them those duties that are proper (from an inferior to a superior). Whosoever does so, shall be guilty of a dukka*t*a.'

4.

1. Now Mahâ-pa*g*âpatî the Gotamî went up to the place where the Blessed One was, and bowed down before him, and stood respectfully on one side. And, so standing, Mahâ-pa*g*âpatî the Gotamî said to the Blessed One: 'What course, Lord, shall we pursue with reference to those precepts for the

Bhikkhunîs which are applicable also to the Bhikkhus?'

'Train yourselves, Gotamî, therein in the same manner as the Bhikkhus do.'

'And what course, Lord, should we pursue in reference to those precepts for the Bhikkhunîs which are not applicable also to the Bhikkhus?'

'Train yourselves, Gotamî, therein according to the substance thereof, as they are laid down.'

5.

1. Now Mahâ-pagâpatî the Gotamî went to the Blessed One [&c., as before], and said: 'May the Blessed One preach to me the Dhamma (truth, doctrine) in abstract; so that, having heard the doctrine of the Blessed One, I may remain alone and separate, earnest, zealous, and resolved[1].'

'Of whatsoever doctrines thou shalt be conscious, Gotamî, that they conduce to passion and not to peace, to pride and not to veneration, to wishing for much and not to wishing for little, to love of society and not to seclusion, to sloth and not to the exercise of zeal, to being hard to satisfy and not to content[2] —verily mayest thou then, Gotamî, bear in mind

[1] These last words are the standing expression for the preparatory stage to Arahatship. Compare Mahâvagga I, 6, 16; Mahâparinibbâna Sutta V, 68. The whole speech frequently occurs in the S*am*yutta Nikâya at the commencement of conversations with the Buddha.

[2] Most of these terms have already occurred in the standing 'religious discourse' which is related to have preceded the enunciation of so many of the rules for Bhikkhus (*K*ullavagga I, 2, 3).

that that is not Dhamma, that that is not Vinaya, that that is not the teaching of the Master. But of whatsoever doctrines thou shalt be conscious, Gotamî, that they conduce to peace and not to passion, to veneration and not to pride, to wishing for little and not to wishing for much, to seclusion and not to love of society, to the exercise of zeal and not to sloth, to content and not to querulousness—verily mayest thou then bear in mind that that is Dhamma, and that is Vinaya, and that the teaching of the Master.'

6.

1. Now at that time the Pâtimokkha was not recited to the Bhikkhunîs.

They told this matter to the Blessed One.

'I allow the Pâtimokkha, O Bhikkhus, to be recited to the Bhikkhunîs.'

Now it occurred to the Bhikkhunîs: 'By whom should the Pâtimokkha be recited to the Bhikkhunîs?'

They told this matter to the Blessed One.

'I allow, O Bhikkhus, the Pâtimokkha to be recited to Bhikkhunîs by Bhikkhus.'

Now at that time Bhikkhus went to the residence of the Bhikkhunîs and recited the Pâtimokkha to the Bhikkhunîs there. The people murmured, and were indignant, saying: 'There are their wives, there are their mistresses; now will they take pleasure together.'

The Bhikkhus heard this, and told the matter to the Blessed One.

'Bhikkhus are not, O Bhikkhus, to recite the

Pâtimokkha to the Bhikkhunîs at their residence. Whosoever does so, shall be guilty of a dukkata. I allow Bhikkhunîs, O Bhikkhus, to recite the Pâtimokkha to the Bhikkhunîs.'

The Bhikkhunîs did not know how to recite the Pâtimokkha. They told this matter to the Blessed One.

'I allow Bhikkhus, O Bhikkhus, to tell Bhikkhunîs how to recite the Pâtimokkha.'

2. Now at that time the Bhikkhunîs did not confess the faults (they had committed).

They told this matter to the Blessed One.

'A Bhikkhunî, O Bhikkhus, is not to leave a fault unconfessed. Whosoever does so, shall be guilty of a dukkata.'

The Bhikkhunîs did not know how to confess their faults. They told this matter to the Blessed One.

'I allow Bhikkhus, O Bhikkhus, to tell Bhikkhunîs how they should confess their faults.'

Then it occurred to the Bhikkhus: 'By whom ought the confession of a fault to be received from the Bhikkhunîs?' They told this matter to the Blessed One.

'I allow Bhikkhus, O Bhikkhus, to receive the confession of a fault from Bhikkhunîs.'

Now at that time Bhikkhunîs, on seeing a Bhikkhu on the road, or in a street closed at one end, or at the place where four cross-roads met, would place their bowl on the ground, and arranging their robes over one shoulder, would crouch down on their heels, and stretch forth their joined hands, and confess a fault. The people murmured, were indignant, and complained, saying: 'There are their wives, there are their mistresses; they are asking pardon now after having treated them scornfully overnight.'

They told this matter to the Blessed One.

'Bhikkhus are not, O Bhikkhus, to receive the confessions of a fault from Bhikkhunîs. Whosoever does so, shall be guilty of a dukka*t*a. I allow Bhikkhunîs, O Bhikkhus, to receive the confession of a fault from Bhikkhunîs.'

The Bhikkhunîs did not know how to receive the confession of a fault. They told this matter to the Blessed One.

'I allow Bhikkhus, O Bhikkhus, to tell Bhikkhunîs how to receive the confession of a fault.'

3. Now at that time disciplinary proceedings (Kammas) were not carried out against Bhikkhunîs. They told that matter to the Blessed One.

'I allow disciplinary proceedings, O Bhikkhus, to be carried out against Bhikkhunîs.'

Then the Bhikkhus thought: 'By whom ought disciplinary proceedings to be carried out against Bhikkhunîs?' They told this matter to the Blessed One.

'I allow Bhikkhus, O Bhikkhus, to carry out disciplinary proceedings against Bhikkhunîs.'

Now at that time Bhikkhunîs who had been subjected to disciplinary proceedings, on seeing a Bhikkhu on the road, or in a street closed at one end, or at the place where four cross-roads met, would place their bowls on the ground, and arranging their robes over one shoulder, would crouch down on their heels, and stretching out their joined palms would ask for pardon, thinking that that was the proper time for doing so. The people murmured [&c., as before].

They told this matter to the Blessed One.

'Bhikkhus are not, O Bhikkhus, to carry out disciplinary proceedings against the Bhikkhunîs. Whosoever does so, shall be guilty of a dukka*t*a.' I allow Bhikkhunîs, O Bhikkhus, to carry out disciplinary proceedings against Bhikkhunîs.'

The Bhikkhunîs did not know how to carry out the disciplinary proceedings. They told this matter to the Blessed One.

'I allow Bhikkhus, O Bhikkhus, to tell the Bhikkhunîs how to carry out disciplinary proceedings.'

7.

1. Now at that time Bhikkhunîs in Sa*m*gha assembled, having fallen into quarrel, strife, and dispute, got to blows, and were unable to settle the point at issue. They told this matter to the Blessed One.

'I allow Bhikkhus, O Bhikkhus, to settle for Bhikkhunîs a point at issue.'

Now at that time Bhikkhus were settling for Bhikkhunîs a point at issue, and as the point at issue was being enquired into, it was found that both Bhikkhunîs competent to take part in an official act[1], and Bhikkhunîs who had been guilty of an offence (had taken part in the Sa*m*gha during the official act (the Kamma) at which the point in issue arose).

The Bhikkhunîs said: 'It would be well if you, Sirs, would carry out disciplinary proceedings against the guilty Bhikkhunîs, or absolve their offence: for

[1] Kammappattâ; on which see Parivâra XIX, 6, 7.

thus has it been laid down by the Blessed One: "Bhikkhus are to settle for the Bhikkhunîs a point at issue."'

They told this matter to the Blessed One.

'I allow Bhikkhus, O Bhikkhus, to set on foot[1] an official act for Bhikkhunîs, and then to give it in charge for Bhikkhunîs to carry out the official act against Bhikkhunîs. And I allow Bhikkhus to set on foot the (dealing with an) offence for Bhikkhunîs, and then to give it in charge for Bhikkhunîs to accept the confession thereof.'

8.

1. Now at that time a Bhikkhunî, a pupil of the Bhikkhunî Uppalava*nn*â, followed the Blessed One for seven years, learning the Vinaya; but she, being forgetful, lost it as fast as she received it. And that Bhikkhunî heard that the Blessed One was about to go to Sâvatthi. Then she thought: 'For seven years have I followed the Blessed One, learning the Vinaya; and, being forgetful, I have lost it as fast as I received it. Hard is it for a woman to follow the Blessed One her life long. What now shall I do?'

And that Bhikkhunî told this matter to the Bhikkhunîs, and they told it to the Bhikkhus, and the Bhikkhus told it to the Blessed One.

'I allow Bhikkhus, O Bhikkhus, to teach the Vinaya to Bhikkhunîs.'

Here ends the First Portion for Recitation.

[1] Ropetu*m*, on which Buddhaghosa says: Ta*gg*aniyâdîsu ima*m* nâma kamma*m* etissâ kâtabban ti eva*m* ropetvâ.

9.

1. Now when the Blessed One had stayed at Vesâlî as long as he thought fit, he sat out towards Sâvatthi; and, journeying straight on, he in due course arrived thereat. And there, at Sâvatthi, the Blessed One remained in the *G*etavana, Anâtha Pi*nd*ika's Park.

Now at that time the *Kh*abbaggiya Bhikkhus threw dirty water over Bhikkhunîs, thinking, perhaps, they would fall in love with them[1].

They told this matter to the Blessed One.

'A Bhikkhu is not, O Bhikkhus, to throw dirty water at a Bhikkhunî. Whosoever does so, shall be guilty of a dukka*t*a. I allow a penalty, O Bhikkhus, to be imposed on that Bhikkhu.

Then the Bhikkhus thought: 'What penalty is it that ought to be imposed on him?' They told this matter to the Blessed One.

'That Bhikkhu is to be declared to be one who is not to be saluted by the Bhikkhunî-sa*m*gha[2].'

Now at that time the *Kh*abbaggiya Bhikkhus uncovered their bodies, or their thighs, or their private parts, and showed them to Bhikkhunîs, or addressed Bhikkhunîs with wicked words, or associated with Bhikkhunîs, thinking, perhaps, they would fall in love with them[3].

They told this matter to the Blessed One.

---

[1] On sâra*gg*eyyun compare sâra*gg*ati at V, 3, 1.

[2] On this decision compare the 'sending to Coventry' of *Kh*anna for levity of conduct towards Bhikkhus at Mahâ-parinibbâna Sutta VI, 4, and *K*ullavagga XI, 1, 12 (where the penalty is called Brahma-da*nd*a).

[3] On sampayo*g*eti compare *K*ullavagga I, 5, at the end.

'A Bhikkhu is not, O Bhikkhus, to do [any of these things]. Whosoever does, shall be guilty of a dukka*t*a. I allow, O Bhikkhus, a penalty to be imposed on that Bhikkhu.'

Then the Bhikkhus thought: 'What penalty is it that ought to be imposed on him?' They told this matter to the Blessed One.

'That Bhikkhu is to be declared to be one who is not to be saluted by the Bhikkhunî-sa*m*gha.'

2. [The last section repeated of the *Kh*abbaggiya Bhikkhunîs, the decision being the same down to]

Then the Bhikkhus thought: 'What penalty is it that ought to be imposed on her?' They told this matter to the Blessed One.

'I allow you, O Bhikkhus, to prohibit her (from entering a Vihâra)[1].'

When the prohibition was laid upon them, they would not accept it. They told this matter to the Blessed One.

'I allow you, O Bhikkhus, to inhibit them from the Exhortation.'

3. Then the Bhikkhus thought: 'Is it lawful to hold Uposatha with a Bhikkhunî who has been inhibited from the Exhortation, or is it not lawful?'

They told this matter to the Blessed One.

'You are not, O Bhikkhus, to hold Uposatha with a Bhikkhunî who has been inhibited from the Exhortation until such time as her case has been settled.'

Now at that time the venerable Udâyi, after having inhibited the Exhortation (to one or more Bhikkhunîs), went away on a journey. The Bhik-

[1] Âvara*n*an ti vihârapavesane nivâra*n*a*m*, says Buddhaghosa.

khunîs murmured, were indignant, and complained, saying: 'How can the venerable Udâyi [act so]?'

They told this matter to the Blessed One.

'You are not, O Bhikkhus, to go on a journey after having inhibited the Exhortation. Whosoever does so, shall be guilty of a dukka*t*a.'

Now at that time foolish and incompetent Bhikkhus inhibited the Exhortation.

They told this matter to the Blessed One.

'The Exhortation is not, O Bhikkhus, to be inhibited by a foolish, incompetent Bhikkhu. When such a one does so, he shall be guilty of a dukka*t*a.'

Now at that time Bhikkhus inhibited the Exhortation without grounds and without cause.

They told this matter to the Blessed One.

'You are not, O Bhikkhus, to inhibit the Exhortation without ground and without cause. Whosoever does so, shall be guilty of a dukka*t*a.'

Now at that time Bhikkhus, who had inhibited the Exhortation, would not give a decision (on the matter out of which the inhibition arose).

They told this matter to the Blessed One.

'When, O Bhikkhus, you have inhibited the Exhortation, you are not to abstain from giving a decision (on the matter out of which the inhibition arose). Whosoever does so, shall be guilty of a dukka*t*a.'

4. Now at that time Bhikkhunîs did not go to the Exhortation. They told this matter to the Blessed One.

'A Bhikkhunî, O Bhikkhus, is not to omit going to the Exhortation. Whosoever does so, shall be dealt with according to the rule [1].'

---

[1] Bhikkhunî Pâ*k*ittiya LVIII.

Now at that time the whole Bhikkhunî-sa*m*gha went to the Exhortation together. The people murmured, were indignant, and complained, saying: 'There are their wives, there are their mistresses; now will they take pleasure together.'

They told this matter to the Blessed One.

'The whole Bhikkhunî-sa*m*gha is not, O Bhikkhus, to go to the Exhortation together. And if it should so go, it is guilty of a dukka*t*a. I allow, O Bhikkhus, four or five Bhikkhunîs to go together.'

[The same when four or five went the decision ending,]

'I allow, O Bhikkhus, two or three Bhikkhunîs to go together to Exhortation; and let them go up to some one Bhikkhu, and arrange their robes over one shoulder, and, sitting down on their heels, let them stretch forth their joined palms, and thus address him: "The Bhikkhunî-sa*m*gha salutes the feet of the Bhikkhu-sa*m*gha, and requests permission to come for the purpose of the Exhortation being held; may that be granted, they say, to the Bhikkhunî-sa*m*gha."

'Then he who is entrusted with the recitation of the Pâtimokkha is to ask: "Is there any Bhikkhu who has been appointed to hold the Exhortation of the Bhikkhunîs?"

'If a Bhikkhu has been appointed thereto, the reciter of the Pâtimokkha is to say: "Such and such a Bhikkhu has been appointed to hold Exhortation to the Bhikkhunîs. Let the Bhikkhunî-sa*m*gha come to him accordingly."

'If no Bhikkhu has been appointed thereto, the reciter of the Pâtimokkha is to say: "Which of the venerable ones is able to hold Exhortation to the Bhikkhunîs?" If any one is able to do so, and is possessed of the eight qualifications[1], he is to appoint him thereto, and is to say: "Such and such a Bhikkhu is appointed to hold Exhortation to the Bhikkhunîs. Let the Bhikkhunî-sa*m*gha come to him."

'If no one is able to do so, the reciter of the Pâtimokkha is to say: "There is no Bhikkhu appointed to hold Exhortation to the Bhikkhunîs. May the Bhikkhunî-sa*m*gha obtain its desire in peace[2]."'

5. Now at that time Bhikkhus did not accept the (office of holding) Exhortation. They told this matter to the Blessed One.

'The Exhortation is not, O Bhikkhus, to be declined. Whosoever shall not accept it, shall be guilty of a dukka*t*a.'

Now at that time a certain Bhikkhu was stupid. To him the Bhikkhunîs went, and said: 'Sir, please to accept the (duty of holding) Exhortation.'

'I, sister, am stupid. How can I accept the Exhortation?'

'You should take it, Sir; for thus has it been laid down by the Blessed One: "Bhikkhus are to accept the (duty of holding) Exhortation to the Bhikkhunîs."'

They told this matter to the Blessed One.

'I allow, O Bhikkhus, all the rest, save the stupid, to accept the Exhortation.'

[The same repeated of a sick Bhikkhu, and a

[1] These are given at length in the Sutta Vibhaṅga, Pâ*k*ittiya XXI, 2, 1.

[2] Pâsâdikena sampâdetu, on which Buddhaghosa has no note. Perhaps 'by means of faith' would be a better rendering.

Bhikkhu on a journey. The same case put of a Bhikkhu living in the jungle. The decision is,]

'I allow a Bhikkhu living in the jungle, O Bhikkhus, to accept the Exhortation, and to appoint a time and place for the meeting[1], saying: "There will I perform it."'

Now at that time Bhikkhus accepted the Exhortation, but did not perform it. They told this matter to the Blessed One.

'The Exhortation, O Bhikkhus, is not to be neglected. Whosoever does so, shall be guilty of a dukka*t*a.'

Now at that time Bhikkhunîs did not attend at the place appointed. They told this matter to the Blessed One.

'A Bhikkhunî is not, O Bhikkhus, to omit attending at the place appointed. Whosoever does so, shall be guilty of a dukka*t*a.'

10.

1. Now at that time Bhikkhunîs wore long girdles, and out of them they arranged fringes[2]. The people murmured, were indignant, and complained, saying: 'As the women who are still enjoying the pleasures of the world do!'

---

[1] On sa*m*keta*m*, see our note above on Mahâvagga VIII, 23, 3.

[2] Pâsuke namentîti gihidârikâyo viya ghanapa*tt*akena kâyabandhanena pâsuke namanatthâya bandhanti, says Buddhaghosa. Pâsuka is probably equal to the Sanskrit pâr*s*vaka, and means a fringe arranged round the body, as shown in Plate LI of Cunningham's 'Bharhut Tope,' being so called from the rib-like arrangement of the strings or cloth or other substance of which it was made. On corresponding girdles worn by men and forbidden to Bhikkhus, see *K*ullavagga V, 29, 2.

'A Bhikkhunî is not, O Bhikkhus, to wear a long girdle. Whosoever does so, shall be guilty of a dukka*t*a. I allow a Bhikkhunî, O Bhikkhus, a girdle that will go once round the body[1], and fringes are not to be arranged in it. Whosoever does so, shall be guilty of a dukka*t*a.'

Now at that time Bhikkhunîs arranged fringes in cloth of bambû fibre[2], or in leather, or in white cotton cloth[3], or in plaited cotton cloth[4], or in fringed cotton cloth[5], or in white or in plaited or in fringed *k*ola cloth[6], or in plaits or fringes made of thread. The people murmured, were indignant, and complained, saying: 'As the women who are still enjoying the pleasures of the world do!'

They told this matter to the Blessed One.

'A Bhikkhunî is not, O Bhikkhus, to wear any of these things. Whosoever does so, shall be guilty of a dukka*t*a.'

2. Now at that time Bhikkhunîs had their backs scrubbed with the steak-bone of an ox, or slapped with the jaw-bone of an ox; and had their fore-arms[7],

---

[1] Ekapariyâkatan ti ekavâra*m* parikkhipanaka*m*, says the Samanta Pâsâdikâ.

[2] Vilivena pattenâti (sic) sa*n*heti ve*l*uvi*l*ivehi (sic) katapa*tt*ena.

[3] Dussapa*tt*enâti setavatthapa*tt*ena.

[4] Dussave*n*iyâti dussena kataveniyâ.

[5] Dussava*tt*iyâti dussena katava*tt*iyâ.

[6] *K*olapa*tt*âdisu *k*olakâvâsa*m* *k*olan ti veditabba*m*.

[7] Hattha*m* ko*tt*âpentîti agga*m* bâha*m* ko*tt*âpetvâ morapattâdîhi *k*ittaka*m* karonti, says Buddhaghosa. The meaning is not clear. No. 10 of the tattoo marks figured on Plate LII of Cunningham's 'Bharhut Tope,' referred to in the note on the next section, is a representation of a peacock's feathers. On a*tth*illa, see Buddhaghosa's note at p. 327 of the text. Compare the prohibition of the use by Bhikkhus of back-scratchers and other like things (*K*ullavagga V, 1, 1) connected with shampooing or luxurious bathing.

and the backs of their hands[1], and their calves[2], and the upper part of their feet[3], and their thighs, and their faces, and their gums, so slapped. The people murmured, were indignant, and complained, saying: 'As the women who are still enjoying the pleasures of the world do!'

They told this matter to the Blessed One.

'A Bhikkhunî is not, O Bhikkhus, to [do any of these things]. Whosoever does so, shall be guilty of a dukka*t*a.'

3. Now at that time the *Kh*abbaggiya Bhikkhunîs [&c., down to]

'[4] A Bhikkhunî is not, O Bhikkhus, to anoint her face, nor to rub ointments on to her face[5], nor to put chunam on to her face, nor to smear red arsenic on to her face, nor to paint her body, nor to paint her face, nor to paint her body and face. Whosoever does so, shall be guilty of a dukka*t*a.'

4. [Similar paragraph concluding,]

'A Bhikkhunî is not, O Bhikkhus, to make (tattoo marks) by the corners of her eyes[6], or on her cheeks[7], nor to peep out of window[8], nor to stand in the

---

[1] Hattha-ko*kkh*an ti pi*tth*i-hattha*m*.

[2] Pâdan ti *g*aṅgha*m*.

[3] Pâda-ko*kkh*an ti pi*tth*i-pâda*m*.

[4] This paragraph has already occurred above, V, 2, 5 of the Bhikkhus.

[5] These two injunctions are found also in the 90th and 91st Bhikkhunî Pâ*k*ittiyas.

[6] Avaṅga*m* karontîti avanga-dese adhomukha*m* lekha*m* karonti (B.). Avaṅga=Sanskrit apâṅga.

[7] Visesaka*m* karontîti ga*nd*a-padese vi*k*itra-sa*nth*âna*m* visesaka*m* karonti (B.). A number of tattoo marks on the cheeks are figured in Plate LII of Cunningham's 'Bharhut Tope.'

[8] Olokentîti vâtapâna*m* vivaritvâ vîthi*m* olokenti (B.).

light (of a half-opened door)[1], nor to have dances performed, nor to keep courtesans, nor to keep a tavern, nor to keep a slaughter-house, nor to open a shop, nor to practise usury, nor to supply men slaves or women slaves, or men servants or maid servants, or animals, nor to carry on the business of florist and seedsman[2], nor to carry the razor case[3].'

[Similar paragraph concluding,]

'A Bhikkhunî is not, O Bhikkhus, to wear robes that are all of a blue, light yellow, crimson, black, brownish-yellow, or dark yellow colour: nor to wear robes with skirts to them which are not made of torn pieces of cloth, or are long, or have flowers worked on them, or cobras' hoods; nor to wear jackets, nor dresses made of the fibre of the Tirîtaka plant[4]. Whosoever does so, shall be guilty of a dukka*t*a.'

11.

1. Now at that time a certain Bhikkhunî, when on her death-bed, said: 'After I am gone, let my set of necessaries[5] belong to the Sa*m*gha.' Then the

[1] Sâloke ti*tth*antîti dvâro*m* vivaritvâ upa*ddh*a-kâya*m* dassentiyo ti*tth*anti (B.). Compare Theri-gâthâ 73.

[2] Harîtaka-pa*nn*ika*m* paki*n*antîti harîtaka*ñ k*' eva pa*nn*iñ *k*a paki*n*anti, paki*nn*akâpa*n*a*m* pasârentîli vutta*m* hoti (B.). Compare pa*nn*ika-upâsako in the *G*âtaka I, 411=II, 180.

[3] Namataka*m* dhâreti. See V, 27, 3, and our note above on V, 11, 1. The expression evidently means here 'to be a barber.'

[4] This paragraph has already occurred above, in respect to the Bhikkhus (Mahâvagga VIII, 29), where see our notes on the various items.

[5] Parikkhâro; that is, the eight things over which a member

Bhikkhus and the Bhikkhunîs disputed as to it, saying: 'It belongs to us; it belongs to us.'

They told this matter to the Blessed One.

'If, O Bhikkhus, a Bhikkhunî, or a novice under training to become one (a Sikkhamânâ), when on her death-bed, should say: "After I am gone, let my set of necessaries belong to the Sa*m*gha," then it is the Bhikkhunî-sa*m*gha it belongs to; the Bhikkhu-sa*m*gha is not the owner thereof. If a Bhikkhu, O Bhikkhus, or a novice under training to become one (a Sâma*n*era), when on his death-bed, should say: "After I am gone, let my set of necessaries become the property of the Sa*m*gha," then it is the Bhikkhu-sa*m*gha it belongs to; the Bhikkhunî-sa*m*gha is not the owner thereof[1].'

12.

1. Now at that time a certain woman, who had formerly belonged to the clan of the Mallas[2], had entered the Order of the Bhikkhunîs. She, seeing a weakly Bhikkhu on the road, struck up against him with the edge of her shoulder, and knocked him over. The Bhikkhus murmured, were indignant, and complained, saying: 'How can a Bhikkhunî assault a Bhikkhu?'

They told this matter to the Blessed One.

'A Bhikkhunî is not, O Bhikkhus, to assault a

of the Buddhist Order was allowed proprietary rights—the three robes, the alms-bowl, razor, needle, girdle, and water-strainer.

[1] By the rule laid down in the Mahâvagga VIII, 27, the set of robes and the bowl are to be assigned by the Sa*m*gha to those that waited on the sick—at least in the case of Bhikkhus,—and the analogy would doubtless hold good of the Bhikkhunîs also.

[2] Well known as wrestlers.

Bhikkhu. Whosoever does so, shall be guilty of a dukka*t*a. I prescribe that a Bhikkhunî, O Bhikkhus, on seeing a Bhikkhu, should get out of the way when still at a distance, and make room for him.'

13.

1. Now at that time a certain woman, while her husband was on a journey, became with child by a paramour. She had a premature delivery, and asked a Bhikkhunî, a confederate of hers, to carry away the foetus in her bowl. And that Bhikkhunî put it into her bowl, and, covering it over with her upper robe, went away.

Now at that time a certain Bhikkhu, who was on an alms-pilgrimage, had made a vow not to partake of the first food given to him until he had already given of it either to a Bhikkhu or to a Bhikkhunî. On seeing the Bhikkhunî, that Bhikkhu said: 'Come, sister! take some food.'

'No thank you, Sir.'

[And a second and a third time the Bhikkhu made the same request, and received the same reply. Then he said,]

'Sister! I have made a vow not to partake myself of the first food given to me until I have already given of it either to a Bhikkhu or to a Bhikkhunî. Come, sister! take the food.'

Then that Bhikkhunî, being so pressed by the Bhikkhu, pulled out her bowl, and showed him what was inside of it. And the Bhikkhu was indignant, and annoyed, and remonstrated, saying: 'How can you do such a thing?' And he told the Bhikkhus, and they were indignant, &c., and told the Blessed One.

'A Bhikkhunî is not, O Bhikkhus, to carry away a foetus in her bowl. Whosoever does so, shall be guilty of a dukka*t*a. I allow a Bhikkhunî, O Bhikkhus, on seeing a Bhikkhu, to pull out her bowl, and show it to him.'

The following short section will scarcely bear translating into modern English.

15.

1. Now at that time the people gave food to the Bhikkhus, and the Bhikkhus gave to the Bhikkhunîs. The people murmured, were indignant, and complained, saying: 'How can their reverences give away to others what was given for them to have—as if we did not know how to give gifts?'

They told this matter to the Blessed One.

'A Bhikkhu, O Bhikkhus, is not to give away to others what was given for them themselves to have. Whosoever does so, shall be guilty of a dukka*t*a.'

Now at that time the Bhikkhus had come into the possession of some (meat for) food. They told this matter to the Blessed One.

'I allow you, O Bhikkhus, to give it to the Sa*m*gha.'

Too much came into their possession.

They told this matter to the Blessed One.

'I allow you, O Bhikkhus, to give away that which was given to special individuals (and to keep that which had come into the possession of the Sa*m*gha as a whole[1]).'

[1] Puggalika*m* dâtu*m*. On this phrase compare the similar one below at X, 24. Buddhaghosa has no note either here or there.

Now at that time food, which had been stored up for the Bhikkhus, had come into their possession.

They told this matter to the Blessed One.

'I allow food that has been stored up to be enjoyed by the Bhikkhunîs after they have had it given over to them by the Bhikkhus.'

2. [The same repeated, reading Bhikkhunî for Bhikkhu, and vice versâ.]

16.

1. Now at that time the Bhikkhus had come into the possession of some bedding, and the Bhikkhunîs had none. The Bhikkhunîs sent a messenger to the Bhikkhus, saying: 'It would be well if their reverences the Bhikkhus would give us some bedding on loan[1].'

They told this matter to the Blessed One.

'I allow you, O Bhikkhus, to give bedding to the Bhikkhunîs on loan.'

2. Now at that time Bhikkhunîs, in their courses, sat down or lay down on stuffed bedsteads and chairs, and the stuffing was soiled with blood.

They told this matter to the Blessed One.

'A Bhikkhunî is not, O Bhikkhus, to sit down or lie down on a stuffed bedstead or chair. Whosoever does so, shall be guilty of a dukka*t*a. I allow the use, O Bhikkhus, of an indoor's robe[2].'

The indoor's robe got soiled.

---

[1] Tâvakâlika*m*. See the passages quoted in our note above on *K*ullavagga VI, 18.

[2] Âvasatha-*k*îvara*m*. See the Old Commentary on this word as occurring in the 47th Bhikkhunî Pâ*k*ittiya.

They told this matter to the Blessed One.

'I allow, O Bhikkhus, the use of a thigh-cloth (a cloth to reach nearly down to the knee [1]).'

The thigh-cloth slipped down.

They told this matter to the Blessed One.

'I allow it, O Bhikkhus, to be fastened by a thread to be tied round the thigh.'

The thread broke.

They told this matter to the Blessed One.

'I allow, O Bhikkhus, a loin-cloth, and a string going round the hips (to keep it up)[2].'

Now at that time the *Kh*abbaggiya Bhikkhunîs used to wear the hip-string always. The people murmured, &c., saying: 'Like the women who still enjoy the pleasures of the world!' They told this matter to the Blessed One.

'A Bhikkhunî is not, O Bhikkhus, to wear a hip-string for constant use [3]. I allow its use to one who is in her courses.'

---

[1] Â*n*i-*k*olaka*m*. Buddhaghosa has no note on this. Â*n*i must be here 'that part of the leg immediately above the knee, the front of the thigh.' Compare Böhtlingk-Roth s. v. No. 2.

[2] Sa*m*velliya*m* ka*t*i-suttaka*m*. The sa*m*velliya*m* is the ordinary undress as worn for the sake of decency, even now, by a labourer working in muddy paddy fields, or at any severe task. It is a wedge-shaped strip of cotton cloth about a foot and a half long, about five inches wide at one end, and tapering down to one inch in width at the other. The broad end is fixed on to a string going round the waist (*k*a*t*i-suttaka*m*), and hangs down, when put on, in front of the legs. When worn under other clothes, it remains so; but when the other clothes are taken off for work the narrow end is passed under the body between the legs, and twisted round the hip-string behind (at the small of the back) so as to keep it fast. Its use is forbidden to Bhikkhus at V, 29, 5, where Buddhaghosa says, 'Such as wrestlers and labourers wear.'

[3] Its use is also forbidden to Bhikkhus (above, *K*ullavagga V, 2, 1).

17.

1. Now at that time there were found among the Bhikkhunîs some who were [deformed in one or other of eleven ways][1].

They told this matter to the Blessed One.

'I prescribe, O Bhikkhus, that a woman on whom the upasampadâ initiation is being conferred, is to be questioned as touching the four-and-twenty Disqualifications[2]. And thus, O Bhikkhus, is she to be questioned:

(1–11) "Have you any one or other of the eleven deformities [each repeated as above]?"

(12–16) "Have you any of the following diseases—leprosy, boils, dry leprosy, consumption, or fits?"

(17) "Are you a human being[3]?"

(18) "Are you a female?"

(19) "Are you a free woman?"

(20) "Are you free from debts?"

(21) "Are you not in the king's service?"

(22) "Have your father and mother given their consent?"

(23) "Are you full twenty years of age?"

(24) "Are you duly provided with robes and alms-bowl?"

"What is your name?"

---

[1] Here follow a number of abnormities, deformities, or diseases, all of which have reference to the womb or its accessories. Some of them are unintelligible to us. Compare the corresponding section in respect to Bhikkhus at Mahâvagga I, 68.

[2] Of these twenty-four, eleven are the deformities just referred to, and the rest are the same as those for Bhikkhus at Mahâvagga I, 76. The number of questions is, in fact, twenty-six, but the last two do not refer to Disqualifications.

[3] For the reason of this, see Mahâvagga I, 63.

"What is the name of your proposer[1]?"'

2. Now at that time Bhikkhus put the questions as touching the Disqualifications to Bhikkhunîs[2], and they who were seeking after the upasampadâ initiation became disconcerted and perplexed, and were unable to answer.

They told this matter to the Blessed One.

'I prescribe, O Bhikkhus, that initiation is to be conferred in the Bhikkhu-sa*m*gha upon a Bhikkhunî who has been initiated on the one side in the Bhikkhunî-sa*m*gha, and has there cleared herself (from the Disqualifications).'

Now at that time the Bhikkhunîs questioned those who desired to receive the upasampadâ initiation about the Disqualifications, without having had them instructed beforehand (how to answer). The persons who desired to be ordained became disconcerted and perplexed, and were not able to answer[3].

They told this matter to the Blessed One.

'I prescribe, O Bhikkhus, that you first instruct the women about to be initiated (how to answer), and that you then question them as to the Disqualifications.'

Then they instructed the candidates in the midst of the assembly, and they still became disconcerted, and could not answer.

They told this matter to the Blessed One.

---

[1] Pavattinî; corresponding to upa*ggh*âya in the case of Bhikkhus.

[2] This is in accordance with the rule laid down in X, 2, 2, that Bhikkhus, and not Bhikkhunîs, are to confer the upasampadâ.

[3] This paragraph is word for word the same as Mahâvagga I, 76, 2 of the Bhikkhus.

'I prescribe, O Bhikkhus, that they be instructed aside, and then questioned in the midst of the assembly.

'And thus, O Bhikkhus, ought they to be instructed:—First they ought to be made to choose an instructor[1]; when they have chosen an instructor their robes and bowl must be shown to them: "This is your alms-bowl, this is your waist-cloth, this is your upper garment, this is your under garment, this is your vest, this is your bathing dress[2]. Go and stand in such and such a place."'

3. Ignorant and incompetent (Bhikkhunîs) instructed them, and they became disconcerted, perplexed, and unable to answer.

They told this matter to the Blessed One.

'They are not to be instructed, O Bhikkhus, by unlearned, incompetent Bhikkhunîs. Whosoever does so, shall be guilty of a dukka*t*a. I prescribe, O Bhikkhus, that they be instructed by learned and competent Bhikkhunîs.'

4. Bhikkhunîs not appointed (to the office of doing so) instructed them.

They told this matter to the Blessed One.

'Let no one, O Bhikkhus, instruct them without

[1] Upa*gg*h*am*. It should be observed that this expression is found only here, and in the corresponding section for the Bhikkhus, at Mahâvagga I, 76, 3. Elsewhere, throughout, Upa*gg*h*â*ya is the form used for Bhikkhus, and Pavattinî for Bhikkhunîs. The word is probably here also, as in the Mahâvagga I, 76, 3, to be taken as a masculine.

[2] These last two are omitted in the corresponding section for the Bhikkhus, Mahâvagga I, 76, 3. On Sa*m*ka*kkh*ika*m*, see the note of the Old Commentator on the 96th Bhikkhunî Pâ*k*ittiya, and on Udaka-sâ*t*ikâ, the same on the 22nd Bhikkhunî Pâ*k*ittiya.

having been appointed thereto. Whosoever does so, shall be guilty of a dukka*t*a. I prescribe, O Bhikkhus, that a Bhikkhunî appointed to the office instruct them.

'And thus, O Bhikkhus, ought she to be appointed—one may either appoint herself, or one may be appointed by another. And how is a Bhikkhunî to appoint herself? Let a learned, competent Bhikkhunî lay the following motion (*ñ*atti) before the Sa*m*gha: "Let the Sa*m*gha, reverend Ladies, hear me. N. N. desires to receive the upasampadâ initiation from the venerable lady, M. M. If it seem meet to the Sa*m*gha, I will instruct N. N." Thus may a Bhikkhunî appoint herself.

'And how is a Bhikkhunî to be appointed by another? Let a learned, competent Bhikkhunî lay the following resolution before the Sa*m*gha: "Let the Sa*m*gha, reverend Ladies, hear me. N. N. desires to receive the upasampadâ initiation from the venerable lady, M. M. If it seem meet to the Sa*m*gha, let A. A. instruct N. N." Thus may one Bhikkhunî be appointed by another.

5. 'Then let that so appointed Bhikkhunî go to the person who is seeking to be initiated, and thus address her: "Listen to me, N.N. This is the time for you to speak the truth, to declare that which is. When you are asked about what has happened before the Sa*m*gha, you ought, if it is so, to answer: "That is so;" if it is not so, to answer: "That is not so." Be not perplexed, be not disconcerted. I shall ask you thus: "Are you deformed (&c., down to the end of the twenty-six questions in § 1)."'

(After the instruction was over, the instructor and the candidate) returned together to the assembly.

'They are not to return together. Let the instructor return first, and lay the following resolution before the Sa*m*gha: "Let the Sa*m*gha, reverend Ladies, hear me. N. N. desires to receive the upasampadâ initiation from the venerable lady, M. M.; and she has been instructed by me. If it seem meet to the Sa*m*gha, let N. N. come forward." Then let her be told to come forward. Then let her be told to adjust her upper robe over one shoulder only, to bow down before the Bhikkhunîs, to sit down on her heels, and stretching forth her joined palms, to ask for the upasampadâ initiation, saying: "I ask the Sa*m*gha, reverend Ladies, for initiation. May the Sa*m*gha, reverend Ladies, raise me up (out of the worldly life), having pity on me." And a second and a third time is she to repeat that request.

6. 'Then let a learned and competent Bhikkhunî lay the following resolution before the Sa*m*gha: "Let the Sa*m*gha, reverend Ladies, hear me. This person, N. N., desires to receive the upasampadâ initiation from M. M.; and she has been instructed by me. If it seem meet to the Sa*m*gha, let me question N. N. as touching the Disqualifications. Listen to me, N. N. [as before, down to the end of the questions]."

7. 'Then let a learned and competent Bhikkhunî lay the following motion before the Sa*m*gha: "Let the Sa*m*gha, reverend Ladies, hear me. This person, N. N., desires to receive the upasampadâ initiation from the venerable lady, M. M. She is free from the Disqualifications, and is duly provided with alms-bowl and robes. This person, N. N., asks the Sa*m*gha for the upasampadâ initiation, the vene-

rable lady, M. M., being her proposer. If it seem meet to the Sa*m*gha, let the Sa*m*gha receive N. N., the venerable lady, M. M., being her proposer. That, then, is the motion.

'"Let the Sa*m*gha, venerable Ladies, hear me. N. N. desires to receive the upasampadâ, the lady, M. M., being her proposer. The Sa*m*gha confers the upasampadâ upon N. N., the lady, M. M., being her proposer. Whosoever of the venerable ones agrees thereto, let her keep silence; whosoever agrees not thereto, let her speak. A second time I say the same thing." [The whole of this paragraph repeated.] And a third time I say the same thing. [Paragraph repeated.]

'The Sa*m*gha has conferred the upasampadâ upon N. N., the lady, M. M., being her proposer. The Sa*m*gha agrees thereto. Therefore is it silent. Thus do I understand.'

8. 'Then, further, let her be taken before the Bhikkhu-sa*m*gha, and there told to arrange her robe over one shoulder only, to bow down before the Bhikkhus, and, sitting down on her heels, to stretch forth her joined palms, and say: "I, Sirs, N. N., who, being desirous of receiving the upasampadâ initiation from M. M., have received it on the one side (of the Sa*m*gha, from the Bhikkhunîs), and have there been declared free (from the Disqualifications), do hereby ask the Sa*m*gha for the upasampadâ." [The rest of the proceedings are the same as before the Bhikkhunî-sa*m*gha.] "May the Sa*m*gha, reverend Sirs, raise me up (out of the worldly life), having pity on me." And a second time do I hereby ask [&c., repeated]. And a third time do I hereby ask [the same repeated].

[The rest of the proceedings are the same as in the last sections 6 and 7, putting 'Bhikkhu' for 'Bhikkhunî,' and 'reverend Sirs' for 'reverend Ladies.']

'Then, further, let them (the Bhikkhus) measure the shadow, tell (the newly-received Bhikkhunî) what season and what date it is, tell her what part of the day it is, tell her the whole formula[1], and tell the Bhikkhunîs: "You are to teach her what are the three things allowed[2], and what are the eight things interdicted[3]."'

18.

Now at that time Bhikkhunîs wasted their time in the dining-hall, doubting as to which should take which seat.

They told this matter to the Blessed One.

'I prescribe, O Bhikkhus, that the senior eight Bhikkhunîs shall take their seats according to seniority, and the rest as they happen to come in.'

Now at that time Bhikkhunîs, on the ground that the Blessed One had so prescribed, let the eight senior Bhikkhunîs in every other place take

[1] Sa*m*gîti. On the meaning of this curious use of the word, see our note on the corresponding section for the Bhikkhus (Mahâvagga I, 77).

[2] The three Nissayas, which are doubtless the same as the 1st, 2nd, and 4th of the four Resources mentioned in the corresponding paragraph for Bhikkhus (Mahâvagga I, 77). The third is forbidden to Bhikkhunîs, below, X, 23.

[3] A*tth*a akara*n*îyâni. These must bear the same relation to the eight Bhikkhunî Pârâ*g*ikas as the four Interdicts in the corresponding paragraph for the Bhikkhus (Mahâvagga I, 78) do to the four Bhikkhu Pârâ*g*ikas.

exclusive possession (of the first eight seats), and the rest arranged themselves as they came in.

They told this matter to the Blessed One.

'I prescribe, O Bhikkhus, as above, only in the case of the dining-hall. Everywhere else let there be no exclusive right to seats by seniority.'

19.

1. Now at that time the Bhikkhunîs did not hold Pavâra*n*â.

They told this matter to the Blessed One.

'A Bhikkhunî is not, O Bhikkhus, to omit holding Pavâra*n*â. Whosoever does so, shall be dealt with according to law[1].'

Now at that time the Bhikkhunîs held Pavâra*n*â by themselves, and not in the Bhikkhu-sa*m*gha.

They told this matter to the Blessed One.

'A Bhikkhunî is not, O Bhikkhus, to hold Pavâra*n*â apart, and not in the Bhikkhu-sa*m*gha. Whosoever does so, shall be dealt with according to law[2].'

Now at that time Bhikkhunîs holding Pavâra*n*â with the Bhikkhus only, and not apart by themselves, disturbed (the meeting of the Bhikkhu-sa*m*gha).

They told this matter to the Blessed One.

'A Bhikkhunî is not, O Bhikkhus, to hold Pavâra*n*â with the Bhikkhu-sa*m*gha only. Whosoever does so, shall be guilty of a dukka*t*a[2].'

Now at that time Bhikkhunîs spent all their time

---

[1] The 57th Bhikkhunî Pâ*k*ittiya, which is the same as the 4th Garudhamma above, X, 1, 4.

[2] See last note.

before noon holding Pavâra*n*â [and so had no time left for the early meal].

They told this matter to the Blessed One.

'I prescribe, O Bhikkhus, that they hold Pavâra*n*â in the afternoon.'

When holding Pavâra*n*â in the afternoon, they had not time enough [to conclude their own ceremony that day, and take part in that of the Bhikkhus].

They told this matter to the Blessed One.

'I allow them, O Bhikkhus, to hold their own Pavâra*n*â one day, and that with the Bhikkhus the next day.'

2. Now at that time the whole of the Bhikkhunî-sa*m*gha declaring, each one for herself, her Pavâra*n*â before the Bhikkhu-sa*m*gha, disturbed (the proceedings).

They told this matter to the Blessed One.

'I prescribe, O Bhikkhus, that some one learned and competent Bhikkhunî be deputed to make the Pavâra*n*â invitation on behalf of the Bhikkhunî-sa*m*gha before the Bhikkhu-sa*m*gha. And thus, O Bhikkhus, is she to be deputed:

'"First, the Bhikkhunî is to be asked (whether she be willing to serve). When that has been done, a learned and discreet Bhikkhunî is to lay this motion before the Sa*m*gha: Let the Sa*m*gha, venerable Ladies, hear me. If it seem meet to the Sa*m*gha, let the Sa*m*gha depute N. N. to make the Pavâra*n*â invitation on behalf of the Bhikkhunî-sa*m*gha before the Bhikkhu-sa*m*gha. That is the motion.

'"Let the Sa*m*gha, venerable Ladies, hear me. The Sa*m*gha deputes N. N. to make the Pavâra*n*â invitation on behalf of the Bhikkhunî-sa*m*gha before the Bhikkhu-sa*m*gha. Whosoever of the venerable ones approves thereof, let her keep silence. Whosoever approves not thereof, let her speak.

'"N. N. is deputed by the Sa*m*gha to make the Pavâra*n*â invitation on behalf of the Bhikkhunî-sa*m*gha before the Bhikkhu-sa*m*gha. The Sa*m*gha approves thereof. Therefore is it silent. Thus do I understand."'

3. 'When that Bhikkhunî has been deputed, she, accompanied by the Bhikkhunî-sa*m*gha, is to go before the Bhikkhu-sa*m*gha, arrange her robe over one shoulder, bow down before the Bhikkhus, and sitting on her heels, to stretch forth her joined palms, and say: "The Bhikkhunî-sa*m*gha invites the Bhikkhu-sa*m*gha (to point out to them any faults they may have committed) in respect of things heard, or seen, or suspected. May the Bhikkhu-sa*m*gha speak to the Bhikkhunî-sa*m*gha (if there be anything wherein they have offended) out of compassion toward them. Then will they, if they perceive the offence, confess the same. And a second time the Bhikkhunî-sa*m*gha . . . . . . [the whole repeated]. And a third time . . . . . . [the whole repeated][1]."'

20.

Now at that time Bhikkhunîs inhibited Bhikkhus from the Uposatha, or from the Pavâra*n*â, or from the Exhortation, or issued commands to them, or asked them to give them leave to rebuke them, or warned them of some offence they supposed they

[1] This, of course, is the same form that each separate member of the Order uses before his or her own Sa*m*gha. Compare our notes above on the corresponding passage in the Mahâvagga, IV, 1, 4.

were committing, or called upon them to remember whether or not they had committed an offence[1].

They told this matter to the Blessed One.

'A Bhikkhunî is not, O Bhikkhus, to perform any one of these official acts towards a Bhikkhu. Should she do so, the act is itself invalid, and she is guilty of a dukka*t*a.'

Now at that time Bhikkhus inhibited Bhikkhunîs [&c., as before, giving the contrary decision].

21.

Now at that time the *Kh*abbaggiya Bhikkhunîs had themselves carried in vehicles to which cows were yoked with a bull between them[2], or bulls were yoked with a cow between them. People were annoyed, murmured, and became indignant, saying: 'That is what is done at the feast of the Gaṅgâ, and the Mahî[2].'

They told this matter to the Blessed One.

'A Bhikkhunî is not, O Bhikkhus, to be carried in a vehicle. Whosoever does so, shall be dealt with according to law[3].'

Now at that time a certain Bhikkhunî was sick, and unable to go on foot.

They told this matter to the Blessed One.

'I allow the use of a carriage, O Bhikkhus, to a sick (Bhikkhunî)[4].'

---

[1] On all these official acts of a Bhikkhunî, see the notes above on *K*ullavagga I, 5.

[2] On all these expressions, see our notes above at Mahâvagga V, 9, 3, where they recur word for word.

[3] This is the 85th Bhikkhunî Pâ*k*ittiya.

[4] This is repeated from the 85th Bhikkhunî Pâ*k*ittiya. The corresponding permission is given to Bhikkhus by Mahâvagga V, 10, 2.

Now the Bhikkhunîs thought: 'Should the carts be yoked with cows or bulls?'

They told this matter to the Blessed One.

'I allow, O Bhikkhus, a cart yoked with cows or bulls, or drawn by hand[1].'

Now at that time a certain Bhikkhunî was much distressed by the jolting of the cart.

They told this matter to the Blessed One.

'I allow, O Bhikkhus, the use of a litter or sedan chair[2].'

22.

1. Now at that time a courtesan named *Addh*akâsî[3] had adopted the religious life under the Bhikkhunîs, and she wanted to go to Sâvatthi to be received as full member of the Order (to receive the upasampadâ initiation) by the Blessed One himself. And men of abandoned life heard of it, and beset the road. And when *Addh*akâsî, the courtesan, heard that they had done so, she sent a messenger to the Blessed One, saying: 'I want to receive the upasampadâ initiation: what course of action should I adopt?'

Then the Blessed One, in that connection, addressed the Bhikkhus, after delivering a religious discourse[4], and said: 'I allow you, O Bhikkhus, to confer the upasampadâ initiation (upon Bhikkhunîs) even by a messenger[5].'

---

[1] Hattha-va*tt*aka*m*. See the note on Mahâvagga V, 10, 3.

[2] So also for Bhikkhus at Mahâvagga V, 10, 3.

[3] On the meaning of this nickname or epithet, compare our note on Mahâvagga VIII, 2 (and see also VIII, 1, 1, and 3).

[4] As set out in *K*ullavagga I, 1; Mahâvagga I, 35, 6.

[5] The ordinary rule, no doubt, required, as in the case of Bhik-

2. They conferred it by (sending) a Bhikkhu as the messenger.

They told this matter to the Blessed One.

'You are not, O Bhikkhus, to confer the upasampadâ initiation on a Bhikkhunî by sending a Bhikkhu as messenger. Whosoever does so, shall be guilty of a dukkaṭa.'

They conferred it by sending a female student . . . . . a male novice . . . . . a female novice . . . . . an ignorant, incompetent Bhikkhunî, as the messenger.

[Similar decision in each case.]

'I allow you, O Bhikkhus, to confer the upasampadâ initiation by sending a learned, competent Bhikkhunî as a messenger.'

3. 'That Bhikkhunî messenger is to go before the Saṃgha, and arranging her robe over one shoulder, is to bow down before the Saṃgha, and sitting on her heels, to stretch forth her joined palms, and say: "N. N., having been desirous of receiving the upasampadâ initiation with the lady, M. M. (as her proposer), has received it on the one hand from the Bhikkhunî-saṃgha, and has there been declared free (from the Disqualifications [1]). But she is prevented by some danger or other from coming before the Saṃgha (to have her initiation confirmed) [2]. N. N. asks the Saṃgha for initiation. Let the Saṃgha raise her up (out of the worldly life) out of compassion upon her.' [To be said thrice.]

khus, a Saṃgha of not less than ten persons (Mahâvagga I, 31, 2, and IX, 4, 1), each of ten years standing or more (Mahâvagga I, 31, 8). But even for Bhikkhus there were, under special circumstances, certain relaxations of this rule (Mahâvagga V, 13, 11).

[1] See above, X, 17, 1, for the twenty-four Disqualifications.

[2] Compare above, X, 1, 4, and X, 17.

'Then let a learned, competent Bhikkhu lay the motion before the Sa*m*gha. "Let the Sa*m*gha, venerable Sirs, hear me. N. N., having been desirous . . . . . [statement of fact, as before]. If it seem meet to the Sa*m*gha, let the Sa*m*gha confer the upasampadâ initiation upon N. N., M. M. being her proposer. That is the motion.

'"Let the Sa*m*gha, venerable Sirs, hear me. N. N., ... [statement of fact, as before]. The Sa*m*gha hereby confers the upasampadâ initiation upon N. N., M. M. being her proposer. Whosoever of the venerable ones approves thereof, let him keep silence. Whosoever approves not thereof, let him speak. And a second time I say the same thing. N. N., ... (&c., down to) let him speak. And a third time I say the same thing. N. N., ... (&c., down to) let him speak.

'"The Sa*m*gha has hereby conferred the upasampadâ initiation upon N. N., M. M. being her proposer. The Sa*m*gha approves thereof. Therefore is it silent. Thus do I understand."'

'Then, further, let them (the Bhikkhus) measure the shadow, tell (the messenger that she may tell the newly-received Bhikkhunî) what season and what date it is, tell her what part of the day it is, tell her the whole formula; and tell the Bhikkhunîs to teach her what are the three things allowed, and what are the eight things interdicted[1].'

23.

Now at that time Bhikkhunîs dwelt in the forest, and men of abandoned life violated them.

[1] See above, X, 17, 8.

They told this matter to the Blessed One.

'A Bhikkhunî is not, O Bhikkhus, to adopt the forest life. Whosoever does so, shall be guilty of a dukka*t*a[1].'

24.

1. Now at that time a certain lay disciple had given to the Bhikkhunî-sa*m*gha a servant's lodge[2] (to live in).

They told this matter to the Blessed One.

'I allow, O Bhikkhus, the use of a stable.'

It did not satisfy (their wants)[3]. They told this matter to the Blessed One.

'I allow, O Bhikkhus, a separate residence for Bhikkhunîs.'

That did not satisfy their wants. They told this matter to the Blessed One.

'I allow, O Bhikkhus, building operations[4] (to be carried on for the benefit of Bhikkhunîs).'

---

[1] Compare Mahâvagga I, 30, 4, and I, 77, and our note above on X, 17, 8.

[2] This word has already occurred, in a list of various buildings, at Mahâvagga III, 5, 9, where we have rendered it stable. Buddhaghosa says here uddositan (MS. udosita) ti bha*nd*a-sâlâ, and as at Mahâvagga I, 61, assa-bha*nd*â and hatthi-bha*nd*â are evidently grooms attending on horses or elephants (compare *G*âtaka I, 62, 3), bha*nd*a-sâlâ may mean a servant's hall for the use of that particular class of servants. A lawsuit about an uddosita forms the Introductory Story to the 1st Bhikkhunî Sa*m*ghâdisesa, but the passage throws no light on the special meaning of the term. See also the Sutta-vibhaṅga on Nissaggiya II, 3, 5, and Khudda Sikkhâ III, 19. The Sanskrit equivalent might perhaps be udavasita, if the reading of the Samanta Pâsâdikâ had any traditional value; but the dd is not doubtful in the MSS. of the text at any of the passages quoted. Assa-sâlâ is the word for stable at *G*âtaka I, 62, 3.

[3] Na sammati. See the note on V, 13, 3.

[4] Navakamma*m*. See the note above at V, 13, 3.

That did not satisfy their wants. They told this matter to the Blessed One.

'I allow Bhikkhunîs, O Bhikkhus, to assign certain places to live in to individual members of the Order[1].'

25.

1. Now at that time a certain woman who had already conceived, but did not know it, was received into the Order among the Bhikkhunîs. Afterwards her womb moved within her[2]. Then that Bhikkhunî thought: 'How shall I now conduct myself towards this child?'

They told this matter to the Blessed One.

'I allow her, O Bhikkhus, to bring it up till it have attained to years of discretion[3].'

Then the Bhikkhunî thought: 'It is not permissible for me to live alone, nor for any other Bhikkhunî to live with a male child. What course ought I to pursue?'

They told this matter to the Blessed One.

'I allow the Bhikkhunîs, O Bhikkhus, to depute any one Bhikkhunî, and give her as a companion to that (first-mentioned) Bhikkhunî.'

---

[1] Puggalika*m* kâtu*m*. See the note above on X, 15, 1.

[2] There is a touching story founded on a similar incident which is given as the Introductory Story to No. 12 of the *G*âtakas, translated in Rh. D.'s 'Buddhist Birth Stories,' pp. 199–205. By the 61st Bhikkhunî Pâ*k*ittiya it is lawful or unlawful to initiate a pregnant woman according as she is unconscious or conscious of the fact of her conception.

[3] Viññutam pâpu*n*âti. That is, no doubt, to puberty. Compare the opening phrases of the Introductory Story referred to in the last note (*G*âtaka I, 231) and also *G*âtaka III, 437.

'And thus, O Bhikkhus, is she to be appointed: First that Bhikkhunî ought to be asked (whether she be willing to undertake the duty). After she has been asked, a learned and competent Bhikkhunî ought to lay the motion before the Sa*m*gha, saying:

'"Let the Sa*m*gha, venerable Ladies, hear me. If it seem meet to the Sa*m*gha, let the Sa*m*gha depute N. N. as a companion to M. M. That is the motion.

'"Let the Sa*m*gha,"' [&c., as usual, to the end of the Kammavâ*k*â.]

2. Then that companion Bhikkhunî thought: 'Now how should I conduct myself towards this child?'

They told this matter to the Blessed One.

'I prescribe that the Bhikkhunîs, O Bhikkhus, conduct themselves towards that child precisely as they would towards other men, save only as regards the sleeping under the same roof[1].'

3. Now at that time a certain Bhikkhunî, who had been guilty of a grievous offence, was living subject to the Mânatta penance[2]. Then that Bhikkhunî thought: 'It is not permissible for me to live alone, and it is not permissible for any other Bhikkhunî to live with me. What now ought I to do?'

They told this matter to the Blessed One.

'I allow the Bhikkhunîs, O Bhikkhus, to depute any one Bhikkhunî, and to give her as a companion to that Bhikkhunî. And thus, O Bhikkhus, ought

---

[1] Sâgâra*m*; on which Buddhaghosa has no note.

[2] For what this implied, see *K*ullavagga II, 1, 2, and II, 6, 1, and compare the 5th Garudhamma above, X, 1, 4.

she to be deputed [&c., as in last section but one, down to the end of the Kammavâkâ].'

26.

1. Now at that time a certain Bhikkhunî first abandoned the precepts, and then threw off tl robes[1]. Afterwards she came back, and asked th Bhikkhunîs to admit her into the Order again.

They told this matter to the Blessed One.

'A Bhikkhunî ought not, O Bhikkhus, to abandon the precepts. But by having thrown off the robes she is ipso facto incapable of being a Bhikkhunî.'

2. Now at that time a certain Bhikkhunî, though still wearing the orange-coloured robe, joined a sect of the Titthiyas. Afterwards she came back, and asked the Bhikkhunîs to receive her into the Order again.

They told this matter to the Blessed One.

'A Bhikkhunî, O Bhikkhus, who, when still wearing the orange-coloured robe, has gone over to the Titthiyas, is not to be received again[2].'

27.

1. Now at that time Bhikkhunîs, fearing to offend, would not let men salute them, or cut their hair or nails, or dress their wounds.

[1] On the distinction between these two phrases, see the note on Mahâvagga II, 22, 3.

[2] For the similar rule in the case of Bhikkhus, see Mahâvagga I, 38, 1.

They told this matter to the Blessed One.

'I allow them, O Bhikkhus, to permit those things.'

2. Now at that time Bhikkhunîs, when sitting on a divan, allowed (other people thereon) to touch them with their heels.

They told this matter to the Blessed One.

'A Bhikkhunî is not, O Bhikkhus, to sit on a divan[1]. Whosoever does so, shall be guilty of a dukka*t*a.'

Now at that time a certain Bhikkhunî was sick, and without using a divan she could not be at ease.

They told this matter to the Blessed One.

'I allow Bhikkhunîs, O Bhikkhus, to use a half-divan[2].'

3. [Rule as to construction of privies[3].]

4. Now at that time the Bhikkhunîs used chunam at their baths.

People murmured, saying, 'As the women in the world do!'

They told this matter to the Blessed One.

'A Bhikkhunî is not, O Bhikkhus, to use chunam at her bath. Whosoever does so, shall be guilty of a dukka*t*a. I allow, O Bhikkhus, the use of clay and the red powder of rice husks[4].'

---

[1] Pallaṅka*m*. Compare Mahâvagga V, 10, 4, 5; *K*ullavagga V, 37, VI, 8, VI, 14; and the 42nd Bhikkhunî Pâ*k*ittiya.

[2] A*ddh*a-pallaṅka*m*. Probably a cushion, which only one person could use at a time.

[3] Compare the Rules for the Bhikkhus, *K*ullavagga VIII, 9, 10, which we have also left untranslated. Buddhaghosa says here, He*tth*â-viva*t*e upari*kkh*anne ti ettha sa*k*e kûpo khato hoti upari pana padaramattam eva sabba-disâsu pa*ññ*âyati evarûpe pi va*tt*ati.

[4] Kukkusa*m*. Buddhaghosa says here, Kukkusa*m* mattikan

[Similar paragraph, ending]

'A Bhikkhunî is not, O Bhikkhus, to use scented clay at her bath[1]. Whosoever does so, shall be guilty of a dukka*t*a. I allow, O Bhikkhus, the use of common clay.'

Now at that time Bhikkhunîs bathing together in the steam-bath room made a tumult.

They told this matter to the Blessed One.

'Bhikkhunîs are not, O Bhikkhus, to bathe in a steam-bath. Whosoever does so, shall be guilty of a dukka*t*a.'

Now at that time Bhikkhunîs bathing against the stream allowed the rush of water against them.

They told this matter to the Blessed One.

'A Bhikkhunî is not, O Bhikkhus, to bathe against the stream. Whosoever does so, shall be guilty of a dukka*t*a.'

Now at that time Bhikkhunîs bathed in a place not a common bathing-place, and men of abandoned life violated them.

They told this matter to the Blessed One.

'A Bhikkhunî is not, O Bhikkhus, to bathe at a place not a common bathing-place. Whosoever does so, shall be guilty of a dukka*t*a.'

Now at that time Bhikkhunîs bathed at a bathing-place used also by men. People murmured, were indignant, and complained, saying, 'As those women do who are still living in the pleasures of the world[1].'

They told this matter to the Blessed One.

---

ti ku*nd*akañ *k*' eva mattikañ *k*a. The use of these last two was allowed to Bhikkhus by *K*ullavagga VI, 3, 1, for building purposes.

[1] This is apparently covered by the 88th and 89th Bhikkhunî Pâ*k*ittiya.

'A Bhikkhunî is not, O Bhikkhus, to bathe at a bathing-place used also by men. Whosoever does so, shall be guilty of a dukka*t*a. I allow, Bhikkhunîs, O Bhikkhus, to bathe at a bathing-place used by women.'

End of the Third Portion for Recitation.

End of the Tenth Khandhaka, the Bhikkhunî-Khandhaka.

ELEVENTH KHANDHAKA.

On the Council of Râ*g*agaha.

1[1].

1. Now the venerable Mahâ Kassapa addressed the Bhikkhus, and said: 'Once I was travelling along the road from Pâvâ to Kusinârâ with a great company of the Bhikkhus, with about five hundred Bhikkhus. And I left the high road and sat myself down at the foot of a certain tree.

'Just at that time a certain naked ascetic (â*g*îvaka), who had picked up a Mandârava[2] flower in Kusinârâ, was coming along the road towards Pâvâ. And I saw him coming in the distance, and on seeing I said to him:

'"O, friend! surely thou knowest our Master?"

'"Yea, friend, I know him. This day the Sama*n*a Gotama has been dead a week. That is how I obtained this Mandârava flower."'

'Then, Sirs, of those of the Bhikkhus who were not yet free from their passions, some stretched out

---

[1] The following section differs from the corresponding passage in the 'Book of the Great Decease' (VI, 36–41) in the very curious and instructive way pointed out by H. O. in the Introduction to his edition of the text, p. xxvi, on which see the remarks of Rh. D. at p. xiii of the General Introduction to his 'Buddhist Suttas.'

[2] This was a flower which was supposed to grow only in heaven, and its appearance on earth showed that the devas, on some special occasion, had been casting down heavenly flowers upon the earth.

their arms and wept; and some fell headlong on the ground; and some reeled to and fro in anguish at the thought: "Too soon has the Blessed One died! Too soon has the Happy One passed away! Too soon has the Light gone out in the world!"'

'But those of the Bhikkhus who were free from the passions (the Arahats) bore their grief, collected and composed at the thought: "Impermanent are all component things. How is it possible [that they should not be dissolved]?"

'Then I, Sirs, spake thus to the Bhikkhus: "Enough, Sirs! Weep not, neither lament! Has not the Blessed One already declared to us that it is the very nature of all things near and dear unto us that we must divide ourselves from them, leave them, sever ourselves from them? How then, Sirs, can this be possible—that whereas anything whatever born, brought into being, and organised, contains within itself the inherent necessity of dissolution—how then can this be possible that such a being should not be dissolved? No such condition can exist!"

'Then at that time[1], Sirs, one Subhadda, who had gone out from the world in his old age, was seated there in the company of Bhikkhus. And Subhadda, the late-received one, said to the Bhikkhus: "Enough, Sirs! Weep not, neither lament! We are well rid of the great Sama*n*a. We used to be annoyed by being told, 'This beseems you, this beseems you not.' But now we shall be able to do whatever we like; and what we do not like, that we shall not have to do[1]."

[1] In the 'Book of the Great Decease' the following speech comes before the preceding one.

'Come, Sirs, let us chant together the Dhamma and the Vinaya before what is not Dhamma is spread abroad, and what is Dhamma is put aside; before what is not Vinaya is spread abroad, and what is Vinaya is put aside; before those who argue against the Dhamma become powerful, and those who hold to the Dhamma become weak; before those who argue against the Vinaya become powerful, and those who hold to the Vinaya become weak!'

2. 'Let then the venerable Thera choose out Bhikkhus.'

Then the venerable Mahâ Kassapa chose out five hundred Arahats less one. And the Bhikkhus said to the venerable Mahâ Kassapa: 'Lord, this venerable one, Ânanda, although he have not yet attained [to Nirvâ*n*a], yet is he incapable of falling into error through partiality, or malice, or stupidity, or fear, and thoroughly have the Dhamma and the Vinaya been learnt by him from the Blessed One himself. Therefore let our Lord choose the venerable Ânanda. And the venerable Mahâ Kassapa chose also the venerable Ânanda.'

3. Then it occurred to the Thera Bhikkhus: 'In what place shall we now chant over together the Dhamma and the Vinaya?' And it occurred to the Thera Bhikkhus: 'In Râ*g*agaha is alms plentiful, and there is abundance of lodging-places. What, now, if we were to spend the rainy season at Râ*g*agaha, and chant the Dhamma and the Vinaya together there: and if no other Bhikkhus were to go up to Râ*g*agaha for the rainy season[1]?'

4. Then the venerable Mahâ Kassapa laid the

[1] This last was necessary, for if other Bhikkhus spent the Was at Râ*g*agaha, either they must take part in the council, or its

resolution before the Sa*m*gha: 'Let the venerable Sa*m*gha hear me. If the time seems meet to the Sa*m*gha, let the Sa*m*gha appoint that these five hundred Bhikkhus take up their residence during the rainy season at Râ*g*agaha, to chant over together the Dhamma and the Vinaya, and that no other Bhikkhus go up to Râ*g*agaha for the rainy season. This is the resolution. Let the venerable Sa*m*gha hear. The Sa*m*gha appoints accordingly. Whosoever of the venerable ones approves thereof, let him keep silence. Whosoever approves not thereof, let him speak. The Sa*m*gha has appointed accordingly. Therefore is it silent. Thus do I understand.'

5. So the Thera Bhikkhus went up to Râ*g*agaha to chant over together the Dhamma and the Vinaya. And the Thera Bhikkhus thought: 'The Blessed One has spoken in praise of the repair of dilapidations. Let us, then, during the first month of the rainy season repair such dilapidations, and during the middle month let us chant over the Dhamma and the Vinaya together.' And during the first month they repaired dilapidation.

6. And the venerable Ânanda—thinking, 'To-morrow is the assembly, now it beseems me not to go into the assembly while I am still only on the way (towards Arahatship)'—spent the whole night with mind alert. And at the close of the night, intending to lie down, he inclined his body, but before his head reached the pillow, and while his feet were still far from the ground, in the interval he became

decisions would have been invalid through its being incompletely constituted (want of vaggatta).

free from attachment to the world, and his heart was emancipated from the Âsavas (that is to say, from sensuality, individuality, delusion, and ignorance)[1].

7. And the venerable Mahâ Kassapa laid the resolution before the Sa*m*gha: 'If the time seem meet to the Sa*m*gha, I will question Upâli concerning the Vinaya.' And the venerable Upâli laid a resolution before the Sa*m*gha: 'Let the venerable Sa*m*gha hear me. If the time seems meet to the Sa*m*gha, I, when questioned by the venerable Mahâ Kassapa, will give reply.'

Then the venerable Mahâ Kassapa said to the venerable Upâli: 'Venerable Upâli, where was the first Pârâ*g*ika promulgated?'

'In Vesâlî, Sir.'

'Concerning whom was it spoken?'

'Concerning Sudinna, the son of Kalanda.'

'In regard to what matter?'

'Sexual intercourse.'

Thus did the venerable Mahâ Kassapa question the venerable Upâli as to the matter, as to the occasion, as to the individual concerned, as to the (principal) rule, as to the sub-rule[2], as to who would be guilty, and as to who would be innocent[3], of the first Pârâ*g*ika.

---

[1] In other words, he became an Arahat. Some MSS. omit the clause about the feet.

[2] Anupa*ññ*atti. Turnour (Journal of the Asiatic Society of Bengal, 1837, p. 19) translates this word, which is not in Childers, by 'the sequel or application of the exhortation.' We think the pa*ññ*atti refers to the principal rule (as laid down in the Sutta Vibhaṅga at the close of I, 5, 11), and the anupa*ññ*atti to the additions made to it in the following sections.

[3] This last clause doubtless refers to the closing words in the account given in the Sutta Vibhaṅga of each rule.

'Again, venerable Upâli, where was the second Pârâgika promulgated?'

'At Râgagaha, Sir.'

'Concerning whom was it spoken?'

'Dhaniya, the potter's son.'

'In regard to what matter?'

'The taking of that which had not been given[1].'

Thus did the venerable Mahâ Kassapa question the venerable Upâli as to the matter, and as to the occasion, and as to the individual concerned, and as to the (principal) rule, and as to the sub-rule, and as to who would be guilty, and as to who would be innocent of the second Pârâgika.

'Again, venerable Upâli, where was the third Pârâgika promulgated?'

'At Vesâlî, Sir.'

'Concerning whom was it spoken?'

'A number of Bhikkhus.'

'In regard to what matter?'

'Human beings[2].'

Thus did the venerable Mahâ Kassapa question the venerable Upâli as to [all the particulars, as before] of the third Pârâgika.

'Again, venerable Upâli, where was the fourth Pârâgika promulgated?'

'At Vesâlî, Sir.'

'Concerning whom was it spoken?'

'The Bhikkhus dwelling on the banks of the Vaggumudâ river.'

'In regard to what matter?'

---

[1] That is, 'theft.'

[2] That is, murder or manslaughter. 'The slaying of' is to be understood.

'Superhuman conditions.'

Thus did the venerable Mahâ Kassapa question the venerable Upâli as to [all the particulars, as before] of the fourth Pârâ*g*ika. And in like manner did he question him through both the Vinayas[1]; and as he was successively asked, so did Upâli make reply.

8. Then the venerable Mahâ Kassapa laid a resolution before the Sa*m*gha: 'Let the venerable Sa*m*gha hear me. If the time seems meet to the Sa*m*gha, I would question Ânanda concerning the Dhamma.'

And the venerable Ânanda laid a resolution before the Sa*m*gha: 'Let the venerable Sa*m*gha hear me. If the time seems meet to the Sa*m*gha, I, as questioned by the venerable Mahâ Kassapa, will give reply.'

And the venerable Mahâ Kassapa said to the venerable Ânanda: 'Where, venerable Ânanda, was the Brahma*g*âla spoken?'

'On the way, Sir, between Râ*g*agaha and Nalanda, at the royal rest-house at Ambala*tth*ikâ[2].'

'Concerning whom was it spoken?'

'Suppiya, the wandering ascetic, and Brahmadatta, the young Brâhman.'

Thus did the venerable Mahâ Kassapa question

---

[1] Ubhato-vinaye. That is, relating on the one hand to Bhikkhus, and on the other to Bhikkhunîs (not Sutta Vibhaṅga and Khandhakas). The Burmese MS. at Berlin reads ubhato-vibhaṅge, suggested possibly by Buddhaghosa's expression in the corresponding part of his accounts of this Council at the commencement of the Sumaṅgala Vilâsinî and the Samanta Pâsâdikâ (see Turnour, loc. cit., and H. O., Vinaya III, 290.)

[2] In the text read râ*g*âgârake, as suggested in the notes at p. 329, and confirmed by the Sutta itself (ed. Grimblot).

the venerable Ânanda as to the occasion of the Brahmagâla, and as to the individuals concerning whom it was spoken.

'And again, venerable Ânanda, where was the Sâmaññâ-phala spoken?'

'At Râgagaha, Sir; in Gîvaka's Mango Grove.'

'And with whom was it spoken?'

'With Agâtasattu, the son of the Vedehî.'

Thus did the venerable Mahâ Kassapa question the venerable Ânanda as to the occasion of the Sâmaññâ-phala, and as to the individual concerned. And in like manner did he question him through the five Nikâyas, and as he was successively asked, so did Ânanda make reply.

9. Then the venerable Ânanda spake thus to the Thera Bhikkhus: 'The Blessed One, Sirs, at the time of his passing away, spake thus to me: "When I am gone, Ânanda, let the Samgha, if it should so wish, revoke all the lesser and minor precepts[1]."'

'Did you then, venerable Ânanda, ask the Blessed One which were the lesser and minor precepts?'

'No, Sirs.'

Some Theras then said that all the rules save the four Pârâgikas; others that all save those and the thirteen Samghâdisesas; others that all save those and the two Aniyatas; others that all save those and the thirty Nissaggiyas; others that all save those and the ninety-two Pâkittiyas; others that all save those and the four Pâtidesaniyas were lesser and minor precepts.

Then the venerable Mahâ Kassapa laid a resolution before the Samgha: 'Let the venerable

[1] 'Book of the Great Decease,' VI, 3.

Sa*m*gha hear me. There are certain of our precepts which relate to matters in which the laity are concerned. Now the laity know of us that "such and such things are proper for you Sama*n*as who are Sakyaputtiyas, and such and such things are not." If we were to revoke the lesser and minor precepts, it will be said to us: "A set of precepts was laid down for his disciples by the Sama*n*a Gotama to endure until the smoke should rise from his funeral pyre[1]. So long as their teacher remained with these men, so long did they train themselves in the precepts. Since their teacher has passed away from them, no longer do they now train themselves in the precepts.'

'If the time seems meet to the Sa*m*gha, not ordaining what has not been ordained, and not revoking what has been ordained, let it take upon itself and ever direct itself in the precepts according as they have been laid down. This is the resolution.

'Let the venerable Sa*m*gha hear me. [These things being so[2]] the Sa*m*gha takes upon itself the precepts according as they have been laid down. Whosoever of the venerable ones approves thereof, let him keep silence. Whosoever approves not thereof, let him speak. The Sa*m*gha has taken upon itself the precepts according as they were laid down. Therefore does it keep silence. Thus do I understand.'

10. Now the Thera Bhikkhus said to the vener-

[1] Dhûmakâlika*m*. See our note above on VI, 17, 1. Buddhaghosa says here, Dhûmakâlikan ti yâva samanassa Gotamassa parinibbâna-*k*itika-dhûmo pa*ññ*âyati tâvakâlo ti attho.

[2] The whole repeated.

able Ânanda: 'That was ill done by thee, friend Ânanda, in that thou didst not ask the Blessed One which were the lesser and minor precepts. Confess thy fault.'

'Through forgetfulness was it, Sirs, that I did not ask that of the Blessed One. I see no fault therein. Nevertheless, out of my faith in you, I confess that as a fault[1].'

'This also, friend Ânanda, was ill done by thee, in that thou steppedst upon the Blessed One's rainy-season garment to sew it. Confess thy fault.'

'It was not, Sirs, through any want of respect to the Blessed One that I did so. I see no fault therein. Nevertheless, out of my faith in you, I confess that as a fault.'

'This also, friend Ânanda, was ill done by thee, in that thou causedst the body of the Blessed One to be saluted by women first[2], so that by their weeping the body of the Blessed One was defiled by tears. Confess that fault.'

'I did so, Sirs, with the intention that they should not be kept beyond due time. I see no fault therein. Nevertheless, out of my faith in you, I confess that as a fault.'

'This too, friend Ânanda, was ill done by thee, in that even when a suggestion so evident and a hint so clear were given thee by the Blessed One, thou didst not beseech him, saying, "Let the Blessed One remain on for a kalpa! Let the Happy One remain on for a kalpa for the good and happiness of the

---

[1] Compare Mahâvagga X, 1, 8, at the end.

[2] It is worthy of notice that this episode is not referred to in the 'Book of the Great Decease' (VI, 23-26. Compare V, 46-51).

great multitudes, out of pity for the world, for the good and the gain and the weal of gods and men[1]!" Confess that fault.'

'I was possessed (by the Evil One)[2], friends, when I refrained from so beseeching him. I see no fault therein. Nevertheless, out of my faith in you, I confess that as a fault.'

'This also, friend Ânanda, was ill done by thee, in that thou exertedst thyself to procure admission for women into the Dhamma and Vinaya proclaimed by the Tathâgata[3]. Confess that fault.'

'That did I do, friends, thinking of Mahâ Pa*g*âpatî the Gotamî, the sister of the Blessed One's mother; his nurse and comforter, who gave him milk; how she, when she who had borne him was dead, herself suckled him as with mother's milk. I see no fault therein. Nevertheless, out of my faith in you, I confess that as a fault.'

11. Now at that time the venerable Purâ*n*a was wandering through the Southern Hills with a great company of Bhikkhus, with five hundred Bhikkhus. And when the Thera Bhikkhus had completed the chanting over together of the Dhamma and the Vinaya, he, having stayed in the Southern Hills as long as he thought fit, went on to Râ*g*agaha to the Ve*l*uvana, to the Kalandaka Nivâpa, where the Thera Bhikkhus were, and having greeted the Thera Bhikkhus, he took his seat on one side.

---

[1] This refers to the conversations in the 'Book of the Great Decease,' III, 1–4, and 43–60 (especially 56).

[2] Pariyu*tth*ita-*k*itto. The words in parentheses are supplied from the 'Book of the Great Decease,' III, 4, where see Rh. D.'s note on the spelling of the word.

[3] Pabba*gg*a*m*, admission into the Order.

When he was so seated, the Thera Bhikkhus said to him:

'The Dhamma and the Vinaya, friend Purâ*n*a, have been chanted over together by the Thera Bhikkhus. Do thou, then, submit thyself to and learn the text so rehearsed by them[1].'

'The Dhamma and the Vinaya, Sirs, have been well sung by the Theras. Nevertheless, even in such manner as it has been heard by me, and received by me from the very mouth of the Blessed One, in that manner will I bear it in my memory.'

12. Now the venerable Ânanda said to the Thera Bhikkhus: 'The Blessed One, Sirs, said to me at the time of his death: "Let then the Sa*m*gha, Ânanda, when I am dead, impose the higher penalty on *Kh*anna the Bhikkhu[2]."'

'Didst thou then, friend Ânanda, ask the Blessed One what the higher penalty was?'

'I did, Sirs, (and the reply was): "Let *Kh*anna the Bhikkhu, Ânanda, say whatever he may wish; but the Bhikkhus should neither speak to him, nor exhort him, nor admonish him."'

'Do thou, then, friend Ânanda, let *Kh*anna the Bhikkhu know that the higher penalty has been imposed upon him.'

'How can I, Sirs, do so? Passionate is that Bhikkhu, and rough.'

'Go then, friend Ânanda, in company with a number of other Bhikkhus.'

'Even so, Sirs,' said Ânanda, in assent to the Thera Bhikkhus. And he took with him a number

[1] Saṅgîti*m* upehi.

[2] See 'Book of the Great Decease,' VI, 4.

of Bhikkhus, to wit, five hundred Bhikkhus, and embarked on a boat going up stream, and disembarked at Kosambî, and not far from king Udena's park he took his seat at the foot of a certain tree.

13. Now at that time king Udena was enjoying himself in the park together with the ladies of his palace. And the ladies heard that their teacher, the venerable Ânanda, was seated at the foot of a tre not far from the park. And they said to king Udena:

'They say that our teacher, the venerable Ânanda, is seated at the foot of a tree not far from the park. We desire, Lord, to go and see him.'

'Go, then, and see the Sama*n*a Ânanda.' And they went and saluted the venerable Ânanda, and took their seats on one side. And he instructed, and aroused, and incited, and gladdened them with religious discourse. And when that discourse was concluded, they presented the venerable Ânanda with five hundred robes, and exalted and thanked him for his discourse, and arose from their seats, and saluted him, and keeping him on their right sides as they passed him, they departed thence.

14. And king Udena saw the ladies coming from the distance. And on seeing them he said to them:

'Well, did you succeed in seeing the Sama*n*a Ânanda?'

'We saw him, Sire.'

'Did you present the Sama*n*a Ânanda with any gift?'

'We gave, Sire, to the venerable Ânanda five hundred robes.'

Then king Udena was indignant and annoyed, and became angry, saying:

'How can the Sama*n*a Ânanda accept so many robes? Would he set up as a hawker in cloths, or would he open a shop[1]?'

And king Udena went to where the venerable Ânanda was, and after exchanging with him the greetings and compliments of friendship and civility, sat down by his side. And when he was so seated, he said to him:

'Did our ladies come hither, Ânanda?'

'Yes, great king.'

'Did they give anything to your reverence?'

'They gave me, great king, five hundred robes.'

'And what does your reverence intend to do with those five hundred robes?'

'I shall divide them, great king, among those of the Bhikkhus whose robes are worn out.'

'And what do you intend, Ânanda, to do with the worn-out robes?'

'Of those, great king, we shall make counterpanes.'

'And what do you intend to do, Ânanda, with the old counterpanes?'

'Of those, great king, we shall make bolster cases.'

'And what do you intend to do, Ânanda, with the old bolster cases?'

'Of those, great king, we shall make carpets.'

'And what do you intend to do, Ânanda, with the old carpets?'

'Of those, great king, we shall make towels for the washing of the feet.'

'And what do you intend to do, Ânanda, with the old towels?'

---

[1] Paggâhika-sâlâ, on which Buddhaghosa says nothing.

'Of those, great king, we shall make dusters.'

'And what do you intend to do, Ânanda, with the old dusters?'

'Those, great king, we shall tear in shreds, and beat up with mud, and use them for making flooring of clay.'

Then king Udena thought: 'These Sakyaputtiya Sama*n*as make general use of everything in a conscientious way, and take nothing as one man's peculiar property[1].' And he presented other five hundred pieces of cloth to the venerable Ânanda.

15. But Ânanda went on to the Ghosita Ârâma, and sat down then on the seat spread out for him. And the venerable *Kh*anna went to the place where he was and saluted him, and took his seat beside him. And when he was so seated, Ânanda said to him:

'The Sa*m*gha, friend *Kh*anna, has imposed upon you the higher penalty.'

'What then, friend Ânanda, is the higher penalty?'

'You, friend *Kh*anna, may say to the Bhikkhus whatever you wish; but the Bhikkhus are neither to speak to you, nor exhort you, nor admonish you.'

'Shall I not be even a slain man, friend Ânanda, so long as I am neither spoken to, nor exhorted, nor admonished by the Bhikkhus?' said *Kh*anna, and he fainted and fell.

Then the venerable *Kh*anna, pained, grieved, and seized with remorse through the higher penalty, remained alone and separate, earnest, zealous, and resolved. And ere long he attained to that supreme

[1] Na kulâva*m* gâmenti, on which Buddhaghosa says nothing.

goal[1] of the higher life for the sake of which men even of good family go out from all and every household gain and comfort to become houseless wanderers—yea, that supreme goal did he, by himself, and while yet in this visible world, bring himself to the knowledge of, and continue to realise, and to see face to face! And he became conscious that rebirth was at an end for him, that the higher life had been fulfilled, that all that should be done had been accomplished, and that, after this present life, there would be no beyond[2]!

So the venerable *Kh*anna became yet another among the Arahats. And after he had attained to Arahatship, the venerable *Kh*anna went to the venerable Ânanda, and said:

'Remove from me now, friend Ânanda, the higher penalty.'

'From the moment, friend *Kh*anna, that you had realised Arahatship, from that moment was the higher penalty removed from you.'

16. Now whereas five hundred Bhikkhus, without one failing, without one more, took part in this rehearsal of the Vinaya, therefore is that rehearsal of the Vinaya called 'that of the five hundred[3].'

Here ends the Eleventh Khandhaka, on the Rehearsal by the Five Hundred.

[1] That is, Arahatship, Nirvâ*n*a.

[2] This Nirvâ*n*a paragraph is constantly recurring (e.g. 'Book of the Great Decease,' V, 68; Mahâvagga V, 1, 18; Sa*m*yutta VII, 1).

[3] Compare XII, 2, 9.

TWELFTH KHANDHAKA.

On the Council of Vesâlî.

1.

1. Now at that time, a century[1] after the death of the Blessed One, the Bhikkhus of Vesâlî, Va*g*-*g*ians, promulgated at Vesâlî the ten theses:—(1) that storing salt in a horn vessel was permissible; (2) that the midday meal might be eaten when the sun's shadow showed two finger breadths after noon; (3) that he who intends to go into the village could begin to eat again after he had once left off; (4) that a number of Bhikkhus residing within the same boundary might hold Uposatha separately; (5) that a Sa*m*gha not at unity within itself might carry out an official act, undertaking to inform Bhikkhus of it; (6) that it was permissible for a Bhikkhu to do anything adopted as a practice by his Upa*ggh*âya; (7) that curds might be eaten by one who had already finished his midday meal; (8) that it was permissible to drink unfermented toddy; (9) that a rug or mat need not be of the limited size prescribed if it had no fringe; (10) that it was permissible to receive gold and silver[2].

---

[1] As pointed out at p. xxii of our Introduction, we believe this number ought not to be taken too literally, but to be considered a round number.

[2] The above terms are explained below, §§ 1, 10, and 2, 8.

Now at that time the venerable Yasa, the son of Kâka*nd*aka, who was wandering through the Va*gg*ian country, arrived at Vesâlî; and there the venerable Yasa stayed at the Mahâvana, in the Kû*t*âgâra Hall.

Now at that time the Va*gg*ian Bhikkhus of Vesâlî, on Uposatha day, filled a copper pot with water and placed it in the midst of the Bhikkhu-sa*m*gha, and said to such of their Vesâlian lay disciples as came there: 'Give, Sirs, to the Sa*m*gha a kahâpa*n*a[1], or half a one, or a pâda, or a mâsaka. It will be wanted for the Sa*m*gha, for the provision of various utensils.'

When they had thus spoken, the venerable Yasa, the son of Kâka*nd*aka, said to the lay disciples: 'Do, Sirs, nothing of the kind. The use of gold and silver is not allowed to the Sakyaputtiya Sama*n*as. The Sakyaputtiya Sama*n*as neither allow it to be given to them, nor take charge of it. The Sakyaputtiya Sama*n*as are men whose gems and jewelry have been laid aside, and who are without silver and without gold.'

Though the lay disciples from Vesâlî had been thus addressed by the venerable Yasa, the son of Kâka*nd*aka, they gave money to the Sa*m*gha. And the Va*gg*ian Bhikkhus of Vesâlî, at the close of the night, reserving one portion[2], divided that money according to the number of the Bhikkhus. And they said to the venerable Yasa, the son of Kâka*nd*aka:

'This, friend Yasa, is thy due portion of the money.'

[1] About a penny; on this and the following terms, see Rh. D.'s 'Ancient Coins and Measures, &c.,' p. 6.

[2] Pa*t*iviso. See Mahâvagga VIII, 27, 4.

'I have no due portion in that money. I do not allow any money to be given to me.'

2. Then the Vaggian Bhikkhus of Vesâlî said one to another: 'This brother, Yasa, the son of Kâka*nd*aka, upbraids and reviles, and renders dissatisfied believing and faithful followers. Come, let us carry out against him the Act of Reconciliation [1].' And they did so.

Then the venerable Yasa, the son of Kâka*nd*aka, said to them: 'It has been laid down, Sirs, by the Blessed One, that a companion shall be appointed to go as messenger with a Bhikkhu against whom the Act of Reconciliation has been carried out [2]. Appoint, Sirs, a Bhikkhu, as companion messenger to me.' And the Vaggian Bhikkhus of Vesâlî deputed a Bhikkhu to that work, and gave him as a companion messenger to the venerable Yasa.

And the venerable Yasa, taking the companion Bhikkhu with him, entered into Vesâlî, and said to the believing laymen there:

'I am said, Sirs, to be upbraiding and reviling, and rendering dissatisfied believing and faithful followers, thereby that I have said what is against the Dhamma to be against the Dhamma, and what is Dhamma to be Dhamma, and what is against the Vinaya to be against the Vinaya, and what is Vinaya to be Vinaya.

3. 'Now the Blessed One was once, Sirs, staying at Sâvatthi in the *G*etavana, Anâtha Pi*nd*ika's pleasure-ground. And there, Sirs, the Blessed One exhorted the Bhikkhus, and said:

[1] Pa*t*isâra*n*iya-kamma. See *K*ullavagga I, 18.
[2] On Anudûta, see *K*ullavagga I, 20–22.

'"There are, O Bhikkhus, four obstructions of the sun and moon, by which when the sun and moon are affected, they give no heat and they give no light, and they are no longer glorious. And what are the four? They are clouds and fog and dusty smoke and Râhu[1], by which when the sun and the moon are affected they give neither heat nor light nor sheen. Just so, O Bhikkhus, there are four stains by which when Sama*n*as and Brâhmans are affected they give neither heat nor light nor sheen. And what are the four? There are some Sama*n*as and Brâhmans who drink strong drink, and things intoxicating, abstaining not therefrom[2]. This is the first of such stains. And further, O Bhikkhus, there are some Sama*n*as and Brâhmans who practise sexual intercourse, and abstain not therefrom. This is the second of such stains. And further, O Bhikkhus, there are some Sama*n*as and Brâhmans who accept silver and gold, abstaining not from the use thereof. This is the third of such stains. And lastly, O Bhikkhus, there are some Sama*n*as and Brâhmans who gain their livelihood by low arts[3], abstaining not from such means of life. This is the fourth of such stains."

'Thus spoke, Sirs, the Blessed One: and when the Happy One had thus spoken, the Master further said:

'"Stained by lust and malice, some Sama*n*as and
Brâhmans,

[1] That is, eclipse.

[2] It is curious that this matter is not, like all the following, referred to in the Sîlas. See Rh. D.'s 'Buddhist Suttas,' p. 190.

[3] Those, namely, which are set out in the Mahâ Sîla (Rh. D.'s 'Buddhist Suttas,' pp. 196-203).

Men blinded by ignorance, praise things that seem to have delight.
Strong drink they drink and fierce, indulge in sensual acts,
Devoid of wisdom, silver and gold they take.
And by low arts some Samanas and Brâhmans live.
Stains are such actions called by the Buddha of the Solar race,
Stains—by which defiled some Samanas and Brâhmans,
Impure brutes and unclean, give neither heat nor light.
Covered rather by darkness, purblind, enslaved by craving lusts,
They enlarge the realm of death[1], and dread rebirth they gain."

'It is for upholding this opinion that I, Sirs, have been said to be upbraiding and reviling and rendering dissatisfied believing and faithful followers, in that I have said what is against the Dhamma to be against the Dhamma, and what is Dhamma to be Dhamma; what is against the Vinaya to be against the Vinaya, and what is Vinaya to be Vinaya.

4. 'And once the Blessed One was staying, Sirs, at Râgagaha, in the Veluvana, at the Kalandaka Nivâpa. Now at that time among the royal attendants sitting together in the women's apartment in the palace, the following saying was heard: "Silver and gold is allowed to the Sakyaputtiya Samanas.

[1] That is, by being repeatedly reborn they continually die. Vaddhenti katasin ti punappunam kalevara-nikkhipamâna-bhûmim vaddhenti, says Buddhaghosa. The word occurs at Gâtaka I, 146.

The Sakyaputtiya Sama*n*as accept it, and take it in charge." Now at that time Ma*n*i*k*û*l*aka, a village headman, was present. And he said to the people there: "Say not so, Sirs. Neither is silver and gold allowed to the Sakyaputtiya Sama*n*as, nor do they accept it, nor take it in charge. The Sakyaputtiya Sama*n*as are men who have laid aside gems and jewelry, and are without silver, and without gold." And the headman, Ma*n*i*k*û*l*aka, succeeded in satisfying them.

'Then the headman, Ma*n*i*k*û*l*aka, went to the place where the Blessed One was and saluted him, and took his seat on one side. And he told the Blessed One the whole matter[1], and said:

'"Now am I, Lord, in maintaining as I did, one who speaks according to the word of the Blessed One, one who does not falsely represent the Blessed One, one who does not put forth minor matters in the place of the true Dhamma? And is there anything that leads to blame in such discussion, this way and that, as touching the observance of the rules of the order[2]?"

'"Most certainly, Ma*n*i*k*û*l*aka, in maintaining thus you speak in accordance with my word, and do not represent me falsely, nor put forth minor matters as the true Dhamma. Nor is there anything leading to blame in such discussions. For gold and silver is not allowed, Ma*n*i*k*û*l*aka, to the Sakyaputtiya Sama*n*as, nor ought they to accept it, nor take it in charge. Men who have laid aside gems and jewelry are the Sakyaputtiya Sama*n*as,

[1] The whole is repeated in the text.

[2] The whole of this speech recurs, nearly word for word, in the Mahâvagga VI, 31, 4.

men without silver and without gold. For to whomsoever, Ma*n*i*k*û*l*aka, gold and silver are allowed, to him also the five kinds of sensual pleasure[1] are allowed. And to whomsoever these five kinds of pleasure are allowed, him you may know of a certainty to be following neither the rule of the Sama*n*as, nor the rule of the sons of Sâkya. Although, Ma*n*i*k*û*l*aka, I have said that he who is in need of grass may seek for grass, and he who is in need of wood may seek for wood, and he who is in need of a conveyance may seek for a conveyance, and he who is in need of a servant may seek for a servant; yet have I never said in any way whatever that gold or silver may be sought after or accepted."

'It is for maintaining this opinion that I, Sirs, have been said to be upbraiding and reviling and rendering dissatisfied believing and faithful followers, in that I have said what is against the Dhamma to be against the Dhamma, and what is Dhamma to be Dhamma; that what is against the Vinaya is against the Vinaya, and what is Vinaya is Vinaya.'

5. 'And once, Sirs, the Blessed One at the same place, at Râ*g*agaha, on the occasion of the matter of Upananda, the Sâkyan, distinctly laid down a precept by which gold and silver were forbidden[2].

'It is for maintaining this opinion that I, Sirs, have been said to be upbraiding and reviling and rendering dissatisfied believing and faithful followers, in that I have said what is against the

[1] Compare *K*ullavagga VII, 1, 2.

[2] This is set out in full in the Sutta Vibhaṅga in the Introduction to the 18th Nissaggiya Pâ*k*ittiya.

Dhamma to be against the Dhamma, and what is Dhamma to be Dhamma; that what is against the Vinaya is against the Vinaya, and what is Vinaya is Vinaya.'

6. When he had thus spoken, the lay brethren said to Yasa, the son of Kâka*nd*aka: 'There is but one, Sirs[1], who is a Sakyaputtiya Sama*n*a, our master, Yasa, the son of Kâka*nd*aka. All the rest are no Sama*n*as, neither Sakyaputtiyas. Let the venerable Yasa, the son of Kâka*nd*aka, dwell among us. We will exert ourselves to provide him with robes, and food, and medicine, and the necessaries for the sick.'

Then the venerable Yasa, the son of Kâka*nd*aka, having gained over the lay brethren, returned with the companion Bhikkhu to the Ârâma.

7. And the Va*gg*ian Bhikkhus of Vesâlî asked the companion Bhikkhu: 'Did Yasa, the son of Kâka*nd*aka, obtain, Sir, the forgiveness of the lay brethren?'

'Evil, Sirs, hath been wrought against us. Yasa, the son of Kâka*nd*aka, and he alone has been decided to be a Sakyaputtiya Sama*n*a, and all of us neither Sama*n*as nor Sakyaputtiyas.'

Then the Va*gg*ian Bhikkhus of Vesâlî said: 'The venerable Yasa, the son of Kâka*nd*aka, without being deputed by us, has proclaimed to laymen (a false doctrine)[2]. Come, let us carry out the Act of Suspension[3] against him.' And

---

[1] They are speaking to Yasa and the anudûta.

[2] This cannot refer to the 9th Pâ*k*ittiya, which only speaks of making known grievous offences. Aṅguttara II, 5, 2 refers to laymen as well as to sâma*n*eras.

[3] Ukkhepaniya-kamma. See *K*ullavagga I, 25.

they assembled together with the intention of doing so.

But the venerable Yasa, the son of Kâka*nd*aka, rose up into the sky and descended at Kosambî. And he sent messengers to the Bhikkhus of the Western country, and of Avanti, and of the Southern country[1], saying, 'Let your reverences come! We must take in charge this legal question before what is not Dhamma is spread abroad, and what is Dhamma is put aside; before what is not Vinaya is spread abroad, and what is Vinaya is put aside; before those who argue against the Dhamma become powerful, and those who argue in favour of the Dhamma become weak; before those who argue against the Vinaya become powerful, and those who argue in favour of the Vinaya become weak.'

8. Now at that time the venerable Sambhûta Sâ*n*avâsî[2] was dwelling on the Ahoganga Hill[3]. And thither the venerable Yasa, the son of Kâka*nd*aka, went; and on his arrival he saluted the venerable Sambhûta Sâ*n*avâsî, and took his seat on one side: and being so seated he said to him:

'Lord, these Va*gg*ian Bhikkhus of Vesâlî have

---

[1] On these terms, compare note on Mahâvagga VII, 1, 1.

[2] Sâ*n*avâsî is, literally, he who wears a hempen dress. In the traditions of the Sanskrit Buddhist literature we find mentioned a Sâ*n*avâsika, said to be a predecessor, in the teacher and pupil line, of Upagupta (Wassilief, p. 44). The Nepalese call him So*n*avâsî (Rajendralâl Mitra, 'Sanskrit Buddhist Literature of Nepâl,' p. 10). He is the hero of the Sâ*n*avâsi Avadâna part of the Bodhisatva Avadâna Kalpalatâ (Mitra, p. 67, Bendall 'Catalogue of Cambridge MSS.,' p. 42), where the name is explained: 'I wished for an ochre-coloured robe (so*n*a); hence I was called Sâ*n*avâsi.'

[3] See, for the position of this mountain, our note last quoted.

put forward ten theses.' And he told him what they were[1], and added: 'Come now, Lord, let us take in charge this last question before what is not Dhamma is spread abroad, and what is Dhamma is put aside; before what is not Vinaya is spread abroad, and what is Vinaya is put aside; before those who argue against the Dhamma become powerful, and those who argue in favour of the Dhamma become weak; before those who argue against the Vinaya become powerful, and those who argue in favour of the Vinaya become weak.'

'Even so, Lord,' said the venerable Sambhûta Sâ*n*avâsî, in assent to the venerable Yasa Kâka*n*-*d*aka-putta.

Then about sixty Bhikkhus from the Western country, all of whom were hermits, all of whom lived only on alms, all of whom dressed only in cast-off clothes, and kept only three robes, and all of whom were Arahats, assembled together at the Ahogaṅga Hill. And about eighty-eight from Avanti and the Southern country, some of whom were hermits, and some of whom lived only on alms, and some of whom dressed only in cast-off clothes, and some of whom kept only three robes, but all of whom were Arahats, met together with them on the Ahogaṅga Hill.

9. And the Thera Bhikkhus, consulting together, came to this conclusion: 'This legal question, now, is hard and subtle. How can we obtain such support that we may have the greater power at the decision thereof[2]?'

[1] In the text the full words of I, 1 are here repeated.

[2] Compare below, XII, 2, 1.

Now at that time the venerable Revata was dwelling at Soreyya, and he was wise in the traditions, one who had learned the Âgamas (the four Nikâyas), and knew by heart the Dhamma, the Vinaya, and the Mâtikâs; intelligent, discreet, and wise, modest, conscientious, devoted to the precepts[1]. And the Thera Bhikkhus thought that if they could gain him over to their side, they would attain their end.

And the venerable Revata, by the divine ear, clear and surpassing that of men, heard the Thera Bhikkhus as they were thus consulting together; and he thought: 'This legal question is both hard and subtle, it would not become me to hold back therefrom. But even now those Bhikkhus (the Va*gg*ians) will be coming. It would be unpleasant travelling for me were I to fall in with them. Let me go on before them.'

So the venerable Revata went from Soreyya to Sa*m*kassa. And when the Thera Bhikkhus went to Soreyya, and asked: 'Where is the venerable Revata?' they said: 'He is gone to Sa*m*kassa.'

Now the venerable Revata had gone on from Sa*m*kassa to Ka*nn*aku*gg*a. And when the Thera Bhikkhus came to Sa*m*kassa, and asked: 'Where is the venerable Revata?' they said: 'He is gone on to Ka*nn*aku*gg*a.' And in the same way they followed him thither, and to Udumbara, and to Aggalapura, and to Saha*g*âti, and there they met with the venerable Revata.

10. And the venerable Sambhûta Sâ*n*avâsî said to the venerable Yasa, the son of Kâka*nd*aka:

---

[1] These adjectives have occurred above at Mahâvagga X, 1, 2, and *K*ullavagga I, 11, 1.

'Friend, the brother Revata is wise in the traditions, has learnt the Âgamas, knows by heart the Dhamma, the Vinaya, and the Mâtikâs, he is intelligent, discreet, and wise, modest, conscientious, and devoted to the precepts. If we ask the venerable Revata a puzzling question, he is capable of spending the whole night on that one question. And even now the venerable Revata will call upon a Bhikkhu who is an intoner[1], and a pupil of his. Do you, therefore, when the Bhikkhu has concluded, go to the venerable Revata and ask him concerning these ten theses (points).'

'Even so, Sir,' said the venerable Yasa, the son of Kâka*nd*aka, in assent to the venerable Sambhûta Sâ*n*avâsî.

And the venerable Revata called upon the Bhikkhu, the pupil of his, the intoner. And when the Bhikkhu had concluded, the venerable Yasa, the son of Kâka*nd*aka, went to the venerable Revata, and saluted him, and took his seat beside him. And, so seated, he said to the venerable Revata[2]:

'Is the horn-salt-license, Lord, allowable?'

'What, Sir, is this horn-salt-license?'

'Is it allowable, Lord, to carry about salt in a horn with the intention of putting it into food which has not been salted?'

'No, Sir, it is not allowable.'

'Is the two-inch-license, Lord, allowable?'

'What, Sir, is this two-inch-license?'

'Is it allowable, Lord, to eat the midday meal

---

[1] Sarabhâ*n*aka*m*. See our note above at *K*ullavagga V, 3, 2.

[2] The whole of the following questions and answers recur below at XII, 2, 8, where the reasons of the answers also appear.

beyond the right time, provided only that the shadow has not yet turned two inches?'

'No, Sir, it is not allowable.'

'Is the village-trip-license, Lord, allowable?'

'What, Sir, is this village-trip-license?'

'Is it allowable, Lord, for one who has once finished his meal, and refused any more, to eat food which has not been left over, on the ground that he is about to proceed into the village?'

'No, Sir, it is not allowable.'

'Is the circuit-license, Lord, allowable?'

'What, Sir, is this circuit-license?'

'Is it allowable, Lord, for a number of Bhikkhus who dwell within the same circuit, within the same boundary, to hold separate Uposathas?'

'No, Sir, it is not allowable.'

'Is the indemnity-license, Lord, allowable?'

'What, Sir, is this indemnity-license?'

'Is it allowable, Lord, for a Sa*m*gha, which is not legally constituted[1], to perform an official act on the ground that they will afterwards obtain the sanction of such Bhikkhus who may subsequently arrive?'

'No, Sir, it is not allowable.'

'Is the precedent-license, Lord, allowable?'

'What, Sir, is this precedent-license?'

'Is it allowable, Lord, to do a thing on the ground that, "My preceptor (upa*ggh*âya) has practised this; or my teacher (â*k*ariya) has practised that?"'

'In some cases, Sir, this is allowable, and in some not[2].'

---

[1] Vaggena. See our note on the 21st Pâ*k*ittiya, and *K*ullavagga V, 2, 1.

[2] That is, of course, according as the thing enjoined is, or is not,

'Is the churn-license, Lord, allowable?'

'What, Sir, is this churn-license?'

'Is it allowable, Lord, for one who has once finished his meal, and has refused any more, to drink milk not left over from the meal, on the ground that it has left the condition of milk, and has not yet reached the condition of curds[1]?'

'No, Sir, it is not allowable.'

'Is it allowable, Lord, to drink toddy?'

'What, Sir, is this toddy?'

'Is it allowable, Lord, to drink spirits which have left the condition of not being spirits, and yet have not acquired intoxicating properties[2]?'

'No, Sir, it is not allowable?'

'Is a rug or mat (when it is beyond the prescribed size) lawful, Lord, because it is unfringed?'

'No, Sir, it is not allowable.'

'Is gold and silver, Lord, allowable?'

'No, Sir, it is not allowable.'

'These are the ten theses, Lord, which these Va*gg*ian Bhikkhus of Vesâlî have put forth. Come, Lord, let us take this legal question in hand before that which is not Dhamma is spread abroad, and that which is Dhamma is put aside; before that which is not Vinaya is spread abroad, and that which is Vinaya is put aside; before those who argue against the Dhamma become powerful, and those

lawful. Eka*kk*o kappatî ti ida*m* dhammika*m* â*kinnam* sandhâya vutta*m*, says Buddhaghosa.

[1] That is, which is neither liquid nor solid: something apparently like buttermilk.

[2] It is a question constantly arising under the excise laws in India and Ceylon, whether the liquor in the case has become arrack, or is only arrack in the making, and unfermented. This last is called unfermented toddy.

who argue in favour of the Dhamma become weak; before those who argue against the Vinaya become powerful, and those who argue in favour of the Vinaya become weak.'

'Even so, Sir,' said the venerable Revata, in assent to the venerable Yasa, the son of Kâka*nd*aka.

Here ends the First Portion for Recitation.

2.

1. Now the Va*gg*ian Bhikkhus of Vesâlî heard the rumour: 'Yasa, they say, the son of Kâka*nd*aka, wishing to take this legal question in hand, is seeking about for support, and support they say he is succeeding in getting.' And they thought: 'This legal question, now, is hard and subtle. How can we obtain such support that we may have the greater power at the decision thereof[1]?'

And they thought: 'The venerable Yasa, who dwells at Soreyya, is wise in the traditions, and is one who has learnt the Âgamas, who knows by heart the Dhamma, the Vinaya, the Mâtikâs, is intelligent, discreet, and wise, modest, conscientious, and devoted to the precepts. If we could gain him over to our side, we should attain our end.'

Then the Va*gg*ian Bhikkhus of Vesâlî got together much property, requisites, a number of things of the Sama*n*as' life—to wit, bowls and robes, and rugs, and needlecases, and girdles, and filters, and regulation-pots[2]. And, taking this property with

[1] Compare above, XII, 1, 9.
[2] On Dhamma-karaka, see our note at *K*ullavagga V, 13, 1.

them, they went up stream by boat to Saha*g*âti, and there disembarked, and took their meal at the foot of a certain tree.

2. Now to the venerable Sâ*lh*a, who retired apart and was plunged in meditation, there occurred this doubtful problem: 'Are the Bhikkhus of the East, or the Bhikkhus of the West, the more in accordance with the Dhamma in the opinion that they hold?' And having gone over the Dhamma and the Vinaya in his mind, he came to the conclusion, 'The Bhikkhus of the East are not, and the Bhikkhus of the West are, in accordance with the Dhamma in the opinion that they hold.'

And a certain one of the deities in the Pure Abode[1] perceived how this doubtful problem had arisen in the venerable Sâ*lh*a's mind, and as quickly as a strong man could stretch forth his bent arm, or draw it in again when it was outstretched, so quickly did that deity vanish from the Pure Abode, and appeared before the venerable Sâ*lh*a; saying to him: 'Thou art quite right, Sâ*lh*a; it is the Eastern Bhikkhus whose opinions are against the Dhamma, and the Western Bhikkhus whose opinions accord therewith. Do thou, therefore, O Sâ*lh*a, even as the Dhamma is, so take thy stand!'

'Both formerly, O deity, and now, also, do I take my stand even as the Dhamma is. Notwithstanding, I shall not make manifest my opinion until (the Sa*m*gha) shall have appointed me (judge) over this question[2].'

3. Now the Va*gg*ian Bhikkhus of Vesâlî, taking with them the aforesaid property, went to the place

[1] The Heaven, so called.

[2] Compare below, § 6.

where the venerable Revata was, and said to him: 'Let the venerable Thera receive at our hands these requisites of a Sama*n*a's life.'

But he refused to receive it, saying, 'Not so, my friends. I have all the things[1] I want.'

Now at that time a Bhikkhu named Uttara, who had been twenty years admitted into the Order[2], was the attendant upon the venerable Revata. And the Va*gg*ian Bhikkhus of Vesâlî went to him, and said: 'Let your reverence receive at our hands these requisites of a Sama*n*a's life.'

But he made the same reply.

Then they said: 'People used to offer such requisites to the Blessed One. If he received them, they were happy. If he did not receive them, they used to offer them to the venerable Ânanda, saying, "Let the venerable Thera receive these requisites of a Sama*n*a's life: that will be just as if the Blessed One had received them." Let the venerable Uttara receive these things: that will be as if the Thera had received them.'

Then the venerable Uttara, being thus importuned by the Va*gg*ian Bhikkhus of Vesâlî, accepted one robe, saying, 'You may tell me, friends, what you want.'

'Let the venerable Uttara say thus much for us to the Thera: "Let the venerable Thera say thus much in the meeting of the Sa*m*gha—'It is in the regions of the East that the Buddhas, the Blessed Ones, are born. It is the Bhikkhus of the East who hold opinions in accord with the Dhamma, whereas the Bhikkhus of the West do not.'"'

---

[1] Literally, 'I have the three robes.'

[2] Vîsativasso; that is, since his upasampadâ.

'Even so, Sirs,' said the venerable Uttara, in assent to the Va*gg*ian Bhikkhus of Vesâlî. And he went to Revata, and told him what they had said.

'Thou urgest me, O Bhikkhu, to that which is against the Dhamma,' said the Thera, and sent away the venerable Uttara[1].

And the Va*gg*ian Bhikkhus of Vesâlî said to the venerable Uttara: 'What, friend Uttara, did the Thera say?'

'It is an evil you have wrought me, Sirs. The Thera has sent me away, saying, "Thou urgest me, O Bhikkhu, to what is against the Dhamma."'

'Are you not, Sir, of full age, of twenty years (since your upasampadâ)?'

'Yes, Sirs, I am.'

'Then do we take the nissaya under you as your pupils[2].'

4. Now the Sa*m*gha met together with the intention of deciding the legal question. And the venerable Revata laid a resolution before the Sa*m*gha, saying,

'Let the venerable Sa*m*gha hear me. If we were to settle this question, it might be that those Bhikkhus who had at first taken the matter in hand might raise it again[3]. If it seem meet to the Sa*m*gha, let the Sa*m*gha settle it at that place where it arose.'

---

[1] Pa*n*âmesi. That is, permanently from attendance upon him. Compare Mahâvagga I, 27, 2, where the word is used of the formal dismissal or turning away of a pupil.

[2] Garu-nissaya*m* ga*n*hâma; on which Buddhaghosa has nothing, though the phrase does not occur elsewhere in the Khandhakas.

[3] Compare the 63rd Pâ*k*ittiya.

Then the Thera Bhikkhus went to Vesâlî, with the intention of settling the matter there.

Now at that time the eldest Thera in the world, Sabbakâmî by name, one who was of a hundred and twenty years' standing from the date of his upasampadâ, and who had been a pupil[1] of the venerable Ânanda, was living at Vesâlî. And the venerable Revata said to the venerable Sambhûta Sâ*n*avâsî:

'I shall go to that Vihâra in which the Thera Sabbakâmî dwells. Do you go betimes to the venerable Sabbakâmî, and question him as touching these ten points.'

'Even so, Lord,' said the venerable Sambhûta Sâ*n*avâsî, in assent to the venerable Revata.

And the venerable Revata came to that Vihâra in which the venerable Sabbakâmî lived; and a sleeping-place was made ready for the former in the inner chamber, and for the latter in front thereof. And the venerable Revata, thinking, 'This Thera, though so old, does not care to sleep,' did not go to rest. And the venerable Sabbakâmî, thinking, 'This Bhikkhu, though a traveller and tired, does not care to sleep,' did not go to rest.

5. Then when the night was far spent, the venerable Sabbakâmî said to the venerable Revata:

'By what manner of life, beloved one, have you lived now these so many years?'

'By continuing in the sense of love, honoured friend, have I continued thus so many years.'

'They say that you have continued thus, beloved one, by easiness of life: and that indeed, beloved one, is an easy life, (I mean) the continuing in love.'

[1] Literally, 'had dwelt in the same Vihâra with.'

'Even long ago, Sir, when I was a layman, was much love laid up in my heart, therefore is it that now also I live much in the sense of love, and indeed since long I have attained to Arahatship. And by what manner of life have you lived now these many years?'

'By continuing in the sense of the emptiness (of worldly things) have I, beloved one, lived these many years.'

'They say that you, honoured friend, have continued thus by the sense of being a man born to greatness[1]; and that indeed, honoured friend, is the same feeling, (I mean) the sense of the emptiness of things.'

'Even long ago, beloved one, when I was a layman, had I a strong sense of the emptiness of things, therefore is it that now also I live much in that feeling, and indeed since long I have attained to Arahatship.'

6. Now[2] this conversation between the Thera Bhikkhus was still unfinished when the venerable Sambhûta Sâ*n*avâsî arrived there. And he went up to the venerable Sabbakâmî, and saluted him, and took his seat beside him. And, so seated, he said to the venerable Sabbakâmî:

'These Va*gg*ian Bhikkhus of Vesâlî have put forth in Vesâlî these ten points;' and he told them all[3]. 'Now you, O Thera, have mastered much Dhamma and Vinaya at the feet of your preceptor.

[1] Mahápurisa. On the subsequent history of which word, see Senart's 'Légende du Buddha,' pp. 54, 107.

[2] *K*arahi. Compare 'Book of the Great Decease,' III, 53; Childers, p. 32.

[3] The text repeats XII, 1, 1.

What, then, is the conclusion to which you, O Thera, come as you lay over in your mind the Dhamma and the Vinaya;—whose opinion is in accordance with the Dhamma, that of the Bhikkhus of the East, or that of the Bhikkhus of the West?'

'You also, Sir, have mastered much Dhamma and Vinaya at the feet of your preceptor. What, then, is the conclusion to which you, Sir, come as you lay over in your mind the Dhamma and the Vinaya;—whose opinion is in accordance with the Dhamma, that of the Bhikkhus of the East, or that of the Bhikkhus of the West?'

'The conclusion to which I come, Lord, as I so lay over in my mind the Dhamma and the Vinaya, is this—that the Bhikkhus of the East hold an opinion that is not in accord with the Dhamma, while the Bhikkhus of the West are in accord with the Dhamma. Notwithstanding, I do not intend to make manifest my opinion until (the Sa*m*gha) shall have appointed me (referee) over this question [1].'

'The conclusion to which I also have come, Sir, as I lay over in my mind the Dhamma and the Vinaya, is this—that the Bhikkhus of the East hold an opinion that is not in accordance with the Dhamma, while the Bhikkhus of the West are in accord with the Dhamma. Notwithstanding, I do not intend to make manifest my opinion until (the Sa*m*gha) shall have appointed me (referee) over this question.'

7. Then the Sa*m*gha met together with the intention of enquiring into this legal question. But while they were enquiring into it, both was much pointless speaking brought forth and also the sense

[1] Compare above, § 2.

in no single speech was clear[1]. Then the venerable Revata laid a resolution before the Sa*m*gha:

'Let the venerable Sa*m*gha hear me. Whilst we are discussing this legal question, there is both much pointless speaking, and no sense is clear in any single speech. If it seem meet to the Sa*m*gha, let the Sa*m*gha settle this legal question by referring it (to a jury)[2].'

And he chose four Bhikkhus of the East and four Bhikkhus of the West—from the Bhikkhus of the East the venerable Sabbakâmî, and the venerable Sâ*lh*a, and the venerable Khu*gg*a-sobhita, and the venerable Vâsabha-gâmika—and from the Bhikkhus of the West, the venerable Revata, and the venerable Sambhûta Sâ*n*avâsî, and the venerable Yasa, the son of Kâka*nd*aka, and the venerable Sumana. Then the venerable Revata laid a resolution before the Sa*m*gha:

'Let the venerable Sa*m*gha hear me. During the enquiry into this matter there has been much pointless talk among us, and in no single utterance is the sense clear. If it seem meet to the Sa*m*gha, let the Sa*m*gha delegate four Bhikkhus of the East and four Bhikkhus of the West to settle this question by reference. This is the resolution.

'Let the venerable Sa*m*gha hear me. During the enquiry into this matter there has been much pointless talk among us, and the sense in any single utterance is not clear. The Sa*m*gha delegates four Bhikkhus of the East and four Bhikkhus of the West to settle this question by reference. Whoso-

[1] So above in *K*ullavagga IV, 14, 19, where the proceeding adopted in the subsequent sentences is laid down for use on such an occasion.

[2] Ubbâhikâya. See the passage quoted in the last note.

ever of the venerable ones approves thereof, let him keep silence. Whosoever approves not thereof, let him speak. The delegation is made accordingly. The Sa*m*gha approves thereof. Therefore is it silent. Thus do I understand.'

Now at that time a Bhikkhu named A*g*ita, of ten years' standing, was the reciter of the Pâtimokkha to the Sa*m*gha. Him did the Sa*m*gha appoint as seat regulator[1] to the Thera Bhikkhus.

Then the Thera Bhikkhus thought, 'At what place, now, ought we to settle this legal question?' And it occurred to them: 'This Vâlika Ârâma is a pleasant place, quiet and undisturbed. Let us settle the matter there.' And thither the Thera Bhikkhus proceeded to enquire into the question.

8. Then the venerable Revata laid a resolution before the Sa*m*gha[2]: 'Let the venerable Sa*m*gha hear me. If it seem meet to the Sa*m*gha, I will question the venerable Sabbakâmî as touching the Vinaya.' And the venerable Sabbakâmî laid a resolution before the Sa*m*gha: 'If it seem meet to the Sa*m*gha, I, when asked by Revata touching the Vinaya, will give reply.'

And the venerable Revata said to the venerable Sabbakâmî: 'Is the horn-salt-license, Lord, allowable?'

---

[1] Âsana-paññâpaka*m*. This office is not mentioned in the other Khandhakas. We should expect to find it at *K*ullavagga VI, 21, 2. The reason of this is that it is no office of authority. The different referees would take their seats in the order of their seniority, and all that the âsana-paññâpaka would have to do would be to see that they were provided with everything they required (it was not much, chiefly mats or rugs to sit upon) in the hall or grove where they met.

[2] Here, of course, consisting of the eight referees.

'What, Sir, is this horn-salt-license ?'

'Is it allowable, Lord, to carry about salt in a horn with the intention of putting it into food which has not been salted ?'

'No, Sir, it is not allowable.'

'Where was such a claim rejected ?'

'At Sâvatthi, in the Sutta Vibhaṅga.'

'Of what offence is the person, who does so, guilty ?'

'Of Pâkittiya, in eating food which has been put by[1].'

'Let the venerable Samgha hear me. This first point, having been examined into by the Samgha, has been found to be false Dhamma and false Vinaya, and not contained in the teaching of the Master. Thus do I cast the first vote.'

'Is the two-inch-license, Lord, allowable ?'

'What, Sir, is this two-inch-license ?'

'Is it allowable, Lord, to eat the midday meal beyond the right time, provided only that the shadow of the sun has not yet turned two inches ?'

'No, Sir, it is not allowable.'

'Where has such a claim been rejected ?'

'At Râgagaha, in the Sutta Vibhaṅga.'

'Of what offence is he, who does so, guilty ?'

'Of Pâkittiya, in eating at the wrong time[2].'

'Let the venerable Samgha hear me. This second point, having been examined into by the Samgha, has been found to be false Dhamma and false Vinaya, and not contained in the teaching of the Master. Thus do I cast the second vote.'

'Is the village-trip-license, Lord, allowable ?'

---

[1] Pâkittiya XXXVIII.

[2] Pâkittiya XXXVII.

'What, Sir, is this village-trip-license?'

'Is it allowable for one who has once finished his meal, and has refused any more, to eat food which has not been left over, on the ground that he is about to proceed into the village?'

'No, Sir, it is not allowable.'

'Where was such a claim rejected?'

'At Sâvatthi, in the Sutta Vibhaṅga.'

'Of what offence is he, who does so, guilty?'

'Of Pâkittiya, in eating food which has not been left over[1].'

'Let the venerable Saṃgha hear me. This third point, having been examined into by the Saṃgha, has been found to be false Dhamma and false Vinaya, and not contained in the teaching of the Master. Thus do I cast the third vote.'

'Is the circuit-license, Lord, allowable?'

'What, Sir, is this circuit-license?'

'Is it allowable, Lord, for a number of Bhikkhus who dwell within the same circuit, within the same boundary, to hold separate Uposathas?'

'No, Sir, it is not allowable.'

'Where was such a claim rejected?'

'At Râgagaha, in the Uposatha Saṃyutta[2].'

'Of what offence is he, who does so, guilty?'

'Of Dukkaṭa, in neglecting the Vinaya.'

'Let the venerable Saṃgha hear me. This fourth point, having been examined into by the Saṃgha, has been found to be false Dhamma and false Vinaya, and not contained in the teaching of the Master. Thus do I cast the fourth vote.'

[1] Pâkittiya XXXV.

[2] Saṃyutta must here be used for Khandhaka. The passage referred to is Mahâvagga II (the Uposatha Khandhaka), 8, 3.

'Is the indemnity-license, Lord, allowable?'

'What, Sir, is this indemnity-license?'

'Is it allowable, Lord, for a Saṃgha which is not legally constituted to perform an official act, on the ground that they will afterwards obtain the sanction of such Bhikkhus as subsequently arrive?'

'No, Sir it is not allowable.'

'Where was such a claim rejected?'

'In the *K*ampeyyaka section, in the body of the Vinaya[1].'

'Of what offence is he, who does so, guilty?'

'Of Dukka*t*a, in neglecting the Vinaya.'

'Let the venerable Saṃgha hear me. This fifth point, having been examined into by the Saṃgha, has been found to be false Dhamma and false Vinaya, and not contained in the teaching of the Master. Thus do I cast this fifth vote.'

'Is the precedent-license, Lord, allowable?'

'What, Sir, is this precedent-license?'

'Is it allowable, Lord, to do a thing on the ground that "My preceptor (upa*ggh*âya) has practised this," or "My teacher (â*k*ariya) has practised that?"'

'In some cases, Sir, it is allowable, and in some not[2].'

'Let the venerable Saṃgha hear me. This sixth point, having been examined into by the Saṃgha, has been found to be false Dhamma and false Vinaya, and not contained in the teaching of the Master. Thus do I cast this sixth vote.'

'Is the churn-license, Lord, allowable?'

'What, Sir, is this churn-license?'

---

[1] Vinaya-vatthu. Here used as a title, apparently of the Khandhakas. The passage referred to is in the *K*ampeyyaka Khandhaka (Mahâvagga IX, 3, 5).

[2] See the note above on XII, 1, 10.

'Is it allowable, Lord, for one who has once finished his meal, and has refused any more, to drink milk not left over from the meal, on the ground that it has left the condition of milk and has not yet reached the condition of curds?'

'No, Sir, it is not allowable.'

'Where was such a claim rejected?'

'At Sâvatthi, in the Sutta Vibhaṅga.'

'Of what offence is he, who does so, guilty?'

'Of Pâkittiya, in eating food which has not been left over[1].'

'Let the venerable Samgha hear me. This seventh point, having been examined into by the Samgha, has been found to be false Dhamma and false Vinaya, and not contained in the teaching of the Master. Thus do I cast this seventh vote.'

'Is it allowable, Lord, to drink toddy?'

'What, Sir, is this toddy?'

'Is it allowable, Lord, to drink spirits which have not yet become spirits and have not yet acquired intoxicating properties?'

'No, Sir, it is not allowable.'

'Where was it rejected?'

'At Kosambî, in the Sutta Vibhaṅga.'

'Of what offence is he, who does so, guilty?'

'Of Pâkittiya, in the drinking of fermented liquors and strong drink[2].'

'Let the venerable Samgha hear me. The eighth point, having been examined into by the Samgha, has been found to be false Dhamma and false Vinaya, and not contained in the teaching of the Master. Thus do I cast this eighth vote.'

[1] Pâkittiya XXXV.

'Is the unfringed-seat, Lord, allowable[1]?'

'No, Sir, it is not allowable.'

'Where has it been rejected?'

'At Savatthi, in the Sutta Vibhaṅga.'

'Of what offence is he, who uses such a seat, guilty?'

'Of Pâkittiya, in using a thing which ought to be cut down (to the proper size)[2].'

'Let the venerable Saṃgha hear me. This ninth point, having been examined into by the Saṃgha, has been found to be false Dhamma and false Vinaya, and not contained in the teaching of the Master. Thus do I cast this ninth vote.'

'Is gold and silver, Lord, allowable?'

'No, Sir, it is not allowable.'

'Where was it forbidden?'

'At Râgagaha, in the Sutta Vibhaṅga.'

'Of what offence is he, who takes it, guilty?'

'Of Pâkittiya, in accepting gold and silver[3].'

'Let the venerable Saṃgha hear me. This tenth point, having been examined into by the Saṃgha, has been found to be false Dhamma and false Vinaya, and not contained in the teaching of the Master. Thus do I cast this tenth vote.'

'Let the venerable Saṃgha hear me. These ten points, having been examined into by the Saṃgha, have been found to be false Dhamma and false Vinaya, and not contained in the teaching of the Master.'

---

[1] That is, does the fact of its being unfringed make legal a mat or rug otherwise illegal by reason of its size? See above, XII, 1, 10.

[2] Pâkittiya LXXXIX.

[3] The 18th Nissaggiya Pâkittiya.

'[1] This legal question, Sir, has been concluded; and being settled, it is settled once for all. Nevertheless, Sir, do you question me on these ten points in the midst also of the Sa*m*gha[2], in order to persuade those Bhikkhus[3].'

So the venerable Revata questioned the venerable Sabbakâmî on the ten points also in the midst of the Sa*m*gha, and as he was questioned on one after the other, the venerable Sabbakâmî gave reply.

9. Now whereas at this rehearsal of the Vinaya seven hundred Bhikkhus, without one more, without one being wanting, took part, therefore is that rehearsal of the Vinaya called 'That of the seven hundred[4].'

Here ends the Twelfth Khandhaka, on the Rehearsal by the Seven Hundred.

[1] It is clear from the word tva*m* âvuso, that Sabbakâmî is here addressing Revata.

[2] That is not only of the referees, but of all the Bhikkhus there at Vesâlî.

[3] Bhikkhûna*m* sa*ññ*attiyâ. See the use of this phrase at *K*ullavagga IV, 14, 26, and VII, 4, 1, and our note on the latter of those two passages.

[4] Compare XI, 1, 15.

NOTE ON THE BHÂ*N*AVÂRAS.

As the division into Bhâ*n*avâras or Portions for Recitation is of some value in the history of the way in which the books were handed down, and is now overshadowed by the more practical division for modern purposes adopted in this translation into chapters and sections, the following table may be of use :—

MAHÂVAGGA.

Present division.	Pâli title.	Page in text.	Extent in text.
KHANDHAKA I.			
Chapter 6.	Pa*th*ama-bhâ*n*avâra*m*	14	14
„ 14.	Dutiyaka-bhâ*n*avâra*m*	24	10
„ 21.	Uruvela-pâ*t*ihâriya*m* tatiyaka-bhâ-*n*avâra*m* ni*tth*ita*m*	35	11
„ 24.	*K*atutthaka-bh. ni*tth*ita*m* . . .	44	9
„ 30.	Upa*ggh*âya - vatta - bh. ni*tth*ita*m* pañ*k*ama*m*	58	14
„ 33.	*Khatth*a*m* bhâ*n*avâra*m*	61	3
„ 38.	Sattama*m* bhâ*n*avâra*m*	71	10
„ 53.	Abhayûvara-bh. ni*tth*ita*m* . . .	81	10
„ 79.	. . . .	98	?17
KHANDHAKA II.			
Chapter 16.	A*ññ*a-titthiya-bh. ni*tth*ita*m* . .	115	16
„ 27.	*K*odanâ-vatthu-bh. ni*tth*ita*m* . .	128	13
„ 36.	Uposatha-khandhake tatiya*m* bhâ-*n*avâra*m*	136	8
KHANDHAKA III.			
Chapter 8.	Vassâvâsa-bh. ni*tth*ita*m*	148	11
„ 14.	. . . .	155	7
KHANDHAKA IV.			
Chapter 6.	Pa*th*ama-bh. ni*tth*ita*m*	164	9
„ 18.	. . . .	178	14
KHANDHAKA V has no Bhâ*n*avâras, and ends in the text on page		198	2

Khandhaka VI.
Chapter 15. Bhesagga-anuññâta-bh. pathamam 209 10
" 30. Likkhavi-bh. nitthitam 233 24
" 33. Katu-vîsati-bh. nitthitam . . . 240 7
" 40. . . . . 251 11
Khandhaka VII.
Chapter 7. Âdâya-bh. nitthitam 259 7
" 13. . . . . 265 6
Khandhaka VIII.
Chapter 1. Pathamaka-bh. nitthitam . . . 281 14
" 15. Visâkhâ-bhânavâram 294 13
" 32. . . . . 310 16
Khandhaka IX.
Chapter 4. Vâsabha-gâma-bhânavâram pathamam 322 11
" 6. Upâli-pukkhâ-bhânavâram dutiyam 328 6
" 7. . . . . 333 5
Khandhaka X.
Chapter 2. Dîghâvu-bhânavâram pathamam 349 13
" 6. . . . . 359 10

KULLAVAGGA.

Khandhaka I–IV. None.
Khandhaka V.
Chapter 21. Dutiya-bhânavâram 129 25
" 37. . . . . 143 14
Khandhaka VI.
Chapter 3. Bhânavâram nitthitam pathamam 154 9
" 11. Dutiya-bhânavâram 167 13
" 21. . . . . 177 10
Khandhaka VII.
Chapter 2. Pathamaka-bhânavâram nitthitam 188 9
" 3. Bhânavâram nitthitam dutiyam . 198 10
" 5. Bhânavâram nitthitam tatiyam . 206 8
Khandhaka VIII.
Chapter 4. Bhânavâram pathamam . . . 215 8
" 12. Dutiya-bhânavâram 231 16
" 14. . . . . 231 —

KHANDHAKA IX.			
Chapter	3. Pathamo bhânavâro[1]	247	12
"	5.	251	4
KHANDHAKA X.			
Chapter	8. Pathama-bhânavâram	261	9
"	16. Dutiya-bhânavâram	271	10
"	27. Tatiya-bhânavâram	281	10
KHANDHAKA XI has none		292	9
KHANDHAKA XII.			
Chapter	1. Pathama-bhânavâram	301	8
"	2.	307	6

On this it may be observed—

1. The last Bhânavâra in each Khandhaka is not referred to either by name or by number, except in Mahâvagga II, and in Kullavagga VII and X. In the Mahâvagga fourteen of the Bhânavâras have special titles, independent of their number in the particular Khandhaka.

2. Probably two Bhânavâras in Mahâvagga V, all the Bhânavâras in Kullavagga I–IV, and the first in Kullavagga V, are not noticed in the printed text.

3. Making allowance for these we have in the Mahâvagga 31 (? 32) Bhânavâras, occupying about 350 pages of Pâli text, and about 610 pages in our translation. In books V–XII of the Kullavagga we have 20 Bhânavâras, occupying about 200 pages of Pâli text, and about 350 pages in our translation. Total 51 (? 52) Bhânavâras, occupying about 550 pages of Pâli, and about 960 pages of translation.

4. As in the printed text repetitions have been avoided by a mode of reference to former passages which was impossible in the MSS the average length of the matter contained in a Bhânavâra, as written much more in full in the MSS., would be somewhat greater than its average length as actually printed. It would probably amount to what, if printed verbatim, would occupy in space not much less than a sheet of the size and type used in the edition of the text. Thus the three Bhânavâras in Mahâvagga VIII, which owing to the subject-matter are printed with only a few such contractions, occupy respectively 14, 13, and 16 pages of the text.

[1] Sic. This is the only instance in the Vinaya of a masculine use of the word.

5. The recital in the usual sara-bha*ññ*a (or intonation, see *K*ullavagga V, 3) of such a 'portion for recitation' would occupy in time about half-an-hour.

6. Spence Hardy informs us in his 'Eastern Monachism' (p. 168) that the Dîgha Nikâya contains 64, the Ma*ggh*ima Nikâya 80, the Sa*m*yutta Nikâya 100, and the Aṅguttara Nikâya 120 Bhâ*n*avâras. In fact it is only a few of the longer Suttas in the first two collections which are actually divided into Bhâ*n*avâras in the MSS.; and only the longer Nipâtas in the Aṅguttara. There are no Bhâ*n*avâras in the Eka- and Duka-Nipâtas of that collection; and there are also none in the Sa*m*yutta Nikâya, and none in any of the books of the later literature contained in the Abhidhamma Pi*t*aka (including all those in the Khuddaka Nikâya) as yet published.

7. The division into Bhâ*n*avâras is not made use of in many books of the Pi*t*akas themselves, or in the fifth-century commentaries of Buddhaghosa and others. In the Sutta-vibhaṅga it is only used in Pârâ*g*ikas I–III, and in the Parivâra not at all. When Spence Hardy says therefore (loc. cit. p. 172) that the Pi*t*akas and commentaries combined contain 5347 Bhâ*n*avâras, he must be referring to a mere calculation and not to the actual use of the MSS. On the other hand, the fact of Bhâ*n*avâras being used in the Dîpava*m*sa and the Khudda-sikkhâ may possibly afford some clue to the age in which those works were composed.

INDEX TO VINAYA TEXTS,

PARTS I, II, III,

VOLUMES XIII, XVII, XX.

INDEX OF SUBJECTS.

References to the Introduction are in Roman numerals only, those to the Text have P., M., or *K.* prefixed, according as they occur in the Pâtimokkha, the Mahâvagga, or the *K*ullavagga, respectively. The numerals refer after P. to the pages, after M. and *K.* to the chapters and sections.

Absolution, M. ii, 27; *K.* iv, 14, 30-32; v, 20, 5; vii, 37.
Abuse, P. 32; *K.* x, 22, 1.
Accoucheur, M. viii, 1, 4.
Acquittal of the consciously innocent, *K.* i, 4.
Age, when it begins to run, M. i, 75.
Agriculture forbidden to Bhikkhus, P. 33.
— blight and mildew, *K.* x, 1, 6.
— scare-crows, M. i, 50.
— ploughshares, M. vi, 26, 7.
— gleaning, M. vi, 32, 1.
— shape of rice-fields, M. viii, 12.
— list of farming operations, *K.* vii, 1, 2.
Ague, intermittent, M. vi, 14, 4; M. i, 6, 1, 2.
Alligator's fat, as medicine, M. vi, 2, 2.
Ambrosia of Arahatship, M. i, 5, 7, 12; 6, 8, 12.
Animals, conduct towards, P. 46; M. iii, 1.
— not to be members of the order, M. i, 63; ii, 22, 3.
— not to be killed, M. v, 9, 2; 10, 9; vi, 31, 14.
— various, not to be eaten, M. vi, 23.
— song of love to, *K.* v, 6.
Annihilation, sense in which Buddha teaches, M. vi, 31, 7.
Aperient myrobolan, M. viii, 1, 28.
Arahatship, M. v, 1, 18-28; *K.* i, 4, 1; xii, 2, 5.
Architecture (see also Rest-house).
Buddhist Vihâra, size of, P. 8, 9.
— building of, P. 35; *K.* vi, 4, 10; vi, 5; vi, 17.
— cleansing of, M. i, 25, 15.
— rooms, various, M. i, 25, 19; *K.* vi, 33, 6.
— buildings, list of various, M. iii, 5, 6; *K.* vi, 10, 4.
— the five kinds of, M. i, 30, 4; ii, 8, 1; vi, 33, 2; viii, 7; *K.* vi, 1, 2.
— earthenware huts, M. iii, 12, 9; *K.* v, 37.
— loomsheds, *K.* v, 11, 6.
— roofs of skins, *K.* v, 11, 6; 14, 2; vi, 2, 2; other kinds, *K.* vi, 3, 11.
— doors, drains, chimneys, *K.* v, 14, 3; vi, 1, 2; 3, 8.
— wells, building and machinery of, *K.* v, 16, 2.
— artificial lakes, *K.* v, 17.
— windows, *K.* vi, 22; viii, 3, 5.
— plastering, &c., of walls, *K.* vi, 3, 1.
— ceiling cloth, *K.* vi, 3, 5.
— entrance porch, *K.* v, 14, 4; vi, 3, 9, 10.
— verandahs, *K.* vi, 14.
Arithmetic, M. i, 49.
Asceticism, definition of Buddhist, M. vi, 31, 8.
Assemblies, fortnightly, duty of attending, M. ii, 1.

Astringent herbs, list of, M. vi, 4.
Astrology condemned, *K*. v, 33, 2.
Astronomy, elementary, to be learned, *K*. viii, 6, 3.

Back scratcher, *K*. v, 1, 4.
Banishment of guilty Bhikkhus, *K*. i, 13-17.
Barbers, M. vi, 37; *K*. v, 27, 3; Bhikkhunîs not to be, *K*. x, 10, 4.
Bark garments forbidden, M. viii, 28, 2.
Barter, P. 21-24, when allowed to Bhikkhus, *K*. vi, 19.
Bathing, P. 44; M. i, 25, 12; v, 13, 6; *K*. viii, 4, 2.
 Shampooing, *K*. v, 1.
 Steam baths, M. vi, 14, 3; *K*. v, 14, 1, 3.
 — etiquette in, *K*. viii, 8; forbidden to Bhikkhunîs, *K*. x, 27, 4.
 Bathing dresses for nuns, M. viii, 15, 11.
 Rules for Bhikkhunîs at the bath, *K*. x, 27.
 Forbidden methods of, *K*. v, 1.
— in the open air, *K*. v, 17.
Beans, eating of, M. vi, 16.
Bears' fat as medicine, M. vi, 2, 2.
Beasts of prey, M. iii, 9, 1.
Bedsteads, *K*. vi, 2, 3; form of, *K*. viii, 1, 4.
Bewitched, cure for those, M. vi, 14, 7.
Bhikkhunîs, eight chief rules for, *K*. x, 1, 4; six rules for novices, ibid.; rules for reciting the Pâtimokkha before, x, 6, 1; disciplinary proceedings against, x, 6, 3; settlement of disputes among, x, 7; inhibition of, x, 9, 2; exhortation of, x, 9, 3; girdles, x, 10; shampooing, x, 2; dress of, x, 4, x, 16; devolution of property of, x, 11; disqualifications for initiation as, x, 17, 1; rules for initiation, x, 17, x, 20; rules for Pavâra*n*â of, x, 19; children of, x, 25, 1, 2; reinitiation of, x, 26.
Bladder, rice-milk good for the, M. vi, 24, 5.
Bleeding, surgical, M. vi, 14, 4.
Bolsters, *K*. vi, 2, 7.
Boots, various forbidden kinds of, M. v, 2, 3.
Border countries, list of, M. v, 13, 12.
Bowls, wooden, forbidden, *K*. v, 8, 2.
— of iron and clay allowed, *K*. v, 9, 1.
— not to be painted, *K*. v, 9, 2.
— 'turning down' of, *K*. v, 20.
— proper modes of carrying, *K*. viii, 5, 2; 6, 3.
Boy-Bhikkhus, M. i, 49.
Brahman used for Arahat, M. i, 1, 3, 7; M. i, 2, 3.
Brass, *K*. v, 37, 1.
Brooms, *K*. v, 22.
Buddha, a, description of, M. i, 22, 2; vi, 34, 11.

Cannibalism, M. vi, 23, 9.
Castration forbidden, *K*. v, 7.
Casuistry, *K*. v, 33, 2.
Chain of Causation, M. i, 1, 2.
Chairs, M. v, 11; *K*. vi, 2, 4; vi, 8.
Chapter of five Bhikkhus, M. ix, 4.
— of ten, M. i, 31, 4.
— of twenty, P. 14.
Chicken, fable of, *K*. i, 18, 4.
Chunam, M. vi, 9, 2; *K*. v, 1-2; not to be used at the bath by Bhikkhunîs, *K*. x, 27, 4.
Civil law, M. vi, 3, 9; *K*. iv, 9; vi, 4, 10.
Cloister, use of, for exercise, *K*. v, 14, 1.
Cloths, not to be walked on, *K*. v, 21, 2, 3.
Clyster, use of, forbidden, M. vi, 22, 4.
Cobras' hoods as ornament, M. viii, 29.
Cobwebs, M. i, 25, 15.
Commentary, the Old, xvi.
Common property of the order, *K*. vi, 15.
Concealing offences, *K*. iii, passim.
Conscience, *K*. i, 4, 9.
Conversion, M. i, 7, 10.
Corpse, belief that the sea always throws out a, *K*. viii, 1, 3.
Council of Râgagaha, *K*. xi, passim.
— Vesâlî, *K*. xii, passim.
Covering over as with grass, *K*. i, 13.

Coverlets, used in South India, M. v, 13, 6.
Cow and calf, story of, M. v, 10.
Crocodiles' teeth as pins, *K.* v, 1, 4; v, 9, 2.
Cupping, for fever, M. vi, 14, 4.
Curds, not to be eaten after mid-day, *K.* xii, 1, 10.
Cuttle-fish bones for soup, *K.* v, 22.

Dangers, the ten, M. ii, 15, 4; ii, 35; *K.* ix, 3, 4.
Date of the Vinaya, xxi.
Debtors, imprisonment of, M. i, 46.
Dedication by water, M. i, 22, 18.
Demons troubling Bhikkhus, M. iii, 9, 2.
Devil-worshippers, *K.* v, 10, 2; v, 27, 5.
Disabilities, the eighteen, of a Bhikkhu, *K.* i, 5.
Discourse, to laymen, M. i, 75, 6.
— to the Bhikkhus, M. i, 25, 6; v, 1, 9; *K.* vi, 4, 5; i, 1, 3.
Diseases, the five, M. i, 39; i, 76, 1.
Disqualifications, the twenty-three, after initiation, M. ii, 36; iv, 14; viii, 30.
— for initiation of men, M. i, 76.
— of women, *K.* x, 17, 1.
Dogs, not to be eaten, M. vi, 23, 12.
Doubts of conscience, M. iii, 6, 4.
Drains for water, *K.* v, 14; v, 16; v, 17.
Dress, P. 18-24, 28-30, 45, 54; M. vii, viii, passim; viii, 4, n.; *K.* v, 29; of women, *K.* x, 10.
Drinks, list of, allowable, M. vi, 35, 6.
Dung, medical use of, M. vi, 9; vi, 14, 6.
Dwarfs, *K.* iv, 14, 5.
Dyeing robes, M. i, 26, 11; viii, 10.

Earth, diving into the, M. v, 1, 5.
Elephants, speaking, M. vi, 20, 2.
— not to be eaten, M. vi, 23, 10.
— fable of the old and young, *K.* vii, 4, 5.
— story of the rogue, *K.* vii, 3, 11.
— of men = Buddha, *K.* vii, 3, 12.
Embryo, consciousness of, M. i, 75.
Emissary, eight qualifications of a good, *K.* vii, 3, 6.
Emptiness of worldly things, *K.* xii, 2, 5.
Etiquette, rules of, P. 59-67; M. vi, 36, 4; *K.* vi, 13; on arrival at a Vihâra, viii, 1; at meals, viii, 4; when on begging rounds, viii, 5; towards fellow-lodgers, viii, 7.
Eunuchs, M. i, 38, 5; i, 61; iii, 11, 4; *K.* v, 7.
Exhortation of Bhikkhunîs, P. 35, 36.
Expulsion of Bhikkhus, M. i, 60.
— of a nun, *K.* i, 4, 9.
Extremes, the two, M. i, 617.
Eye of the Truth, M. i, 7, 6.
— ointments, M. vi, 11.

Fairies, curious belief as to, M. vi, 28, 8.
Faith, works, and insight, M. v, 1, 21-25.
False charges, P. 9, 10.
False pretensions, P. 5.
Famine, M. vi, 19, 2; vi, 32, 2; *K.* vi, 21.
Fat, as medicine, M. vi, 2.
Feathers, not to be used for dress, M. viii, 28, 2.
Feet, washing of, M. i, 25, 11.
— the Buddha washes disciples, M. x, 4, 3.
Festivals, the ash*t*akâ, M. i, 20, 15.
Fever, M. vi, 14, 4; cure for, M. vi, 20.
Fines of money, M. vi, 36, 1.
Fire, sacred, M. i, 15, 2.
— sacrifice to, M. i, 20, 19; vi, 35, 8.
— sermon on, M. i, 21.
— by friction, *K.* viii, 6, 1.
Fistula, M. vi, 22; viii, 1, 14, *K.* v, 27, 4.
Flowers, right and wrong use of, *K.* v, 18.
Fly whisks, three kinds of, allowed, *K.* v, 23.
Food, P. 37-42, 56, 57; *K.* v, 5; vii, 5-7.
Freedom, M. i, 6, 46; i, 7, 11; i, 11, 1; *K.* vi, 4, 4.
Frescoes, *K.* vi, 3, 2.
Fruits, which, may be eaten, *K.* vi, 5.
Furniture, P. 34, 53, 54; M. i, 25, 16; *K.* v, 19; v, 37; vi, passim.
— list of, in a Vihâra, *K.* viii; 1, 3; 3, 3.
Future life, M. v, 1, 20.

Gall bladder, *K.* vii, 2, 5.
Games, list of, forbidden to Bhikkhus, *K.* i, 13, 2.
Gems, list of the ten, *K.* ix, 1, 3.
Ghost stories, M. v, 6, 3.
Gift of a Vihâra, M. i, 22, 18.
Girdles, rules for, *K.* v, 29.
Gleaning, M. vi, 32, 1.
Goblins in hollow trees, M. iii, 12, 2.
Gods envy the Arahats, *K.* vii, 1, 6.
Gold and silver, the Bhikkhus not to accept, P. 26; *K.* xii, 1-7, 10.
Gotamaka *K*etiya, M. viii, 13, 2.
Gotama's Ford, M. vi, 28, 12.
Gotama's Gate, M. vi, 28, 12.
Gotamî, M. x, 5, 7; *K.* x, 1, 1; xi, 1, 9.
Gourds as water-pots, *K.* v, 10, 1.
Gravel, *K.* v, 14, 3; v, 22
Grindstone, M. vi, 3, 2.
Gums, medical, list of, M. vi, 7.

Hair on the soles of the feet, M. v, 1.
Hair-garments, forbidden, M. viii, 28, 2.
Hair, modes of wearing, forbidden, *K.* v, 2, 3; v, 27, 4.
Handicraft allowed to Bhikkhus, *K.* v, 28.
Happiness, the highest, M. i, 3, 4.
Harmony of mental powers, M. v, 1, 17.
Headache, cures for, M. vi, 13.
Heresy of Bhikkhus, punishment of, *K.* i, 32.
— of laymen, how to be treated, *K.* v, 20.
Hermaphrodites, M. i, 69.
High places, worship on, *K.* v, 2, 6; vi, 2, 7.
High treason, punishment for, M. ix, 2, 9; *K.* vii, 3, 4.
Horns to carry salt in, *K.* xii, 1, 10.
Horse-flesh not to be eaten, M. vi, 23, 11.
House-warming, *K.* v, 21.
Humours, of the body, M. vi, 14; 24, 5; viii, 1, 30; *K.* v, 14, 1.

Iddhi, M. v, 1, 5, 7; vi, 15, 8; of laymen, vi, 34; *K.* i, 4, 4; v, 8; vii, 1, 4; 2, 1; 3, 2; of the Buddha, vii, 3, 9; sermon on, vii, 4, 3; a lesser thing than Arahatship, vii, 4, 7; flying, *K.* xii, 1, 7.
Ill-will, P. 33.
Impurity, P. 7.
Initiation into the order, M. i, 12, 4; i, 28 and foll.
Insane offender, treatment cf, *K.* i, 5.
Insects, destruction of, M. v, 6, 3.
Insubordination, P. 12.
Interdictions, the iorm, M. i, 78.
Intoning, *K.* v, 3.
Inward struggles, M. iii 6, 3.
Iron, M. vi, 26, 7.
Itch-cloth, M. viii, 17.

Jails, public, M. i, 42.
Jains, xi.
Jaundice, M. vi, 1; vi, 14, 7; viii, 1, 23.
Jewelry for men, *K.* v, 2, 1.
Judges, what four things they should avoid, *K.* iv, 9.
— what ten characteristics they should have, *K.* iv, 14, 19.
Judicial office, four qualifications for, *K.* i, 9.
Jury in different cases, *K.* iv, 14, 19.

Karma, *K.* vii, 3, 9.
Kingdom of Righteousness, M. i, 6, 30.
Knives, *K.* v, 11, 1.

Lamps, etiquette as to lighting, *K.* viii, 7, 4.
Landmarks, M. ii, 6.
Language, each Buddhist to learn the word in his own, *K.* v, 33.
Lattices for windows, *K.* vi, 2, 2; etiquette as to, *K.* viii, 7, 4.
Legal questions, settlement of, P. 68, 69; *K.* i, 14.
Legend of Buddha, growth cf, M. i, 7, 1.
Lever used at wells, *K.* v. 16, 2.
Licenses, the ten, disallowed at Vesâlî, *K.* xii, 1, 10.
Lies, P. 2, 32; M. ii, 7.
Life begins in the womb, M. i, 75.
Light (so let your light shine forth), M. v, 4, 2; ix, 2, 20; *K.* vi, 6, 4.

Lions' flesh not to be eaten, M. vi, 23, 14.
Litigiousness, P. 46.
Lodging-places, regulation of, *K.* i, 4; vi, 11.
Longing of pregnant women, M. ix, 2, 4.
Loons, *K.* v, 11.
Love, power of, M. vi, 36, 4; sense of, *K.* xii, 2, 5.
Luck, walking over cloths for good, *K.* v, 21, 4.
Luck in sneezing, *K.* v, 33, 3.
Lunacy (?), M. vi, 10.
Lusts, *K.* i, 32, 2.
Lute, parable of the, M. v, 1, 15, 16.

Madness, rules in case of, M. ii, 25.
Magical powers (of laymen), M. vi, 34, 1, 2.
Matricide, M. i, 64, 69.
Measures of capacity, M. viii, 1, 11.
Medicaments, the five ordinary, M. vi, 1, 3.
Medicine, P. 27; M. vi, passim; school of, M. viii, 1.
Mice, *K.* vi, 12.
Middle country, the boundaries of, M. v, 13, 12.
Miracles by the Buddha, M. i, 15-21; vi, 23, 6.
Miraculous powers. See Iddhi.
Mission of the sixty-one disciples, M. i, 11.
Money changing, M. i, 49.
— pieces of, M. vi, 35, 1; viii, 1, 1, 3, 13; *K.* v, 8, 2.
Mosquito curtains, *K.* v, 13.
— fans, *K.* v, 23, 1.
Mules, cannot produce young, *K.* vii, 2, 5.
Murder, P. 4.

Nails, to be cut short, *K.* v, 27.
— custom of polishing, *K.* v, 27.
Nakedness forbidden, M. i, 70; viii, 28.
Names too venerable to be uttered, M. i, 74, 1.
Needles, *K.* v, 11, 2.
Needle-cases, P. 86; *K.* v, 11.
Nirvâ*n*a, M. i, 5, 2; i, 6, 8, 17, 18; v, 1, 18, 28; *K.* xi, 1, 15 (see also Arahatship).
Noble eightfold path, xii; M. i, 6, 18.
Noble ones, discipline of, M. ix, 1, 9.
Noble states, the ten, M. i, 22, 13.
Noble truths, xii; M. i, 6, 19-22; vi, 29.
Non-human beings, M. i, 7, 3; ii, 15, 4.
— disease, M. vi, 10.
Nose, giving of medicine through the, M. vi, 13; viii, 1, 13.
Novices, rules for, M. i, 56.
— punishment of, M. i, 57-70.
Nuns (see Bhikkhunîs).

Ocean, parable of the, *K.* ix, 1, 3.
Offences, five kinds of and seven kinds of, *K.* ix, 3, 3.
Onions, not to be eaten, *K.* v, 34.

Painting the face, *K.* v, 2, 5.
— bowls, *K.* v, 9, 2.
— walls, *K.* vi, 3, 2.
Paricide, M. i, 65, 69.
Parishes or districts, M. ii, 6-8.
Partridge, fable of, *K.* vi, 6, 3.
Pasenadi, king, story of, M. iii, 14.
Patchwork coverlets, *K.* vi, 2, 7.
Pâtimokkha, x-xxiii; P. 2, 51; M. i, 36, 14; ii, 3-5, 15-21; *K.* ix, 2.
Pavâra*n*â ceremony, M. iv, passim.
Penance and probation, distinctions between, *K.* ii, 6.
Perfumes, list of, permitted, M. vi, 11.
Pestle and mortar, M. vi, 9, 2.
Pingoes, *K.* v, 30.
Pins and needles in one's limbs, *K.* v, 14, 3.
Plants, injury of, M. iv, 1; v, 7, 1.
— seeds of, not to be destroyed, *K.* v, 5.
Practical joking, P. 41, 46.
Precedent, no ground for change of rules, *K.* xii, 1-10.
Precepts, the ten, M. i, 56.
Present, who must be, at a judicial proceeding before the Chapter, *K.* iv, 14, 16.
Prevarication, P. 33.
Probation, P. 14; M. i, 38; *K.* ii, iii.
Property in a robe, when it passes, M. viii, 31.

Propriety of demeanour, P. 59-61.
Punishments, M. i, 40, 3; i, 44; ix, 2, 9.
Pupils and preceptors, duties of, M. i, 25-27.

Rations, apportioner of, *K.* i, 4; vi, 21.
Rebuke of guilty Bhikkhus, *K.* i, 1-8.
Reconciliation, act of, *K.* i, 18-24.
Refuges, the three, M. i, 4, 5; i, 38, 2.
Requisites, the four, P. 43.
Reservoirs, *K.* v, 17.
Res judicata, *K.* iv, 14, 25.
Respect, want of, P. 33.
Rest-house, public, P. 37; M. vi, 28, 3.
Reviews not to be witnessed by Bhikkhus, P. 43.
Rice-milk, praise of, M. vi, 24, 5.
Riddles in casuistry, *K.* i, 14, 15.
*R*ishis, Vedic, list of, M. vi, 35, 2.
Rivers, ancient worship of, M. v, 9, 3; *K.* x, 21.
— list of principal, *K.* ix, 1, 3.
Robes, donation of, eight grounds for, M. viii, 32.
Roots, medical, lists of, M. vi, 3, 4.
Rugs, P. 24-27; M. v, 10; *K.* vi, 19.
Ruminator, story of the human, *K.* v, 26.

Sabbath (see Uposatha).
Salt, M. x, 4, 1.
— various kinds of, M. vi, 8.
Sama*n*as, xii.
Sandals, P. 66; *K.* viii, 1, 3; 6, 2.
Sanitary arrangements, *K.* v, 35.
Savages, M. iv, 15.
Sâvatthi (the hymn), M. vi, 35, 8.
Scabs, cure for, M. vi, 9.
Schism, P. 10, 11; distinguished from disunion, *K.* vii, 5, 1.
— eighteen kinds of, *K.* vii, 5, 2.
Schismatics, conduct towards, M. x, 5, 8; *K.* i, 4; vii, 4, 4.
Scissors, *K.* vi, 21, 3.
Sects, non-Buddhistic, P. 41.
Seedlings, ancient law of, M. vi, 39.
Seeds, fruits containing life, not to be eaten, *K.* v, 5.
Self (or soul), M. i, 6, 38-41.
Sexual intercourse, P. 4; M. i, 78.
Shampooing, *K.* v, 1.
Shoes, M. i, 25, 8; v, 1, 29; 8, 3; v, 12; v, 13, 13; *K.* v, 12.
Sick Bhikkhus, M. ii, 23; iii, 6; iv, 3; 17, 7; viii, 26, 27; *K.* vi, 10.
— relatives, M. iii, 7.
— Bhikkhu, story of the Buddha nursing a, M. viii, 26.
Silence, vow of, forbidden, M. iv, 1.
Singing the Dhamma forbidden, *K.* v, 3.
Skins, not to be used for dress, M. viii, 28, 2.
— to be used for roofing, *K.* v, 11, 6; 14, 3.
— for water-vessels, *K.* v, 16, 2.
Skulls as bowls, *K.* v, 10, 2.
Sky, walking in the, M. v, 1, 7.
Slander, P. 32.
Slaughter-house for oxen, M. v, 1, 13.
Slaves, runaway, M. i, 47.
Snakes in form of men, M. i, 3, 3; i, 63; vi, 23, 13.
— of supernatural power, M. i, 15.
— girdle of, *K.* vii, 2, 1.
— bite of, cure for, M. vi, 14, 6.
— — charm against, *K.* v, 6.
— not to be eaten, M. vi, 23, 13.
— in houses, *K.* vi, 2, 5; vi, 3, 4; viii, 1, 1.
Sneezing, curious custom connected with, *K.* v, 33, 3.
Snow, M. i, 20, 15.
Sodomy, M. i, 52.
Soldiers may not enter the order, M. i, 40.
Sorcery, M. vi, 14, 7.
Spittoon, *K.* viii, 1.
Spoons, *K.* viii, 5, 2.
Sporting in water, P. 44.
Staves, *K.* v, 24.
Subordination of guilty Bhikkhus, *K.* i, 9-12.
Suffering, M. i, 6, 20-22.
Sugar, M. vi, 26.
Sunshades, *K.* v, 9, 5; v, 23; etiquette as to, P. 65; *K.* viii, 1, 3.
Suspension of Bhikkhus, M. i, 79; *K.* i, 25.

Tailor, story of his building, *K.* vi, 5.
Tanks, *K.* v, 17.

Tathâgatas (= Buddhas), habits of, M. i, 4, 4.
— death of, *K.* vii, 3, 10.
Teetotalism, P. 44.
Theft, P. 4.
Thimbles, *K.* v, 11, 5.
Thoughts, understanding their, M. i, 22, 4; v, i, 7.
Titthiyas, M. i, 38; vi, 31; 34, 12; 35, 1; viii, 28.
Toddy drinking forbidden, *K.* xii, 1, 10.
Toleration, duty of, M. vi, 31, 11.
Tooth-sticks, rules for, *K.* v, 31.
Treasure trove, P. 53.

Upanishads, x.
Uposatha (seventh day), x; M. ii, passim.

Validity of official acts of the Sa*m*gha, M. ix, passim.
Vedas, sacred verses of, M. vi, 35, 2, 8.
Vehicles, use of, forbidden, M. v, 9.
Vihâra = cave, M. v, 1, 5.
Voting in the Chapters of the Order, *K.* iv, 9-10; 14, 25; vii, 4.
Vultures, training of, *K.* i, 32.

Walking up and down thinking, M. v, 1, 14; *K.* ii, 1, 4; v, 14, 1.
Wandering ascetics, non-Buddhistic, M. i, 23.
Was, keeping of, M. i, 13, 1; iii, passim.
Waste tub, *K.* viii, 4, 4.
Water, pouring out of, as dedication ceremony, M. i, 22, 18; viii, 30, 4; used as looking-glass, *K.* v, 2, 4; strainers, *K.* v, 13.
Weapons, P. 65; *K.* v, 37, 1; vii, 3, 4, 7.
Wells, *K.* v, 16, 2.
Wheel and axle machinery, *K.* v, 16, 2.
White ants, *K.* v, 9, 4; vi, 1, 2; viii, 3, 2.
Wind in the stomach, M. vi, 14, 1; 16, 3; 17; *K.* v, 34.
Window spaces, M. i, 25, 15, 18; *K.* viii, 1, 5; three kinds of lattices for, *K.* vi, 2, 2.
Winter, M. i, 20, 15.
Wishing-gift, what it is, *K.* i, 4, 5.
Women, first disciples, M. i, 8, 3.
— See Bhikkhunî.
— story of the lost, M. i, 14.
Worldly talk, specimens of, M. v, 6, 3.
Worms in the head, M. viil, 1, 18.
Writing, xxxii-xxxv; M. i, 49.

INDEX OF PROPER NAMES.

Abhaya, M. viii, 1, 4 seq., 13 seq.
A*ddh*akâsî, *K*. x, 22, 1.
A*g*apâlanigrodha, M. i, 2, 1; 3, 1; 5, 1.
A*g*âtasattu, *K*. vii, 2, 1, 5; 3, 4 seq.; xi, 1, 7.
Agga*l*apura, *K*. xii, 1, 9.
Aggâ*l*ava *k*etiya, *K*. vi, 17, 1.
A*g*ita, *K*. xii, 2, 7.
A*g*ita Kesakambalî, *K*. v, 8, 1.
Ahirâ*g*akulâni, *K*. v, 6.
Ahogaṅga pabbata, *K*. xii, 1, 8.
Âkâsagotta, M. vi, 22, 1.
A*k*iravatî, M. v, 9, 1; viii, 15, 11; *K*. ix, 1, 3 seq.
Â*l*âra Kâlâma, M. i, 6, 1, 2.
Â*l*avakâ bhikkhû, *K*. vi, 17, 1.
Â*l*avî, *K*. vi, 17, 1; 21, 1.
Amanussa, M. i, 6, 3; vii, 1, 26.
Ambala*tth*ikâ, *K*. xi, 1, 7.
Ambapâlî (°pâlikâ), M. vi, 30; viii, 1, 1 seq.
Ambapâlivana, M. vi, 30, 6.
Ânanda, M. i, 4, 9, 5; 51; 53; v, 13, 8; 9, 1; 17; 24, passim.
Anâthapi*nd*ika, M. x, 5, 8; *K*. vi, 4; 9. See Sudatta and *G*etavana.
Andhakavinda, M. ii, 12, 1; vi, 24, 1; 26, 1; viii, 15, 10.
Andhavana, M. viii, 23, 3.
Aṅgâ, M. i, 19, 1, 3.
Aṅgirasa, M. i, 15, 7; vi, 35, 2.
Aṅguttarâpa, M. vi, 34, 17.
A*ññ*âko*nd*a*ññ*a, M. i, 6, 31 seq.
Anotattadaha, M. i, 19, 2, 4.
Antaka, M. i, 11, 2; 13, 2. See Mâra.
Anupiyâ, *K*. vii, 1, 1; 2, 1.
Anuruddha, M. x, 4; 5, 6; *K*. i, 18, 1; vii, 1, 1 seq.
Âpa*n*am, M. vi, 35, 1; 36, 1.
Ârâmikagâma, M. vi, 15, 4.
Ari*tth*a, *K*. i, 32 seq.
Ariya*m* âyatana*m*, M. vi, 28, 8.
Assa*g*i, M. i, 6, 36; 23.
Assa*g*ipunabbasukâ bhikkhû, *K*. i, 13 seq.; vi, 16.
Asurâ, *K*. ix, 1, 3.
A*tth*aka, M. vi, 35, 2.
Âtumâ, M. vi, 37; 38.
Avantî, M. v, 13, 1.
Avantidakkhi*n*âpatha, M. v, 13.
Avantidakkhi*n*âpathakâ bhikkhû, *K*. xii, 1, 7, 8.

Bâlakalo*n*akâragâma, M. x, 4, 1.
Bârâ*n*asî, M. i, 6, 6, 10, 30; 7, 1; 9, 1, 2; 14, 1; v, 7, 1; 8, 1; vi. 23, 1 seq.; 24, 1; viii, 1, 22; 14, 1; 15, 1; x, 2, 3.
Bela*tth*a Ka*kk*âna, M. vi, 26.
Bela*tth*asîsa, M. vi, 9, 1; viii, 17.
Bela*tth*iputta. See Sa*ñg*aya.
Bhaddasâlâ, M. x, 4, 6 seq.
Bhaddavaggiyâ, M. i, 14.
Bhaddiya (the place), M. v, 8, 1; 9, 1; vi, 3, 4.
Bhaddiya (the Bhikkhu), M. i, 6, 33; *K*. vii, 1, 3 seq.
Bhaggâ, *K*. v, 21, 1; 22, 1.
Bhagu, M. vi, 35, 2; viii, 24, 6; x, 4, 1; *K*. vii, 1, 4.
Bhallika, M. i, 4.
Bhâradvâ*g*a, M. vi, 35, 2; *K*. v, 8.
Bhesaka*l*âvana, *K*. v, 21, 1.
Bhummâ devâ, M. i, 6, 30.
Bhumma*g*aka. See Mettiyabhumma*g*akâ.
Bhûsâgâra, M. vi, 37, 4.
Bimbisâra (râ*g*â Mâgadha Seniya), M. i, 22; 39; 40; 42; 46; ii. 1; iii, 4, 3, passim; *K*. v, 5; vi, 3, 11; vii, 3, 5.
Bodhi, *K*. v, 21.
Brahma, *K*. vii, 3, 16.
Brahmadatta, M. x, 2, 3 seq.; *K*. xi, 1, 7.
Brahmakâyikâ devâ, M. i, 6, 30.
Brahmâ Sahampati, M. i, 5, 18; 6, 30.

Dabba Mallaputta, *K*. iv, 4; v, 20.

Dakkhi*n*âgiri, M. i, 5, 3; viii, 12, 1; *K*. xi, 1, 10.
Dakkhi*n*âpatha. See Avantidakkh°.
Dakkhi*n*âpathaka, *K*. i, 18, 3.
Devadatta, M. ii, 16, 8; *K*. vii, 1, 4; 2 seq. See Godhiputta.
Devaputta, *K*. vii, 2, 2.
Devalâ, M. i, 4; 6, 2, 4; 20; vi, 28, 7; 11; viii, 16, 3.
Dhaniya, *K*. xi, 1, 6.
Dîghâvu, M. x, 2, 8 seq.

Erâpatha, *K*. v, 6.

Gagga, M. ii, 25; *K*. iv, 5.
Gaggarâ, M. ix, 1, 1.
Gandhabbâ. *K*. ix, 1, 3.
Gaṅgâ, M. v, 9, 4; vi, 28, 12 seq.; *K*. ix, 1, 3 seq.
Gavampati, M. i, 91, 2.
Gayâ, M. i, 6, 7; 21, 1.
Gayâkassapa, M. i, 15, 1; 20, 22.
Gayâsîsa, M. i, 21, 1; 22, 1; *K*. vii, 4, 1.
Ghositârâma, M. x, 1, 1; *K*. i, 25, 1; 31; vii, 2, 1; xi, 1, 14.
Gi*gg*h*akû*t*a, M. ii, 1, 1; 5, 4; v, 1, 1, 3, 14, 17; *K*. iv, 4, 4; viii, 3, 9.
Gi*ñg*akâvasatha, M. vi, 30, 6.
Giribba*g*a, M. i, 24, 5, 6, 7. See Râ*g*agaha.
Godhiputta, *K*. vii, 3, 2. See Devadatta.
Gama*t*akandarâ, *K*. iv, 4, 4.
Gopaka, M. viii, 24, 6.
Gosâla. See Makkhali.
Gotama (Buddha), M. i, 2, 2, 6, 10, 15; 22, 2, passim; (Buddha's father), M. i, 54, 4.
Gotamadvâra, M. vi, 28, 12.
Gotamaka *K*etiya, M. viii, 13, 2.
Gotamatittha, M. vi, 28, 12.
Gotamî. See Mahâpa*g*âpatî.

*G*ambudîpa, M. i, 20, 7 seq.
*G*âtiyâvana, M. v, 8, 1; vi, 34, 10.
*G*eta, *K*. vi, 4, 9 seq.
*G*etavana, M. i, 55; iii, 5, 1, passim; *K*. i, 1, 1; 13, 5; 18, 5, passim.
*G*îvaka Komârabha*kk*a, M. i, 39; viii, 1, 4 seq.; 2; *K*. v, 14, 1.
*G*îvakambavana, *K*. iv, 4, 4; xi, 1, 7.

Himavanta, *K*. vi, 6, 3.

Inda. See Sakka.
Isibhatta, M. viii, 24, 5.
Isidâsa, M. viii, 24, 5.
Isigili, *K*. iv, 4, 4.
Isipatana, M. i, 6, 6, 10, 30; 7, 7; v, 7, 1; vi, 23, 1; viii, 14, 1.

Ka*g*aṅgala, M. v, 13, 12.
Kâka, M. viii, 1, 26 seq.
Kâka*nd*aka putta, *K*. xii, 1, 1 seq.; 2, 1 seq.
Ka*kk*âna, Ka*kk*âyana. See Pakudha, Bela*tth*a, Mahâka*kk*âna.
Kakudha, *K*. vii, 2, 2; (Devaputta), *K*. vii, 2, 2.
Kâlâma. See Â*l*âra.
Kalandakanivâpa. See Ve*l*uvana.
Kalandaputta, *K*. xi, 1, 6.
Kâ*l*asilâ, *K*. iv, 4, 4.
Ka*nd*aka, M. i, 52; 60.
Ka*nd*akâ, M. i, 60.
Ka*n*hâgotamâ, *K*. v, 6.
Kaṅkhârevata, M. vi, 16.
Ka*nn*aku*gg*a, *K*. xii, 1, 9.
Kapilavatthu, M. i, 54, 1; 55, 1; *K*. x, 1, 1.
Kâsi, M. i, 6, 8; vi, 17, 8 seq.; ix, 1, 1, 5, 7; *K*. i, 13, 3; 18, 1.
Kâsirâ*g*â, M. viii, 2; x, 2, 3 seq.
Kassapa, M. i, 15 seq.; 22, 5; vi, 35, 2.
Kassapagotta, M. ix, 1.
Ka*t*amorakatissaka, *K*. vii, 3, 14.
Keniya, M. vi, 35.
Kesakambalî. See Agita.
Kha*nd*adevî, *K*. viii, 3, 14.
Khu*gg*asobhita, *K*. xii, 2, 7.
Kimbila, M. x, 4; *K*. vii, 1, 4.
Ki*t*âgiri, *K*. i, 13 seq.; vi, 16; 17, 1.
Kokâlika, *K*. vii, 3, 14; 4, 2 seq.
Kokanada, *K*. v, 21.
Kolita, M. i, 24, 3.
Ko*l*ivisa. See So*n*a.
Ko*l*iyaputta, *K*. viii, 2, 2.
Komârabha*kk*a. See *G*îvaka.
Ko*nd*a*ññ*a, M. i, 6, 29, 31.
Kosalâ, M. i, 73, 1, 2; ii, 15, 3; iii, 5, 1; 9, 1; 11, passim; *K*. v, 13, 2; 32, 2.
Kosalarâ*g*â, M. x, 2, 3 seq.
Kosambakâ bhikkhû (upâsakâ), M. x, 4, 6; 5.
Kosambî, M. viii, 1, 27; x, 1, 1; 3; *K*. i, 25, 1; 28, 1; vii, 2, 1, 5; xi, 1, 11; xii, 1, 7; 2, 8.
Kosinârakâ Mallâ, M. vi, 36, 1.
Ko*t*igâma, M. vi, 29 seq.
Kukku*t*ârâma, M. viii. 24, 6.

Kumârakassapa, M. i, 75.
Kuraraghara, M. v, 13, 1.
Kuru. See Uttarakuru.
Kusinârâ, M. vi, 36, 1, 6; 37, 1; *K.* xi, 1, 1.
Ku*t*ika*nn*a. See So*n*a.

*K*ampâ, M. v, 1, 1; ix, 1; 2.
*K*ampeyyaka, *K.* xii, 2, 8.
*K*âtumahârâ*g*ikâ devâ, M. i, 6, 30.
*Kh*abyâputtâ, *K.* v, 6.
*Kh*anna, *K.* i, 25; 28; 30; 31; iv, 14; xi, 1, 11, 14.
*K*itta, *K.* i, 18; 22 seq.
*K*odanâvatthu, M. ii, 17, 1; 18, 1.
*K*orapapâta, *K.* iv, 4, 4.

La*tth*ivanuyyâna, M. i, 22, 1, 2.
Li*kkh*avi, M. vi, 30; 31, 1; *K.* v, 20.
Lohitaka. See Pa*nd*ukalohitaka.

Maddaku*kkh*i, M. ii, 5, 3; *K.* iv, 4, 4.
Magadhâ, M. i, 5, 7; 19, 1, 3; 24, 5, 6, 7; 39, 1.
Mâgadha. See Bimbisâra.
Mâgadhaka, M. i, 22, 3 seq.; 24, 5; *K.* vii, 2, 2.
Magadha-khetta, M. viii, 12, 1.
Magadha-mahâmatta, M. vi, 28, 7 seq.
Ma*gg*h*i*mâ *g*anapadâ, *K.* i, 18; 22 seq.
Mahaka, M. i, 52.
Mahâka*kk*âna, M. v, 13; x, 5, 6; *K.* i, 18, 1.
Mahâkappina, M. v, 13; x, 5, 6; *K.* i, 18, 1.
Mahâkassapa, M. i, 74; ii, 12, 1; viii, 21, 1; x, 5, 6; *K.* xi, 1, 1 seq.
Mahâko*tth*ita, M. x, 5, 6; *K.* i, 18, 1.
Mahâ*k*unda, M. x, 5, 6; *K.* i, 18, 1.
Mahâmoggallâna, M. i, 23; 24; vi, 20; *K.* i, 18, 1; v, 8, 1; 34, 2; vii, 2, 2; 4, 2; ix, 1. See Sâriputtamoggallânâ.
Mahânâma, M. i, 6, 36; *K.* vii, 1, 1.
Mahâpagâpatî Gotamî, M. x, 5, 7; *K.* xi, 1 seq.; xi, 1, 9.
Mahârâgâno, M. i, 4, 4; 16.
Mahâsâlâ, M. v, 13, 12.
Mahâvana, M. vi, 30, 6; *K.* v, 13, 3; vi, 5, 1; x, 1, 2; xii, 1, 1.
Mahî, *K.* ix, 1, 3 seq.
Makkhali Gosâla, *K.* v, 8, 1.
Ma*kkh*ikâsa*nd*a, *K.* i, 18; 22 seq.
Malla, M. vi, 36; viii, 19; *K.* vii, 1, 1.
Mallaputta. See Dabba.
Mallî, *K.* x, 12.
Mandâkinî, M. vi, 20.
Ma*n*i*k*û*l*aka, *K.* xii, 1, 4.
Mâra, M. i, 6, 30; 11, 2; 13, 2; *K.* xi, 1, 9. See Antaka.
Mârasenâ, M. i, 1, 7.
Me*nd*aka, M. vi, 34.
Mettiya, *K.* iv, 4, 8.
Mettiyabhummagakâ, *K.* iv, 4, 5 seq.; v, 20.
Migâramâtâ, *K.* ix, 1, 1. See Visâkhâ.
Moggallâna. See Mahâmoggallâ
Mu*k*alinda, M. i, 3; 4, 1.

Nadî Kassapa, M. i, 15, 1; 20, 30.
Nâga, M. i, 15; 63; *K.* ix, 1, 3.
Nâ*l*andâ, *K.* xi, 1, 7.
Nanda, M. i, 54, 5.
Nâtaputta, M. vi, 31; *K.* v, 8, 1.
Nâtikâ, M. vi, 30, 6.
Nera*ñ*garâ, M. i, 1, 1; 15, 6; 20, 15.
Nigrodhârâma, M. i, 54, 1; *K.* x, 1, 1.
Nilavâsî, M. viii, 24, 25.
Nimmânaratî devâ, M. i, 6, 30.

Paggota (râgâ), M. viii, 1, 23 seq.; 24.
Pâ*k*înakâ (bhikkhû), *K.* xii, 2, 2 seq.
Pâ*k*înava*m*sadâya, M. x, 4, 1 seq.
Pa*kk*antimâ *g*anapadâ, M. v, 13, 16 seq.
Pakudha Ka*kk*âyana, *K.* v, 8, 1.
Pa*nd*ukalohitaka, *K.* i, 1; 6, 8.
Paranimmitavasavattî devâ, M. i, 6, 30.
Pârileyyaka, M. x, 4, 6 seq.; 5, 1.
Pasenadi (râgâ Kosala), M. iii, 14.
Pâ*t*aligâma, M. vi, 28.
Pâ*t*aliputta, M. vi, 28, 8; viii, 24, 6.
Pâ*th*eyyakâ bhikkhû, M. vi., 1, 1 seq.; *K.* xii, 1, 7, 8; 2, 2 seq.
Pâvâ, *K.* xi, 1, 1.
Phalikasandâna, M. viii, 24, 6.
Pilinda-gâma, M. vi, 15, 4, 7.
Pilindava*kkh*a, M. vi, 13 seq.
Pi*nd*olabhâradvâga, *K.* v, 8.
Pisâ*k*illika, *K.* v, 10 3; 27, 5.
Pubbârâma, *K.* ix, 1, 1.
Punabbasuka. See Assagipunabbasukâ.
Pu*nn*agi, M. i, 9, 1, 2.
Purâ*n*a, *K.* xi, 1, 10.
Pûra*n*a Kassapa, *K.* v, 8, 1.
Puratthimâ *g*anapadâ, *K.* i, 18, 3; xii, 2, 3.

Râgagaha, M. i, 22, 1, 2, 13; 23, 1 seq.; 28, 2; 30, 1; 49, 1; 53, 1, passim; K. iv, 4, 15; v, 1, 1; 2, 6, passim.
Râgagahaka, M. viii, 1, 2, 16 seq.; K. v, 8; vi, 1; 4, 1, 6 seq.
Râgâyatana, M. i, 4, 1, 2; 5, 1.
Râhu asurinda, K. xii, 13.
Râhula, M. i, 54; 55; x, 5, 6; K. i, 18, 1.
Râhulamâtâ, M. i, 54.
Rakkhitavanasa*nd*a, M. x, 4, 6 seq.
Râmaputta. See Uddaka.
Revata, M. viii, 31, 1; x, 5, 6; K. i, 18, 1; xii, 1, 9 seq.; 2, 1 seq. See Kaṅkhârevata.
Ro*g*a, M. vi, 36; viii, 19.

Sabbakâmî, K. xii, 2, 4 seq.
Sâgata, M. v, 1, 3 seq.
Sahagâti, K. xii, 1, 9; 2, 1.
Sâketa, M. i, 66, 1; vii, 1, 1; viii, 1, 8; 13, 7.
Sâkiya, M. i, 38, 11; K. vii, 1, 4; x, 1, 2; 2, 1.
Sakka, M. i, 17; 20; 22, 13 seq.
Sakkâ, M. i, 54; K. vii, 1, 1 seq.; x, 1, 1, 2.
Sakya, K. vii, 1, 3.
Sakyakula, M. i, 22, 2; 23, 4; vi, 34, 11; 35, 1.
Sakyakumarâ, K. vii, 1, 1 seq.
Sakyaputta. See Upananda.
Sâkyaputtiya, M. i, 24, 7 seq., passim.
Sakyarâ*g*â, K. vii, 1, 3 seq.
Sâlavatî, M. viii, 1, 3 seq.
Sâ*l*ha, K. xii, 2, 2 seq.
Sallavatî, M. v, 13, 12.
Sambhûta, K. xii, 1, 8 seq.; 2, 4 seq.
Sa*m*kassa, K. xii, 1, 9.
Samuddadatta, K. vii, 3, 14.
Sâ*n*a, M. viii, 24, 6.
Sâ*n*avâsî, M. viii, 24, 6; K. xii, 1, 8 seq.; 2, 4 seq.
Sa*ñg*aya, M. i, 23; 24; K. v, 8, 1.
Sa*ñg*ikâputta, K. vi, 21 1 seq.
Sappaso*nd*ikapabbhâra, K. iv, 4, 4.
Sarabhû, K. ix, 1. 3 seq.
Sâriputta, M. 1, 23; 24; 28, 2, 3; 54, passim; K. i, 18, 1; v, 34; 2; vi, 6, 1; 7; vii, 3, 2 seq.; 4; viii, 4, 1. See Sâriputtamoggallânâ.
Sâriputtamoggallânâ, K. i, 13, 16; 16; vi, 16, 1; vii, 3, 1; 4, 1 seq.
Sattapa*nn*iguhâ, K. iv, 4, 4.
Sâvatthi, M. 1, 55; 66, 1; 67; iii, 5, 1, passim; K. i, 1, 1; 13, 3, 5; 18, 4, passim.
Senânigama, M. i, 11, 1.
Seniya. See Bimbisâra.
Setaka*nn*ika, M. v, 13, 12.
Seyyasaka, K. i, 9 seq.
Sîha, M. vi, 31.
Sîtavana, M. v, 1, 12 seq.; 17; K. iv, 4, 4; vi, 4, 3 seq.
Sîvaka (yakkha), K. vi, 4, 3.
Siveyyaka, M. viii, 1, 29, 34.
So*n*a Ko*l*ivisa, M. v, 1.
So*n*a Ku*t*ika*nn*a, M. v, 13.
Soreyya, K. xii, 1, 9.
Sudatta, K. vi, 4, 4. Cf. Anâthapi*nd*ika.
Suddhâvâsâ devâ, Suddhâvâsakâyikâ devatâ, K. xii, 2, 2.
Suddhodana, M. i, 54.
Sudhamma, K. 1, 18; 22 seq.
Sudinna, K. xi, 1, 6.
Sumana, K. xii, 2, 7.
Su*m*sumâragira, K. v, 21, 1.
Sunidha, M. vi, 28, 7 seq.
Supassa nâgarâ*g*â, M. vi, 23, 13.
Supati*tth*a *K*etiya, M. i, 22, 1, 2.

Takkasilâ, M. viii, 1, 5 seq.
Tapodakandarâ, K. iv, 4, 4.
Tapodârâma, K. iv, 4, 4.
Tapussa, M. i, 4.
Tâvati*m*sa, M. i, 6, 30; 20, 10; vi, 28, 8; 30, 5.
Tekula. See Yame*l*utekulâ.
Thûna, M. v, 13, 12.
Tissaka. See Ka*t*amorakatissaka.
Tusitâ devâ, M. i, 6, 30.

Udâyi, M. ii, 16, 7; K. iii, 1; x, 9, 3 seq.
Uddaka Râmaputta, M. i, 6, 3, 4.
Udena, M. iii, 5; K. xi, 1, 11 seq.
Udumbara, K. xii, 1, 9.
U*gg*enî, M. viii, 1, 23.
Ukkala, M. i, 4, 2.
Upaka, M. i, 6, 7 seq.
Upâli, M. i, 62; 64; ix, 6; K. i, 18, 1; ii, 2; 7, passim.
Upâli (of Râgagaha), M. i, 49.
Upananda, M. i, 52; 60; iii, 14; vi, 19; viii, 25; K. vi, 10, 1; 12; xii, 1, 5.
Upasena Vaṅgantaputta, M. i, 31.
Upatissa, M. i, 24, 3.
Uppalava*nn*â, K. x, 8.

Uruvelâ, M. i, 1, 1; 6, 6; 11, 1; 14, 1; 15, 1; 22, 4.
Uruvelakassapa, M. i, 15; 22, 4; *K.* v, 37.
Usîraddhaja, M. v, 13, 2.
Uttara, *K.* xii, 2, 3.
Uttarakuru, M. i, 19, 2, 4.
Uvâ*l*a, *K.* iv, 11; 12, 5.

Va*ddh*a, *K.* v, 20.
Vaggi, M. vi, 28.
Vaggiputtaka, *K.* vii, 4, 1; xii, 1, 1 seq.; 2, 1 seq.
Vaggumudâtîriya, *K.* xi, 1, 6.
Vâlikârâma, *K.* xii, 2, 7.
Vâmadeva, M. vi, 35, 2.
Vâmaka, M. vi, 35, 2.
Vaṅgantaputta, M. i, 31.
Vappa, M. i, 6, 33.
Vâsabhagâma, M. ix, 1, 1, 5, 7.
Vâsabhagâmika, *K.* xii, 2, 7.
Vâse*tth*a, M. vi, 35, 2.
Vassakâra, M. vi, 28, 7 seq.
Vebhâra, *K.* iv, 4, 4.
Vedehiputta, *K.* xi, 1, 7.
Ve*l*uvana, M. i, 22, 18; 24, 3; iii, 1, 1; vi, 17, 1, 8; 22, 1; 27; viii, 1, 1; *K.* iv, 4, 1, 4; v, 1, 1; vi, 1, 1; 21, 1; vii, 2, 5; 4, 3; xi, 1, 11; xii, 1, 4.
Vesâlî, M. vi, 30, 31, 4, 10 seq.; 32, 1; viii, 1, 1 seq.; 13; 14, 1; *K.* v, 12, 1; 13, 3; 14, 1; 21, 1; vi, 5, 1; 6, 1; x, 1, 2; 9, 1; xi, 1, 6; xii, 1, 1 seq.; 2, 4 seq.
Vesâlika, *K.* vii, 4, 1; xii, 1, 1 seq.
Vessâmitta, M. vi, 35, 2.
Videha. See Vedehiputta.
Vimala, M. i, 9, 1, 2.
Virûpakkhâ, *K.* v, 6.
Visâkhâ Migâramâtâ, M. iii, 13; viii, 15; 18; x, 5, 9; *K.* v, 22; vi, 14.

Yakkha, *K.* vi, 4, 3.
Yâmâ devâ, M. i, 6, 30.
Yamataggi, M. vi, 35, 2.
Yame*l*utekulâ, *K.* v, 33, 1.
Yamunâ, *K.* ix, 1, 3 seq.
Yasa, M. i, 7 seq.; *K.* xii, 1, 1 seq.; 2, 1 seq.
Yasoga, M. vi, 33, 5.

INDEX OF PÂLI WORDS

FXPLAINED OR REFERRED TO IN THE NOTES.

The references are to parts i, ii, iii, and pages.

akappakata, part ii, p. 155.
akara*n*îya, iii, 355.
akuppa, ii, 435.
akkanâ*l*a, ii, 247.
akkavâ*t*a, iii, 178.
agga, iii, 202.
agga*l*a, ii, 215.
agga*l*ava*tt*i, iii, 106.
aṅgana, iii, 295.
a*k*akkhussa, iii, 147.
a*k*elaka, i, 41.
a*kk*ibaddha, ii, 207.
a*kk*eka*k*îvara, i, 29.
a*kkh*upiyati, iii, 83.
a*g*inakkhipa, ii, 247.
a*ñg*ana, ii, 50.
a*ñg*ani, iii, 141.
a*ññ*â, ii, 10; iii, 303.
a*ññ*âta, iii, 186.
a*tt*âna, iii, 67.
A*tth*aka, ii, 130.
a*tth*akavagga, ii, 37.
a*tth*apadaka, iii, 167.
a*tth*illa, iii, 341.
a*ddh*akâsika, ii, 195 seq.
a*ddh*akusi, ii, 209.
a*ddh*apallaṅka, iii, 367.
a*ddh*ama*nd*ala, ii, 209.
a*ddh*ayoga, i, 174.
a*ddh*arûka, iii, 138.
attakâmapâri*k*ariyâ, i, 8.
attâdâna, iii, 313.
atthavasa, iii, 263.
atthâra, ii, 148 seq.
atthâraka, ii, 155.
adesanâgâmî, ii, 333.
addhâna, i, 26.
adhi*tth*ahati, iii, 101, 117.
adhi*tth*ita, ii, 40, 151, 152.
adhisîla, ii, 23.
ana*kkh*ariya, i, 85.
anantarika, iii, 285.
anapadâna, ii, 272.
anabhâva, ii, 113.
anabhirati, iii, 77.
anavasesa, ii, 316; iii, 35.
anâdariya, i, 44.
anâmanta*k*âra, ii, 150.
anîka, ii, 13.
anupakha*gg*a, i, 42; iii, 285.
anupa*ññ*atti, iii, 374.
anupada*gg*eyya, i, 29.
anubhâga, iii, 203.
anullapanâ, iii, 36.
anuvâta, ii, 154; ii, 231; iii, 93.
anuviva*tt*a, ii, 209.
anusampavaṅkatâ, iii, 36.
ane*l*agala, ii, 37.
antaggâhika, i, 344.
antaraghara, i, 56, 59, 65; iii, 286.
antaravâsaka, ii, 212.
antarâkâ*g*a, iii, 146.
antimavatthu, i, 276.
apagabbha, ii, 111, 112.
apatissara*n*a, iii, 175.
apalokana, iii, 37.
apassenaphalaka, iii, 219.
appuyya, iii, 183.
appo*th*eti, ii, 349.
abbhussahanatâ, iii, 36.
abhayûvara, i, 207.
abhisa*m*khârika, iii, 9.
abhisanna, ii, 60.
abhisannakâya, iii, 102.
abhiha*tth*u*m*, i, 21; ii, 440.
ambakâ, ii, 107.
ara*n*isahita, iii, 292.
ariyavâsa, i, 141.
alakkhika, iii, 250.
ala*m*kammaniya, i, 16.
avakkârapâtî, iii, 287.
avaga*nd*akâraka*m*, i, 64.

avaṅga, iii, 342.
avippavâsa, i, 20, 255.
asaddhamma, iii, 262.
asamâdâna*k*âra, ii, 151.
asambhoga, iii, 120.
ahivâtakaroga, i, 204.
Ahogaṅga, ii, 146.

âgamma, ii, 237.
â*k*amanakumbhi, iii, 280.
â*k*ariya, i, 178 seq.
â*k*ariyaka, ii, 140.
â*k*âra, i, 184.
â*nik*olaka, iii, 348.
âdeyyavâ*k*a, iii, 186.
ânantarika, iii, 198, 246.
âpâyika, iii, 262.
âma*l*akava*nt*ikapî*th*a, iii, 165.
âmisa, i, 36.
âmisakhâra, ii, 60.
âyataka, iii, 72.
âyatikâ, iii, 115.
âyoga, iii, 141.
ârâma, i, 23.
ârâmika, iii, 282.
âlambanabâhâ, iii, 96.
âlinda, iii, 175.
âvara*n*a, iii, 336.
âvasathapi*nd*a, i, 37.
âvâsaparamparâ, ii, 371.
âvi*ñkh*ana, iii, 106.
âsa*gg*ana*m*, iii, 264.
âsatti, iii, 183.
âsanantarikâ, ii, 292.
âsanapa*ññ*âpaka, iii, 408.
âsandi, ii, 27.
âsandika, iii, 165.
âsâdeti, ii, 373.
âsittakûpadhâna, iii, 117.
âsevanavitthaka, iii, 95.
âha*kk*apâdaka, iii, 164.
âhundarika, i, 205.

ikkâsa, iii, 171.
iddhi, i, 119; ii, 136; iii, 230.
indakhîla, i, 52.

ukkapi*nd*aka, ii, 70.
ukkâsika, iii, 68.
ukku*t*ika*m*, iii, 16.
ukku*t*ikâ, i, 62.
u*kk*inatha, i, 194.
u*kkh*edavâda, ii, 111.
u*n*hîsa, iii, 97.
utu, ii, 236.
uttara*kkh*ada, ii, 27.
uttarapâsaka, iii, 106.
uttarâsaṅga, ii, 212; iii, 123.
uttaribhaṅga, iii, 9, 179.
utti*tth*apatta, i, 152.
udakaniddhamana, iii, 108.
udakasa*m*gaha, ii, 147.
udakasâ*t*ika, ii, 225.
udukkhalika, iii, 105.
udda, ii, 16.
uddesa, i, 12.
uddosita, iii, 363.
uddhasudhâ, iii, 174.
upa*ggh*a, iii, 351.
upa*ggh*âya, i, 178 seq.
upa*tth*âpeti, i, 49.
upadhi, i, 85, 138.
upanandhati, iii, 100.
upanikkhitta, i, 26.
uparipi*tth*ita, iii, 273.
upalâpeti, i, 49.
uposathapamukha, i, 252.
ubbâ*lh*a, ii, 314.
ubbâhikâ, iii, 49.
ubbha*nd*ita, ii, 210.
ubbhâra, i, 19; ii, 157.
ubbhida, ii, 48.
ubhatolohitakûpa, dhâna, ii, 28.
ubhatovinaya, iii, 376.
ubhatovibhaṅga, iii, 376.
ummattakâlaya, iii, 21.
ura*kkh*ada, ii, 348.
ullikhita, ii, 153.
ulloka, iii, 169.
ussâdeti, iii, 202, 301.
ussâvanâ, ii, 120.
ussîra, ii, 23.
usse*lh*eti, ii, 349.

ûha*ññ*i, iii, 277.

eka*kk*iya, ii, 212.
ekapariyâkata, iii, 341.
ekapalâsika, ii, 13.
ekuddesa, i, 11.
eragu, ii, 35.
e*l*akapâdakapî*th*a, iii, 165.

okirati, ii, 231.
oko*t*imaka, iii, 40.
ogumphiyati, ii, 31.
oti*nn*a, i, 7.
ottharaka, iii, 102.
onîta, i, 83.
onogana, ii, 386.
opâna, ii, 115.
obhoga, i, 156.

ova*tt*ika, iii, 69.
ova*tt*iyakara*n*a, ii, 153.
ovaddheyya, ii, 154.
ovâda, i, 35.
osaraka, iii, 175.

ka*m*sapattharikâ, iii, 140.
kakka, ii, 58.
ka*t*a*kkh*uparissâvana, iii, 100.
ka*t*asî, iii, 390.
ka*t*isuttaka, iii, 69, 142, 348.
ka*th*ina, i, 18 seq.; ii, 148 seqq.; iii, 92 seq.
ka*n*â*g*aka, iii, 9.
ka*nd*usakara*n*a, ii, 153.
ka*nn*akita, iii, 91.
katâkata, iii, 309.
katikasa*nth*âna, iii, 8.
kattarada*nd*a, ii, 20.
kattari, iii, 138.
kattarikâ, iii, 139.
kattika, i, 29 seq.
kapalla, ii, 50.
kapisîsaka, iii, 106.
kappa*tth*ika, iii, 254.
kappiyakâraka, ii, 59.
kappiyaku*t*î, i, 303.
kaba*l*ikâ, ii, 58.
kamala, ii, 23.
kambala, ii, 23.
kambalamaddana, ii, 154.
kammârabha*nd*u, i, 200.
karaka*t*aka, iii, 112.
kalâbuka, iii, 143.
ka*l*iṅgara, iii, 127.
ka*l*imbhaka, iii, 94.
kavâ*t*a, iii, 88, 160.
kavâ*t*api*tth*a, iii, 105.
kasâva, iii, 172.
kâ*k*a, iii, 82.
kâya, ii, 224.
kâyura, iii, 69.
kâ*l*aka, i, 25.
ki*ñk*ana, i, 139.
ki*t*ika, iii, 174, 176.
kukkukata, ii, 154.
kukkusa, iii, 367.
ku*dd*anâda, iii, 107.
ku*nd*akamattikâ, iii, 171.
kuttaka, ii, 27.
kupita, i, 309.
kumbhakârikâ, iii, 156.
kumbhatthena, iii, 325.
kuruvindakasutti, iii, 67.
kulaṅkapâdaka, iii, 174.
kulâva, iii, 384.
kulîrapâdaka, iii, 164.
kusi, ii, 208.
ko, i, 138.
ko*kkh*a, i, 34; iii, 165.
ko*tt*âpeti, iii, 341.
ko*tth*aka, ii, 219; iii, 11, 109, 177.
kopeti, ii, 435.
komudî, i, 324.

kha*nd*a, iii, 191.
khandhakavatta, i, 185.
khallaka, ii, 15.
khâdaniya, i, 39.
khârikâ*g*a, i, 132.
khuddânukhuddaka, i, 50.
khurabha*nd*a, ii, 141.
khurasipâ*t*ikâ, iii, 138.
khe*l*âpaka, iii, 239.

ga*n*amagga, i, 269.
ga*nth*ika, iii, 144.
ga*nd*ikâdhâna, iii, 213.
ga*nd*umattikâ, iii, 172.
gatigata, iii, 26.
gandhabbahatthaka, iii, 67.
gabbha, iii, 173.
gahapati*k*îvara, ii, 194.
gâmapoddava, iii, 66.
gâmûpa*k*âra, i, 256.
giraggasama*gg*a, iii, 71.
gîveyyaka, ii, 209.
gu*n*aka, iii, 143.
guhâ, i, 174.
geruka, ii, 50.
gerukaparikamma, iii, 97.
goka*nt*aka, ii, 34.
gogha*m*sikâ, iii, 98.
go*k*ara, iii, 275.
gonisâdika, ii, 121.
golomika, iii, 138.

gha*t*aka, iii, 130.
gha*t*ika*t*âha, iii, 88.
gha*t*ikâ, iii, 106.
gharadinnaka, ii, 60.

*k*akkabheda, iii, 251.
*k*akkalikâ, iii, 163.
*k*akkava*tt*aka, iii, 112.
*k*aṅkama, ii, 7; iii, 103.
*k*atuka*nn*aka, iii, 145.
*k*andanaga*nth*î, iii, 78.
*k*ammakha*nd*a, iii, 113.
*k*âleti, ii, 49.
*k*itta, ii, 224.
*k*imilikâ, iii, 167.

*k*îvara, ii, 199.
*k*etâpeti, i, 22.
*k*elapa*tt*ikâ, iii, 128.
*k*o*k*a, ii, 132.
*k*olaka, iii, 86.

*kh*akana, ii, 49.
*kh*atta, iii, 133.
*kh*adana, i, 35.
*kh*anda, i, 277.
*kh*andaso, iii, 150.
*kh*ava, iii, 239.
*kh*avi, iii, 169.
*kh*âdeti, ii, 42; iii, 147.
*kh*inniriyâpatha, i, 225.
*kh*eppâ, ii, 24.

*g*aṅgheyyaka, ii, 209.
*g*a*t*ila, i, 118; ii, 129, 134.
*g*anatâ, iii, 72.
*g*antâghara, i, 157; iii, 103.
*g*antu, ii, 35.
*g*âla, iii, 162.
*g*e, ii, 217.

*gh*âyî, iii, 7.

*ñ*atti, i, 169.
*ñ*atti*k*atuttha, i, 169.
*ñ*attidutiya, i, 169.

ta*tt*ikâ, ii, 35.
tathâgata, i, 82.
tantibaddha, ii, 256.
talasattikâ, i, 51.
tassapâpiyyasikâ, iii, 28.
tâla*kkh*idda, iii, 106.
tâlava*nt*a, iii, 131, 145.
tâvakâlika, iii, 217.
ti*k*îvara, i, 20; i, 255.
ti*n*agahana, iii, 148.
ti*n*asanthâraka, iii, 86.
tittirapattika, ii, 15.
Tittiriya, iii, 194.
tira*kkh*ânavi*gg*â, iii, 152.
tirîtaka, ii, 248.
tumbaka*t*âha, iii, 88.
tulâ, iii, 112.
tulikâ, iii, 167.
tûla, i, 54.
tûlapu*nn*ika, ii, 15.
tora*n*a, iii, 178.

thakîyati, iii, 161.
thavikâ, iii, 293.
thinna, ii, 206.
thulla*kk*aya, i, xxv.
thûpato, i, 63.
theyyasa*m*khâta, i, 4.

dakako*tth*aka, ii, 57.
da*nd*aka*th*ina, iii, 93.
da*nd*aparissâvana, iii, 102.
da*nd*asatthaka, iii, 90.
dantaka*tth*a, iii, 146.
dantapo*n*a, i, 40.
damaka, ii, 71.
da*l*h*i*karana, ii, 153.
dâ*th*ikâ, iii, 138.
di*tth*âvikamma, iii, 34.
dukka*t*a, i, xxv.
dukkha, ii, 224.
du*tth*agaha*n*ika, ii, 60.
du*tth*ulla, ii, 316.
dubba*k*a, i, 12.
dubbalya, i, 4.
dummaṅku, iii, 251.
dumma*ññ*u, iii, 251.
de*dd*ubhaka, iii, 143.
dvâra, iii, 160.
dvârakosa, i, 35.

dhamanisantata, ii, 41.
dhamma, iii, 193, 262.
dhammakaraka, iii, 100.
dhâna, ii, 28.
dhuvakâra, ii, 254.
dhûmakâlika, iii, 214, 378.
dhûmanetta, iii, 107.
dhotapâdaka, iii, 219.

na*m*, iii, 19.
natthukamma, ii, 53.
natthukara*n*î, ii, 54.
nandimukhî, ii, 211; iii, 299.
namataka, iii, 90, 343.
nalâ*t*ika, ii, 349.
navakamma, iii, 101, 189 seq.
navakammika, ii, 359.
nâgadanta, iii, 68, 98.
nâ*l*ikâgabbha, iii, 173.
nâsanâ, i, 236.
nâseti, ii, 377.
niga*nth*a, i, 41.
nigg*h*âpeti, iii, 2.
ni*dd*âpeti, iii, 225.
nippurisa, iii, 225.
nibbu*ggh*ati, ii, 349.
nimitta, ii, 9.
nimittakata, ii, 154.
nillekha*g*antâghara, iii, 115.
nissaggiya, ii, 155.

nissaya, ii, 337; iii, 355.
nekkhamma, i, 104.
negama, iii, 185.
netthâ, ii, 339.
nerayika, iii, 262.

pa*m*sukûla, ii, 157.
pakata, ii, 343.
pakatatta, ii, 340; iii, 266.
pa*k*âsaniyakamma, iii, 239.
pakutta, iii, 175.
pakkhasa*m*kanta, i, 178.
pakkhika, iii, 220.
paggâhikasâlâ, iii, 383.
paghana, iii, 175.
pa*kk*akkhâta, i, 275.
pa*kk*akkhâti, i, 4.
pa*kk*aya, i, 146.
pa*kk*uddharati, ii, 152.
pa*ñk*aka, ii, 155.
pa*ñk*apa*t*ika, iii, 97.
pa*t*ikâ, ii, 3, 27.
pa*t*iggaha, iii, 90, 95.
pa*t*i*kkh*âdaniya, ii, 81.
pa*t*i*kkh*âdi, iii, 111.
pa*t*ibhâna, iii, 13.
pa*t*ibhâna*k*itta, iii, 172.
pa*t*ibhâneyyaka, ii, 140.
pa*t*isâra*n*îya, ii, 364.
pa*tt*a, iii, 341.
pa*n*âmeti, iii, 403.
pattaka*nd*olikâ, iii, 86.
pattakkhandha, iii, 13.
pattamâ*l*aka, iii, 86.
patthaddha, iii, 244.
pannaloma, iii, 232.
para, ii, 307.
paradavutta, iii, 232.
parampara bho*g*ana, i, 38.
parikathâkata, ii, 154.
parikammakata, iii, 218.
parikkhâra, iii, 343.
pari*g*ita, iii, 75.
parittâna*k*i*t*ika, iii, 174.
parinibbuta, iii, 183.
paribbâ*g*aka, i, 41.
paribha*nd*a, ii, 154, 231; iii, 85, 93.
paribha*nd*akara*n*a, iii, 213.
paribhoga, iii, 208.
paribhoganîya, iii, 8.
parima*nd*ala*m*, i, 59.
parimâ*n*a, ii, 421.
parimukha, iii, 138.
parimu*tth*a, ii, 307.
pariyanta, ii, 386.
pariyâya, i, 47.
pariyu*tth*ita*k*itta, iii, 380.
parive*n*a, iii, 109; iii, 203.
parisâ, i, 12.
pala, ii, 178.
palâsî, iii, 38.
palibodha, ii, 157.
pallaṅka, iii, 367.
pallatthikâ, i, 62; iii, 141.
pavattama*m*sa, ii, 81.
pavattinî, iii, 350.
pavananta, iii, 143.
pavâra*n*âsa*m*gaha, i, 353.
pavârita, i, 39.
pavâreti, i, 21.
pasata, ii, 178.
pahara*n*î, iii, 156.
pâ*k*ittiya, i, 32.
Pâ*th*eyyaka, ii, 146.
pâtimokkha, i, xxvii seq.
pâdakathalika, i, 92; ii, 373.
pâdakhîlâbâdha, ii, 19.
pâdapî*th*a, i, 92.
pâpa*n*ika, ii, 157.
pâmaṅga, iii, 69.
pârâ*g*ika, i, 3.
pârisuddhi, i, 242, 274.
pâligu*nth*ima, ii, 15.
pâlibaddha, ii, 208.
pâsaka, iii, 144.
pâsâda, i, 174; iii, 178.
pâsâdika, iii, 339.
pâsuka, iii, 340.
pi*tth*akhâdaniya, ii, 139.
pi*tth*amadda, iii, 171.
pi*tth*asa*m*ghâ*t*a, iii, 105.
pi*nd*ukkhepaka*m*, i, 64.
pitta, iii, 237.
pidalaka, iii, 94.
pilo*t*ikâ, ii, 157.
pisâ*k*illika, i, 318; iii, 139.
pî*th*a, iii, 278.
pî*th*ikâ, iii, 165.
pu*kkh*ati (vassa*m*), i, 310.
pu*ñkh*anî, iii, 114.
pu*t*abaddha, ii, 15.
puthupâ*n*iya, iii, 68.
pûva, i, 39.
peyyâla, i, 291.
potthaka, ii, 247.
pothugganika, iii, 230.
posit*um*, iii, 169.

pha*n*aka, iii, 70.
phalaka, ii, 246; iii, 165.
phâtikammattha, iii, 217.
phulla, iii, 191.

bandhana, ii, 153.
bandhanamatta, iii, 141.
bahukata, ii, 135; iii, 214.
bâhanta, ii, 209.
bâhullika, iii, 254.
bidalamañkaka, iii, 164.
bila, ii, 48.
bilaṅga, iii, 9.
bundikâbaddha, iii, 164.
byâ, ii, 378.

bhaṅga, ii, 57.
bhaṅgodaka, ii, 57.
bhandâgâra, ii, 201.
bhandika, iii, 213.
bhatikamma, iii, 83.
bhattikamma, iii, 169.
bhaddapîtha, iii, 165.
bhasmâ, iii, 264.
bhikkhugatika, i, 312.
bhisi, ii, 210; iii, 163.
bhummattharana, iii, 278.
bhoganiya, i, 39.
bhoggayâgu, ii, 89.

makaradantaka, iii, 68.
makasakutikâ, iii, 102.
makkhavâlaka, iii, 145.
maggâru, ii, 35.
mañka, iii, 278.
mañkuka, ii, 140.
mañgarikâ, ii, 347.
mañgu, ii, 140.
mandala, ii, 209.
mandalikâ, iii, 107.
matakakîvara, ii, 151.
mattikâdonikâ, iii, 107.
maddavîna, iii, 143.
madhusitthaka, iii, 92.
manam, i, 254.
mantha, i, 39.
mandâmukhî, i, 130.
marumba, iii, 109.
mallaka, iii, 68.
mallamutthika, iii, 66.
malorikâ, iii, 117.
masâraka, iii, 164.
mahânâma, ii, 14.
mahâraṅga, ii, 14.
mahâseda, ii, 56.
Mahî, ii, 25.
mâtikâ, i, 273; ii, 157; iii, 2.
mâsakarûpa, iii, 80.
migabhûta, iii, 232.
midhanta, iii, 85.
midhi, iii, 163.

missaka, ii, 432.
mukhamattikâ, iii, 107.
muttaharîtaka, ii, 60.
mendavisânabandhika, ii, 15.
mokkhakikâ, ii, 184.
moghasuttaka, iii, 94.
moka, ii, 132.
moragu, ii, 35.

yathâdhammo, i, 203.
yantaka, iii, 162.
yâgu, ii, 89.

raganapakka, ii, 49.
ratanasammata, i, 53.
rûpa, i, 201.
rûpiyakkhaddaka, i, 27.
rûhati, ii, 414.
ropeti, iii, 334.

latthivana, i, 136.
luggati, iii, 111.
lûka, ii, 16.
lekha, iii, 78.
lesakappa, iii, 200.
lona, ii, 48.
loma, ii, 339.

vagga, iii, 27.
vaggulî, iii, 163.
vakanapatha, iii, 324.
vakkapâdukâ, ii, 24.
vatamsaka, ii, 347.
vatti, iii, 341.
vanta, ii, 347.
vatthikamma, ii, 80.
varâha, iii, 261.
vallikâ, iii, 69.
vassupanâyikâ, i, xxxvii.
vâtapâna, iii, 162.
vâtamandalikâ, iii, 85.
Vâmaka, ii, 130.
vâraka, iii, 113.
vâha, ii, 13.
vikanna, ii, 230; iii, 92.
vikappanâ, i, 45.
vikâla, i, 53.
vikâsika, ii, 59.
vigayha, iii, 68.
vikkhikâlika, ii, 16.
viññu, i, 33.
vidha, iii, 143.
vidhutikâ, ii, 347.
vinandhana, iii, 94.
vinayapâmokkha, i, xiii.
vinayavatthu, iii, 411.

vinidhâya, iii, 269.
vineyya, iii, 183.
vipa*kk*atâya, iii, 36.
vipari*n*ata, i, 7.
vipâ*t*eti, iii, 90.
vippakata, iii, 214.
vibbhamati, i, 275.
vibhaṅga, ii, 325.
viva*tt*a, ii, 209.
visibbanâ, i, 44.
visesaka, iii, 342.
visesâdhigama, iii, 263.
vissara, iii, 273.
vihâra, ii, 386.
vihesaka, i, 33.
vî*n*â, ii, 8.
vuddhapabba*g*ita, ii, 140.
vûpakâseti, i, 161.
vokkamma, iii, 285.
vodaka, iii, 84.
ve*n*i, iii, 341.
vedikâ, iii, 162.
veyyâyika, iii, 185.
ve*l*uriya, iii, 82.
vyâbâdheti, iii, 235.

sa*m*velliya, iii, 348.
sa*m*sara*n*aki*t*ika, iii, 176.
sa*m*harati, iii, 168.
sagu*n*a, i, 155.
sa*m*ka*kkh*ika, iii, 351.
sa*m*kassara, iii, 300.
sa*m*kâpayati, i, 298.
sa*m*keta, ii, 234.
saṅkhanâbhi, ii, 51.
sa*m*khâra, i, 76.
sa*m*gîti, iii, 355.
sa*m*ghâ*t*i, ii, 212.
sa*m*ghâ*t*ipallatthikâ, iii, 12.
sa*m*ghâdisesa, i, 7.
sa*ññ*a ti, iii, 257.
sa*nd*âsa, iii, 140.
satavallikâ, iii, 145.
sati, i, 119.
sativepullappatta, iii, 16.
sattaṅga, iii, 165.
sattalûkha, ii, 209.
satthuhâraka, i, 4 seq.
satthu, iii, 92.
santaruttara, i, 21; ii, 233.
sannidhikata, ii, 154.
sapadâna, i, 63.
sabhogana, i, 41.
sama*n*uddesa, i, 48.
samatittika, i, 62; ii, 104.
samanubhâsati, i, 11.
samasûpaka, i, 62.
samukase, i, xxvi.
samuddaphe*n*aka, iii, 131.
samodhâna, ii, 405, 409.
sampavâreti, i, 110.
sambhâraseda, ii, 56.
sambhinna, ii, 145.
sambhu*n*âti, ii, 159.
sammukha, ii, 332.
sammukhâvinaya, iii, 3.
sammosa, iii, 87.
sayana, iii, 279.
sarakutti, iii, 72.
sarati, iii, 14.
sarabha*ññ*a, iii, 73.
sarâvaka, iii, 108.
saritaka, iii, 92.
saritasârita, iii, 26.
saritasipâ*t*ikâ, iii, 92.
salâka, iii, 162.
salâkabhatta, iii, 220 seq.
salâkodhâniya, iii, 53.
sava*k*anîya, ii, 338, 386.
sahadhammika*m*, i, 12.
Sahampati, i, 86.
sâ*t*iya, iii, 223.
Sâ*n*avâsî, iii, 394.
sâradika, ii, 41.
sârâ*n*îya, ii, 364.
sâloka, iii, 343.
sâvasesa, ii, 316; iii, 35.
sâsapaku*tt*a, iii, 171.
sikkhâsâ*g*îva, i, 4.
sitthatelaka, iii, 171.
sindhava, ii, 48.
sivâ*t*ikâ, ii, 47.
sivikâgabbha, iii, 173.
siveyyaka, ii, 190.
sîtâlo*l*î, ii, 60.
sîla, i, 184.
sukha, ii, 224.
sugata, i, 54 seq.
sugatavidatthi, i, 8.
su*ññ*âgâra, ii, 101.
sutta, i, xxix.
suttadhara, i, xxviii.
suttanta, i, xxix seq.
suttalûkha, ii, 209, 230.
suttavibhaṅga, i, xxix seq.
suddhaka, ii, 433.
suddhanta, ii, 417.
suppavâyita, i, 28.
sûkarantaka, iii, 143.
sû*k*i, iii, 97.
sû*k*ikâ, iii, 106, 162.
sû*k*inâ*l*ikâ, iii, 91.

sekha, i, 185; ii, 138.
sekhasammata, i, 57.
se*tth*i, i, 102.
seda, ii, 56.
senesika, ii, 42.
seyyagga, iii, 202.
sotâpattiphala, iii, 230.
sobha*n*a, iii, 143.

hatthabhitti, iii, 169.
hatthava*tt*aka, ii, 27.
hatthavikâra, i, 326.
hatthavilaṅghaka, i, 326.
hatthinakhaka, iii, 208.
hatthiso*nd*aka, iii, 145.
hammiya, i, 174.
hammiyagabbha, iii, 173.
harîtaka, ii, 60.
harîtakapa*nn*ikâ, iii, 343.
hintâla, ii, 23.
huhuṅkagâtika, i, 79.
hetu, i, 146.

TRANSLITERATION OF ORIENTAL ALPHABETS ADOPTED FOR THE TRANSLATIONS OF THE SACRED BOOKS OF THE EAST.

CONSONANTS.	MISSIONARY ALPHABET. I Class.	II Class.	III Class.	Sanskrit.	Zend.	Pehlevi.	Persian.	Arabic.	Hebrew.	Chinese.
Gutturales.										
1 Tenuis	k	...	....	क	𐬐	[illegible]	ک	ك	כּ	k
2 „ aspirata	kh	...	....	ख	𐬑	[illegible]	...	...	כ	kh
3 Media	g	...	....	ग	𐬔	[illegible]	گ	...	גּ	...
4 „ aspirata	gh	...	....	घ	𐬖	[illegible]	...	...	ג	...
5 Gutturo-labialis	q	...	....	...	....	...	ق	ق	ק	...
6 Nasalis	ṅ (ng)	...	....	ङ	𐬧 (ng) / 𐬣 (N)	...	...	...	...	...
7 Spiritus asper	h	...	....	ह	𐬵 (𐬓 *hv*)	[illegible]	ه	ه	ה	h, hs
8 „ lenis	'	...	....	...	....	...	ا	ا	א	...
9 „ asper faucalis	‘h	...	....	...	....	...	ح	ح	ח	...
10 „ lenis faucalis	’h	...	....	...	....	...	ع	ع	ע	...
11 „ asper fricatus	...	‘*h*	....	...	....	...	خ	خ	ח	...
12 „ lenis fricatus	...	’*h*	....	...	....	...	...	...	...	...
Gutturales modificatae (palatales, &c.)										
13 Tenuis	...	*k*	....	च	𐬗	[illegible]	چ	...	...	*k*
14 „ aspirata	...	*kh*	....	छ	....	...	...	...	...	*kh*
15 Media	...	*g*	....	ज	𐬘	[illegible]	ج	ج	...	...
16 „ aspirata	...	*gh*	....	झ	....	...	غ	غ	...	...
17 „ Nasalis	ñ	...	....	ञ	....	...	...	...	...	...

CONSONANTS (*continued*).	MISSIONARY ALPHABET. I Class.	II Class.	III Class.	Sanskrit.	Zend.	Pehlevi.	Persian.	Arabic.	Hebrew.	Chinese.
18 Semivocalis	y	...	...	य	[illegible], [illegible] init.	[illegible]	ي	ي	י	y
19 Spiritus asper	...	($\acute{y}$)	...	...	...	...	...	...	...	...
20 „ lenis	...	($\grave{y}$)	...	...	...	...	...	...	...	...
21 „ asper assibilatus	...	*s*	...	श	[illegible]	[illegible]	ش	ش	...	...
22 „ lenis assibilatus	...	*z*	...	...	[illegible]	[illegible]	ژ	...	...	*z*
Dentales.										
23 Tenuis	t	...	...	त	[illegible]	[illegible]	ت	ت	תּ	t
24 „ aspirata	th	...	...	थ	[illegible]	...	...	...	ת	th
25 „ assibilata	...	...	TH	...	...	...	ث	ث	...	...
26 Media	d	...	...	द	[illegible]	[illegible]	د	د	דּ	...
27 „ aspirata	dh	...	...	ध	[illegible]	...	...	...	ד	...
28 „ assibilata	...	...	DH	...	...	...	ذ	ذ	...	...
29 Nasalis	n	...	...	न	[illegible]	[illegible]	ن	ن	נ	n
30 Semivocalis	l	...	...	ल	...	[illegible]	ل	ل	ל	l
31 „ mollis 1	...	*l*	...	ळ	...	...	...	...	...	...
32 „ mollis 2	...	...	L	...	...	...	...	...	...	...
33 Spiritus asper 1	s	...	...	स	[illegible]	[illegible]	س(ث)	س	ש	s
34 „ asper 2	...	...	s (ʃ)	...	...	...	...	...	ס	...
35 „ lenis	z	...	...	...	[illegible]	[illegible]	ز (ذ)	ز	ז	z
36 „ asperrimus 1	...	...	z (ʒ)	...	...	...	ص	ص	צ	ʒ, ʒh
37 „ asperrimus 2	...	...	ẓ (ʒ)	...	...	...	ض	...	...	...

Dentales modificatae (linguales, &c.)										
38 Tenuis	...	*t*	...	ट	...	...	ط	ط	ט	...
39 „ aspirata	...	*th*	...	ठ	...	...	ط	ط	...	...
40 Media	...	*d*	...	ड	[illegible]	[illegible]	...	...	...	...
41 „ aspirata	...	*dh*	...	ढ	...	...	...	ض	...	...
42 Nasalis	...	*n*	...	ण	[illegible]	...	...	...	...	...
43 Semivocalis	r	...	...	र	𐬭	[illegible]	ر	ر	ר	...
44 „ fricata	...	*r*	...	...	...	...	...	...	...	*r*
45 „ diacritica	...	...	R	...	...	...	...	...	...	...
46 Spiritus asper	sh	...	...	ष	[illegible]	[illegible]	...	...	...	sh
47 „ lenis	zh	...	...	...	...	...	...	...	...	...
Labiales.										
48 Tenuis	p	...	...	प	𐬞	[illegible]	پ	...	פּ	p
49 „ aspirata	ph	...	...	फ	...	...	...	...	פ	ph
50 Media	b	...	...	ब	𐬠	[illegible]	ب	ب	בּ	...
51 „ aspirata	bh	...	...	भ	...	...	...	...	ב	...
52 Tenuissima	...	*p*	...	...	...	...	...	...	...	...
53 Nasalis	m	...	...	म	𐬨	[illegible]	م	م	מ	m
54 Semivocalis	w	...	...	...	[illegible]	...	...	...	...	w
55 „ aspirata	hw	...	...	...	...	...	...	...	...	...
56 Spiritus asper	f	...	...	...	𐬟	[illegible]	ف	ف	...	f
57 „ lenis	v	...	...	व	„	[illegible]	و	و	ו	...
58 Anusvâra	...	*m*	...	अं	[illegible] ã	...	...	...	...	...
59 Visarga	...	*h*	...	अः	...	...	...	...	...	...

VOWELS.	I Class.	II Class.	III Class.	Sanskrit.	Zend.	Pehlevi.	Persian.	Arabic.	Hebrew.	Chinese.
1 Neutralis	0	. . .	. . . .	. . . .	. . . .	. . .	. . .	. . .	ְ	ă
2 Laryngo-palatalis	ĕ	. . .	. . . .	. . . .	. . . .	. . .	. . .	. . .	. . .	. . .
3 „ labialis	ŏ	. . .	. . . .	. . . .	. . . .	𐭠 fin.	. . .	. . .	. . .	. . .
4 Gutturalis brevis	a	. . .	. . . .	अ	𐬀	𐭠 init.	ـَ	ـَ	ַ	a
5 „ longa	â	(*a*)	. . . .	आ	𐬁	𐭠	ـَا	ـَا	ָ	â
6 Palatalis brevis	i	. . .	. . . .	इ	𐬌	. . .	ـِ	ـِ	ִ	i
7 „ longa	î	(*i*)	. . . .	ई	𐬍	𐭩	ـِي	ـِي	ִי	î
8 Dentalis brevis	*li*	. . .	. . . .	ऌ	. . . .	. . .	. . .	. . .	. . .	. . .
9 „ longa	*lî*	. . .	. . . .	ॡ	. . . .	. . .	. . .	. . .	. . .	. . .
10 Lingualis brevis	*ri*	. . .	. . . .	ऋ	. . . .	. . .	. . .	. . .	. . .	. . .
11 „ longa	*rî*	. . .	. . . .	ॠ	. . . .	. . .	. . .	. . .	. . .	. . .
12 Labialis brevis	u	. . .	. . . .	उ	𐬎	. . .	ـُ	ـُ	ֻ	u
13 „ longa	û	(*u*)	. . . .	ऊ	𐬏	𐭥	ـُو	ـُو	וּ	û
14 Gutturo-palatalis brevis . . .	e	. . .	. . . .	. . .	𐬈(e) 𐬆(*e*)	. . .	. . .	. . .	ֶ	e
15 „ longa . . .	ê (ai)	(*e*)	. . . .	ए	𐬉, 𐬇	𐭩	. . .	. . .	ֵ	ê
16 Diphthongus gutturo-palatalis	âi	(*ai*)	. . . .	ऐ	. . . .	. . .	ـَيْ	ـَيْ	. . .	âi
17 „ „	ei (ĕi)	. . .	. . . .	. . .	. . . .	. . .	. . .	. . .	. . .	ei, êi
18 „ „	oi (ŏu)	. . .	. . . .	. . .	. . . .	. . .	. . .	. . .	. . .	. . .
19 Guttur.-labialis brevis	o	. . .	. . . .	. . .	𐬊	. . .	. . .	. . .	ָ	o
20 „ longa	ô (au)	(*o*)	. . . .	ओ	𐬋	𐭥	. . .	. . .	וֹ	. . .
21 Diphthongus gutturo-labialis	âu	(*au*)	. . . .	औ	𐬁𐬎 (*au*)	. . .	ـَوْ	ـَوْ	. . .	âu
22 „ „	eu (ĕu)	. . .	. . . .	. . .	. . . .	. . .	. . .	. . .	. . .	. . .
23 „ „	ou (ŏu)	. . .	. . . .	. . .	. . . .	. . .	. . .	. . .	. . .	. . .
24 Gutturalis fracta	ä	. . .	. . . .	. . .	. . . .	. . .	. . .	. . .	. . .	. . .
25 Palatalis fracta	ï	. . .	. . . .	. . .	. . . .	. . .	. . .	. . .	. . .	. . .
26 Labialis fracta	ü	. . .	. . . .	. . .	. . . .	. . .	. . .	. . .	. . .	ü
27 Gutturo-labialis fracta	ö	. . .	. . . .	. . .	. . . .	. . .	. . .	. . .	. . .	. . .